Urban Poverty and Climate Change

T0361136

The urban poor face greatly increased levels of vulnerability due to the impacts of climate change. Even small shocks can be damaging, as they have few assets to cushion themselves, and lack access to formal risk-reduction mechanisms. High rates of urbanisation occurring in low- and middle-income countries make such vulnerability a major challenge for global poverty reduction goals.

Urban Poverty and Climate Change pulls together the work of leading scholars to offer a policy-relevant narrative that aims to deepen our understanding of the everyday experiences of climate change – both the impacts on and responses of urban poor households and communities in 13 towns and cities in 7 countries across Asia, Africa and Latin America. The book contributes to the evolution of more effective pro-poor climate change policies in urban areas by local, national governments and international organisations. A number of key questions are posed; how do innovative adaptation practices emerge and flourish? How do they vary within, between and across communities and countries? What are the potential enablers, barriers and forms of urban governance that emerge?

This book is a valuable and important contribution to policy makers, students and scholars interested to learn about the lived experiences of urban poverty and climate change.

Manoj Roy is Lecturer in Sustainability at Lancaster Environment Centre, Lancaster University, UK.

Sally Cawood is a doctoral researcher at the Global Development Institute, University of Manchester, UK.

Michaela Hordijk is Assistant Professor of International Development Studies at the University of Amsterdam, the Netherlands and at UNESCO-IHE Institute for Water Education, Delft, the Netherlands.

David Hulme is Professor of Development Studies at the Global Development Institute, University of Manchester, UK.

Routledge Advances in Climate Change Research

Urban Poverty and Climate Change

Life in the slums of Asia, Africa and Latin America

Edited by Manoj Roy, Sally Cawood, Michaela Hordijk and David Hulme

Routledge
Taylor & Francis Group

LONDON AND NEW YORK

First published 2016
by Routledge

2 Park Square, Milton Park, Abingdon, Oxfordshire OX14 4RN
711 Third Avenue, New York, NY 10017

Routledge is an imprint of the Taylor & Francis Group, an informa business

First issued in paperback 2017

British Library Cataloguing in Publication Data
A catalogue record for this book is available from the British Library

Library of Congress Cataloguing in Publication Data
Names: Roy, Manoj, editor. | Hordijk, Michaela, editor. |
Hulme, David, editor. | Cawood, Sally, editor.
Title: Urban poverty and climate change : life in the slums of Asia,
Africa and Latin America / edited by Manoj Roy, Sally Cawood,
Michaela Hordijk, David Hulme.
Other titles: Routledge advances in climate change research.
Description: New York, NY : Routledge, 2016. |
Series: Routledge advances in climate change research
Identifiers: LCCN 2015045848 | ISBN 9781138860506 (hb) |
ISBN 9781315851105 (ebook)
Subjects: LCSH: Urban poor–Developing countries. | Climatic changes–Social aspects–Developing countries. | Climatic changes–Effect of human beings on–Developing countries. | City planning–Environmental aspects–Developing countries. | Urban ecology (Sociology)–Developing countries. | Urban health–Developing countries. | Urban policy–Developing countries.
Classification: LCC HV4173. U75 2016 | DDC 362.5091732–dc23
LC record available at http://lccn.loc.gov/2015045848

ISBN: 978-1-138-86050-6 (hbk)
ISBN: 978-0-8153-6448-1 (pbk)

Typeset in Goudy
by Out of House Publishing

Contents

Figures

Tables and box

Tables

Box

Editors and contributors

Editors

Manoj Roy is Lecturer in Sustainability at Lancaster Environment Centre, Lancaster University, UK. Working with David Hulme at the Global Development Institute, University of Manchester, Roy led the ClimUrb project. He specialises in urban poverty analysis through multidisciplinary methods combining technical analysis (e.g. architectural and planning, spatial analysis and modelling) with a social (e.g. livelihoods, wellbeing) and political (governance, institutional) analysis. His other research projects include CLUVA and EcoPoor.

Sally Cawood is Doctoral researcher at the Global Development Institute (GDI), School of Environment, Education and Development, University of Manchester, UK. Sally's research interests include urban geography, social policy and grassroots initiatives in low-income settlements in the Global South. Sally conducted her PhD fieldwork in Dhaka, Bangladesh on the role of community-based organisations in accessing basic services.

Michaela Hordijk is human geographer and assistant professor of International Development Studies at the Governance for Inclusive Development (GID) programme group, University of Amsterdam and at UNESCO-IHE Institute for Water Education, Delft, the Netherlands. Michaela was adjunct scientific coordinator in Chance2sustain. Her expertise lies in urban water governance, the politics of knowledge in urban water governance, participatory urban governance, climate change adaptation and resilience.

David Hulme is Professor of Development Studies, Executive Director of the Global Development Institute and CEO of the Effective States and Inclusive Development Research Centre at the University of Manchester. He has worked on rural development, poverty and poverty reduction, microfinance, the role of NGOs in development, environmental management, social protection and the political economy of global poverty for more than 30 years. His recent books include *Global Poverty* (Routledge, 2015), *Governance, Management and Development* (Palgrave, 2015) and *Just Give Money to the Poor* (Kumarian Press, 2010).

Contributors

A. F. M. Ashraful Alam, Faculty of Architecture Discipline in Khulna University and now PhD candidate in the Department of Geography and Planning at Macquarie University. His work falls under the broad umbrella of political ecology in urban built environment in the cities of the Global South. He is interested in the everyday human-nature relations at home in transitional spaces that are constantly in flux due to religious and ethnic conflicts, transnational migration and climate change.

Rumana Asad, Faculty of Architecture Discipline in Khulna University, Bangladesh. Her research falls under the fields of climate change, disaster adaptation, urban design and urban informal settlements focusing on water issues to ensure sustainability for developing countries.

Nicola Banks, ESRC Future Research Leader (grant reference number ES/K009729/1) at the Global Development Institute, University of Manchester. Her current research explores young people's experiences of urban poverty in Tanzania.

Eric K. Chu is Assistant Professor of Urban Studies in the Department of Geography, Planning and International Development Studies at the University of Amsterdam. His teaching and research is at the intersection of climate change adaptation, urban development and environmental justice in the Global South.

María Evangelina Filippi is a PhD candidate at the Development Planning Unit, University College London. At the UCL Institute for Global Prosperity she supported London-based projects on the impacts of regeneration and experimenting with co-designed research and the involvement of citizen scientists. In Chance2Sustain she worked in the areas of water governance, participatory (spatial) knowledge and climate change adaptation in Arequipa, Peru.

Arabella Fraser is a Research Associate at the King's Centre for Integrated Research on Risk and Resilience in the Geography Department, King's College London. Her present research interests are in the governance and politics of environmental risk, in particular in contexts of rapid urbanisation and urban informality.

Barbara Harriss-White, FAcSS, is Emeritus Professor of Development Studies at Oxford University where she established the MPhil in Development Studies and the Contemporary South Asian Studies Programme, and directed Queen Elizabeth House. Since 1969, she has researched rural and small-town development through fieldwork in India. Widely published, her book *Rural Commercial Capital* won the Edgar Graham Prize for originality in development studies in 2009.

Syed Hashemi has a long career in teaching, research and managing programmes for the poor. He taught Economics at Jahangirnagar University in Bangladesh, directed an anti-poverty research programme at Grameen Trust, and set up a development institute and chaired the Department of Economics and Social Sciences at BRAC University. He spent nine years with CGAP, at the World Bank, focusing on financial inclusion of the poorest. He also headed a multi-country programme to develop new pathways to graduate out of food insecurity. Hashemi continues to be Senior Advisor for the graduation programme at CGAP. He has a PhD in Economics from the University of California at Riverside.

Kelvin Haule is an urban geographer with a keen interest in urban ecosystem services. He holds an MA in Development Studies, BA in Geography and Environmental Studies and Postgraduate Diploma in Poverty and Policy Analysis. Haule is an Assistant Lecturer at the University of Dodoma in the Department of Geography and Environmental Studies. He is currently pursuing a PhD on land markets and livelihoods dynamics in peri-urban areas in Tanzania. He has participated in writing two book chapters and published articles on land use dynamics and on water resources in the Serengeti ecosystems.

Anirudh Krishna is the Edgar T Thompson Professor of Public Policy in the Sanford School of Public Policy and a professor of political science at Duke University. His research investigates how poor communities and individuals in developing countries cope with the structural and personal constraints that result in poverty and powerlessness.

Caroline Moser is an urban social anthropologist / social policy specialist. She is Emeritus Professor at the University of Manchester. Until 2012 she was Director of the Global Urban Research Centre. Previous positions include Lead Specialist Social Development, World Bank, Lecturer at LSE, and at DPU, UCL. She has undertaken research on gender and development, urban violence and insecurity, intergenerational asset accumulation and poverty, and on asset adaptation to climate change.

Iddi Mwanyoka is an experienced researcher and consultant who has done a number of research and consultancy assignments and has co-authored and published papers in reputable journals. He holds a Masters in Integrated Water Resource Management. Mwanyoka is a 'hands-on' person with vast practical experience in conservation having worked for prominent conservation and development organisations such as WWF, CARE and UNDP for over seven years in the areas of Environmental Policy, Payments for Ecosystem Services (PES) and Sustainable Land Management. Currently, Mwanyoka is an Assistant Lecturer at the University of Dodoma in the Department of Geography and Environmental Studies, where he teaches on a range of courses.

Aftab Opel is a social anthropologist currently working at WaterAid in Bangladesh. He has over two decades of research experience in different

South and East Asian countries on a range of development issues. His current research focus includes issues related to water, sanitation and hygiene leading to programme development and policy influence. Opel's career also includes research and programme development in the areas of climate change, poverty and vulnerability, migration, alternative livelihoods, education and early childhood development. Most recently, he completed several projects in Bangladesh on impacts of climate change on water, water privatisation and its impacts on the poor, issues of faecal sludge management, and hygiene behaviour change. He developed and advised several WASH programmes for WaterAid Bangladesh. He led a team of experts at BRAC University Institute of Educational Development on early childhood programme and curriculum development, and an Afghanistan Research and Evaluation Unit in Afghanistan on several multi-country projects on livelihoods, vulnerability and cross-border population movements, and has worked with the Royal Foundation in Thailand on alternative livelihoods, and with Plan Bangladesh on education projects.

Afroza Parvin is Professor of Architecture at Khulna University, Bangladesh. She got her Bachelor of Architecture degree from Khulna University, and an MSc in Urban Planning and PhD in Urban Design from The University of Hong Kong. Afroza has been a Commonwealth Academic Fellow at the Development Planning Unit, University College London. She is the recipient of a Fulbright Visiting Research Scholarship hosted by the School of Architecture, The University of Texas at Austin. Afroza's research interests include urban and rural settlement planning, resilient built environment, building process in informal settlements, and space syntax study.

Mamun Ur Rashid is the Executive Director of Development Research Initiative (dRi) since October 2015. Before that, he was a senior research associate at the BRAC Development Institute (BDI), BRAC University. He was a core team member of the DFID-ESRC funded BDI, BRAC University and BWPI, Manchester University joint research project on 'impact of climate change on urban poverty'. Trained as an anthropologist at Jahangirnagar University of Bangladesh, Mr Rashid started his research career at BRAC's Research and Evaluation Division (RED) in 2003.

Noara Razzak completed her undergraduate in Physics and Comparative Literature in Bryn Mawr College, Pennsylvania, US. She then worked in the BRAC Development Institute (BDI), BRAC University under the supervision of Syed M Hashemi as a Junior Research Associate for two years. Now she is in a PhD programme in Economics at Penn State University, State College, USA.

Gilbert Rodrigo, a legally trained activist/researcher with involvement in half a dozen studies and over three decades of field experience in Tamil Nadu, works particularly on the rights, development and education of Fisher folk and Dalits, hence his commitment to the current research on social relations of waste.

Dianne Scott is a human geographer, who is an Honorary Research Fellow at the University of KwaZulu-Natal, Durban, South Africa. Her expertise lies in urban development in the Global South, environmental social science, and the co-production of knowledge for sustainability. Her current research focus is climate change governance and smart cities.

Riziki Shemdoe is Senior Research Fellow at the Institute of Human Settlements Studies, Ardhi University, Dar es Salaam, Tanzania. His research interests include climate change mitigation and adaptation, traditional knowledge in managing natural resources, ecosystem health, biodiversity and sustainable development.

M. S. Sriram is a Visiting Faculty researcher at the Indian Institute of Management, Bangalore and a Distinguished Fellow of the Institute for Development of Research in Banking Technology. He was formerly ICICI Bank – Lalitha Gupte Chair professor of Microfinance at the Indian Institute of Management, Ahmedabad. He researches urban poverty and financial inclusion.

Alfredo Stein is an urban development specialist with 35 years of experience in the design, management and evaluation of low-income housing, post-emergency reconstruction, and poverty reduction policies and projects. He is currently a lecturer in urban development planning at the University of Manchester, with research focusing on climate change adaptation.

Catherine Sutherland is a geographer who focuses on urban environmental governance and sustainability. She is a lecturer in the School of Built Environment and Development Studies at the University of KwaZulu-Natal, Durban, South Africa. Her current research includes the water and climate governance interface, community adaptation in informal and peri-urban settlements and resilience.

Francine van den Brandeler is a PhD student at the University of Amsterdam, researching the metropolitan water governance regimes in São Paulo (Brazil) and Mexico City (Mexico). She was a junior researcher in the Chance2sustain project based at the Centro Brasileiro de Análise e Planejamento (CEBRAP) in São Paulo, Brazil.

Acknowledgements

This book builds on two research programmes: Poverty and Climate Change in Urban Bangladesh (ClimUrb), and Chance2Sustain. The ClimUrb programme was sponsored by the UK Government's ESRC-DFID Joint Fund for Poverty Alleviation Research (RES-167-25-0510). It originates from a Rory and Elizabeth Brooks Foundation-funded research collaboration between the University of Manchester (UK) and BRAC University (Bangladesh), hosted at the Brooks World Poverty Institute (BWPI), now the Global Development Institute (GDI), at the University of Manchester. The editors are particularly grateful to the ClimUrb sponsors and collaborators, as well as the numerous low-income residents and key informants in three Bangladeshi cities – Dhaka, Chittagong and Khulna – who gave so much of their time to ClimUrb researchers. For more information, visit http://www.bwpi.manchester.ac.uk/research/researchprogrammes/climurb/index.htm.

The Chance2sustain programme was sponsored by the Seventh European Union framework programme (FP7 grant no. 244828). We thank FP7 for its support, as well as all partners that took part in the programme: the European Association of Development Research and Training (EADI), Germany; French National Center for Scientific Research (CNRS), Paris, France; School of Planning and Architecture (SPA), Delhi, India; Cities for Life Forum (FORO), Lima, Peru; Centro Brasileiro de Analise e Planejamento (CEBRAP), São Paulo, Brazil; Norwegian Institute for Urban and Regional Research (NIBR), Oslo, Norway; the University of KwaZulu-Natal (UKZN), Durban, South Africa; and the Amsterdam Institute of Social Science Research (AISSR), University of Amsterdam (the Netherlands). For more information on the research programme see http://www.chance2sustain.eu/.

Several chapters in this book also come directly from the best papers presented at a two-day international workshop held at Manchester in September 2013 as part of the ClimUrb project, which was co-sponsored by the Chance2sustain programme. The workshop pulled together works of leading scholars researching urban poverty across Asia, Africa and Latin America to facilitate the exchange and consolidation of knowledge and its policy uptake. We are particularly thankful to these expert workshop participants.

We would like to thank SAGE Publishers for permitting us to re-use some materials published in the *Journal of Environment and Urbanization*. We would also like to thank START Secretariat, the Brooks World Poverty Institute (BWPI), *Jàmbá Journal of Disaster Risk Studies* (particularly Tumpale Sakijege), and Routledge for kindly permitting the re-use of their tables and illustrations.

The initial findings of the book were presented to scholars at two UK research organisations with specialist knowledge on urban poverty and climate change, the International Institute for Environment and Development (IIED) and the Global Urban Research Centre (GURC, University of Manchester). The editors gratefully acknowledge the comments made at these meetings, which have significantly enhanced the intellectual narrative presented in this book.

Finally, the book draws on knowledge being generated as part of another ongoing research programme, EcoPoor (Institutions for Urban Poor's Access to Ecosystem Services: A Comparison of Green and Water Structures in Bangladesh and Tanzania) which is funded by the UK Government's ESPA (Ecosystem Services for Poverty Alleviation) programme (Ref. NE-L001616-1). See http://ecopoor.com/ for further details on the EcoPoor project and http://www.espa.ac.uk/ on the ESPA programme.

Abbreviations

AAS	Association for the Advancement of Society
ACCCRN	Asian Cities Climate Change Resilience Network
ACHR	Asian Coalition for Housing Rights
ADB	Asian Development Bank
APCA	Asset Planning for Climate Change Adaptation
APW	Asset Adaptation Planning Workshop
AR5	IPCC Fifth Assessment Report
BBMP	*Bruhat Bengaluru Mahanagara Palike* (Bengaluru Municipal Authority)
BBS	Bangladesh Bureau of Statistics
BWDB	Bangladesh Water Development Board
CBA	Community-Based Adaptation
CBO	Community-Based Organisation
CDC	Community Development Committee
CEBA	Community Ecosystem-Based Adaptation
Chance2Sustain	Urban Chances-City growth and the sustainability challenge (Research Project)
ClimUrb	Poverty and Climate Change in Urban Bangladesh (Research Project)
CLIMWAYS	Climate change and urban water governance: pathways to social transformation (Research Project)
CLUVA	Climate Change and Urban Vulnerability in Africa (Research Project)
COP	Conference of the Parties
CSO	Civil Society Organisation
DFID	UK Department for International Development
DPAE	Directorate for the Prevention of and Attention to Emergencies
DRR	Disaster Risk Reduction
DSK	*Dushtha Shasthya Kendra* (an NGO)
DWASA	Dhaka Water and Sewerage Authority
EBA	Ecosystem-Based Adaptation

EcoPoor	Institutions for the urban poor's access to ecosystem services (Research Project)
EPCPD	Environmental Planning and Climate Protection Department
ESPA	Ecosystem Services for Poverty Alleviation
ESRC	Economic and Social Research Council
EWS	eThekwini Water and Sanitation Unit
FAO	Food and Agriculture Organisation
FBW	Free Basic Water
FGD	Focus Group Discussion
GDI	Global Development Institute
GDP	Gross Domestic Product
GNP	Gross National Product
GOB	Government of Bangladesh
GOI	Government of India
GURC	Global Urban Research Centre
HAT	Human African Trypanosomiasis
ICDP	Indore City Development Plan
ICRS	Indore City Resilience Strategy
IDS	Institute of Development Studies
IGA	Income-Generating Activity
IIED	International Institute for Environment and Development
IPCC	Intergovernmental Panel on Climate Change
IWRM	Integrated Water Resource Management
JMP	Joint Monitoring Programme
JNNURM	Jawaharlal Nehru National Urban Renewal Mission
KCC	Khulna City Corporation
KDA	Khulna Development Authority
KSDB	Karnataka Slum Development Board
MDGs	Millennium Development Goals
MGNREGA	Mahatma Gandhi Rural Employment Guarantee Act
MHUPA	Indian Ministry of Housing and Urban Poverty Alleviation
MOEF	Ministry of Environment and Forests
MPI	Global Multidimensional Poverty Index
NGO	Non-Governmental Organisation
NSSO	National Sample Survey Organisation
OPHI	Oxford Poverty and Human Development Initiative
PCAA	Participatory Climate Change Asset Adaptation Appraisal
PCR	Polymerase Chain Reaction
PRODEL	Promotion of Local Development
RDP	Reconstruction and Development Programme
RIA	Rapid Institutional Appraisal

SANCOOP	South Africa–Norway Research Cooperation on Climate Change
SDF	Spatial Development Framework
SDGs	Sustainable Development Goals
SDI	Slum/Shack Dwellers International
SSI	Semi-Structured Interview
TTC	Total Thermotolerant Choliform
UDL	Urban Development Line
UEIP	Umgeni Ecological Infrastructure Partnership
UN	United Nations
UN DESA	United Nations Department of Economic and Social Affairs
UNDP	United Nations Development Programme
UNICEF	United Nations Children's Fund
UPPRP	Urban Partnerships for Poverty Reduction Project
WAPDA	Water and Power Development Authority
WHO	World Health Organisation

Part I

Urban poverty and climate change

An overview

1 Introduction

*Michaela Hordijk, Manoj Roy, David Hulme
and Sally Cawood*

No one should experience poverty, yet in this affluent world up to a third of humanity experiences poverty in the form of multiple deprivations, including limited access to basic services, food, potable water and sanitation, clothing and shelter (Hulme 2015). Whilst poverty incidence is in decline, with the proportion of extreme poor in the Global South down from over one half of the population (living on less than US$1.25 per day) in 1990 to 14 percent in 2015, 1.9 billion to 836 million people respectively (UN 2015), poverty in urban areas is rising sharply. Such high levels of poverty in such a wealthy world should be a concern for anyone interested in social justice. Whilst poverty estimates are notoriously unreliable, predictions consistently show an upward trend of poverty in towns and cities across the Global South, with a jump from 17 to 28 percent in the past ten years (Haddad 2012). In East Asia, nearly half of all poverty is now in urban areas, whilst in Sub-Saharan Africa the urban share of poverty is 25 percent (Haddad 2012). Arguably, there are many pitfalls in our understanding of, and efforts to reduce, urban poverty. Two concerns stand out to justify this book.

First, that understanding multifaceted urban poverty requires a conscious consideration of climate change as a global process with local impacts. Critically, climate change is identified as one of the contributing factors to rising numbers of urban poor, as the relative decline of rural poverty is partly due to migration of the rural poor to urban areas as a result of or in reaction to climate related shocks and stressors (DePaul 2012). Second, there is a lack of meaningful action to incorporate and understand climate change impacts on the urban poor. UN Habitat suggests that urbanisation (as a process) should adhere to human rights principles while the city (as an outcome) should meet specific human rights standards (UN Habitat 2012). With the tripling of urban land cover (UN Habitat 2015), and an expected three billion people living in slums by 2030 (UN Habitat 2012a), fulfilling this vision is an enormous challenge.

Whilst there is a growing political momentum to tackle urban poverty, this is largely at the level of policy formulation, and has not yet been converted into policy implementation. In September 2015 the UN General Assembly adopted the Sustainable Development Goals (SDGs), committing *inter alia* to 'end poverty in all its forms everywhere' (SDG1), 'to make cities and human settlements inclusive, safe, resilient and sustainable' (SDG11) and 'to take urgent action to combat climate change and its impacts' (SDG13; UN 2015a). 'Cities and Regions' was also one of the key themes on the 'Lima to Paris Action Agenda' in preparation for the 21st Conference of the Parties (COP 21) to the UN Framework on Climate Change in December 2015. Furthermore, whilst climate change was mentioned only once in the Habitat Agenda (resulting from the Istanbul City Summit in 1996), and only in reference to the need to reduce energy use (hence mitigation), climate change is one of the key themes of the Habitat III conference to be held in Quito in October 2016.

Despite this apparent momentum, the research and policy community have only recently begun to explore climate change impacts in cities, thanks to a flurry of publications and initiatives. These publications include: the World Bank 2008 report on 'Climate Resilient Cities' (Prasad et al. 2009), the Red Cross 2010 World Disaster Report on 'Focus on Urban Risks' (IFRC 2010) and the World Wildlife Fund (who rarely focus on 'urban') release of the 'Mega-Risks in Mega-Cities' report in 2009 (WWF 2009). Initiatives include: the Rockefeller Foundation support for the Asian Cities Climate Change Resilience Network (ACCCRN) since 2008 (Rockefeller Foundation 2015) and the Local Governments for Sustainability (ICLEI) yearly gathering for local government representatives, civil society and private sector actors and academia under the banner 'Resilient Cities' since 2010, with a strong focus on climate change. Finally, in 2014 ESRC-DFID has funded a three-year programme on 'Urban Africa: Risk and Capacity' (Urban ARC; Adelekan et al. 2015).

'Cities are where the battle for sustainable development will be won or lost', noted the High Level Panel on the Post 2015 Development Agenda (UN 2013: 17). However, both the High Level Panel report and UN Resolution A/70/L.1 (by which the SDGs were adopted) are notoriously vague on concrete actions to be taken. As one commentator noted, 'the SDGs may have a lot about what needs to be achieved but not about how, by whom and with what funding and support' (Satterthwaite 2015: unpaged). Comparison of resolution A/70/L.1, the Urban Chapter of the IPCC Fifth Assessment Report (AR5) and issue papers released in preparation for Habitat III in 2016 (UN Habitat 2015; 2015a; 2015b) reveals the repetition of certain core concepts and principles, namely: participation, adaptation, co-creation, resilience and transformation, explored below.

Participation is embedded in resolution A/70/L.1, which seeks 'the participation of all countries, all stakeholders and all people' (UN 2015b: 2). However, fostering genuine participation of vulnerable groups is a difficult task, and participation as a panacea to smoothen exclusion has been heavily criticised (Cooke and Kothari 2001; Hickey and Mohan 2005; Hordijk et al. 2015). Rather, attempts to enable community participation in climate adaptation programmes should learn from decades of 'trial and error' in participatory development (Dodman and Mitlin 2013). Indeed, community-based adaptation (CBA) intends to strengthen local capacities at neighbourhood, community or village level to adapt to climate change through participatory local development initiatives (Dodman and Mitlin 2013). However, despite emphasis on the importance of partnerships with local actors, CBA has been criticised for being too localised, too small scale and isolated, and running the risk of making the poor responsible for their own adaptation (Dodman and Mitlin 2013; Forsyth 2013). Sharply focused questions of *who* participates, *how* and *why* remain critically important.

Adaptation can be defined as 'the process of adjustment to actual or expected climate and its effects. In human systems, adaptation seeks to moderate or avoid harm or exploit beneficial opportunities' (IPCC 2014: 1132). Adaptation to climate change impacts seeks to respond to both increased stresses (gradual negative changes that reduce the quality of life and/or impact on livelihoods, e.g. more frequent waterlogging) and to increases in the frequency or severity of disasters. Where climate change adaptation and disaster risk reduction (DRR) converge with development planning and intervention, significant synergies can emerge (UN Habitat 2015: 7). To ensure such interventions benefit the urban poor does, however, require that risk perceptions and existing experiences of climate change impacts are integrated, meaningfully, into formal DRR and adaptation strategies (Fraser Chapter 13, this volume; Hordijk et al. Chapter 8, this volume; Sutherland et al. Chapter 4, this volume).

Such integration requires the co-creation of knowledge, an idea which often underpins CBA. Co-creation of knowledge takes place when a range of actors develop a shared understanding of complex problems and explore possible solutions. It is often assumed that social learning can shift power relations through including the voices and knowledge of the poor (Ensor and Harvey 2015), and build networks across sectors at different scales (Reed et al. 2013), strengthening linkages on which actors can draw when swift action is needed in times of crises. Co-creation of knowledge is arguably one of the building blocks of resilience (Hordijk et al. Chapter 8, this volume), and underpins the work on networks from ACCCRN (Reed et al. 2013; Rockefeller Foundation 2015). Co-creation of knowledge is also undertaken on the premise that the new shared ways of knowing will lead to changes in practice (Ensor and Harvey 2015). However, while ideas such as CBA (Dodman and Mitlin 2013), adaptive development (Agrawal and Lemos 2015) and rights-based perspectives on adaptive capacity (Ensor et al. 2015) emerge, the urban poor are yet to benefit in practice. A major gap therefore remains in translating this knowledge into local planning practice (Turner et al. 2015; UN Habitat 2015: 4).

Interestingly, the concept of 'resilience' can be found in all three (resolution A/70/L.1, AR5 and Habitat III) documents, demonstrating the popularity of the term in policy circles, despite widespread critique (Fainstein 2015; Peyroux 2015). However, in the SDGs the term remains undefined, as if common understanding is assumed. In the formulation of the 17 SDGs the term refers to resilient infrastructure (SDG 9) and 'inclusive, safe, resilient and sustainable cities' (SDG 13). According to UN Habitat, resilience is both 'aspirational and operational', it 'concentrates on how individuals, communities and business not only cope in the face of multiple shocks and stressors, but also realise opportunities for transformational development' (UN Habitat 2015a: 1). The UN Habitat definition moves beyond the traditional definition of the 'capacity to bounce back' after a shock or disturbance, which underlies AR5's definition of resilience (Revi et al. 2014: 547), and entails the possibility to 'bounce forward' (Manyena et al. 2011) based on learning, creativity and innovation (Berkes et al. 2003).

Reference to 'transformation' is also common in all three documents. Resolution A/70/L.1 is even entitled 'Transforming our world: The 2030 Agenda for Sustainable Development'. Addressing persistent inequalities is acknowledged as a prerequisite for 'transformational development' (UN Habitat 2015a) or 'transformative adaptation' (Revi et al. 2014). However, none of the documents explicitly discuss the prevailing power structures and relations that have caused, maintain or even *deepen* existing inequalities. If climate resilience and climate justice have to be dealt with simultaneously, this requires a drastic shift in existing power structures and the policies these structures bring forward, a shift that puts the needs of the poor high on the agenda, and redirects adaptation finance to address their needs. However, this may be judged by many as too radical and therefore unrealistic as the drastic redistribution of resources needed is beyond the capacity of many local governments (Fainstein 2015).

While the official analyses focus on the role of formal agencies in adaptation (Habitat III and AR5 documents highlight the role of local governments in fostering 'incremental improvement' and 'transformative adaptation'), this book focuses on the *lived experiences* of the urban poor – the everyday realities of urban poverty and responses to vulnerability and climate change. Crucially, emphasis on the lived experience addresses the knowledge gap identified in AR5 on the vulnerabilities of urban populations to direct, second- and third-order impacts of climate change, as well as the impacts of slow-onset processes (Revi et al. 2014). The book explores who shapes these experiences and the role that climate change plays in exacerbating existing (and future) multidimensional poverty in towns and cities of the Global South. Finally, it asks how and when 'do-able actions' (i.e. incremental improvements) can be taken, without losing sight of the need for radical change to achieve climate justice. The book draws from two recently completed research programmes – Climate Change and Urban Poverty in Bangladesh (ClimUrb) and Chance2Sustain, as well as a series of papers emerging from research on urban poverty and climate change across Africa, Asia and Latin America, presented at the ClimUrb conference in September 2013 in Manchester, UK.

Finally, the editors have thought long and hard about what term to use when referring to the settlements in which poor urban people live. Different authors and agencies use different terms, each with positive and negative connotations and assumptions. At present, there is no 'agreed' term – slums, informal settlements, low-income settlements, squatter settlements, shanties, *favelas*, *bustees* and others. Each term also refers to very different realities (see, for instance, Sriram and Krishna Chapter 3, this volume). The term 'informal settlement' might appear more value neutral, but in the varied and complex examples in this volume, some of our cases are formally registered in legal terms. 'Low-income settlement' is a term that Hulme and Roy have used extensively in their ClimUrb work in Bangladesh, but this fails to recognise that in other countries such settlements may include the compounds of families who have become very wealthy.

In South Asia, the vernacular term *bustee* is probably most relevant – but again, this has little or no currency for other continents. Whilst acknowledging critique (e.g. Gilbert 2007; 2009), we have opted to use the term 'slum' in the title of the book, and where locally appropriate. We apply this in a purely descriptive sense, certainly *not* in a pejorative sense as some elites do (suggesting illegal economic activities and anti-social behaviours). To respect both context and diversity (and despite the varied critiques), each chapter author was encouraged to apply their own interpretation and locally or regionally relevant framing of the settlements where poor urban people live.

Structure of the book

Part I: Urban poverty and climate change: an overview

Following this introduction, Chapter 2 unpacks the highly complex and value-laden terms 'urban poverty' and 'climate change', with a specific focus on *who* the urban poor are, *where* they live and *how* climate change exacerbates their existing vulnerabilities. With particular emphasis on everyday, lived experiences, the chapter demonstrates how the urban poor are already coping and/or adapting to these impacts in diverse ways. Finally, the chapter draws together the key concepts (e.g. participation, co-creation, resilience and transformation) noted above, exploring their relevance to current policy and planning on urban poverty and climate change. Three key themes drawn from the two research projects and associated papers are used to structure the remainder of the book – i) vulnerability, adaptation and the built environment; ii) understanding change and adaptation: from institutional interface to co-production; and iii) from learning to knowledge, innovation to action.

Part II: Vulnerability, adaptation and the built environment

Where (and how) one lives has dramatic implications for the risks one is exposed to, and adaptation options available. In Chapter 3, Sriram and Krishna demonstrate how heterogeneity within and between Bengaluru (formerly Bangalore) slums in India has implications for household adaptation. In the Indian case the term 'slum' ranges from the official or so-called 'notified' slums (where poverty levels may be low compared to city averages) to 'un-notified' slums (where poverty levels are high). In Durban, South Africa, 'spatially differentiated service provision' is actually an official policy. Where you live therefore determines the level of service provision you are entitled to. In Chapter 4, Sutherland et al. outline how this policy is perceived, both from a justice and adaptation perspective. They explore how an abstract policy is reworked by the everyday practices of the urban poor, offering important insights on the co-creation of knowledge.

In Chapter 5, Parvin et al. explore two spatial domains (settlement and dwelling unit) in which adaptive practices take place in the built environment. In doing so, they highlight how expert-led, top-down climate change policy and planning can neglect innovative adaptation practices of the urban poor. These practices are, however, often affected by (citywide) factors beyond their ability to control, demonstrating the importance of individual and household capacity to engage with external institutions. Characteristics of spatial location and the built environment (both of dwelling and settlement) also have important consequences for the health-related impacts of climate change. Slow-onset (e.g. temperature rise) and rapid weather events (e.g. floods and heavy rain) affect the spread of vector-borne (such as malaria, dengue) and water-borne (such as typhoid, cholera) diseases. In Chapter 6, Mwanyoka et al. provide an overview of these impacts on the urban poor living in low-income settlements in Dar es Salaam, Tanzania, addressing the glaring knowledge gap on health, climate change and urban poverty.

Part III: Understanding change and adaptation: from institutional interface to co-production

This section unpacks the lived experience of urban poverty and climate change further, by focusing on the social and economic differentiation within, among and between slum households, and on their links to external actors. Settlement heterogeneity has important implications for vulnerability and adaptive capacity, and can be a serious barrier for local adaptation. In Chapter 7, Banks outlines the coping strategies of the urban poor in four low-income settlements (*bustees*) in Dhaka, Bangladesh. This reveals how unequal power dynamics and inequality within settlements, particularly between tenants and owners, influences access to social networks and other resources. Vulnerability is ultimately reinforced by internal stratification and informal governance in the *bustee*.

Chapter 8 by Hordijk et al. focuses on community collective capacities for adaptive action. Comparing dynamics of community exposure and response to flood risks in two low-income neighbourhoods in Guarulhos (Brazil) and Arequipa (Peru), it demonstrates how community heterogeneity is linked to the presence or absence of certain capacities (such as social capital, community competence and access to information and knowledge) that supports or erodes community resilience. Both chapters show the importance of the institutional interface, and that successful and sustained local adaptation needs to be linked to wider processes. In Chapter 9, Stein and Moser present a conceptual and operational framework that fosters such links. The 'Asset Planning for Climate Change Adaptation' (APCA) framework presented has been developed through action research (Moser and Stein 2011; Stein and Moser 2014). The findings from Cartagena, Colombia, show how, through engagement with local institutions, participatory asset planning moves beyond traditional CBA.

In Chapter 10, Opel analyses the consequences of two simultaneous trends: rapid urbanisation (in part caused by increased migration from rural hinterlands to coastal cities) and increasing saline contamination (linked to climate change-related stressors). In Paikgacha and Kalaroa, Bangladesh, the consequences for (safe) water availability are such that uncomfortable questions about the inevitability of displacement and relocation must be raised. This is not only relevant for the urban poor, but for entire urban coastal populations. Such relocation would not only require significant financial resourcing, but raises multiple logistical and ethical dilemmas.

Part IV: From learning to knowledge, innovation to action

In this section we explore how innovation and the co-creation of knowledge can spur local adaptation. In Chapter 11, Harriss-White and Rodrigo highlight the role of innovation in India's informal economy (a sector in which many of the urban poor are employed). This valuable contribution raises questions about who innovates and how; it explores the diversity and hybridity of actors and institutions engaged in innovation of various types, and at multiple levels. Drawing on examples from a small town in India, it demonstrates that, until now, the informal economy has been absent from discussions on climate change, yet has implications for climate change mitigation and a 'low carbon' agenda.

In Chapter 12, Hashemi et al. present an experimental asset transfer programme, which reaches the poorest of the poor. It shows that a poverty alleviation programme which reduces vulnerabilities (such as employment, food, dwelling and health insecurities) simultaneously enables households to change from being 'risk prone' to being 'risk averse'. Although as a short-term donor-funded project it faces many challenges, the results support calls to incorporate both development (i.e. infrastructure improvement) *and* adaptation (i.e. damage resilient livelihoods) into NGO, donor and government policy, planning and practice.

The two subsequent chapters analyse what role multiple knowledge can (and should) play in local adaptation action. In Chapter 13, Fraser describes the mismatch between expert-led understandings of landslide risks and the risks perceived by low-income communities on the hill-slopes of Bogota, Colombia. The 'actual risks' as calculated by experts based on probability of occurrence (in the future) hardly ever match what residents perceive as risk based on past and current experience. Risk notions inform actions. If these different notions of risk are not contested or debated, then opportunities for joint adaptive action might go astray. In Chapter 14, Chu chronicles what can be achieved if policies and actions are built upon the local community's knowledge and experience. Collective action plays a significant role throughout this process. Navigating the possibilities offered by ACCCRN and recognising the need for adaptation planning, local communities in Indore, India, were able to integrate their adaptive actions with existing struggles to overcome poverty. They engage with a responsive state which (even though it has funded little adaptation action) attracted and enabled a number of adaptation projects through multilevel adaptation governance. Chu's chapter highlights the contribution of the co-creation of knowledge but also the importance of an experienced community with a history of collective action.

In Chapter 15, the conclusion, we draw out key ideas and recommendations about 'the way forward', bringing the recent policy developments (AR5, the

SDGs, COP 21 and Habitat III) into dialogue with the rich material presented in this book. Evidently, context is central to understanding adaptation processes. The types of impact that climate change imposes and the responses of households, communities and municipal authorities to those impacts are very much dependent on the specific environmental, socio-economic and institutional context. In almost all cases presented here, households and communities are actively adapting but the effectiveness of those adaptations varies greatly both within and between cases. Towards the end of the conclusion, we re-engage with the 'ladder of adaptive capacity' presented in Chapter 2, to shape our understanding of the diverse forms of adaptation across the chapters. This framework is proposed as an analytical device rather than a 'best practice' prescription. In an ideal world all adaptation would be transformative, but in reality, with households and communities having very different levels of capacity for collective action and highly varied external institutions to partner with, moving from acquiescence to coping and/or from coping to progressive adaptation may be a 'best fit' approach.

References

Adelekan I Johnson C Manda M Matyas D Mberu B U Parnell S Pelling M Satterthwaite D and Vivekananda J 2015 Disaster risk and its reduction: an agenda for urban Africa *International Development Planning Review* 37(1) 33–43

Agrawal A and Lemos M C 2015 Commentary: adaptive development *Nature Climate Change* 5 185–187

Berkes F Colding J and Folke C (eds) 2003 *Navigating Social–Ecological Systems: Building Resilience for Complexity and Change* Cambridge, UK: Cambridge University Press

Cooke W and Kothari U 2001 *Participation: The New Tyranny?* London: Zed Books

DePaul M 2012 Climate change, migration, and megacities: addressing the dual stresses of mass urbanization and climate vulnerability *Paterson Review of International Affairs* 12 145–162

Dodman D and Mitlin D 2013 Challenges for community-based adaptation: discovering the potential for transformation *Journal of International Development* 25(5) 640–659

Ensor J and Harvey B 2015 Social learning and climate change adaptation: evidence for international development practice *Wiley Interdisciplinary Reviews: Climate Change* 6(5) 509–522

Ensor J E Park S E Hoddy E T and Ratner B D 2015 A rights-based perspective on adaptive capacity *Global Environmental Change* 31 38–49

Fainstein S 2015 Resilience and Justice *International Journal of Urban and Regional Research* 39(1) 157–167

Forsyth T 2013 Community-based adaptation: a review of past and future challenges *Wiley Interdisciplinary Reviews: Climate Change* 4(5) 439–446

Gilbert A 2007 The return of the slum: does language matter? *International Journal of Urban and Regional Research* 31(4) 697–713

Gilbert A 2009 Extreme thinking about slums and slum dwellers: a critique *SAIS Review of International Affairs* 29(1) 35–48

Haddad L 2012 Poverty is urbanising and needs different thinking on development Available from: http://www.theguardian.com/global-development/poverty-matters/2012/oct/05/poverty-urbanising-different-thinking-development [Accessed: 10/09/15]

Hickey S and Mohan G 2005 Relocating participation within a radical politics of development *Development and Change* 36(2) 237–262

Hordijk M L Sara M L Sutherland C and Scott D 2015 Participatory Instruments and Practices in Urban Governance in Gupta J Pfeffer K Verrest H and Ros-Tonen M (eds) *Geographies of Urban Governance: Advanced Theories, Methods and Practices* Springer (Online) chapter 7 127–146

Hulme D 2015 *Global Poverty: Global Governance and Poor People in the Post-2015 Era* Abingdon UK: Routledge

International Federation of the Red Cross (IFRC) 2010 '*Focus on Urban Risk*' *World Disasters Report 2010* International Federation of Red Cross and Red Crescent Societies Geneva

Intergovernmental Panel on Climate Change (IPCC) 2014 *Climate Change 2014: Impacts, Adaptation, and Vulnerability Part A: Global and Sectoral Aspects. Contribution of Working Group II to the Fifth Assessment Report of the Intergovernmental Panel on Climate Change* Cambridge and New York: Cambridge University Press

Manyena S B O'Brien G O'Keefe P and Rose J 2011 Disaster resilience: a bounce back or bounce forward ability? *Local Environment* 16(5) 417–424

Moser C and Stein A 2011 Implementing urban participatory climate change adaptation appraisals: a methodological guideline *Environment and Urbanization* 23(2) 463–486

Peyroux E 2015 Discourse of urban resilience and 'inclusive development' in the Johannesburg Growth and Development Strategy 2040 *The European Journal of Development Research* 27(4) 560–573

Prasad N Ranghieri F Shah F Trohanis Z Kessler E Sinha R 2009 *Climate Resilient Cities: A Primer on Reducing Vulnerabilities to Disasters* Washington DC: The World Bank

Revi A Satterthwaite D Aragón-Durand F Corfee-Morlot J Kiunsi R B R Pelling M Roberts D C and Solecki W 2014 Urban Areas in: Field C B Barros V R Dokken D J Mach K J Mastrandrea M D Bilir T E Chatterjee M Ebi K L Estrada Y O Genova R C Girma B Kissel E S Levy A N MacCracken S Mastrandrea P R White L L (eds) *Climate Change 2014: Impacts, Adaptation, and Vulnerability. Part A: Global and Sectoral Aspects. Contribution of Working Group II to the Fifth Assessment Report of the Intergovernmental Panel on Climate Change* Cambridge, UK: Cambridge University Press 535–612

Reed S Friend R Toan C V Thinphanga P Sutarto R and Singh D 2013 'Shared learning' for building urban climate resilience: experiences from Asian cities *Environment and Urbanization* 25(2) 393–412

Rockefeller Foundation 2015 *Insights from the Asian Cities Climate Change Resilience Network: Ten Cities, Four Countries, Five Years: Lessons on the Process of Building Urban Climate Change Resilience* Available from: https://assets.rockefellerfoundation.org/app/uploads/20150102000721/Ten-Cities-Four-Countries-Five-Years-Lessons-on-the-Process-of-Building-Urban-Climate-Change-Resilience.pdf [Accessed: 27/10/15]

Satterthwaite D 2015 The SDGs and 'a new urban agenda'? IIED Blogpost September 8th Available from: http://www.iied.org/sdgs-new-urban-agenda [Accessed: 27/10/15]

Stein A and Moser C 2014 Asset planning for climate change adaptation: lessons from Cartagena, Colombia *Environment and Urbanization* 26(1) 166–183

Turner M Hulme D and McCourt W 2015 *Governance, Management and Development: Making the State Work* London: Palgrave Macmillan (2nd edition)

United Nations (UN) 2013 A new global partnership: Eradicate poverty and transform economies through sustainable development *Final Report of the UN High-Level Panel of Eminent Persons on the Post-2015 Development Agenda* Available from: http://www.un.org/sg/management/pdf/HLP_P2015_Report.pdf [Accessed: 27/10/15]

United Nations (UN) 2015 The Millennium Development Goals Report 2015 Available from: http://www.un.org/millenniumgoals/2015_MDG_Report/pdf/MDG%202015%20 rev%20(July%201).pdf [Accessed: 27/10/15]

United Nations (UN) 2015a *Sustainable Development Goals* Available from: https:// sustainabledevelopment.un.org/topics [Accessed 16/10/15]

United Nations (UN) 2015b *Transforming our world: the 2030 Agenda for Sustainable Development* General Assembly Resolution 70/1 Available from: http://www.un.org/ga/ search/view_doc.asp?symbol=A/RES/70/1&Lang=E [Accessed: 27/10/15]

UN Habitat 2012 *City Prosperity Initiative* Available from: http://unhabitat.org/urban-initiatives/initiatives-programmes/city-prosperity-initiative/ [Accessed 27/10/15]

UN Habitat 2012a *Housing and Slum Upgrading* Available from: http://unhabitat.org/ urban-themes/housing-slum-upgrading/ [Accessed: 27/10/15]

UN Habitat 2015 Cities and Climate Change and Disaster Risk Management *Habitat III Issue Paper 17* UN Habitat Available from: http://unhabitat.org/wp-content/ uploads/2015/04/Habitat-III-Issue-Paper-17_Cities-and-Climate-Change-and-Disaster-Risk-Management-2.0.pdf [Accessed: 27/10/2015]

UN Habitat 2015a Urban Resilience *Habitat III Issue Paper 15* UN Habitat Available from: http://unhabitat.org/wp-content/uploads/2015/04/Habitat-III-Issue-Paper-15_Urban-Resilience-2.0.pdf [Accessed: 27/10/15]

UN Habitat 2015b Inclusive Cities *Habitat III Issue Paper 1* UN Habitat Available from: http://unhabitat.org/wp-content/uploads/2015/04/Habitat-III-Issue-Paper-1_Inclusive-Cities-2.0.pdf [Accessed: 27/10/2015]

World Wildlife Fund (WWF) 2009 *Mega-Stress for Mega-Cities: A Climate Vulnerability Ranking of Major Coastal Cities in Asia* Gland: WWF International

2 The lived experience of urban poverty and climate change

Impacts and adaptation in slums

Manoj Roy, David Hulme, Michaela Hordijk and Sally Cawood

Introduction

This book concerns two potentially irreversible global trends. The first is rapid urbanisation across the Global South and the associated rise in the scale of urban poverty. More than half of the world's eight billion people already live in cities and towns, and by 2050 the urban share of global population is expected to rise to 66 percent, nearly five billion people (UN DESA 2014). Whilst the Global North has stabilised, and is in fact shrinking in terms of urban share of global population, Asia is dominating and will continue to do so over the next two decades. By 2050, a predicted 63 percent of the world's urban population will live in Asia's towns and cities (Rahman 2011). Africa is catching up with Asia, but will outpace all other regions in the rate of urbanisation (UN DESA 2014).

The single most worrying prospect that this urbanisation trend brings is the rapid increase in population that live in slums, low-income or informal settlements across Asia, Africa and, to a lesser extent, Latin America. Poverty and deprivations are rampant in slums (Pauleit et al. 2015). Indeed, high rates of urbanisation in developing regions are already regarded as a major challenge for global poverty reduction goals (Hulme 2015). It should be noted that a significant proportion of slum dwellers are classed as 'non-poor' by many poverty lines. This is because urban poverty is not simply a matter of low income but a combination of multiple deprivations (Alkire and Seth 2015) which are not covered by these poverty lines. It can also be because over time the urban poor accumulate assets, increase wealth and hence are socially mobile, but continue to live in the dwellings in low-income settlements for which they struggled so hard (Hordijk et al. Chapter 8, this volume; Sriram and Krishna Chapter 3, this volume). In Latin America, for example, 30 to 40 percent of the population are living on US\$4 to US\$10 per day, and regarded as the 'strugglers'. They have not yet reached the income security of the 'real middle classes' and are still vulnerable to shocks (Birdsall et al. 2014).

Paradoxically, rapid urbanisation in the Global South can also be regarded as one of the most important contributors to poverty reduction. For example, Dobbs et al. (2011) estimate that in emerging economies, secondary cities of over 150,000 inhabitants will deliver nearly 40 percent of global growth by 2025, more than the entire developed world and emerging market megacities combined. Urbanisation creates big problems but also brings opportunity. China and India, two of the most populous and fastest urbanising countries in the world, are where the drop in extreme poverty rates has been the highest – approximately 33 percentage points reduction over the past three decades (Olinto et al. 2015). Commentators such as Glaeser (2011: 70) argue: 'cities aren't full of people because cities make people poor, but because cities attract poor people with the prospect of improving their lot in life. The poverty rate among recent arrivals to big cities is higher than the poverty rate of long-term residents, which suggests that, over time, city dwellers' fortune can improve considerably'. Rapid urbanisation is thus both a concern and an opportunity.

The second trend is climate change. The IPCC Fifth Assessment Report (AR5), the most authoritative source, concludes that warming of the climate system is unequivocal, with 95 percent certainty that humans have contributed to global warming (IPCC 2014). The report confirms that by the turn of this century a 2°C rise in average global temperature is unavoidable, yet the worst case scenario indicates an increase of up to 4.8°C. The risks associated with these changes are already increasing for local and national economies and ecosystems. There is general consensus that ignoring climate change will eventually damage global economic growth, while the benefits of strong, early action considerably outweigh the costs (Stern 2006). At the same time, these predictions can act to turn climate change risk from a negative phenomenon to a development opportunity, although reaching a global agreement to seize this opportunity is proving elusive (see the section on COP 21 in Chapter 15, p263). Despite this failure to produce a coordinated international response to climate change, the urban scale has shown concrete action is possible, although its success is relative (Aylett forthcoming).

In a 2012 global survey, respondents[1] from local governments confirmed that their cities already experienced the effects of climate change. Eighty-one percent noted an increase in natural disasters, others noted increased intensity of storms (41 percent), longer periods of drought (31 percent), inland flooding (30 percent) and coastal flooding (13 percent). Higher temperatures were reported throughout the world, though most notably in Asia (91 percent) and Africa (70 percent). Sixty percent reported changes in precipitation levels. Two-thirds of the respondents indicated that their cities engaged in adaptation planning (Carmin et al. 2012). Very little of such adaptation planning has, however, yet reached implementation stages (Aylett forthcoming). Some authors are very optimistic about the potential synergies if adaptation action is streamlined with or even spurs other urban development priorities (Wilbanks 2003). This then offers the opportunity to address direct needs and long-term goals simultaneously.

Concepts such as 'adaptive development' (Agrawal and Lemos 2015) and 'climatising development' (Boyd et al. 2008) have started to emerge, and receive increasing policy attention. Sadly, being regarded as illegal occupiers in the eyes of governments and political elites (Banks et al. 2011), slum dwellers are usually excluded from access to such formal risk reduction mechanisms (Christoplos et al. 2009). However, as noted in Chapter 1, the recent ratification of the UN Sustainable Development Goals (SDGs) and framing of UN Habitat III demonstrate that a pathway for the urban poor to better tackle the threats posed by climate change risk is finally being created. Whether these pathways and opportunities reach the poorest and most vulnerable is yet to be seen, and requires sustained critical engagement.

In this chapter we conceptualise *how* and *why* these two trends can (and should) be integrated to inform future policy, planning and practice on urban poverty and climate change. Building on recent scholarship, we argue that even small shocks can damage the livelihoods of poor urban households, as they have few assets to deploy to cushion themselves from negative impacts. A series of small shocks can often accumulate to trigger a collapse in household viability, with disastrous consequences for all members – men, women and children. In turn, this may disrupt, or even reverse, the broader processes that might have broken the intergenerational transmission of poverty. Climate variability and climate change are rapidly increasing the urban poor's exposure to minor shocks and major disasters at a time when rapid migration to urban areas is fuelled by the destruction of rural livelihoods (Park et al. 2003). Such high levels of vulnerability can ultimately undermine national development prospects, community improvements and local aspirations. The twofold concerns of urban poverty (fuelled by rapid urbanisation) and climate change (characterised by slow-onset, rapid or sudden and cascade effects) are therefore intertwined. Before exploring these interconnections, the discussion turns to 'who' the urban poor are, and where they live.

Profiling the urban poor

There are ongoing, intense debates around how to define and measure poverty (Ravallion and Chen 2013; Hulme 2015), and urban poverty in particular (Mitlin and Satterthwaite 2013). Broadly speaking, there are two distinct approaches to understanding poverty, focusing on whether poverty is defined in absolute or relative terms. Urban poverty appears to be best understood through the relative perspective, but the absolute measure of poverty dominates official and formal practices of poverty assessment and monitoring. The absolute measure of poverty uses levels of consumption as a basis for classifying people (or households) as being poor or non-poor (a headcount measure). There are various methods of defining the consumption levels – in Bangladesh for example, the 'cost of basic needs' approach is used to define poverty lines. This utilises a fixed food bundle, consisting of 11 key items based on a concept of 'minimum nutritional intake' (Banks 2010). Food poverty lines are computed by pricing this bundle using the average price of each item for each of Bangladesh's 15 geographical areas (BBS 2006). A number of critics, notably Baud et al. (2008), Bapat (2009) and Mitlin and Satterthwaite (2013), have argued that the absolute measure produces underestimations of poverty in urban areas. Four main critiques are, outlined below:

I. The national poverty lines do not reflect the costs of basic necessities in urban areas. Low-income urban households must meet all of their food costs, high monthly rent and transport costs, as well as the high costs of water and electricity, and health and education costs.

II. Poverty lines do not capture the (lack of) assets that households have, which reduces their vulnerability in the long run. If consumption is steady, but assets are being depleted, then a household's vulnerability to future poverty increases.

III. The health situation of family members can be an asset or a liability (when labour is directed to the care economy and ill family members cannot work).

IV. Spatial segregation and social exclusion among poor households are not covered in such approaches, despite the fact that they reduce household access to important state- and/or community-provided resources.

The relative approach, in contrast, assesses poverty in relational terms. In other words, it recognises that *access* to a variety of assets makes a household capable of producing wellbeing for its members, or a lack of assets prevents them from doing so (Baud et al. 2008). These capabilities represent the set of alternative commodity bundles that the household can command in a society, using the totality of its rights and opportunities (Sen 1999). They constitute various 'endowments' that people need to realise their full set of 'freedoms' as human beings. Sen emphasises the role and responsibility of the state in providing for these freedoms, and the importance of the voices of all to be included in the deliberation on the goals of development. His work underlies the human rights based approach to development. Mitlin and Satterthwaite (2004; 2013; 2014) observe that it is the lack of endowments of various kinds that characterises urban poverty, as summarised in Figure 2.1.

This figure adequately illustrates the complexity of urban poverty and the interrelatedness of the multiple deprivations the urban poor experience, such as inadequate income, housing, access to services, but also the immediate causes that make it impossible for the urban poor to overcome these deprivations. The Multidimensional Deprivation Index (MPI), developed by Oxford Poverty and Human Development Initiative (OPHI), has grouped a number of these deprivations as far as they can be quantitatively measured and compared internationally (Alkire et al. 2015). Therewith they miss out, for instance, indicators of powerlessness vis à vis the bureaucracy. This is important, since the first global study on how people experience poverty has proven that the poor themselves consider this powerlessness, being discriminated or marginalised by authorities, not being heard, as a very important aspect of poverty (Narayan et al. 2000). The MPI does, however, complement traditional income-based poverty measures (i.e. the absolute measure) by capturing the severe deprivations of each person with respect to education, health and living standards.

Of course the MPI is an important step forwards for monitoring changes in global, national and regional poverty statistics, as it allows the measurement of the *intensity* and *depth* of poverty. People are considered poor when they score

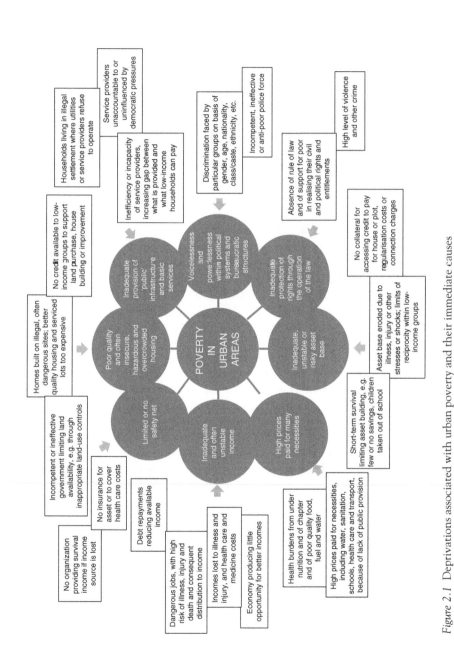

Figure 2.1 Deprivations associated with urban poverty and their immediate causes

Source: Mitlin and Satterthwaite (2014: 241).

below a certain cut-off point in the index. They are considered intensely poor when they are deprived in, for instance, five out of ten dimensions of the index, hence when many deprivations coincide. People are considered deeply poor when (on a number of dimensions) they score considerably lower than the moderately poor: being, for instance, very malnourished, illiterate and possessing hardly any assets (Alkire and Seth 2015). A third important characteristic is the *duration* of poverty – that households can move in and out of poverty. Small shocks can lead to a chain of events that throw households back into poverty. The longer poverty persists, the more difficult it becomes to escape. People that have been poor for more than five years are more likely to remain poor for the rest of their lives, and even pass poverty on to subsequent generations. Chronic poverty then becomes intergenerational poverty (Hulme and Shepherd 2003).

Putting the lived experience at the centre of the poverty debate, recent accounts of 'wellbeing' (instead of welfare) incorporate subjective and relational dimensions. Wellbeing is as much about 'doing well' as about 'feeling good' (White 2010). 'It is not only wealth that matters, it's peace of mind too' (Brock 1999). 'Doing well' or the material aspects include well-known endowments such as income levels, housing quality, tenure status, employment and livelihoods opportunities, availability/quality of services and amenities, infrastructure and accessibility (e.g. public transport), access to information, quality of the environment. The *subjective* dimension is people's satisfaction with and perception of these elements.

Confirming Narayan and Brock's findings, it is the relationships with others that are critically important. This *relational* dimension refers both to relations of love and care and social obligations at the household and community level, and to relations with the state – law and politics. It also includes scope for personal and collective action. The subjective aspect is people's satisfaction with and perception of these, as well as the sense of meaning/meaninglessness. This has a strong, collective moral dimension, grounded in shared understandings of how the world is and should be (White 2010). Wellbeing is ultimately an iterative 'network', in which interdependency is key and the factors and dimensions complement and overlap (Knoeff 2015). Both Sen's capability approach and the wellbeing approach are actor-oriented, focusing on what people value being and doing (Sen 1999), emphasising strengths, rather than needs (White 2009; 2010). If we analyse poor people's innovations and strategies for survival, we can see how development actions can support their personal and collective aspirations and agency (McKean 2009). Thus, we posit that poor urban people are innovative and diverse individuals with their own agency, cultural resources and economic strategies. They constantly seek to improve their lives, whether this is individually, collectively and/or by engaging in co-productive arrangements with state and non-state actors and agencies (e.g. NGOs, community-based organisations, private businesses, local politicians, planners, technicians, etc.). Co-production is concerned with the provision of public services through regular, long-term relationships between state agencies and citizen groups, with both making substantial resource contributions (Joshi and Moore 2004). Building on state capacity and local collective action is therefore increasingly seen as a means of improving service delivery in urban areas (EcoPoor 2013–2016[2]).

It is important to note, however, that the actor-oriented or agency approach has often been criticised for neglecting the structural inequalities in wealth and power. In practice, the urban poor rely predominantly on their own collective action, with some co-production and a bundle of (often exploitative) vertical relationships with local elite (e.g. landlords, politicians). Success depends upon the strength and direction of their social relationships, particularly with regards to collective action. The experience of such exploitative relations and inequalities is already accounted for in what Mitlin and Satterthwaite (2013) regard as 'voicelessness and powerlessness in political systems', and the quality of relations with the state and rule of law, as in the wellbeing framework. It is these small-scale *everyday practices* and engagements in which structural inequalities are constantly reproduced (Ekers and Loftus 2008).

Climate change's impacts on the risk bundle for the urban poor

Nature of climate change impacts on urban poor

Climate change may be conceptualised in several ways. Armah et al. (2015), for example, distinguish between two approaches. First, it may refer to systematic trends in aspects of climate (e.g. precipitation, temperature ranges) that deviate from relatively recent patterns. Secondly, it may refer to changing conditions that are seen in regular environmental fluctuations (e.g. predictable seasonal changes) and in stochastic events of perturbations (e.g. 50-year droughts or floods). What is common for both approaches is that the process of climate change projection is inherently uncertain, and the level of accuracy of climate models decreases as we move from the global to national or city level (Karl and Trenberth 2003). As such, instead of relying on climate models, research on climate change impacts within cities and especially at the slum settlement level tends to apply a *perception-based* approach (Moser and Stein 2011; McEvoy et al. 2014; Stein and Moser 2014).

Another notable aspect of the climate change debate is how popular discourse distinguishes between climate and weather, reflecting everyday lived experience of climate change more closely. In defining climate, Hulme (2009) observes that climate is frequently attached to aggregated meteorological measurements and eventually to the predictive natural sciences. According to the Merriam-Webster online dictionary, climate may also mean the prevailing attitudes, standards or environmental conditions of a group, period or place, whereas weather is the state of the atmosphere with respect to heat or cold, wetness or dryness, calm or storm, clearness or cloudiness. Hulme (2009) argues that the discourse moves between talk of 'climate' and talk of 'weather', depending on the relationship with the present. We can only assess 'weather' for the next few days or for the past few centuries. The further back in time we look, the more our reconstructions of the past rely upon notions of climate, rather than weather, and this process of understanding requires specialised knowledge. For the general public, it is the short-term and medium-range weather forecast that is most important and comprehensible.

Our discussion of climate change impacts in poor urban contexts, therefore, needs to focus more on weather events and climate variability than on long-term climate change. After all, causes of climate change may be global and historic, yet in its effects climate change is decidedly local (Moser and Ekstrom 2010). Changes in the global climate will be increasingly manifested in important and tangible ways, such as changes in extremes of temperature and precipitation, decreases in seasonal and perennial snow and ice extent, and sea level rise. The effect will be felt differently in different locations by different people.

With extreme weather events predicted to become more frequent, untimely and severe (Rosenzweig et al. 2011), it becomes an intellectual and policy challenge to understand how these impacts lead to differential outcomes for poor urban people. All too often this relationship is misunderstood as being little different from (or indeed merely a variety of), natural disasters (Simon 2008; Moser et al 2010). Everyday shocks rarely make headlines or cause concern among duty bearers. This is reflected in the way the disaster management community, political leaders, civil servants, charities and other actors respond to extreme weather events such as cyclones or severe flooding. Following rescue operations of perhaps a week's duration, the response shifts to reconstruction – with an emphasis on mitigation to reduce vulnerability to future occurrences – and, perhaps, special assistance to the most vulnerable. In reality, however, many slum dwellers take a long time to recover from a current shock (Chatterjee 2010). Indeed, low-income households experience multiple shocks, and a new shock often occurs before people can recover from the current/previous ones (ClimUrb 2013).

A disaster risk management approach therefore ignores two important dimensions of climate change impacts. First, it ignores the gradual changes in climate variability and the consequent 'piggy-backing' effect on patterns of extreme and severe weather events. Secondly, it ignores many unexpected, hard-to-notice subtle changes in the affected systems as a consequence of both weather events and gradual changes in climate variability. The second forms of impacts are particularly important for poor urban communities. For example, poor urban people usually work as day labourers and lack productive capital, which makes them less able to distribute risk across asset classes and across time. Adelekan et al. (2015) support this line of thinking by (re)defining urban risk for low-income people as *everyday risk*. We therefore posit that the impacts of climate change on poor urban households and communities needs to be divided into three forms (IOM 2010; Roy et al. 2011):

- *Sudden-onset events:* such as floods, cyclones and catastrophic river erosion. Numerous cities and towns are (and will be) highly vulnerable to the threat of sudden-onset events for the foreseeable future, and climate change may well aggravate the situation.

- *Slow-onset processes:* such as coastal erosion, sea-level rise, salt water intrusion, rising temperature, changing rainfall patterns and drought. Many cities and towns are exposed to slow-onset processes.
- *Cascade effects:* a chain of events due to an act affecting a system, such as reduced human security, and domestic and international migration.

It is widely recognised that urban shocks and stressors are unequally distributed both socially and spatially (Pelling 2003). According to the IPCC (2012: 5), 'individuals and communities are differentially exposed and vulnerable based on inequalities expressed through levels of wealth and education, disability, and health status, as well as gender, age, class, and other social and cultural characteristics'. The IPCC therewith recognises the structural inequalities as root cause of risk exposure and vulnerability, acknowledging the knowledge gap when it comes to the vulnerability of citizens to climate change in general, but to sudden shocks and slow onset events in particular (Revi et al. 2014: 550).

Spectrum of shocks and stressors

In the context of slum settlements, impacts are felt both directly and indirectly. Directly – homes are flooded, drainage systems fail, water becomes scarcer, livelihoods are disrupted, incomes fall and health burdens increase. Indirectly – rural livelihoods are destroyed and millions migrate to towns and cities, placing additional demand on already overstressed housing facilities and services (ClimUrb 2013). Poor urban communities are places where physical (spatial and external) and social (internal) vulnerabilities coincide (Simon 2008), creating 'dual vulnerability'. Physical vulnerability refers to those locations that are most likely to be affected by an extreme event (e.g. coastal areas to tidal surge, floodplains to floods, and steep slopes to landslides). It relates to the external dimension of vulnerability, and comprises the potential damage caused by external shocks or trends. Social vulnerability, in contrast, refers to the internal dimensions, namely household and community resources, institutions and relationships, and relates to how these are affected by external shocks/trends and how people deal with them (Duarte et al. 2007). Moser et al. (2010) differentiate this further into socio-economic and legal-political vulnerability. As a common trend, poor urban people generally live in vulnerable locations, where shelter is cheaper, or on vacant land available for illegal/informal occupancy. At the same time, they have high social vulnerability, in that they have weaker social networks and/or face discrimination, and experience lack of voice, neglect from authorities. This coincidence of vulnerable places and vulnerable people is a major concern in poor urban communities (Douglas et al. 2008).

Impacts are also spatially and temporally variable. Krishna et al. (2014) have shown how slum communities have different life experiences along the gradients of new arrivals to third generation slum-dwellers. Roy et al. (2011) observe

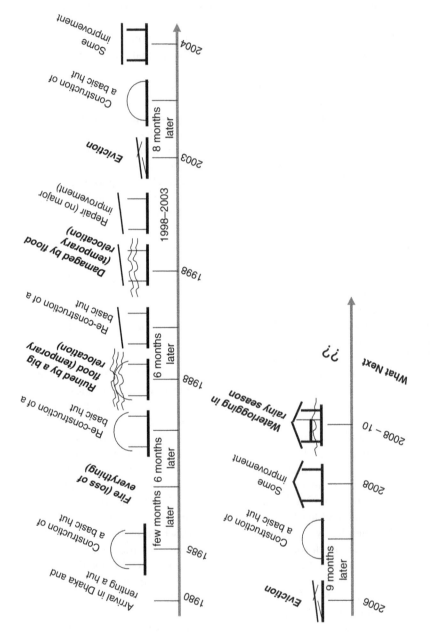

Figure 2.2 Risk bundle for slum dwellers in Dhaka, Bangladesh

Source: ClimUrb (2013: 4).

contrasting lived experiences between 'squatter' households who 'own' their land and those of tenants who rent dwellings from private landlords. Likewise, Jabeen and Guy (2015) identify fluidity in the way slum communities respond to shocks. Even within a single slum, some areas are affected by certain shocks (e.g. water logging) while others are not (Hordijk et al. Chapter 8, this volume). It is, however, the combination and concentration of climatic and non-climatic shocks that overlap in a complex manner, that form a risk bundle for the urban poor. Figure 2.2 indicates the 'risk bundle' for one household in a Dhaka slum. The household portrayed here shows how, even after 40 years in the same settlement, it has barely been able to improve its dwelling. This is partly due to recurrent weather events such as flooding and water logging, as well as non-climatic events such as eviction and fire (Roy et al. 2011).

Framing a response to climate change

Adaptation involves changes in social-ecological systems in response to actual and expected impacts of climate change in the context of interacting non-climatic changes (Moser and Ekstrom 2010). Adaptation strategies and actions can range from short-term coping to longer-term, deeper transformations, aiming to meet more than climate change goals alone, and may or may not succeed in moderating harm or exploiting beneficial opportunities. Three analytical angles stand out from this definition:

- First, adaptation must not consider climate change alone and may be initiated or undertaken in the context of non-climatic factors.
- Second, we must acknowledge mixed outcomes. Whether harm will be moderated and beneficial opportunities exploited through adaptation is contingent on many factors, not just on the adaptive action itself.
- Third, local adaptations of an individual, household or community can be supported, constrained or undermined by extra-local interventions. Thus examination of who acts is also important to understand effective adaptation.

Of course, the need for, type and scale of adaptation depends on the kind of changes taking place, as well as the vulnerability of people and natural systems to this change (Hammill et al. 2008). Recent studies of adaptation have classified adaptation practices into a variety of categories (Table 2.1). The classification drawn out by Smithers and Smit (1997) addresses intentionality, duration and form of adaptation, focusing on the 'how', 'who' or 'what' of adaptation, and referring to social-ecological systems in general. Agrawal's (2010) approach is relevant for examining how climate-related risks affect livelihood capabilities over time, across space, across asset classes and across households. Yet, the approach is developed with reference to rural contexts only. Moser et al. (2010) build upon a participatory appraisal of the physical, socio-economic and legal-political vulnerabilities the poor experience, and the assets they can mobilise to address this (see also Stein and Moser Chapter 9,

Table 2.1 Selected examples of adaptation practice categorisation

Source	Category of adaptation practices
Smithers and Smit (1997)	*Intent* – incidental versus purposeful adaptation practices.
	Duration – short-term adjustments versus permanent adaptation; tactical (short-term) versus strategic (enduring and/or anticipatory) adjustments.
	Form – technological, behavioural and/or institutional.
	Effect – buffering a system from climate perturbation (enhancing stability) versus attempting to facilitate a shift or evolution to a new state (enhancing 'bounce forward' resilience or flexibility).
Pelling and High (2005)	*Individual action on the environment* – material adaptations.
	Managing resources – to improve adaptive capacity.
	Learning to learn (deutero-learning) – learning to operate with ongoing adaptation.
	Learning from experience (single/double/triple loop learning) – reflecting on the merits of improving what is being done or doing something new.
	Institutional modification – attempts to change the social context, for example by realigning their connections of social capital or by challenging or supporting particular institutions. This can also include lobbying on behalf of a policy coalition.
	Collective action on the environment – group reappraisal of past actions, reflection on the use of resources, and changing institutions (but these are not expanded on in this figure, where the focus is on the experience of an individual acting within an organisation).
Agrawal (2010)	*Mobility* – the distribution of risk across space.
	Storage of past surpluses – the distribution of risk across time.
	Diversification – the distribution of risk across asset classes.
	Communal pooling – the distribution of risk across households.
	Market exchange – the purchase and sale of risk via contracts, which may substitute for any of the other four categories when households have access to markets.

Chatterjee (2010)	*Structural adjustments* – these include physical structural mechanisms to raise the building to stabilise the process of sinking, to live with this risk and minimise losses.
	Support network after the event – refers to a household's ability to access resources from multiple sources (e.g. government, non-government, private and local agencies) simultaneously during relief and recovery phase.
	Long-term recovery and network of loss redistribution – how slum dwellers diversify loss redistribution system to recover and reconstruct after flood loss.
	Network for diverse slum communities – socio-cultural characteristics that render households more or less vulnerable during, immediately after and at recovery stages.
	Variety in support network – support network needs to be of different kinds (not limited to distribution of relief material and economic assistance. Such networks could also be designed to provide physical, informational, and legal assistance to slum households to reduce risks and overcome losses).
	Consolidation of existing networks – how poor urban people secure networks that are already informally in place and operating successfully.
Moser et al. (2010)	*Household-level adaptation* – adapting household as the most important asset, protecting human capital, and mobilisation of urban and rural networks.
	Adaptation by small business – maintaining stock, protecting produce by covering it with plastic, or storing it in containers; reduction of range of perishable goods on offer; buying extra stock to profit from scarcity (if having greater liquidity) or reducing stock (if limited liquidity).
	Collective adaptation – maintenance of wells; house sharing; structural adjustments to houses; taking children to safer places (as a form of rescue); strengthening civic buildings, such as schools.
Pelling (2010)	*Nature of adaptation:*
	Degree of collaboration – individual or collective
	Degree of focus – purposeful, incidental
	Degree of forethought – spontaneous or planned
	Phasing – proactive or reactive.
	Scope of impact:
	Target – proximity, intermediary or root causes of risk
	Timescale – immediate or delayed
	Future wellbeing – climate proofing (integration of mitigation) or mal-adaptation
	Social consequences – progressive or regressive (depending on the redistributive consequences)
	Developmental orientation autonomous (isolated and contained) or integrated (seeking synergies).

Source: Authors' elaboration.

this volume). Both Moser et al.'s and Chatterjee's categorisations are based on urban contexts, and address certain aspects of the 'how' and 'what' of adaptation. Chatterjee, for instance, shows how slum residents in Mumbai have made both temporary and permanent adaptations to flooding. It is interesting to note the importance of mobilising social capital and networks, both horizontally and vertically, in both categorisations. In addition, Pelling and High (2005) emphasise the 'institutional modifications' which aim to change the context to reduce vulnerabilities, and the importance of (social) learning, which is increasingly recognised as a catalyser of adaptation practices (Ensor and Harvey 2015). Pelling (2011) also categorises adaptation practices in terms of the scope of their impact. The latter categorisation is informed by justice concerns. For example, to what extent do adaptation practices address root causes of vulnerability? Do they have a distributional component and consider the wellbeing of future generations?

Social learning and the co-creation of knowledge

Whereas in the co-production of services diverse actors collaborate to improve planning and/or delivery, in the co-creation of knowledge different actors bring different sets of knowledge to the table to develop a shared understanding of reality, inform decision-making, and undertake action. The importance of this 'co-creation' for climate adaptation is increasingly recognised (Ensor and Harvey 2015) as it can improve the quality and legitimacy of local-level assessments. Given that climate science is inherently uncertain, and becomes even more uncertain when downscaled to local levels, creating a shared understanding drawing on different knowledge is of crucial importance.

An example of this is provided in Hordijk et al. (Chapter 8, this volume), which highlights how residents have far more precise knowledge on the localised impacts of floods than what is recognised by experts, with implications for adaptation measures. The 'actual' risk as measured by experts rarely matches the 'perceived' risk as experienced by laypersons (Jasanoff 1998). Fraser (Chapter 13, this volume) examines how expert-led mapping of landslide risk has in turn created additional risks of displacement and loss of livelihood in Bogota, Colombia. Other scholars also conclude that expert-led risk assessments can have little or no regard of the lived experiences of (actual or perceived) risks for poor people on the ground (Dickson et al. 2012).

Since scientific knowledge, even when presented as unbiased and neutral, is socially embedded and constructed, it can reinforce existing power structures and, intentionally or unintentionally, exclude alternative views. Social learning, understood as iterative 'cycles of knowledge sharing and joint action, to co-create knowledge, relationships and practices' (Ensor and Harvey 2015: 509), can therefore have the dual purpose of improving the knowledge base, and giving voice to those affected. Expert-led risk assessments, for instance, often underpin major decisions to construct large-scale infrastructure such as seawalls or dykes. Such infrastructure commonly protects major economic assets, but can come with a portrayed necessity of relocating urban poor living on marginal lands, on the grounds that they are 'at risk'.

There are two aspects of social learning that we wish to highlight. First, social learning for climate change often draws on organisational learning literature and increasingly distinguishes between single loop learning (to improve existing practices), double loop learning (which questions the frame of reference, and can lead to change in guiding assumptions), and triple loop learning (challenging the underlying value systems, which can lead to paradigm changes or regime shifts) (Pahl-Wostl et al. 2007; Huntjens et al. 2012; Hordijk et al. 2014). When actors engage in the co-creation of knowledge, single loop learning can gradually develop into double or even triple loop learning. Social learning processes can empower communities and raise awareness of their rights. Given its cyclical process, co-creation can foster trust and the development of bridging and linking social capital between different actors. This not only provides a basis for action, but can also evolve in challenging guiding assumptions and underlying values, hence contesting the status quo.

A second aspect of social learning is that it can foster a culture of experimentation and innovation (Sutherland et al. Chapter 4, this volume; Chu Chapter 14, this volume). Arguably, in the highly uncertain context of climate change, there is a need for incremental action and learning from these efforts.

Resilience – transition – transformation

The IPCC Fifth Assessment Report (AR5) presents a categorisation of cities' adaptive capacities from very little, some or adequate adaptive capacity to 'bounce back', to absorb or cope with the consequences of climate change without losing basic functionality. A fourth category is climate resilience (bouncing forward), and the highest category is transformative (Revi et al. 2014) or 'radical' (Dodman et al. 2014) adaptation. This categorisation is inspired by Pelling's work on climate resilience, transition or transformation (Pelling 2011; Pelling et al. 2012). In this particular understanding, 'resilience' is mainly concerned with stability, improving current practices yet maintaining the status quo, often through technical interventions. Transition relates to incremental adaptation, where technical and material interventions are combined with the recognition of rights and responsibilities, and the improvement of governance structures. This is often guided by a 'learning by doing' or experimental approach, testing 'what works'. Pelling's original understanding of transformation argues that root causes of inequality are addressed, and not 'the proximate causes such as infrastructure planning or livelihoods management', in which short-term and partial remedies dominate because they best serve established interests (Pelling et al. 2012: 5).

What is needed are 'alternative approaches to policy and political action, which promote ecological integrity, procedural and distributional justice as part of living with, and beyond, crisis' (Pelling et al. 2012: 2), based on a change in world view and values. Although this radical shift is not explicit in the AR5 categorisation, it is implicit in the outcomes chosen to characterise transformative adaptation. In this categorisation, most or all built-up areas are serviced with adequate infrastructure, land use planning provides safe land for housing and takes account of mitigation, development policies and investments have integrated adaptation and development with an understanding of the need for mitigation and ecological sustainability. AR5 also concludes that no city in the world has already reached this category, although some governments have taken initial steps (Revi et al. 2014: 546), including local governments in Durban (South Africa), Rosario (Argentina) and Manizales (Colombia) (Bartlett and Satterthwaite forthcoming).

For the purpose of this volume it is important to recognise that the co-production (of services) and co-creation (of knowledge) can support resilience, transition and transformation. In 'resilience' (as bouncing back) co-production is mainly giving users a voice to improve service performance (operational level), and social learning is directed at improving current practices, without challenging existing practices or structures. In 'transition', users are involved in the planning and design stage of service production, and therefore in strategic decisions. This has the potential to give them a voice in a process that affects their lives, and lead to the questioning of existing structures (social learning). It can inspire change in institutional or governance practices, a change in the rules of the game (Pelling 2011; Osborne and Strokosch 2013). Indeed, co-production of services and co-creation of knowledge have often been associated with empowering local communities, challenging the existing order, challenging the norms and values underlying this order and inspiring a shift in regimes, paradigms or the structures of development (Mitlin 2008; Pelling 2011, Hordijk et al. 2014).

The vulnerability of the urban poor is a consequence of historical and existing patterns of uneven development at the local, national and global level. In turn, climate change unjustly impacts those who have contributed least to the global emissions that cause it. Climate justice – understood as the fair distribution of social and material advantages over time and space (Shi et al. forthcoming) and the recognition of existing forms of inequality and underlying structures (Bulkeley et al. 2014) – therefore requires transformative or radical adaptation. 'Empowerment' of the urban poor will not suffice. Rather, community-based efforts (co-production, co-creation, community-based planning) should be a starting point rather than an endpoint for adaptation planning (Archer et al. 2014). Adaptation practices and strategies aiming to achieve 'just outcomes' involve clear statements on 'who wins' and 'who loses' (Fainstein 2015: 158). Who wins and who loses when protective infrastructure is built? Is adequate compensation offered to those displaced?

The answers require difficult political choices around the redistribution of risks, resources and power (Shi et al. forthcoming) that Fainstein (2015) refers to as 'too radical' and beyond the mandate of local governments and planners. Many local governments lack control over areas key to urban adaptation, such as water infrastructure, energy and transport, but also public housing, building codes, welfare and risk assurance. There is thus a clear scalar mismatch between the transformative adaptation needs and existing mandates, financial schemes and regulations (Shi et al. forthcoming). There is also a mismatch in time, as transformative adaptation requires that short-term development and adaptation needs are addressed, and long-term social and ecological consequences are considered, hence the call for integrating development, adaptation and mitigation (Agrawal and Lemos 2015).

In doing so, it is however important to note that urban poverty and climate vulnerability do not coincide in the same way in all cases. Coetzee (2002) argues that people experiencing vulnerability are not necessarily poor. Amongst poor urban people there are varying levels and patterns of vulnerability. This echoes Hulme's (2009) notion that people are more vulnerable to climate change because they are poor, but not necessarily poor because of climate change. Thus, climate change brings an additional layer of stress for poor people. This suggests that both poverty reduction and vulnerability reduction measures should go side by side. However, though there are some common areas between them, these two objectives are not the same. Poverty reduction measures involve responses that range from promoting economic growth to increasing institutional capacity, securing livelihoods, empowering the poor and increasing freedom (Sen 1999). Vulnerability reduction measures, on the other hand, may include responses that reduce biophysical risks, as well as addressing social and environmental factors that influence wellbeing and people's active strategies to secure this in the face of weather events, climate variability and change. In order to simultaneously address both vulnerability and urban poverty through policy responses and interventions, it is necessary to identify those measures that target the overlap between vulnerability and urban poverty. Eriksen and O'Brien (2007) identify three such approaches:

1. Risk reduction – Reducing risks to current ways of securing wellbeing resulting from climate stresses. This means, for example, reducing risks to people's livelihoods, and household and community resources, such as dwellings and civic facilities.
2. Strengthening adaptation strategies – Strengthening the adaptation strategies of poor people in the face of climate stresses. This includes, for example, finding ways to support people's livelihood diversification, structural adjustments to the built environment and consolidation of support networks.
3. Tackling the causes of vulnerability – Addressing the causes of vulnerability, or specific factors and conditions that make poor people vulnerable to climate stresses, or which can push people into destitution. As noted above, the urban poor's vulnerability is an outcome of their multiple deprivations; in that sense tackling root causes to vulnerability is in fact addressing people's deprivations and inequality.

These three approaches refer to three broad areas, namely: people's livelihood practices (i.e. what people do to earn a living and how they live); how people adapt these practices (i.e. what people do to ensure that they can earn a living and manage to live in the face of extreme weather events, climate variability and change); and the broader structural and political processes that shape where and how people live (i.e. factors influencing their location choice and agency and structural characteristics).

Ways forward: everyday practices as a source of policy-relevant knowledge

Poor people must (and do) ultimately adapt to existing environmental problems, addressing the everyday risks through their everyday practice. There is growing recognition that poor people are already, consciously and/or unconsciously, adapting to climate change impacts, both in physical and behavioural terms. Because the adaptation practices of the urban poor are (i) rarely reflected in the formal mechanisms for poverty reduction and climate adaptation, and (ii) context specific, it is often difficult for policy makers, professionals and practitioners to understand what works for the poor. As Scott (1998) argues in *Seeing like a State*, most formal state-sponsored urban development is unable to resist the temptation to regard the apparent unplanned nature of poor communities as in need of reorganisation, leading to policy attempts to regularise design and planning processes. Yet, as Scott argues, the successful social organisation of community design depends upon the recognition that local, practical knowledge is as important as formal, epistemic knowledge. The inherent uncertainty associated with climate change requires that while we appreciate what people have been doing already, we must not be complacent in believing that existing knowledge would be equally applicable under future climatic conditions. Imagine, for instance, that a slum dwellers' association may have been successful in negotiating long-term tenure security in an area which could be potentially become flood prone in the future. When that actually happens, who will be culpable? Simply relying on what works today for some people is not going to be enough under a changing climate context for society as a whole, nor to secure just outcomes from an intergenerational perspective. Arguably, incremental and transformative adaptation should be pursued simultaneously, not sequentially. We need to support what works for the poor, here and now, without losing sight of the overarching climate justice agenda.

Following this, the alternative perspective taken here (Figure 2.3) is that it is precisely the pragmatism (Guy 2010a) and fluidity (Guy 2010b) of the adaptation practices of the urban poor that require close attention and appreciative analysis. This approach resonates with the work of Agrawal (2010), which calls for governments and other actors to understand, take advantage of, and strengthen already existing practices that poor households and groups use individually or collectively. The construction of specific adaptation practices, however, is dependent on the social and economic resources of households and communities, as well as their ecological location and networks of (and access to) social and institutional relationships.

It is important, as we have done previously, to 'unpack' adaptation within this framework. Efforts should also be made to identify and distinguish between

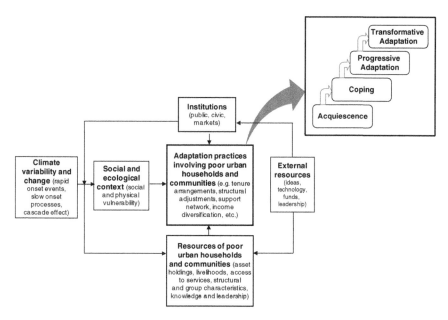

Figure 2.3 Dimensions of adaptation practices and the ladder of adaptive capacity

Source: Roy et al. (2011: 11); the 'ladder of adaptive capacity' is authors' elaboration based on Agrawal (2010), Pelling (2011), Gurran et al. (2013) and Dodman et al. (2014).

four forms of adaptation practices (shown as a blow-up of the central box on the top-right corner of Figure 2.3). In other words, the agenda must distinguish between what people fail to, can and should do (i.e. acquiescence and coping), what and where development agencies should do better, involving gradual transformation (i.e. progressive adaptation), and how society should strive for transformative structural change (i.e. transformative adaptation). This can be seen as a 'ladder' of adaptive capacity in Figure 2.3, further elaborated in Chapter 15. To this end, the remainder of the book provides a rich account of how well (or inadequately) the diverse lived experiences of slum dwellers in 13 towns and cities in 7 countries across Asia, Africa and Latin America add to existing knowledge and deepen our understanding of the policy-relevant development agenda involving a progression from acquiescence, to coping, to progressive adaptation, and ultimately transformative adaptation.

Notes

1 Respondents from 468 cities from five continents filled in (part of) this survey. See Carmin et al. (2012) for more details.

2 EcoPoor is an acronym for a three-year (2013–2016) research programme on 'Institutions for the urban poor's access to ecosystem services: A comparison of green and water structures in Bangladesh and Tanzania'. It is funded by the UK government's

ESPA (Ecosystem Services for Poverty Alleviation) programme (www.espa.com). Visit the EcoPoor website (www.ecopoor.com) to learn more about the project.

References

Adelekan I Johnson C Manda M Matyas D Mberu B U Parnell S Pelling M Satterthwaite D and Vivekananda J 2015 Disaster risk and its reduction: an agenda for urban Africa *International Development Planning Review* 37(1) 33–43

Agrawal A 2010 Local Institutions and Adaptation to Climate Change in R Mearns and A Norton (eds) *Social Dimensions of Climate Change: Equity and Vulnerability in a Warming World* Washington DC: The World Bank 173–197

Agrawal A and Lemos M C 2015 Commentary: adaptive development *Nature Climate Change* 5 185–187

Alkire S and Seth S 2015 Multidimensional poverty reduction in India between 1999 and 2006: where and how? *World Development* 72 93–108

Alkire S Jindra C Aguilar G R Seth S and Vaz A 2015 *Global Multidimensional Poverty Index 2015* Oxford: Poverty and Human Development Initiative, UK

Archer D Almansi F DiGregorio M Roberts D Sharma D Syam D 2014 Moving towards inclusive urban adaptation: approaches to integrating community-based adaptation to climate change at city and national scale *Climate and Development* 6(4) 345–356

Armah F A Luginaah I Hambati H Chuenpagdee R and Campbell G 2015 Assessing barriers to adaptation to climate change in coastal Tanzania: does where you live matter? *Population and Environment* 37(2) 231–263

Aylett A forthcoming Institutionalizing the urban governance of climate change adaptation: results of an international survey *Urban Climate*

Banks N 2010 *Employment and mobility among low-income households in Dhaka, Bangladesh* unpublished PhD thesis University of Manchester UK

Banks N Roy M and Hulme D 2011 Neglecting the urban poor in Bangladesh: research, policy and action in the context of climate change *Environment and Urbanization* 23(2): 487–502

Bapat M 2009 *Poverty Lines and Lives of the Poor: Underestimation of Urban Poverty, the Case of India* Human Settlements Working Paper 20 London: International Institute of Environment and Development (IIED)

Bartlett S and Satterthwaite D (eds) forthcoming *Cities on a Finite Planet: Transformative Responses to Climate Change* London: Routledge

Baud I Sridharan N and Pfeffer K 2008 Mapping urban poverty for local governance in an Indian mega-city: the case of Delhi *Urban Studies* 45(7) 1385–1412

BBS (Bangladesh Bureau of Statistics) 2006 *Preliminary Report on Household Income and Expenditure Survey (HIES) – 2005* Dhaka

Birdsall N Lustig N Meyer C J 2014 The strugglers: the new poor in Latin America? *World Development* 60 132–146

Boyd E Osbahr H Ericksen P J Tompkins E L Lemos M C and Miller F 2008 Resilience and 'climatizing' development: examples and policy implications *Development* 51 390–396

Brock K 1999 *It's Not Only Wealth that Matters – Its Peace of Mind Too: A Review of Participatory Work on Poverty and Ill-being* Washington: World Bank

Bulkeley H Edwards G A S and Fuller S 2014 Contesting climate justice in the city: examining politics and practice in urban climate change experiments *Global Environmental Change* 25 31–40

Carmin J Nadkarni N Rhie C 2012 Progress and Challenges in Urban Climate Adaptation Planning: Results from a Global Survey Available from: http://resilient-cities.iclei.org/fileadmin/sites/resilient-cities/files/Resilient_Cities_2012/Urban_Adaptation_Report_23May2012.pdf [Accessed: 1/1/15]

Chatterjee M 2010 Slum dwellers response to flooding events in the megacities of India *Mitigation and Adaptation Strategies for Global Change* 15(4) 337–353

ClimUrb (Poverty and Climate Change in Urban Bangladesh) 2013 *Climate Change Makes Life Harder for the Urban Poor: Policy-makers Must Act Now* Research Summary Brooks World Poverty Institute, The University of Manchester, UK http://www.bwpi.manchester.ac.uk/medialibrary/research/climurb/output/ClimbUrb_output_summary.pdf [Accessed: 1/11/15]

Christoplos I Anderson S Arnold M Galaz V Hedger M Klein R J T and Goulven K L 2009 *The Human Dimension of Climate Adaptation: The Importance of Local and Institutional Issues* Stockholm: Commission on Climate Change and Development

Coetzee E 2002 Urban Vulnerability: A Conceptual Framework in C Nomdo and E Coetzee (eds) *Urban Vulnerability: Perspectives from South Africa* Cape Town: Periperi Publications

Dickson E Baker J L Hoornweg D and Tiwari A 2012 *Urban Risk Assessments: Understanding Disaster and Climate Risk in Cities* Washington DC: The World Bank

Dobbs R Smit S Remes J Manyika J Roxburgh C and Restrepo A 2011 *Urban World: Mapping the Economic Power of Cities* McKinsey Global Institute Available from: http://www.mckinsey.com/insights/urbanization/urban_world [Accessed: 28/10/15]

Dodman D Archer D and Satterthwaite D 2014 Radical adaptation: how farsighted cities prepare for climate change *IIED Briefing Nov 2014* 1–4

Douglas I Alam K Maghendra M McDonnell Y McLean L and Campbell J 2008 Unjust waters: climate change, flooding and the urban poor in Africa *Environment and Urbanization* 20(1) 187–205

Duarte M Nadelman R H Norton A Nelson D and Wolff J 2007 Adapting to climate change: understanding the social dimensions of vulnerability and resilience *Environment Matters 2007: Adapting to Climate Change* Washington DC: The World Bank

Ekers M and Loftus A 2008 The power of water: developing dialogues between Foucault and Gramsci *Environment and Planning D: Society and Space* 26(4) 698–718

Ensor J and Harvey B 2015 Social learning and climate change adaptation: evidence for international development practice *Wiley Interdisciplinary Reviews: Climate Change* 6(5) 509–522

Eriksen S R and O'Brien K 2007 Vulnerability, poverty and the need for sustainable adaptation measures *Climate Policy* 7(4) 337–352

Fainstein S 2015 Resilience and Justice *International Journal of Urban and Regional Research* 39(1) 157–167

Glaeser E 2011 *Triumph of the City* London: Pan Books

Gurran N Norman B and Hamin E 2013 Climate change adaptation in coastal Australia: an audit of planning practice *Ocean and Coastal Management* 86 100–109

Guy S 2010a Pragmatic ecologies: situating sustainable building *Architectural Science Review* 53(1) 21–28

Guy S 2010b Fluid Architectures: Ecologies of Hybrid Urbanism in D White and C Wilbert (eds) *Technonatures: Environments, Technologies, Spaces and Places in the Twenty-First Century* Waterloo ON: Wilfred Laurier University Press

Hammill A Matthew R and McCarter E 2008 Microfinance and climate change adaptation *IDS Bulletin* 39(4) 113–122

Hordijk M A Miranda Sara L and Sutherland C 2014 Resilience, transition or transformation? A comparative analysis of changing water governance systems in four Southern cities. *Environment and Urbanization* 26(1) 130–146

Hulme D 2015 *Global Poverty* Second edition New York: Routledge

Hulme D and Shepherd A 2003 Conceptualizing chronic poverty *World Development* 31(3) 403–423

Hulme M 2009 *Why We Disagree about Climate Change: Understanding Controversy, Inaction and Opportunity* Cambridge UK: Cambridge University Press

Huntjens P Pahl-Wostl C Rihoux B Schläter M Flachner Z Neto S Koskova R Dickens C and Nabide Kiti I 2012 Adaptive water management and policy learning in a changing climate: a formal comparative analysis of eight water management regimes in Europe, Africa and Asia *Environmental Policy and Governance* 21(3) 145–163

International Organisation for Migration (IOM) 2010 *Assessing the Evidence: Environment, Climate Change and Migration in Bangladesh* Dhaka: IOM

Intergovernmental Panel on Climate Change (IPCC) 2012 *Managing the Risks of Extreme Events and Disasters to Advance Climate Change Adaptation. A Special Report of Working Groups I and II of the Intergovernmental Panel on Climate Change* Cambridge UK: Cambridge University Press

Intergovernmental Panel on Climate Change (IPCC) 2014 *Climate Change 2014: Impacts, Adaptation, and Vulnerability* (Part A: Global and Sectoral Aspects) Cambridge and New York: Cambridge University Press

Jabeen H and Guy S 2015 Fluid engagements: responding to the co-evolution of poverty and climate change in Dhaka, Bangladesh *Habitat International* 47 307–314

Jasanoff S 1998 The political science of risk perception *Reliability Engineering and System Safer* 59 91–99

Joshi A and Moore M 2004 Institutionalised co-production: unorthodox public service delivery in challenging environments *Journal of Development Studies* 40(4) 31–49

Karl T R and Trenberth K E 2003 Modern global climate change *Science* 302 1719–1723

Knoeff J 2015 *Economic Decision-making for Wellbeing: Exploring Household Strategies in a Post-conflict Sri Lankan Fishing Village* MA thesis University of Amsterdam http://dare.uva.nl/cgi/arno/show.cgi?fid=613078 [Accessed: 31/10/2015]

Krishna A Sriram M S and Prakash P 2014 Slum types and adaptation strategies: identifying policy-relevant differences in Bangalore *Environment and Urbanization* 26(2) 568–585

McEvoy D Ahmed I Trundle A Sang L T Diem N N Suu L T T Quoc T B Mallick F H Rahman R Rahman A Mukherjee N and Nishat A 2014 In support of urban adaptation: a participatory assessment process for secondary cities in Vietnam and Bangladesh *Climate & Development* 6(3) 205–215

McKean B 2009 Invisible lives: stories of innovation and transition *Intersections* 10(2) 1–57

Mitlin D 2008 With and beyond the state – co-production as a route to political influence, power and transformation for grassroots organizations *Environment and Urbanization* 20(2) 339–360

Mitlin D and Satterthwaite D 2004 *Empowering Squatter Citizen: Local Government, Civil Society, and Urban Poverty Reduction* London: Earthscan

Mitlin D and Satterthwaite D 2013 *Urban Poverty in the Global South: Scale and Nature* London: Routledge

Mitlin D and Satterthwaite 2014 *Reducing Urban Poverty in the Global South* London: Routledge

Moser C Norton A Stein A and Georgieva S 2010 *Pro-poor Adaptation to Climate Change in Urban Clusters: Case Studies of Vulnerability and Resilience in Kenya and Nicaragua* World Bank Report No. 54947-GLB Washington DC

Moser S C and Ekstrom J A 2010 A framework to diagnose barriers to climate change adaptation. *Proceedings of the National Academy of Sciences of the United States of America (PNAS)* 107(51) 22026–22031

Moser C and Stein A 2011 Implementing urban participatory climate change adaptation appraisals: a methodological guideline *Environment and Urbanization* 23(2) 463–485

Narayan D Patel R Schafft K Rademacher A and Koch-Schulte S 2000 *Voices of the Poor: Can Anyone Hear Us?* World Bank Publications: The World Bank

Olinto P Beegle K Sobrado C and Uematsu H 2015 The State of the Poor: Where are the Poor, Where is Extreme Poverty Harder to End, and What is the Current Profile of the World's Poor? *The World Bank Economic Premier* 125 Available from: http://siteresources.worldbank.org/EXTPREMNET/Resources/EP125.pdf [Accessed: 28/10/15]

Osborne S P and Strokosch K 2013 It takes two to tango? Understanding the co-production of public services by integrating the services management and public administration perspectives *British Journal of Management* 24 31–47

Pahl-Wostl C Craps M Dewulf A Mostert E Tabara D Taillieu T 2007 Social learning and water resources management *Ecology and Society* 12(2) 1–19

Park T Greenberg J Nell E Marsh S Baro M and Mjahed M 2003 Research on urbanization in the developing world: new directions *Journal of Political Ecology* 10 69–94

Pauleit S Coly A Fohlmeister S Gasparini P Jørgensen G Kabisch S Kombe W J Lindley S Simonis I and Yeshitela K (eds) 2015 *Urban Vulnerability and Climate Change in Africa* Future City 4 Heidelberg: Springer

Pelling M 2003 *The Vulnerability of Cities: Natural Hazard and Social Resilience* London: Earthscan

Pelling M and High C 2005 *Social Learning and Adaptation to Climate Change* Benfield Hazard Research Centre Disaster Studies Working Paper 11

Pelling M 2011 *Adaptation to Climate Change: From Resilience to Transformation* London: Routledge

Pelling M Manuel-Navarrete D and Redclift M (eds) 2012 *Climate Change and the Crisis of Capitalism: A Chance to Reclaim Self, Society and Nature* London: Routledge

Rahman H Z 2011 *Urban Bangladesh: Challenges of Transition* Dhaka: Power and Participation Research Centre (PPRC)

Ravallion M and Chen S 2013 A proposal for truly global poverty measures *Global Policy* 4(3) 258–265

Revi A Satterthwaite D Aragón-Durand F Corfee-Morlot J Kiunsi R B R Pelling M Roberts D C and Solecki W 2014 Urban Areas in: Field C B Barros V R Dokken D J Mach K J Mastrandrea M D Bilir T E Chatterjee M Ebi K L Estrada Y O Genova R C Girma B Kissel E S Levy A N MacCracken S Mastrandrea P R White L L (eds) *Climate Change 2014: Impacts, Adaptation, and Vulnerability. Part A: Global and Sectoral Aspects. Contribution of Working Group II to the Fifth Assessment Report of the Intergovernmental Panel on Climate Change* Cambridge, UK: Cambridge University Press 535–612

Rosenzweig S Solechi W D Hammer S A and Mehrotra S (eds) 2011 *Climate Change and Cities: First Assessment Report of the Urban Climate Change Research Network* Cambridge, UK: Cambridge University Press

Roy M with Guy S Hulme D and Jahan F 2011 *Poverty and Climate Change in Urban Bangladesh (ClimUrb): An Analytical Framework* BWPI Working Paper 148, University of Manchester, UK

Scott J C 1998 *Seeing Like a State: How Certain Schemes to Improve the Human Condition Have Failed* New Haven, CT: Yale University Press

Sen A 1999 *Development as Freedom* New York: Knopf

Shi L Chu E Anguelovski I Aylett A Debats J Goh K Schenk T Set K Dodman D Roberts D Timmons Roberts J Van Deveer S forthcoming Roadmap towards justice in urban climate adaptation research *Nature and Climate Change*

Simon D 2008 *When Do You See It? The Challenges of Global Environmental Change for Urban Africa* Urbanisation and Global Environmental Change (UGEC) International Working Papers 08-01 Tempe USA

Smithers J and Smit B 1997 Human adaptation to climatic variability and change *Global Environmental Change* 7(2) 129–146

Stein A and Moser C 2014 Asset planning for climate change adaptation: lessons from Cartagena, Colombia *Environment and Urbanization* 26(1) 166–183

Stern N 2006 *Stern Review on the Economics of Climate Change* London: UK Treasury

United Nations Department of Economic and Social Affairs (UN DESA) 2014 *World Urbanization Prospects: The 2014 Revision* New York: UN DESA

White S C 2009 *Bringing Wellbeing into Development Practice* WeD working paper 09/50 Wellbeing in developing country research group University of Bath UK

White S C 2010 Analysing wellbeing: a framework for development practice *Development in Practice* 20(2) 158–172

Wilbanks T J 2003 Integrating climate change and sustainable development in a place-based context *Climate Policy* 3(1) 147–154

Part II

Vulnerability, adaptation and the built environment

3 Generations of migrants and natures of slums

Distress, vulnerability and a lower-middle class in Bengaluru, India[1]

M. S. Sriram and Anirudh Krishna

Indian slums: the bigger picture

Expanding slums in India's growing cities are attracting increasing official and scholarly attention. For the first time, in 2011 the Census of India undertook a separate enumeration and listing of people in slums,[2] adding to prior knowledge (NSSO 2003; 2009; GOI 2010) about the likely numbers of slums and slum dwellers. The 2011 census data revealed that while the absolute decadal growth of population across the nation was 17.7 percent, the increase in urban population was 31.8 percent, demonstrating a rapid phase of urbanisation. From 17.3 percent of the total population in 1951, the urban share has risen to 31.2 percent as per the 2011 census (GOI 2013). It is expected to rise further on account of three separate trends:

1. Urban incorporation: rural areas reclassified as urban (because of increases in the numbers and densities of population, accompanied by a reduced dependence on agriculture). A total of 2,772 formerly rural areas were reclassified as urban between 2001 and 2011.
2. Rural–urban migration: large-scale migration of people into cities, especially large agglomerations. (Towns with more than 100,000 population account for 70.2 percent of the total urban population).
3. Natural increase: due to the increase of the population in cities, as birth rates outpace death rates.

The above trends are putting pressure on the larger cities, exacerbating the twin issues of urban poverty and urban sprawl. This migration is not only a result of the ongoing fragmentation of land holdings: increased volatility in yields (as a result of climate change impacts, e.g. drought or erratic rainfall) and prices (because of the incursions of global price effects into rural areas) are making it more difficult to maintain a reliable and steady living in rural areas. Climate change and agrarian distress therefore induces the movement of the most vulnerable sections of the rural population into large cities. Part of the urbanisation story is represented by the phenomenon of *urban primacy*, where a single city in a province, such as

Bengaluru[3] in Karnataka, accounts for a significant portion of the overall urban population of the province (Henderson 2005).

As cities (particularly the biggest ones) are growing, slums are growing faster still. Despite this, little is known about the lives of people living in these settlements. Problems of definition, methodology and interpretation collide to create this knowledge gap. The Indian situation, which we discuss below, exemplifies conceptual and practical obstacles noted elsewhere (Mitlin and Satterthwaite 2012; Marx et al. 2013; UN Habitat 2014). Whilst relatively broad, the official definition of a slum (as per the Census of India) is broken down into three categories (listed below) which inform the enumeration process:

I. All notified areas in a town or city notified as 'Slum' by State, Union territories Administration or Local Government under any Act including a 'Slum Act' may be considered as *Notified slums*

II. All areas recognised as 'Slum' by State, Union territories Administration or Local Government, Housing and Slum Boards, which may have not been formally notified as slum under any act may be considered as *Recognised slums*

III. A compact area of at least 300 population or about 60–70 households of poorly built congested tenements, in unhygienic environment usually with inadequate infrastructure and lacking in proper sanitary and drinking water facilities. Such areas should be identified personally by the Charge Officer and also inspected by an officer nominated by Directorate of Census Operations. This fact must be duly recorded in the charge register. Such areas may be considered as *Identified slums.*

(GOI 2013)

Not all government agencies follow the Census definition. The Indian Ministry of Housing and Urban Poverty Alleviation (MHUPA), following the definition adopted by the National Sample Survey Organisation (NSSO), considers a slum to be 'a compact settlement with a collection of poorly built tenements mostly of a temporary nature, crowded together usually with inadequate sanitary and drinking water facilities in unhygienic conditions. Such an area, for the purpose of this survey, was considered as a "non-notified slum" if at least 20 households lived in that area' (GOI 2010: 3). This difference in the qualifying criterion – 20 households per NSSO and 60–70 households in the Census – has led to divergent estimates of people in slums. While the NSSO and MHUPA estimate that 16.5 percent of the urban population in the state of Karnataka live in slums, the corresponding figure provided by the 2011 census was around 12 percent.

Along with uncertainty about the 'true' size of the slum population, another complication emerges when slums are assumed to constitute a homogeneous category of settlements, or when differences are examined only in terms of the gross distinction between notified and non-notified settlements. For example, the description contained in the opening sentence of the MHUPA understanding of slums as 'poorly built tenements mostly of a temporary nature' may not apply to many settlements notified as slums. Once a slum is notified, it could take multiple trajectories depending on the ownership of the land and the type of intervention that the state chooses to implement. For example, there could be resettlement of the slum dwellers in new apartment blocks located elsewhere, *in situ* development providing superior housing, or a handover of property rights so that the dwellers can develop the housing themselves without fear of eviction. Therefore, even within the category of notified slums we see a range between 'poorly built tenements mostly of temporary nature' and multi-storey concrete buildings. Since the statute does not have a provision to de-notify a slum (even when it has been transformed through state intervention into multi-storey buildings), many continue to be listed as slums when there is nothing 'slum-like' about them. At the other extreme, there are settlements (often located alongside notified slums) that look very temporary in nature, with flimsy materials (e.g. blue tarpaulin) as the only protection from the elements, and very few (if any) municipal services provided. In this chapter we distinguish this type as 'first-generation' slums, compared to the notified, recognised or identified slums.

Significant differences characterise the lived experience within slums of different types, and these differences are poorly captured by the gross distinction between 'notified' and 'non-notified'. Whilst notified slums differ from one another depending upon their age and location, even larger differences can be found between non-notified slums. Policies that do not take these distinctions into account are unlikely to be helpful or cost-effective. Even when a slum is notified or recognised (through identification by census or NSSO enumerators), the spatial boundaries of these settlements are not plotted on city maps, making it impossible to know where a particular slum is located, where it begins and where it ends. Slums sprawl over time, stretching the original boundaries. Dwelling spaces acquired in these processes of spatial extension remain in legal limbo, subject to political bargains. Other slums, particularly the flimsiest among the non-notified, are simultaneously dismantled or relocated. As a result, the dynamic landscape of slums remains ever changing and without any firm basis for formulating plans of urban renewal.

Finally, the lack of longitudinal information[4] about these settlements makes it difficult, if not impossible, to respond to basic questions such as, have people who moved into slums improved their living conditions over time? Or, has moving to cities made people, by and large, upwardly mobile? There are no studies (to date) tracking slum households to ascertain if their economic position, access to services and living conditions has improved or deteriorated over time. These aspects are virtually unknown. As a result, it is hard to ascertain whether particular sets of policies have helped or hindered the urban poor.

Broad characterisation of slums across India

The 2011 enumeration indicated that over 5.4 percent of the Indian population live in slums (GOI 2013a). As most slums are located in urban areas, this figure is much higher in towns and cities, at 22 percent. Of those living in slums, around *one-third* live in notified slums, while the rest live in recognised or identified

Table 3.1 Numbers of slum population in comparison with urban population

Demographics	Proportion in urban India (%)	Proportion in urban slums (%)
Proportion of population to total population	31.2	17.4
Scheduled castes to total population	12.6	20.0
Scheduled tribes	2.8	3.4
Literacy rates	84.1	77.7
Work participation rates	35.5	36.4
Work participation rates (male)	53.8	54.3
Cultivators	2.8	2.2
Agricultural labourers	5.5	7.0
Household industry	4.8	5.0

Source: Authors' elaboration based on GOI (2013a).

slums. While the notified and recognised slums are documented in government records, identified slums have limited/no documentation (GOI 2013a). Table 3.1 outlines basic statistical data from the slum census, with a particular focus on the demographic characteristics of the slum population. As indicated, the proportion of scheduled castes and tribes in slums is greater than in urban centres overall, the literacy rates are lower, and a higher proportion report their occupation as agricultural labourers. These numbers require nuanced examination, particularly in the context of climate-induced migration from rural to urban areas.

In the case of Karnataka, the census lists 206 cities and towns as having slums. The largest number of slums and slum residents were concentrated in the largest city, Bengaluru, formerly known as Bangalore. The population of Bengaluru grew by 47.18 percent between 2001 and 2011. Of the three causal processes noted above, 33 percent of this urban growth was on account of jurisdictional change (reclassification of villages and their incorporation within Bengaluru), 22 percent on account of natural growth, but the largest share of the increase, 45 percent, was accounted for by in-migration (JNNURM 2006). The 2011 census also recorded that Bengaluru had 165,341 households with a population of 712,801 residing in slums (GOI 2013a). This number represents 7.4 percent of Bengaluru's population, and 22 percent of the total slum population of the state of Karnataka (GOI 2013b).

If we apply the principle of primacy, then we can see that Bengaluru, the capital city of Karnataka State not only has a significantly high population in slums (compared to all other cities), but also a higher growth rate and proportion of in-migration. Bengaluru accounts for 36.05 percent of the urban population of the state, and 15.75 percent of the total population (NIUA and JNNURM 2011). Unlike the all-India numbers, where about a third equally live in notified, recognised and identified slums, according to the 2011 census (whose numbers are widely regarded to underestimate the true extent of slums), in Karnataka

Table 3.2 Numbers of slum population in comparison with urban population in Karnataka and Bengaluru

Demographics	Proportion in urban Karnataka (%)	Proportion in slums in urban Karnataka (%)	Proportion in Bengaluru to urban Karnataka (%)	Proportion in Bengaluru slums to Bengaluru population (%)
Total population	38.60	13.93	40.72	7.20
Scheduled castes	28.00	30.96	40.22	12.45
Scheduled tribes	19.20	21.01	19.75	10.16
Other details	Urban Karnataka	Karnataka slums	Bengaluru	Bengaluru slums
Literacy rates	85.80	66.00	84.7	69.00
Work participation rates	39.66	40.36	43.83	44.87
Work participation rates (male)	59.43	57.04	61.82	60.57
Occupation: cultivators	2.56	2.70	0.92	0.58
Agricultural labourers	4.47	7.15	1.33	1.01

Source: Authors' elaboration based on *Primary Census Abstract* (GOI 2013), *Primary Census Abstract Data for Slum* (GOI 2013a) and *Primary Census Abstract for Slum (States and UT)* (GOI 2013b).

the proportion of people living in notified slums was more than twice as high at 69 percent. A smaller proportion of 13.5 and 17.5 percent of the population were living in recognised and identified slums respectively.

When we examine the demographic details of slums in Karnataka and Bengaluru (Table 3.2), some key features emerge. The literacy rates in slums in Karnataka are significantly lower than the average for urban Karnataka, and the rates for Bengaluru are marginally better than the average for slums, but significantly lower than the urban averages. The relative proportion of scheduled caste and scheduled tribe populations to the total population in the urban areas are lower, indicating that a relatively larger proportion might be stuck in their rural settings. However, when we look at the sections of population in the slums, we find that these vulnerable caste groups have a disproportionate representation as 'first-generation' migrants in slums.

Research and methodology:[5] first phase

Whilst the 2011 census provided useful data, significant knowledge gaps remain about slums in India and Bengaluru – the focus of this study. To fill these gaps, a research project commenced in 2010 in Bengaluru with the support of the non-profit agency Jana Urban Foundation (see Krishna et al. 2014 for further information). The study focused on 14 slum settlements randomly selected from the extensive list of notified and recognised slums provided by Karnataka Slum Development Board (KSDB). These settlements were far from the official definition of slums as 'poorly built tenements mostly of a temporary nature, crowded together usually with inadequate sanitary and drinking water facilities'. Depending on the type of intervention by the state, we found permanent constructions, with electricity connections and piped water supply commonly available. Residents here were firmly anchored within the city economy, yet mostly in the informal sector. Poverty was low in comparison to the average for the city, with 14 percent of residents reporting incomes below the official poverty line, as against the figure of 26 percent estimated for urban Karnataka.

In terms of income and poverty prevalence, these slum dwellers were located below the middle of the city's economic distribution, constituting Bengaluru's lower-middle classes. Initial surveys in 2010 revealed that television sets, pressure cookers and electric fans were the most common asset types, with more than 80 percent of all slum households reporting ownership of each type. Kerosene or gas stoves were owned by nearly every household. Another commonly possessed asset was a mobile phone, possessed by more than two-thirds of all slum households. Investment in education ranked alongside home ownership as these households' highest spending priority. Yet, few children studied beyond high school (Krishna 2013). Crucially, hardly anyone in these slums was a new migrant to Bengaluru. Out of 152 households interviewed, only 10 percent were 'first-generation' migrants. Even these migrants were not recent arrivals from rural areas, but had lived in Bengaluru for an average of 18 years. On the other hand, the largest number (1,011 or a little more than 70 percent of all respondents) had lived in Bengaluru for *four or more* generations. Knowledge gaps still remained, therefore, about the lives and livelihoods of so-called 'first-generation' migrants in Bengaluru's slums.

Finding and understanding first-generation migrants

Despairing of the poor state of knowledge about Indian slums, many investigators have turned to using remote sensing techniques to deliver accurate and reliable data.[6] This ongoing study in Bengaluru relies similarly on Google Earth images, compared over a ten-year time frame with the objectives of:

(a) identifying low-income settlements and detecting newly arisen slums,
(b) tracking changing slum boundaries, and
(c) distinguishing between slum types.

As home addresses within slums (even long-standing ones) are notoriously hard to locate, with street names and alignments changing frequently, we are additionally:

(d) geo-referencing sample households within slums with the intention of revisiting these households at regular intervals and constructing longitudinal databases.

Using this method, the exercise of identification began by drawing the spatial borders of the area administered by the municipal authority, the *Bruhat Bengaluru Mahanagara Palike* (BBMP).[7] This area was divided into four evenly sized quadrants on Google Earth (going counter-clockwise from the northeast: Quadrant I, II, III and IV) and using the 'ruler' feature to find the midpoints of each line segment and the 'line' feature to draw the quadrant boundaries. We could then take each quadrant separately and analyse a more manageable number of identified settlements (polygons) at a time, enabling ground verification quadrant by quadrant. It is critical to compare settlements at the same height level on Google Earth. We determined that an altitude of 4,000 feet was appropriate, and used it in all analyses of Google Earth images. The following criteria were used to identify slums of varying types:

- Lack of space between blocks.[8]
- Roofs that appear to be low quality, based on brown or weathered grey colouring.
- Hodgepodge pattern of blocks clustered together without organisation.
- Lack of proper roads (if there are roads, they are brown, narrow and unpaved).
- Lack of shadows coming from the blocks, signifying that they are low to the ground, thus not multi-storey.

Based on these criteria, 279 low-income polygons were initially identified. A unique name was provided to each polygon based on the nearest populated place or water body, so that it could be easily identified in the future and verified on the ground. Iterative ground verification exercises led to continuous improvement in our ability to accurately delineate low-income and very-low-income settlements. Some of the notified slums that were of higher living standard were excluded in this exercise. Successive iterations revealed that the most important criteria for determining whether an area was low-income were small block sizes and lack of space between houses. Supporting criteria also included unpaved roads (if they were visible), narrow inner roads (if visible on these images) and brown-roofed blocks.

Interestingly, field visits and neighbourhood surveys indicated that these settlements *did not* represent new migrants into the city. While they were not as well settled as the notified slums studied initially, they had existed for multiple years with various stages of intervention from the state, including a notification in some cases. Despite this, the research team was determined to locate and find more about the most recent 'first-generation' migrants.

Based on these field visits, the research team identified that new settlers lived mostly in temporary settlements, and that the colour of the rooftops were rarely brown. Homes within these newer settlements were in general covered by blue plastic sheets (referred to as tarpaulins, but made of plastic-based material).[9] The recurrent observations that temporary settlements tended to have blue-coloured rooftops provided us with a different set of criteria for identifying the poorest settlements. In exploring these settlements, we used the time slider feature on

Google Earth and noticed that these settlements had come up largely in the past few years. Some, however, had been around for much longer, growing in size over the ten-year period observed. The criteria we used for identifying these first-generation settlements on the satellite images were small block size, blue rooftops and recent establishment. The comparison of 'before' and 'after' satellite imagery indicated the rapid pace of transformation.[10]

The research team identified 61 such settlements. Ground verification revealed that initial identification was accurate in the vast majority of cases. A total of eight settlements no longer existed, perhaps because they had relocated, or were temporary construction sites housing workers. In turn, we could not iden-tify newer settlements as the satellite image data only went up to 2011.[11] As expected, first-generation slums (or blue polygons) were found to be areas where recent migrants from rural areas, mostly northern Karnataka and the adjoining state of Andhra Pradesh, would reside. Residents of these slums retain strong links with their native villages, going back and forth often, with families some-times split between the two locations. Reasons for coming to the city were mainly agrarian crises (brought about by drought and erratic rainfall), and a consequent need to pay off accumulated debts.

The typical abode in a first-generation slum was a 7'×7' tent erected on land hired from a private owner. Families of between three and five people shared these small spaces, with the adult male and female both employed, most often as construction labourers. Some sites, pending the grant of building permits, instead of lying vacant, had been let out temporarily to migrants, thus earn-ing rent for their owners. The monthly rental fee for one of these tiny plots in blue polygons ranged from Rs. 200–400 (approximately US$3–6), with migrants from further afield paying considerably higher amounts. These amounts were paid in advance in cash. None of the sites surveyed were 'encroachments' on public or government-owned land (a common misconception), which is a sig-nificant departure from the stories of large well-settled slums. While there are instances of older, larger slums on private land, in general such slums emerge on government-owned land, adjacent to an open drain or railway line, below high tension wires, or near military defence, forest and other land types.

Research and methodology: second phase

During the second study phase (August to December 2012), we undertook detailed investigations in a randomly selected sample of 18 first-generation set-tlements of this type, conducting interviews with a total of 631 households, a little more than half of all households in the settlements. Households were ran-domly selected for interviews (i.e. every second household starting from a com-mon point), although in a few cases these protocols were broken, since contact with some households proved impossible despite repeat visits.

On average, 70 households, most having migrated from the same rural village or adjoining group of villages, constituted a first-generation settlement, with settle-ment size ranging from 10 to 150 households. About 40 percent of households

Table 3.3 First-generation settlements: SCs, STs and non-Hindus

Neighbourhood	Household count	SC	ST	Muslim or Christian	Proportion to total households (%)
Quadrant I, Polygon-Hudi	80	50	30		100
Quadrant I, Polygon-Whitefield A	35	35			100
Quadrant IV, Polygon-HSR Layout A	150	90	60		100
Quadrant II, Polygon-Peenya Phase B	60	50	10		100
Quadrant II, Polygon-Chikka Venkatappa Lay out	10	6	4		100
Quadrant I, Polygon-Nagavarapallaya B	15	15			100
Quadrant I, Polygon-Manyata Residency	160	120	30		93.75
Quadrant II, Polygon-Atturu	60	60			100
Quadrant II, Polygon-Goraguntepalya	25	25			100
Quadrant III, Polygon-Bangarapanagar A	60	45		15	100
Quadrant III, Polygon-Bangarapanagar B	25	5	20		100
Quadrant III, Polygon-Kenchenhalli	18	18			100
Quadrant III, Polygon-RNS Inst. of Technology	80	80			100
Quadrant IV, Polygon-Kaikondrahalli	58	58			100
Quadrant IV, Polygon-Manjunatha	150	75		30	70
Quadrant IV, Polygon-Thubarahalli	70	60		10	100
Quadrant IV, Polygon-Nallurhalli	130	100		15	88.46
Quadrant IV, Polygon-Pattandur Agrahara	50	50			100
Total	1236	942	154	70	94.33

Source: Original data from 2013 surveys (cited in Krishna et al. 2014: 576).

came to Bengaluru between one and five years ago, and another 40 percent had been in the city between five and ten years, with a smaller proportion (about 15 percent), having stayed in Bengaluru for more than ten years. Crucially, more than 80 percent cited droughts, debt and the general difficulty of making a living in their native villages as the reason for migrating to the city.

Prior to migrating, the principal occupation of 52 percent of residents was agricultural labour. Another 40 percent farmed small plots of land, supplementing these incomes with farm or off-farm labour. While primarily agrarian in origin, as many as 38 percent of these households did not own agricultural land of their own, another 34 percent owned tiny plots of between one and three acres, with only 7 percent owning five or more acres of agricultural land. When we compare this with overall numbers for Bengaluru and Karnataka, as well as our 2010 study, it is evident that these residents have a greater connection with their native village and are still connected to agriculture. A larger number reported cultivation and agricultural wage labour as their occupation, had identity papers in

Table 3.4 Asset ownership (percentage of households owning each type of asset)

Asset type	Fourth-generation residents (notified slums) (%)	First-generation residents (blue polygons) (%)	
		In Bengaluru	Bengaluru or native village
Kerosene or gas stove	98	7	11
Television	84	1	22
Electric fan	84	1	24
Pressure cooker	81	1	3
Dressing table or almirah	43	0	6
DVD or CD player	22	0	6
Bicycle	18	6	22
Motorcycle or scooter	17	3	5
Refrigerator	6	0	0
Sewing machine	6	0	1
Washing machine	4	0	0
Mobile phone	81	75	82

Source: Original data from 2013 surveys (cited in Krishna et al. 2014: 580).

the native village and were indebted to sources in the village. Unlike the larger, well-developed slums, these residents are not fully connected to the city, in spite of spending more than five years in Bengaluru.

A large majority of these residents (72 percent) belonged to Scheduled Castes (SCs), the former 'untouchables' – more than three times the share of this group in the population of Bengaluru – and Scheduled Tribes (STs) or India's aborigines, constituted another 11 percent. Other Backward Castes (OBCs) made up 7 percent of this group. In 8 of the 18 selected neighbourhoods, SCs constituted 100 percent of the settler group. Table 3.3 outlines the caste divisions for all 18 neighbourhoods. Crucially, the statistics are in stark contrast with the proportions for the general population, as well as population in larger, more developed slums, indicating that distress- and vulnerability-induced migration affects these poorer groups to a higher degree.

Caste backgrounds together with prior occupations and land holdings show how this group of households has arisen from among some of the poorest people in rural India, impelled to move from their native villages by diminishing economic prospects linked in the longer term to fragmenting landholdings, and in the immediate term by debts and droughts. This is further reinforced when one considers other aspects of lifestyle, including asset holdings (Table 3.4). As indicated in Table 3.4, there are few possessions within the 7'×7' tent dwellings compared to the notified slums. Clothes were usually stored on wooden planks balanced atop brick or earthen supports; a few battered aluminium cooking vessels, an open wood-burning *chulha* (fireplace) for cooking, a mobile phone, pictures of Hindu gods and goddesses, and one or

Table 3.5 Monthly household expenditures in first-generation slums

Category	Average monthly expenditure (Rs)	Share of total expenditure (%)
Food	4,349	57.3
School fees and tuition	361	4.8
Medical	703	9.3
Debt repayment	1,246	16.4
Travel and remittances	935	12.3
Total	7,593	100.0

Source: Original data from 2013 household surveys (cited in Krishna et al. 2014: 577).

two plastic containers in which water, brought from afar, is stored are typically found within the dwelling.

Blue-polygon settlements exist in an institutional limbo, unconnected to city services and economic opportunities. None of the 18 settlements were connected to the electricity network, and not one was served by street lights. Muddy, narrow, unpaved alleyways and the frequent presence of stray dogs made it imperative to complete household interviews before dark, immediately after householders returned from a day of work. Regarding water, a hand-pump was found in one neighbourhood and a bore-well in another. However, residents of the remaining 16 neighbourhoods had to purchase water from mobile tankers or travel great distances to fill up at public water points. Garbage removal and security services were non-existent. The nearest public bus stop was located within one kilometre of only two settlements, and was more than three kilometres away from another nine. The nearest health clinic (government or private) was on average four kilometres away. There are no signs visible in any neighbourhood of any government, non-governmental organisation (NGO) or other outside support. Residents mostly relied on immediate family members and neighbours, with only a tiny percentage able to call upon support from employers, community leaders, government officials, political parties or NGOs.

Eighty percent of male and female household heads worked on construction sites as irregular, daily-waged labourers, with men earning on average Rs. 300 for each day's work and women earning lower amounts (around Rs. 200) in the same job. Prospects for advancement and permanence were severely compromised on account of frequent absences (often caused by illness), occasioned by visits two or three times a year to one's home in the native village. Such visits were necessary to look after the land and family left behind in the village and to service the debts that originally brought one to seek work in Bengaluru. A great deal of expenditure was incurred on home visits and on monthly debt repayments. Table 3.5 shows the distribution of average monthly expenditures for these blue-polygon households. More than one-quarter went towards obligations connected with the native village, with 16 percent going towards debt repayment and another

12 percent towards travel and remittances. The average household sent a sum of Rs. 1,840 (approximately US$18) to the native village every month. Many households stated that debt repayment in the village limited their chances for self-improvement in the city. Note, for example, in Table 3.5 that only a tiny proportion of household budget (4.8 percent) was spent on education. In fact, only 21 percent of all 631 households spent any amount on tuition, fees and other school-related expenditures. Very few children went to school.

As many as 77 percent of all household members aged 14 years or older had no formal education, having never been to school. Those who attended school did so sporadically, often dropping out after a couple of years. No more than 4 percent attended English-medium schools, an important point of difference with notified slums, where the vast majority of young people attended schools regularly, with more than 60 percent educated in English-medium schools. The itinerant life lived by residents of blue-polygon slums or 'tented cities' makes it harder to keep children in school.

Lack of official identity papers for residents of these settlements is a further barrier to social and economic mobility. The papers that blue-polygon residents possess are related to residence in their native village. Only a tiny proportion were registered as a resident of Bengaluru. Thus, while 69 percent had a Voter ID card in their native village, fewer than 9 percent were registered to vote in Bengaluru. Similarly, 65 percent had a ration card issued in their native village, but only 6 percent had one in Bengaluru. The corresponding proportions for a Unique ID (or *Aadhar*) card are 17 percent and 1 percent respectively. Access to basic services (e.g. health and education) was significantly hampered by lack of official documentation. As we can see in the next section, the situation was very different in notified slums.

Arguably, the lives of first-generation slum residents are doubly precarious. They are exposed to risk in two places – in the city and their native villages. Along with droughts and rainfall failures associated with climate variability, deaths, marriages and health incidents combine to deplete the households' minor savings, fuelling a loan–debt cycle. A total of 447 households (71 percent) reported experiencing a health incident requiring substantial expenditure during the preceding year, incurring (on average) an expense of Rs. 30,285 (approximately US$460). Expenses on marriages added more than Rs. 100,000 (approximately US$1500) over the prior five years to the outstanding debts of 391 households (62 percent).

Whilst the threat of eviction is also ever present in these settlements, some had been in place for ten years or longer, with the average age of settlements being 6.5 years. In contrast, notified slums generally represented higher livelihood opportunities and service provision, with many residents becoming part of a lower-middle class – a result of incremental gains won through a series of political and official accommodations.

Conclusion

The population of urban slums in India has been expanding rapidly. Two inter-related processes, with different internal dynamics and consequently diverse repercussions for policy, have contributed to this growth. One reason for the increase is natural process, i.e. births outpacing deaths. This process is most prevalent within longer-established slums, and particularly visible in our surveys of notified slums, where the majority of residents (more than 85 percent) were born within the slum, and continued living there, incrementally building better lives and accumulating assets.

The second reason, and the focus of this study, is the longer-term diminution of economic prospects in agriculture coupled with the lure of growing cities (Reddy and Mishra 2009), plus factors associated with changing climatic conditions, i.e. heavy rainfall and drought. These processes bring first-generation migrants into the newest and flimsiest settlements, where poverty, uncertainty, risk and vulnerability are more centrally implicated in people's lives and livelihoods, and where resilience is much lower in comparison to notified slums. The largest proportion (81 percent) of our blue-polygon interviewees stated that their principal reason for coming to Bengaluru was related to the increasing frequency of rainfall failures resulting in droughts, difficult working conditions in the village, and accumulating debts. As climate change further raises the precariousness of rural livelihoods, the number of these settlements could rise.

Residents of these blue-polygon slums in Bengaluru have no official documents and no fixity of tenure. They are liable to be evicted, as many of our interviewees had been, with very little notice. Given these circumstances, these families aim not to build a better life within Bengaluru, but to use Bengaluru as a means for paying off the debts that they have contracted back in the village. Children's education is a lesser priority in the face of other more compelling and immediate commitments. Home improvements are neither feasible, given the shortage of income following remittances, nor desirable in situations where the threat of eviction is ever-present.

These situations contrast starkly with those experienced by native-born Bengalurians living in notified slums. Home ownership and children's education are the two highest priorities of people living in the settlements. There is no imminent threat of eviction, and the need to send remittances to other places is a reality for only a few residents. Given these differences in lived experience and future expectations, different kinds of policy support are required for different people in different kinds of slums. For example, notified-slum households are investing heavily in education, but the returns on these investments are currently low. Notified-slum residents, therefore, would benefit most from receiving support that can help raise social mobility, enabling their children to become medical doctors, software engineers, senior business professionals and so on, positions achieved by very few.

In contrast, blue-polygon settlers have a very different set of expressed needs and hopes regarding public assistance. Their basic needs – electricity, clean drinking water, security of person and property, education, secure housing, affordable health care – are largely unmet or require large expenditures. Lacking identity cards in the city (and thus not registering as constituents or voters), blue-polygon dwellers are unable to attract much political patronage or official support.

Drives to acknowledge and register their presence in the city must, therefore, take precedence. Subbaraman et al. (2012: 661), who studied one such settlement in Mumbai, focusing primarily on health outcomes, underline how such slums constitute a 'legal "no-man's land" – a zone absent of policies that address their existence as human beings and citizens of the city'. They 'emphasise the need to establish minimum humanitarian standards for … basic services such as water, sanitation, solid waste collection and restitution after calamities'. Helping first-generation migrants prepare for and address the obstacles they face both in the city and in their native villages will enhance resilience among this vulnerable group. Whether this can be done by providing support for rural livelihoods, or whether – since cities are where Indian planners are pinning their future hopes[12] – to deploy public resources for building improved urban infrastructures, is a critical question, with multiple answers.

The methods presented here are an effort to develop complete slum maps with clearly marked boundaries and with settlements classified in terms of a slum typology. Whilst these methods have been useful in the Bengaluru case, wider application in other large and small Indian cities remains to be seen. In Bengaluru, at least, the existence of substantial differences between the two types studied through detailed neighbourhood analyses and extensive household interviews shows that treating slums as a homogeneous category can result in serious policy mistakes. There is little that residents of first- and fourth-generation slums and slum dwellers have in common that can justify any unitary policy in the context of global climate change.

Notes

1 An earlier version of this chapter is available as a paper: Krishna et al. (2014).
2 This trend began after the last census, conducted in 2001, but since that exercise was confined only to the largest Indian cities, a more complete enumeration was conducted in the 2011 census.
3 The capital city of Karnataka was known by the name Bangalore and has been renamed as Bengaluru.
4 Despite data limitations, some notable investigations have examined longitudinal trends, using innovative methods. See, for example, Bapat (2009), Bhatia and Chatterjee (2010), Krishna (2013), Mitra (2010) and Ramachandran and Subramanian (2001).
5 Field investigations for this study were in large part supported by the Jana Urban Foundation, Bengaluru. The authors are thankful to colleagues in JUF as well as Ms Purnima Prakash (then with the Indian Institute of Management, Bengaluru) who led the field investigation.
6 See, for example, Kit et al. (2013), Livengood and Kunte (2012) and Sudhira et al. (2004).
7 Rather than considering what is colloquially known as Greater Bengaluru (which extends over a wider and fast-expanding area, covering in addition to the BBMP's jurisdiction several smaller peri-urban areas), we selected to focus initially on a well-identified area constituting the core of this city. Our methodology can be extended to Greater Bengaluru at a later stage.
8 We refer to 'blocks' rather than houses because the number of distinct homes (or households) that lie inside any particular block cannot be accurately foretold using only the publicly available Google Earth images.

9   While plastic sheets similar to the blue roofing sheets are available in multiple colors, and people might resort to covering their dwelling with discarded flex banners, we found that blue sheets are the norm in these settlements, representing an affordable compromise between expense and durability.

10 The Google Earth images showing the changes in the satellite imagery are available on a website dedicated to this research at www.urbanindiastories.com.

11 Thus, while our methodology is subject to the error of omission – i.e., not picking up recently established blue polygons – the error of commission, as we could make out from our ground verification exercises, is minimal; there were no false positives in these identifications.

12 See, for example, the report of a high-level committee of the Indian government, which begins by assuming that cities 'are the reservoirs of skills, capital and knowledge. They are the centers of innovation and creativity. They are the generators of resources for national and state exchequers. They are also the hopes of millions of migrants from the rural hinterland and smaller settlements. With growth of the services sector and surge of the knowledge economy, the population pressure on cities is bound to escalate' (GOI 2010: 1).

References

Bapat M 2009 *Poverty Lines and Lives of the Poor: Under-estimation of Urban Poverty – the Case of India* IIED Working Paper London

Bhatia N and Chatterjee A 2010 Financial inclusion in slums of Mumbai *Economic and Political Weekly* October 16 23–26

Government of India (GOI) 2010 *Report of the Committee on Slum Statistics/Census* New Delhi: Government of India, Ministry of Housing and Urban Poverty Alleviation

Government of India (GOI) 2013 *Census of India: Primary Census Abstract (2011)* New Delhi: Office of the Registrar General and Census Commissioner

Government of India (GOI) 2013a *Census of India: Primary Census Abstract for Slum* New Delhi: Office of the Registrar General and Census Commissioner Available from: http://www.censusindia.gov.in/2011-Documents/Slum-26-09-13.pdf [Accessed: 9/6/15]

Government of India (GOI) 2013b *Census of India: Primary Census Data for Slum (India and States/UTs)* Available from: http://www.censusindia.gov.in/2011census/population_enumeration.html [Accessed: 11/6/15]

Henderson J V 2005 Urbanisation and Growth in Aghion P and Durlauf S (eds) *Handbook of Economic Growth* Volume 1B Chapter 24 1543–1591 Amsterdam: Elsevier

Jawaharlal Nehru National Urban Renewal Mission (JNNURM) 2006 *Revised City Development Plan for Bangalore* Available from: http://218.248.45.169/download/pds/finalcdp.pdf [Accessed: 18/5/15]

Kit O Lüdeke M and Reckien D 2013 Defining the bull's eye: satellite imagery-assisted slum population assessment in Hyderabad, India *Urban Geography* 34(3) 413–424

Krishna A 2013 Stuck in place: investigating social mobility in 14 Bangalore slums *Journal of Development Studies* 49(7) 1010–1028

Krishna A Sriram M S and Prakash P 2014 Slum types and adaptation strategies: identifying policy-relevant differences in Bangalore *Environment and Urbanization* 26(2) 568–585

Livengood A and Kunte K 2012 Enabling participatory planning with GIS: a case study of settlement mapping in Cuttack, India *Environment and Urbanization* 24(1) 77–97

Marx B Stoker T and Suri T 2013 The economics of slums in the developing world *Journal of Economic Perspectives* 27(4) 187–210

Mitlin D and Satterthwaite D 2012 Editorial: Addressing poverty and inequality: new forms of urban governance in Asia *Environment and Urbanization* 24(2) 395–401

Mitra A 2010 Migration, livelihood and well-being: evidence from Indian city slums *Urban Studies* 47(7) 1371–1390

National Sample Survey Organization (NSSO) 2003 *Conditions of Urban Slums: Salient Features* NSS 58th Round (July 2002–December 2002) Government of India National Sample Survey Organization

National Sample Survey Organization (NSSO) 2009 *India – Urban Slums Survey: NSS 65th Round: July 2008–June 2009* Government of India National Sample Survey Organization

NIUA and JNNURM 2011 *India's Urban Demographic Transition: The 2011 Census Results* (Provisional) New Delhi: National Institute of Urban Affairs and JNNURM

Ramachandran H and Subramanian S V 2001 Slum Household Characteristics in Bangalore: A Comparative Analysis (1973 and 1992) in Schenk H (ed) *Living in India's Slums: A Case Study of Bangalore* 65–88 New Delhi: Manohar Publishers

Reddy D N and Mishra S 2009 Agriculture in the Reforms Regime in Reddy D N and Mishra S (eds) *Agrarian Crisis in India* 3–43 New Delhi: Oxford University Press

Subbaraman R O'Brien J Shitole T Shitole S Sawant K Bloom D and Patil-Deshmukh A 2012 Off the map: the health and social implications of being a non-notified slum in India *Environment and Development* 24 643–663

Sudhira H S Ramachandra T V and K S Jagadish 2004 Urban sprawl: metrics, dynamics, and modeling using GIS *International Journal of Applied Earth Observation and Geoinformation* 5 29–39

UN HABITAT 2014 *Background Paper on the World Habitat Day* Available from: http://unhabitat.org/wp-content/uploads/2014/07/WHD-2014-Background-Paper.pdf [Accessed: 26/6/15]

4 Emerging practices of community adaptation within innovative water and climate change policies in Durban, South Africa

Catherine Sutherland, Michaela Hordijk and Dianne Scott

Introduction

There is a well-established literature on the multiple scales of governance and extensive network of actors that shape water and climate management in cities. A complex web of international bodies, state and private sector actors (including consultants), non-governmental organisations (NGOs), civil society organisations (CSOs) and ordinary citizens engage, or dis-engage with each other and with the material reality of water and climate change challenges, to develop more sustainable and resilient ways of using water and adapting to climate change (Taylor et al. 2014; Chu Chapter 14, this volume).

This chapter focuses on the relations between the local state and its citizens in Durban, South Africa in the arena of water and climate governance. In a broader sense, the chapter reflects on 'the diverse and often divergent means by which life in liberal societies comes to be managed and modulated in the face of an "urgency" or "crisis"', in this case, in the face of climate change (Braun 2014: 50). It uses the methodological device of presenting vignettes (singular evocative illustrations) to explore the shifts that have taken place as a result of engagement within the state, and between state policies and the everyday lived experiences of ordinary citizens. These vignettes provide insight into 'particular ways in which urban life is managed or administered' by government in reaction to the crisis of water provision and climate change (Braun 2014: 51). It reflects how 'actors appropriate ideas and practices to align them with their own views, ambitions, and projects' (Artur and Hilhorst 2012: 529).

The engagement between the state and its citizens around the provision of services for water, sanitation and climate adaptation provides a lens through which to reflect on the politics and practices that emerge when state-led policies are implemented on the ground. The chapter reflects on the policies and practices of two departments within eThekwini Municipality, the administrative and management entity of the city of Durban. The eThekwini Water and Sanitation Unit (EWS) is responsible for the provision of water and sanitation services, whilst the Environmental Planning and Climate Protection Department (EPCPD) focuses on biodiversity conservation and climate adaptation. The importance of understanding, and working at the interface between, water and climate governance in Durban emerged in 2012 as a result of the strategic intervention of EWS and EPCPD (Sutherland and Roberts 2014).

The chapter draws on research conducted for the Chance2Sustain and CLIMWAYS projects, funded jointly by Norwegian and South African research foundations (SANCOOP).[1] The understandings and interpretations of officials and local communities about water governance and climate change were analysed through data collected between April 2010 and December 2014. Interviews, focus groups, participant observation and policy analysis were undertaken in different sites across the city from municipal offices to five low-income settlements. A multi-sited ethnographic approach was used to generate the data required to construct three vignettes (Artur and Hilhorst 2012). This allowed multiple experiences, knowledge and representations at the scale of the state and local (case study) communities to be collected, informing the analysis presented here. Out of the five low-income settlements, Ocean Drive-In and Quarry Road West are informal, Magwaveni contains one informal settlement, as well as state-subsidised low-cost housing and a transit camp, and Russia in KwaNgcolosi and Mzinyathi are peri-urban settlements (see Figure 4.2).

The chapter first briefly presents the policies and practices that have been developed by the local state to address service provision and climate adaptation. It then uses three vignettes to illuminate the relations between state policies and the everyday lived worlds of the urban poor. The first vignette outlines the significant shift in municipal approaches (of EWS and EPCPD) outlined above. The second explores the ways in which ordinary citizens act in response to state policies and practices and, in doing so, bring about transformation, through the lens of (free) basic water provision. The third vignette considers the conceptualisation of people–environment relations through 'environmental services', where climate and water governance align to address both water and climate challenges in settlements of the urban poor. Vignettes should not be read as comprehensive understandings. Rather, they reveal particular ways in which state–citizen relations are being negotiated through the implementation of policies (Braun 2014). The three vignettes together create a more composite picture of local state–citizen relations in water and climate governance (Artur and Hilhorst 2012), and address questions around the role of learning and knowledge generation in experimental governance.

Abstract constructions and everyday lived worlds

Abstract constructions of society and space, such as policies and maps produced by planners, engineers, architects and scientists to guide and inform the practice of governing cities, need to be considered in relation to the everyday lived worlds of ordinary people. Ordinary citizens respond to (and alter) the policies and practices of the state as they adapt to their everyday realities. Conceptualising and mapping these relations in a complex and fast-changing

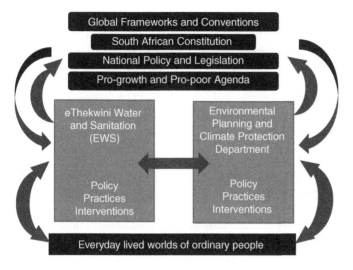

Figure 4.1 Relations in the water and climate governance arena in eThekwini Municipality
Source: Authors' elaboration.

municipality (such as eThekwini) is challenging. However, it is critical to explore how state policies and practices travel to local spaces, which themselves are not homogenous and uniform. Rather, they reflect the inequality and heterogeneity of life in the city.

This chapter focuses on the spaces of the urban poor in relation to water and climate governance in five low-income settlements. Crucially, there are significant differences between and within these settlements. For example, urban poor housing in Durban takes the form of informal settlements, state-provided low-cost housing (known as RDP houses[2]) and/or peri-urban housing (which can be traditional, formal and state-provided low-cost housing). There is also significant variation of service delivery within these settlements, which is dependent on size, physical location, social organisation, politics and status in relation to their inhabitants' rights to the resources of the city. Figure 4.1 outlines the set of relations that exist at various scales in the water and climate governance arena in eThekwini Municipality.

As indicated in Figure 4.1, water and climate change governance in eThekwini Municipality is shaped by global frameworks and conventions, the South African Constitution (1996), national policy and legislation, and macro-level discourses that frame development and transformation in the country. For example, the South African Constitution (1996) states that everyone has the right to sufficient water within available resources, and that water and sanitation services are a local government responsibility. Human dignity (Section 10) and the promotion of equality (Section 9) are also core values of the Constitution that underpins water and sanitation service provision. The provision of Free Basic

Water (FBW) to the urban poor in South Africa is one example of how these values and rights have been translated into policy and practice.

Water and sanitation is considered to be a social good and therefore critical to transformation and development of the country (Tissington et al. 2008). The right to a healthy environment and protection of the environment is also enshrined in the Constitution (Section 24). This provides the moral base for climate change mitigation and adaptation. The policy framework of developmental local government which emerged post 1994, and which draws on the Constitution, strongly supports notions of sustainability and equity (Parnell et al. 2002; Van Donk et al. 2008; Taylor et al. 2014; Scott et al. 2015). Similarly, global conventions to which South Africa is a signatory, such as the Millennium Development Goals (MDGs) and Sustainable Development Goals (SDGs), influence policy making at the national and local government level.

The neo-liberal, pro-growth agenda with its discourses of cost efficiency and cost recovery, and more transformative pro-poor agenda with its discourses of transformation and redistribution, are both mandates of local government. They play a critical role in shaping the policy and practice of local government in Durban. The juxtaposition of these two macro-discourses and tension this raises at the local government level is evident in both water and climate change governance (Sutherland et al. 2015). According to Bond (2012, cited in Lewis 2013), the commodification of water in South Africa means that not everyone will be able to afford to pay for sufficient water, given that the FBW allowance is considered to be insufficient for larger households. This raises concerns as to whether the focus of service delivery is on cost recovery or on social and environmental justice. Likewise, the pressure on environmental resources for economic, pro-growth development undermines the ability of EPCPD in eThekwini Municipality to protect these valuable natural resources for climate adaptation, particularly for the poor.

These abstract constructions, such as international frameworks and national discourses, legislation, policy and plans, create the epistemic frame within which local government operates. These broader-level policy frames are then taken up in the 'spaces' of local government, which are mandated to provide housing, services and income-generating opportunities for their citizens. The Municipal Systems Act (2000) in South Africa legally defines a municipality as including councillors (politicians), administrators (officials) and the local community (Piper and Nadvi 2009). This is significant as it not only promotes participatory governance, but recognises the value of ordinary people and their practices in the foundational praxis of local government. In reality, however, it is argued that the 'spaces' within local government are more bounded, with politicians and officials producing the policy and practices of the municipality with limited input from local communities (Piper and Nadvi 2009; Sutherland 2016). This said, these boundaries can be porous, with local government responding to the knowledge and experiences of local communities in certain instances,

Table 4.1 Governance approaches of EWS and EPCPD

	EWS	EPCPD
Governance approach	Experimental	Experimental
Policy frames	Informed by principle that water and sanitation are a social and economic good.	Informed by the need to support and protect people and the environment. Developed a macro-framework for environmental management based on years of experimentation.
	Clear vision and goals reflected in EWS Customer Services Charter.	
	No overarching 'stable' policy framework.	
	Regular shifts in policy based on incremental learning and public participation: e.g. Free Basic Water Policy.	Range of policies and targets for climate change adaptation that focus on adaptation, but include mitigation through collaboration with the city's Energy Office.
	Policy aligned with concept of Urban Development Line (UDL).[3]	
	Influenced by global policy and research networks.	Influenced by global policy and research networks.
Practice	Strong leadership (champion).	Strong leadership (champion).
	Mandated to provide physical infrastructure (water and sanitation).	Biodiversity conservation through a range of programmes.
	Strong technical capacity.	Integrating climate adaptation into Municipal structures through Municipal Adaptation Plans.
	Strong partnerships which are open and engaging with a wide range of actors: research institutions, civil society organisations and consultants.	Developing a citywide resilience strategy under Rockefeller 100RC.
	Strong international connections.	Strong technical capacity.
	Incremental learning.	Research partnerships with research institutions and consultants carefully controlled by EPCPD.
		Strong international connections.
		Incremental learning.

Source: Adapted from Sutherland et al. (2014) and Taylor et al. (2014).

particularly when experimental governance is adopted. Table 4.1 outlines the broad approach, policies and practices of EWS and EPCPD within eThekwini Municipality.

Analysing the formulation and implementation of policy and practices requires an understanding of the service delivery context in Durban. In 2000, the Municipal Demarcation Act (No. 27 of 1998) restructured the boundaries of municipalities in South Africa, creating wall-to-wall municipalities that combined previously well-off areas with poorer townships, informal and rural areas to pool resources which could be used for redistribution purposes. Under this process, the boundaries of the city were expanded, resulting in a 68 percent increase in the land area of the new municipal entity. This meant that the municipality was now responsible for underdeveloped rural areas on its periphery which had previously been part of the homeland of KwaZulu under the apartheid regime.

This raised significant challenges for the city, many of which relate to what it means to be 'urban' in a city that contains urban, peri-urban and rural spaces and two systems of governance: municipal administration and the Traditional Authority (the Ingonyama Trust is the custodian of traditional land in South Africa and is governed by the Traditional Authority). The expansion added 75,000 rural households to the Municipality in 2000, 60,000 of which did not have access to basic services (Gounden et al. 2006).[4] This placed considerable pressure on EWS who were responsible for providing services to peripheral areas in the city that were remote, under-developed, extremely poor and located on steep topography beyond the existing water-borne service edge.

At the same time, city planners were focusing on how to contain urban sprawl. The principles of densification and the compact city were strong drivers in the production of the first Spatial Development Framework (SDF) in 2002–2007 for the newly formed eThekwini Municipality. Ongoing deliberations between 2000 and 2010 within the local state, including input from consultants who were advising the state on planning issues, led to the delineation of the Urban Development Line (UDL) as a spatial informant for city growth and service provision (Sutherland et al. 2014; Sim et al. 2015; Figure 4.2). Although a planning concept, the UDL was strongly supported by EWS, as it reinforced their efforts to optimise the use of existing wastewater treatment capacities within more centrally located treatment works in the city, before incurring substantial expenses in constructing new treatment works on the outskirts (Sim et al. 2015).

Within this context of service backlogs, water scarcity and increasing demand for water and sanitation services (particularly in peripheral areas that were under-developed during apartheid), and drawing on the concepts of the urban edge and UDL, EWS developed a spatially differentiated service provision model (Sutherland et al. 2014; Sim et al. 2015). As a result, the urban poor now have different access to water and sanitation services to those living in the urban core.

Problematically, this policy and practice juxtaposes the desire of peripheral residents to have the same level of services as those within the urban core. EWS argues that the provision of this level of services across the city, including the rural periphery, is not feasible as a result of historical, technological, financial and environmental constraints (Interview with EWS Official 2015). According to EWS officials, peri-urban areas and the rural periphery raise the most significant challenges due to historical under-development, land ownership falling under the Traditional Authority, low housing densities, population mobility, inaccessible and steep terrain and the financial costs of providing services to the periphery (Gounden et al. 2006).

The spatially differentiated model therefore reflects and reinforces inequality. By rendering the spatial inequalities as abstract, scientific and technical, through

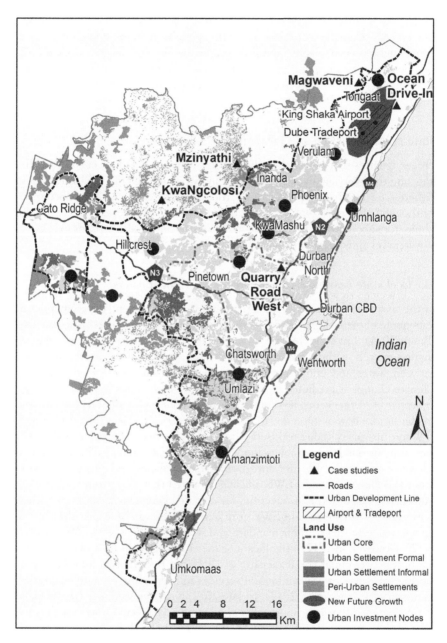

Figure 4.2 The eThekwini Municipality, with its Urban Development Line; the case study
sites for this research are shown on the map

Source: Map produced for authors by Micaela du Sart, EduAction, Durban (2015).

the use of the UDL and its associated spatially differentiated service provision model, the 'politics' is apparently taken out of the process of service delivery. However, the examples below show that the spatially differentiated service provision model has been adapted and reshaped by the 'dreams' and practices of ordinary people as they respond to and reshape the water policies and interventions of the city in their everyday lived worlds. In this way, they have reinserted politics into the practices of the state.

State policy, practice and local spaces

Three vignettes that reflect the relationships between the abstract spaces of the state and the everyday lived worlds of ordinary people are presented here. These vignettes are 'best read as provocations, rhetorical devices designed to open space for thought' (Braun 2014: 60). They are 'singular' in that they can never tell the whole story about a city government and its engagement with citizens in relation to water and climate governance.

The local state water and climate arena: government actors

In the first vignette, we ask what new forms of government have emerged in response to climate change and how these have been located in existing relations (Braun 2014). Given increasing awareness of the risks associated with climate change, as well as the insecurity around water supply in Durban, the interface between water and climate governance began to emerge as a critical issue. Climate change is predicted to result in warmer and wetter weather, a greater frequency of storm events, less consistent rainfall during the summer periods, and greater surface flow of water due to more intense periods of heavy rain in Durban.

Water insecurity is due to insufficient water quantity, poor water quality and increasing demands for potable water. Before 2012, EWS and EPCPD functioned relatively independently, not integrating their policies and practices around water and climate change. EWS officials indicated that they attended EPCPD's Municipal Adaptation Plan meetings for climate change more out of duty than conviction. Many officials in EWS at this time did not believe that the climate agenda was essential to their mandate and work (Interview with EWS Official 2012). However, in 2012, a significant 'game-changing' shift took place.

The EPCPD under the leadership of Dr Debra Roberts had long been promoting the value of environmental services in supporting climate adaptation in the city (Roberts et al. 2012). In late 2012, Neil Macleod, the (then) Head of EWS, argued that new approaches were required to secure water for the city. EWS was increasingly influenced by the extensive body of literature which argues that 'ecological infrastructure can enhance the efficiency of water service delivery through improving water quality, reducing sediment loads, reducing flood risk and increasing yield through increased winter base flows and improve the efficiency of engineering investments' (Grasslands Partnership

2014). At the same time, Macleod attended a presentation prepared by a consultant from the South African Biodiversity Institute (SANBI) and Dr Debra Roberts about the value of ecological infrastructure. As a result, EWS decided to align with the climate adaptation approach promoted by EPCPD, shifting their focus towards protecting and enhancing environmental services to secure water for the Municipality.

Following these changes, a new discourse emerged within the municipality that highlighted water as a 'socio-ecological good' where 'the value of environmental services, or ecological infrastructure[5] in addressing climate adaptation, water scarcity and quality, and poverty [was] increasingly recognised at a local and regional scale' (Sutherland and Roberts 2014: 1). This recognition led to the formation of a partnership between EWS and EPCPD, amongst other actors, to focus on ecological infrastructure in the city both as a means of adapting to climate change and as a way of addressing water scarcity and quality.

Knowledge about the value of ecological infrastructure travelled at an opportune moment from the climate change agenda of EPCPD into the policy space of EWS (Sutherland and Roberts 2014). Climate adaptation thinking (through the ecological infrastructure concept) therefore created an arena where the social negotiation of policy between multiple actors, including provincial and local government, research institutions and NGOs, could take place. This arena became known as the Umgeni Ecological Infrastructure Partnership (UEIP).[6]

Importantly, a new nexus has formed between the two departments that manage water, sanitation and climate adaptation, and new forms of experimental governance and practice have emerged in this space. How this will shape life on the ground is still largely unknown. New policies and practices that connect water and climate through the enhancement of ecological infrastructure still need to be developed. Research within the UEIP, which is adopting a participatory and multi-actor approach to understanding the problem, is providing the platform from which these new policies and practices will emerge. However, working in a trans-disciplinary space which is 'socially embedded' and requires the transfer of knowledge between different disciplines and actors (ranging from scientists to local community members) is difficult. Action research in different sites across the Umgeni Catchment, which includes eThekwini Municipality, is informing the learning. The aim is that by engaging with ordinary people in spaces on the ground, the new policy and practices that emerge will be grounded in the real experiences of water and sanitation insecurity and climate risk faced by the urban poor.

Having considered the shift that has occurred within two local state departments, the second and third vignettes provide a lens through which to explore how abstract state policies and practices relate to (and are reworked by) the everyday lived experiences of the urban poor. The second vignette presents the way ordinary people have adapted to the provision of FBW, while the third reflects on the new climate–water interface (as environmental services) on the ground.

Citizens' responses to state-led policy and practices in the water arena

This vignette asks what happens to state policies and practices when they 'land' in real spaces on the ground. According to the Free Basic Water Policy, indigent households have the right to 9,000 litres of FBW per month in Durban. The delivery of FBW was first introduced by eThekwini Municipality as part of the 'water as a social good' and 'water as an economic good' discourses in the city (Sutherland et al. 2014). FBW was delivered to meet the basic needs of poor households and address the risk of cholera after outbreaks in 2000 and 2002. However, the technology and practices of its delivery were constructed in a manner that ensures limited supply, to counterbalance the efficiencies and costs required to provide water to the rural periphery. Crucially, residents in all five settlements make use of FBW, adapting this system to meet their consumption needs. The majority of residents in peri-urban areas receive 9,000 litres of FBW per month in ground water tanks that are filled daily through a municipal controlled system (Figure 4.3).

Residents who have access to ground water tanks were found to 'borrow' water from their neighbours if they ran out on a particular day. They also store water in water containers if they do not use the full daily quota, ensuring that the tank is empty before it is refilled. In some cases, residents contracted private plumbers to connect second water pipes from EWS's main water infrastructure, using the water from ground water tanks for certain activities (e.g. washing and gardening) and the illegally connected water for others (e.g. drinking water and cooking). Residents in households reported that the water in their self-installed pipes was of higher quality than the water in the tanks, as this water flowed in pipes underground while the water in the tanks was above ground in the sun (see Figure 4.3). They therefore preferred the two systems of water supply, even though technically the water was of the same quality. This differentiation of water is *perceived* rather than actual or real. They ultimately have access to FBW through the state's provision, and their own action, which they do not believe is illegal or 'wrong'. Some residents stated that the water is flowing through the pipes in their area and hence it is there to be used. For many poor people in the city, water is still considered to be a free resource that they have the right to consume.

Residents in informal settlements with communal stand-pipes have access to as much free water as they can carry. However, they often have to queue for this water, especially during the busy times of the day. EWS monitors the use of water in informal settlements to ensure that the free water provided is not used at a level which is higher than the municipal calculations of the requirements of an informal community. Interestingly, Ocean Drive-In residents were concerned that people living outside the community came to their settlement to access the free water supply. They said this wastes 'their' water and impacts on the informal settlers living close to the taps. One resident of Ocean Drive-In complained about the unfairness of 'People [from outside the community] coming to wash their cars and run water to our yard' (Interview with resident 2012).

Figure 4.3 A ground or grey water tank which supplies 9,000 litres of Free Basic Water per month in KwaNgcolosi (peri-urban area)

Source: Author's own.

The 'car-washers' described above drive into the community, exhibiting their higher economic position through the ownership of a car. Figure 4.4 shows how they use the communal taps provided by the state for the poor to fill bucket after bucket of water, washing their cars as a practical chore and a spectacle of status. In a similar way, the availability of 'unlimited' FBW in informal settlements produces an adaptation strategy for formal residents, where formal low-cost housing projects are located adjacent to informal settlements. For example, in one RDP housing project, residents who have access to 9,000 litres of FBW in their houses per month, and who have to pay for their water consumption above this level, cross the road to an informal settlement where they do their washing to access 'unlimited' free water (Interview with Sibongile Buthelezi 2012). Wastage of water is a major problem in areas that have communal standpipes.

As a result of the social learning of the municipality in relation to this problem, all communal standpipes installed by the Municipality now have a tap that is only open if someone holds the tap mechanism up. As soon as it is released, the water stops flowing. However, this has the unintended outcome of potential water contamination from the users' hands coming in contact with the water. This is of concern to informal residents, who have produced their own technology to

Figure 4.4 Free Basic Water being used by outsiders from OceanDrive-In to wash their cars
Source: Author's own.

deal with the problem. They use the cut off end of the top of a plastic two litre soft drink bottle as a funnel to channel water into containers. This technology is shared at some communal tap points, as community members leave the home-made funnels on top of the taps for others to use.

These examples reveal the details of how the technologies and spatial practices of the state are 'captured' by ordinary citizens and altered to meet their needs. Officials of EWS are fully aware of these challenges. They invest resources to manage and at times 'police' the systems they have put in place to govern water provision within the financial and environmental constraints imposed on them. A complex pattern of water supply which is the product of both state policy, practice and community adaptation has emerged in Durban. The final vignette explores the role of ecosystem services in this context.

Community ecosystem-based adaptation (CEBA)

This vignette builds upon EPCPD and EWS's recent acceptance of the con-cept that ecosystem-based adaptation (EBA) is a cost-effective and sustainable approach to improving adaptive capacity to climate change and ensuring water security (Roberts et al. 2012; Sutherland and Roberts 2014). Here, the way in which the concept of environmental services is employed by both the state and local communities is explored. It reflects on the potential of environmental ser-vices in addressing climate and water risk in Durban. Adopting this position in relation to state policy and practice means that the role ecological infrastructure plays 'in improving the quality of life and socio-economic opportunities of the most vulnerable human communities' (Roberts et al. 2012: 167) requires articulation.

Given the importance of the relationship between humans and ecological systems in developing climate adaptation, EBA has now been expanded to the concept of 'community ecosystem-based adaptation' (CEBA; Roberts et al. 2012: 167). According to Artur and Hilhorst (2012: 529), 'adaptation gets incorporated into the everyday politics of politicians, bureaucrats, priests, businessmen, local chiefs and people living in spaces of environmental risk. The integration of the ecological and social systems therefore opens up the possibility of exploring the multiple relations that exist between people and the environment.

EPCPD argues that the value of EBA rests in its proactive capacity to address climate change. Rather than being a reactive intervention (applied once the impacts of climate change set in), ecosystem services provide the foundation for greater resilience, upon which further adaptation strategies can be developed (Roberts et al. 2012). The conservation and restoration of ecosystems support food security, water purification, wastewater treatment and urban development (TEEB 2011 cited in Roberts et al. 2012). The approach of supporting ecosystems for climate adaptation is further supported by the knowledge that the urban poor live at the closest interface to environmental systems, often depending on them for their quality of life.

Through their approach of social learning and experimental governance, EPCPD have provided early insight into how the EBA concept translates into a work stream that is relevant and achievable for local government. Given the notable shift that has taken place in EWS around climate adaptation and ecological infrastructure, officials in (and research partners of) EWS are now exploring similar opportunities that arise from EBA to support state practices. Within both EPCPD and EWS, this is an open and dynamic process, reflecting Roberts et al.'s (2012: 173) notion that local-level adaptation is 'an incremental, iterative and non-linear process that relies on experimentation, flexibility and innovation as the means of achieving progress'. This approach aligns with the culture and practice of both departments, as indicated in Table 4.1.

This vignette explores one set of everyday practices that relate to CEBA. It asks what form EBA takes at the community level, and how the natural environment provides a 'service' for poor people. Reflecting on evidence from the lived experiences of ordinary people in Durban, this vignette reveals that poor communities are already making extensive use of environmental services, sometimes in ways that are detrimental to the service-providing ecosystems. This creates a challenging dichotomy where the very services upon which the urban poor depend are being depleted because of this dependence. The impact of climate change on these systems will exacerbate pressure on valuable services, making it imperative that environmental services are restored. However, it is essential that a CEBA approach uses both existing relations between the urban poor and the environment, and scientific concepts that provide normative ideas about the value of ecosystem services, as its point of departure.

Table 4.2 Flooding and water vulnerabilities in Ocean Drive-In, Magwaveni and Russia, KwaNgcolosi

	Ocean Drive-In (%, n = 29)	Magwaveni (%, n = 40)	Russia, KwaNgcolosi (%, n = 30)
Damage to house from rain	40.4	16.2	36.7
Leaking/flooding house from rain		41.9	24.5
Poor drainage (i.e. muddy pathways)	19.2	27.0	20.4
Collection of dirty/ waste water	30.8	2.7	6.1

Source: Adapted from Lewis (2013).

Among the five settlements, those that had ecological infrastructure to absorb grey water and slow down surface water movement fared far better in terms of reducing the negative impact of wastewater and poor sanitation than those that did not. Low-density informal settlements and peri-urban households in the rural periphery, which still contain the majority of the city's ecosystem services,[7] make use of the ecological infrastructure in their environment to address sanitation needs and grey water disposal. The combination of chronic flooding, inadequate sanitation and the removal of grey water pose significant health threats for poor communities. Table 4.2 shows the reported impact of two of these issues on residents of Ocean Drive-In, Magwaveni and Russia, KwaNgcolosi.

Ocean Drive-In is a low-density informal settlement on a slope, with a reasonable level of environmental services within the settlement. Magwaveni was developed on land that had previously been under sugar cane cultivation and hence has very limited ecosystem services. Russia is a low-density peri-urban area with a wide range of ecosystem services, which are under threat as a result of increasing densification. Households in Ocean Drive-In and Russia are most susceptible to flood damage as a result of them being constructed from plastic, tin, mud and traditional materials. Steep slopes in both these settlements increase the impacts of flooding on households. In Ocean Drive-In, the community has constructed makeshift drainage systems that divert water away from their households. However, because this is not an integrated drainage system, the diversion of water away from one household often results in grey water flowing into another household lower down the slope. This has significant impacts as the water is highly polluted, containing grey water run-off and sewerage from open defecation in pathways during the night. The low density of households in peripheral Russia (with its large gardens and open space still covered in vegetation) helps to ameliorate the impacts of surface water flow in the area. The environmental services provided by the open spaces in Russia therefore play an important role in dealing with run-off. However, where vegetation is removed, significant flood damage occurs.

Although the majority of respondents from Magwaveni live in formal RDP houses, a high proportion of residents reported leaks and flooding during rain. This was attributed to the settlement's location on a floodplain, combined with the low quality of the RDP housing, resulting in flooding of the floors and damp living conditions. As one 57-year-old female resident from Magwaveni explains:

> Water is coming from underground and the back of the house, and doesn't drain away. When it rains water also comes through the back wall at the bottom. I can't do anything about this; I need money to cement the wall.

The development of Magwaveni on a floodplain highlights the challenges the municipality faces given the shortages of cheap and accessible land for low-cost housing and the risks associated with climate change. However, the importance of securing ecosystem services and not building on environmentally challenging sites is a critical consideration for the state in the development of housing for the poor and in addressing climate change adaptation. This argument is used by EPCPD to defend and enhance spaces that contain ecosystem services in the city (Roberts et al. 2012).

In all settlements, residents dispose of wastewater around their houses. The benefits of the larger plots with vegetated open space in Russia are evident as the environment treats and evacuates this wastewater. In Magwaveni and Ocean Drive-In, residents were concerned about the management of grey water and the impact it has on their houses and health, whereas in Russia this was not raised as a concern. Rather, residents commented that their gardens take care of the wastewater and that grey water does not cause problems (Field survey 2012).

The problem of grey water disposal is accentuated during the wet season as water does not drain away on saturated ground. The wetter conditions predicted for Durban as a result of climate change will exacerbate this problem. This supports EPCPD's claim that the protection of basic ecosystem services is essential to the urban poor, who live at the forefront of climate change impacts.

Conclusion

This chapter has critically explored the relationship between the abstract spaces of the state and everyday lived worlds of ordinary people through the presentation of three vignettes. The vignettes share a common argument that knowledge generation and learning, which characterises eThekwini's experimental governance approach, is crucially important.

The first vignette showed how knowledge and discourses from international networks, research within Durban and social engagement at the local scale led to the formation of a multi-stakeholder platform representing actors from different levels of government. This created a governance nexus to address the entangled issues of water scarcity, ecological infrastructure and climate change adaptation. The vignette also indicated that the challenge in this new partnership is how to support the exchange of knowledge within a trans-disciplinary action research framework. Incorporating the lived experience of the community members in the 'ecological buffer zones' is, however, of utmost importance in policy design.

Through engaging in action research, EPCPD and EWS have explored the forms of adaptation that are most appropriate in the Durban context and are still 'learning by doing'. Given that knowledge about climate change adaptation is relatively new, both globally and in South Africa, it is critical that local government develops strong partnerships with local communities to drive this agenda forward.

The second vignette revealed how abstract policy and practices developed in government spaces are reworked through the everyday practices of ordinary people who adapt technical interventions to meet their needs. The vignette showed a certain level of responsiveness of the local state to these reworkings, such as the increase of the Free Basic Water (FBW) supply from 6,000 to 9,000 litres per month, and installation of a self-closing tap on public tap points. Overall, however, EWS mainly invokes highly technical knowledge and interventions which depoliticise decisions. EWS has a well-developed and structured approach to participation, which is orchestrated through the 'technical' participation frames developed by EWS officials. This remains a form of technical managerialism, which can exclude the urban poor.

The third vignette highlights how broadening of ecosystem-based adaptation (EBA) to community ecosystem-based adaptation (CEBA) offers the potential to engage with citizens. Ecosystem services for buffering grey water and heavy rains are essential to protect the inhabitants of poor urban settlements from flooding and health risks, and form an entry point for policy development that addresses residents' needs. The recently established UEIP, with its action research approach and multiple partnerships, provides a further opportunity to develop more participatory processes for the construction of policy in the water–climate governance arena.

Many challenges remain that undermine the potential for deliberation in this new policy space. The rapidly changing urban context, the paucity and difficulty of authentic engagement of communities with the local state (as a result of the political structures in the municipality), the pressure on resources as the city expands and grows in the face of low economic growth, lack of capacity, and the entanglement of formality and informality in urban space make it very difficult for a local state that is under pressure to deliver services and commit to participatory processes that require time and resources. However, evidence-based policy making which is rooted in the lives of those for whom policy interventions are intended, and which recognises the nuances and differences of local spaces within a city, is required if biodiversity interventions are to lead to socio-economic development and the alleviation of poverty in the face of climate change.

Notes

1 The Research Council of Norway (RCN) and South African National Research Foundation (NRF).
2 Low-cost state-subsidised houses in South Africa are known as RDP houses as the post-apartheid large-scale roll-out of free formal housing for the poor was developed through the Reconstruction and Development Programme (RDP).

3 For a detailed account of how the Urban Development Line shapes water and sanitation provision in Durban see Sutherland et al. 2014.
4 In 2011 the service backlog for water provision in the Municipality was 74,481 households and the sanitation backlog was 231,387 households (eThekwini Municipality 2012).
5 Ecological infrastructure is the terminology now used for environmental services as it links these services into the set of 'infrastructure systems' required for society to function.
6 Named as such because its focus on the Umgeni River Catchment as a study area. The UEIP was established in November 2013.
7 For a map of the location of environmental services in the municipality see Roberts et al. 2012.

References

Artur L and Hilhorst D 2012 Everyday realities of climate change adaptation in Mozambique *Global Environmental Change* 22 529–536

Braun B P 2014 A new urban dispositif? Governing life in an age of climate change *Environment and Planning D: Society and Space* 32 49–64

eThekwini Municipality 2012 *Spatial Development Framework 2013/2014* eThekwini, eThekwini Municipality

Gounden T Pfaff B Macleod N and Buckley C 2006 *Provision of Free Sustainable Basic Sanitation: The Durban Experience Conference: Sustainable development of water resources, water supply and environmental sanitation*, 32nd WEDC International Conference, Colombo, Sri Lanka

Grasslands Partnership 2014 *Summary* Available from: www.grasslands.org.za/umngeni-ecological-infrastructure-partnershipsummary [Accessed: 9/07/14]

Lewis B 2013 *A Justice Perspective on Water and Sanitation Delivery* MSc Thesis University of Amsterdam

Parnell S Pieterse E Swilling M and Wooldridge D 2002 *Democratising Local Government: The South African Experiment* Cape Town: University of Cape Town Press

Piper L and Nadvi L 2009 Popular Mobilization, Party Dominance and Participatory Governance in South Africa in Thompson L and Tapscott C (eds) *Citizenship and Social Movements: Perspectives from the Global South* London: Zed Books

Roberts D Boon R Diederichs N Douwes E Govender N Mcinnes A Mclean C O'Donoghue S and Spiers M 2012 Exploring ecosystem-based adaptation in Durban, South Africa: 'learning-by-doing' at the local government coal face *Environment and Urbanization* 24(1) 167–195

Scott D Sutherland C Sim V and Robbins G 2015 Pro-Growth Challenges to Sustainability in South Africa in Hansen A and Wethal U (eds) *Emerging Economies and Challenges to Sustainability: Theories, Strategies, Local Realities* 204–217 London: Routledge

Sim V Sutherland C and Scott D 2015 Pushing the boundaries – urban edge challenges in eThekwini Municipality *South African Geographical Journal* Available from: http://www.tandfonline.com/doi/abs/10.1080/03736245.2015.1052840 [Accessed: 10/07/15]

Sutherland C 2016 Settlement Stories II in Dupont V Jordhus-Lier D Sutherland C and Braathen E (eds) 2016 *The Politics of Slums in the Global South: Urban Informality in Brazil, India, South Africa and Peru* Chapter 6 144–181 London: Routledge

Sutherland C Scott D and Hordijk M 2015 Urban water governance for more inclusive development: a reflection on the 'waterscapes' of Durban, South Africa *European Journal of Development Research* 27 488–504

Sutherland C Hordijk M Lewis B Meyer C and Buthelezi B 2014 Water and sanitation delivery in eThekwini Municipality: a spatially differentiated approach *Environment and Urbanisation* 26(2) 469–488

Sutherland C and Roberts D 2014 *Why Leadership Matters in Water and Climate Governance* Opinion Paper 12 Available from: www.chance2sustain.eu [Accessed: 10/07/15]

Taylor A Cartwright A and Sutherland C 2014 *The Political-Institutional Determinants of Climate Change Adaptation in South African Municipalities* AFD Research Project: 257–2011 AFD Focales Centre France

Tissington K Dettman M Langford M Dugard J and Conteh S 2008 *Water Services Fault Lines: An Assessment of South Africa's Water and Sanitation Provision across 15 Municipalities* Centre for Applied Legal Studies

Van Donk M Pieterse E Swilling M and Parnell S 2008 *Consolidating Developmental Local Government: Lessons from the South African Experience* Cape Town: University of Cape Town Press

5 A built environment perspective on adaptation in urban informal settlements, Khulna, Bangladesh

Afroza Parvin, A. F. M. Ashraful Alam and Rumana Asad

Introduction

The IPCC Fifth Assessment Report (AR5) identifies urban informal settlements as the most vulnerable type of human settlements to climate change (IPCC 2014). Being informal settlers with no legal tenancy, the poor do not get necessary support from formal institutions. Thus, physical growth and socio-economic expansion of informal settlements takes place largely outside any official rules and regulations and in distressed and climate-vulnerable locations (e.g. on flood-plains and the urban fringe). The urban government structure is usually unable or unwilling to address urban problems in informal settlements, let alone develop in line with the process of adaptation to climate-induced urban problems (Satterthwaite et al. 2009). In this way, levels of inequality rise, exacerbating the vulnerability of people and places.

Although inadequate, scholarship on vulnerability and adaptation in informal settlements (or slums) is growing. This chapter contributes to this growing body of literature by looking specifically at the built environment dimension of climate change adaptation in one informal settlement (Rupsha) in Khulna, Bangladesh. The term 'built environment' is generally defined to encompass all buildings, spaces and products that are created or modified by people (Handy et al. 2002; Srinivasan et al. 2003). Using this definition, commentators frequently characterise informal settlements as high-density areas, lacking basic services and infrastructure.

Whilst some studies distinguish between tenure arrangements – such as households built on private land for rental purposes, or those built on occupied government land (Roy et al. 2013) – others point to political ecology to highlight the causal relation of informal dwellings and processes that drive people to live in these areas (Douglas 2012). Arguably, this leads to the creation of particular built environment terminology, such as 'landscape of disaster' (Gandy 2008), 'vernacular architecture' (Aziz and Shawket 2011) and 'fluid engagement' (Jabeen and Guy 2015). Built environment, therefore, is not only a physical aspect of low-income settlements, but is where people live over many generations. It is a visualisation of transitions (and struggles) of people, places and institutions. Thus, it can be used as a rich contextual tool to understand how vulnerabilities are created, reduced and recreated in these areas. This interpretation fits with what Satterthwaite et al. (2009) and Simon (2010) regard as the recreation of vulnerability in poor urban contexts, and Thorn et al.'s (2015) observation that living with such variable experiences requires continuous adaptation through improvisation. The concept of adaptation must therefore be reframed in the context of informal settlements as part of the wider built environment.

Adaptation has a long and multidisciplinary history of inquiry resulting in various interpretations (see Chapters 1 and 2 in this volume). Distinctions are made between autonomous, strategic and planned adaptation. A growing body of literature considers autonomous adaptation as the way of life in informal settlements, while also acknowledging that the presence of planned and transformative adaptation is essential for reduction of multiple vulnerabilities associated with poverty and inequality in the built environment. This study takes a nuanced approach by applying this definition of adaptation to changes in the built environment. Following Satterthwaite et al.'s (2009) 'cycle of vulnerability', this chapter argues that built environment adaptation is mostly (opportunistically) autonomous and reactive. In other words, particular forms of adaptation take hold when an opportunity is presented and used strategically by low-income people. This helps acknowledge spiral or gradual changes in the adaptation process, involving individual and collective action among residents of informal settlements, undertaken both in isolation and/or in tandem with changes to the broader built environment system.

This framing is helpful to explain two interrelated issues – first, how adjustments in the built environmental system enable autonomous and reactive adaptation to rapid-onset weather events in informal settlements; and secondly, how these adaptation practices are organised within the multiple framing of residential activities. Research in one settlement (on occupied government land) – Rupsha slum, in Khulna City, Bangladesh – reveals the everyday actions taken by low-income people to adapt to climate (and non-climate) stresses, and seize opportunities in the built environment system. It also demonstrates causality, in that opportunities for adaptation are usually created at the 'top', with little consideration of the impacts on low-income people at the 'bottom'. These opportunities (such as improved city infrastructure) nonetheless lead to many forms of constrained autonomous and reactive adaptation practices, indicating that informal settlements do not exist in isolation of formal (citywide) planning, policy and process. This is highly policy-relevant, as certain policies (or lack thereof) are clearly manifest and manipulated through the adaptive responses of low-income people at two domains of the built environment: dwelling (or household) and settlement (or neighbourhood) levels. The following section explores the research methods and context in greater depth, before expanding on the debate around built environment systems and adaptation.

Climate change in Bangladesh

Climate change is magnifying existing urban problems in rapidly urbanising towns and cities in Bangladesh (Alam 2004; Alam and Murray 2005; IWM 2010; Banks et al. 2011). This is particularly the case for densely populated informal settlements[1] occupied by the urban poor, which have limited access to resources and services (CUS 2006; Angeles et al. 2009). Millions of poor people are living in these settlements managing food, shelter and livelihoods in the informal sectors, and negotiating daily challenges with different formal and informal stakeholders. In the course of arranging the bare necessities, the urban poor develop diverse adaptation practices to cope with disaster effects as part of their survival strategies. Existing physical planning policy and institutional setup does not address these grassroots adaptive capacities in an integrated manner. Yet, what happens in the built environment planning and management has important knock-on effects for the urban poor living in informal settlements. Thus, we observe a somewhat one-directional unintended influence of the wider urban setting on these settlements.

To understand these processes in context, we focus on a large informal settlement in Khulna, the third largest metropolitan city of Bangladesh. Khulna has a high population density of 15,090 persons per square kilometre,[2] and is located in one of the most vulnerable climatic zones (the south-western coastal belt) of Bangladesh (KDA 2012). As a deltaic plain, Khulna is flat and poorly drained, whilst the whole metropolitan area is only approximately 2.5 metres above mean sea level (KDA 2002). Topographically, large parts of Khulna are situated on a tidal flood plain with lower relief (KDA 2012). This means that drainage from the Rupsha River, which runs through the eastern edge of the city, is impeded during high tides. The city also experiences frequent waterlogging during the rainy season. Key climate change studies at national level (BUP 1993; BIDS 1994; BCAS and BUP 1994; BCAS et al. 1996; MOEF 2009; ADB 2011) and a recent study on Khulna suggest several forms of rapid- and slow-onset impacts for Khulna, such as flooding and waterlogging, and increased salinity in both surface and groundwater (IWM 2010).

In Khulna, there are around 520 informal settlements concentrated in three different parts of the city (KDA 2002; Angeles et al. 2009). The consequences of climate change are expected to be particularly severe for these settlements, due to their geographical location, poor socio-economic and built environment conditions. Urban informal settlements in Khulna are also characterised by overarching non-climatic trends of population growth, rapid urbanisation (with the urbanisation of poverty) and intensification of economic activities. Climate change impacts coupled with these non-climatic trends are magnifying existing urban problems in informal settlements, such as Rupsha.

Research and methodology

Rupsha is located in the administrative unit of Ward no. 22 of Khulna City Corporation (KCC), about 2.5 kilometres southeast from the central business district of Dakbangla (Figure 5.1). There are around 3,700 households in the settlement, who are faced with inadequate basic services such as poor sanitation, inadequate drainage, irregular electricity and water supply. About half

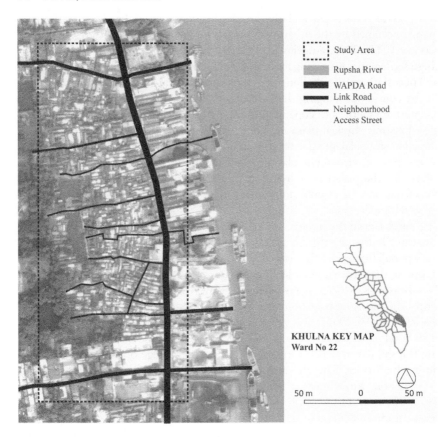

Figure 5.1 Map showing the study area in Rupsha
Source: Authors' elaboration.

of the residents are illiterate, unable to write their name. Most of the settle-ment dwellers are day labourers, the majority of whom (60 percent) work in fish processing industries and others in shipyard, building construction, sawmills and self-employment. Most of the female members (70 percent) of the settle-ment are involved in income-generating activities (IGAs), particularly fish processing works.

Our research in Rupsha revealed four visible impacts of climate change for residents in the last two decades:

1)   more frequent cyclonic storms of higher intensity,
2)   increased river flooding during rainy season and tidal flooding, both in terms of extent and frequency,
3)   increased saline intrusion during low flow conditions, and
4)   summer heat waves.

Table 5.1 Disaster impacts and key built (and socio-economic) environment concerns in urban informal settlements

Disaster impacts in Khulna City	Primary effects on built (and socio-economic) environment
Cyclonic storm with high tide	• Loss of life and damage to dwelling units and properties • Damage to infrastructure and utilities • Inundation of communication lines due to high tide
Tidal flooding and seasonal river flooding	• Submergence of low-lying areas with widespread river flooding • Drainage congestion and waterlogging • Damage to dwelling unit, infrastructure and utilities
Saline water intrusion into rivers and into ground water aquifers	• Ground water salinity • Scarcity of safe drinking water
Increased summer heat	• Heat stress in microclimate of dwelling unit • Damage to health and decline in economic productivity

Source: Authors' elaboration based on MOEF (2009) and ADB (2011).

The effects of these impacts are manifest in the built environmental system of Rupsha settlement in terms of property damage, water logging, salinity in ground water and summer heat stress respectively, as demonstrated in Table 5.1. Together, these effects are aggravating the existing urban problems in the settlement, particularly the lack of access to safe shelter, poor living conditions, inadequate provisioning of public infrastructure, lack of basic services, environmental degradation and inadequate livelihood options.

To understand the adaptation practices in the built environmental system, this research examines three spatial domains: city region, settlement and dwelling unit. Due to a higher level of significance on the lives of Rupsha dwellers, two domains (settlement and dwelling unit) have been explored in greater detail, and divided into the following three sub-domains.

- Settlement domain: (i) land tenure, (ii) land-use and spatial morphology, and (iii) access to utilities and basic services.
- Dwelling unit domain: (i) built form, (ii) space planning, and (iii) construction materials and techniques.

Research in Rupsha involved focus group discussions (FGDs) with a cluster of households living in different *Golis* (or lanes), and semi-structured interviews (SSIs) with selected households. FGDs were conducted in three selected lanes from three different parts of the settlement – 1) Muslim *Goli* (Muslim Lane along a wider path with better living condition); 2) Sat-Bhai *Goli* (Seven Brothers

Lane along a very narrow path with poor living conditions); and 3) Christian *Goli* Bi-Lane (located at low elevation along the east side of the central pond). SSIs were conducted with 15 households, selected based on three criteria:

- income generation from major livelihoods options (fish processing industries – 6 households; building construction 3 households; dockyard 3 households; and day-labourer 3 households);
- household renter (5 households) and household owner (10 households); and
- early settlers (5 households) and new settlers (10 households).

Key informant interviews (KIIs) were also held with local leaders, businesspersons and NGO workers to understand the hidden power relations influencing the adaptation practices. The following section reveals the key findings of the study in terms of adaptation practices in the two main domains of the built environmental system (settlement and dwelling) in Rupsha.

Understanding built environment adaptation in an informal settlement in Khulna

Adaptation in the domain of city region

The analysis reveals two major ways in which the settlement is linked to the city-region built environment domain, namely the construction of a city protection embankment in the 1980s, and the subsequent rise of shrimp processing industries along the Rupsha River. Our KII data reveals the following backdrop of these linkages.

Development of the Rupsha settlement started in the 1930s when economic hardship led people to migrate from the hinterland to the city in search of livelihood opportunities. During the early years, the western bank of the Rupsha River was a low-lying *char* (river bank), which was regularly inundated due to the active tidal flow of the Rupsa–Bhairab–Posur river system. Development of the Rupsha settlement was a consequence of a long process of physical adaptation to widespread river flooding, linked to the high riverbed and filling of channels from increased sedimentation.

Since 1930, the initial settlers spontaneously adapted to the regular tidal inundation at the settlement level by building stilted houses on higher land along the channel. The 'dweller-built' houses were lightweight temporary huts (*kacha ghar*) made of organic materials (wood, bamboo, thatch, plastic sheet, cement bags, etc.) with simple construction techniques. Houses were accessed by a stilted bamboo bridge (*shako*) when inundated with seasonal flooding. Fish trading started in the 1960s along the natural channel of the Rupsha in 'owner-built' trading houses of stilted bamboo construction. During the 1970s and 1980s, the channel had been the arterial communication line for fish trading. During the 1980s and 1990s, the channel gradually filled up, partially by natural deposit (siltation) and partially by fish traders.

Planned adaptation by government agencies started in the 1980s. When the channel filled up, Khulna City Corporation (KCC) constructed a road on the reclaimed land in the late 1980s. To protect the city from drainage congestion and waterlogging caused by widespread river flooding, an embankment was constructed during 1985–90 by the Bangladesh Water Development Board (BWDB). Soon after completion, the Water and Power Development Authority (WAPDA) constructed Rupsha Stand Road (locally called WAPDA road) on the embankment. Even though the embankment construction was primarily the result of a policy decision to protect the city from storm surge and tidal impacts (i.e. 'hard' resilience – see Chapter 8 in this volume), it also immediately protected the settlement and its fish industry from waterlogging and tidal flooding. In turn, it attracted more poor people from hazard-prone rural areas to reside within the 'safer' area that offered both diversified job opportunities and residential space.

Adaptation in the domain of settlement

Adaptation at the settlement level took place in the following three sub-domains.

(i) Land tenure sub-domain

The land[3] of Rupsha settlement is partly owned by KCC and partly by a religious organisation – the Khulna Baptist Church Association (KBCA). Initially, during the 1930s settlers built their houses on KBCA's land in exchange for religious affiliation (i.e. conversion to Christianity) and social engagement in the mission's charitable services. Since the 1970s, KBCA Mission Charitable Trust has declared non-transferable verbal ownership to the dwellers residing on its land. In the 1990s, KCC started to allocate temporary leasehold and has been collecting holding tax from different-sized plots ever since. About 50 percent of the house owners claimed to have holding entitlement of the plot, 20 percent claimed to be in the process of leasehold transfer from previous owners, while the rest (30 percent) were seemingly occupying the plots without any legal status. However, there exists a strong *perceived tenure security* due to the commitment of legalisation from the local political leaders that resulted in activities like permanent house building, renting them and even selling or transferring possession rights without any legal basis. This improvement in tenure security triggered rapid population growth in the settlement. At present, most of the dwellers (70 percent) are house owners, and the remainder (30 percent) are renters.

The data gathered indicates that the status of land tenure is a major determinant of the degree and extent of adaptation practices at the settlement level. Spontaneous adaptations take place only in the case of relatively secure tenure. Leaseholders are found to be actively engaged in adaptation practices to reduce the physical effects of climate change impacts on their assets, infrastructure and basic service provision both at dwelling unit and settlement level. As part of reactive adaptation, they invest in the construction, maintenance and retrofitting of their dwelling units so as to make them more durable and safer in extreme weather events.

They also actively engage with external agencies like KCC, non-governmental organisations (NGOs) and donor agencies like the United Nations Development Programme (UNDP) to undertake settlement and dwelling improvements. One example is the UNDP-funded Urban Partnerships for Poverty Alleviation Project (UPPRP) whereby residents were encouraged to form community groups or Community Development Committees (CDCs) at the neighbourhood level to improve water, sanitation and drainage. Each CDC contained members from 25–30 households on the same lane or bi-lane. Two members from each CDC then formed an upper-level unit (CDC cluster) to represent the settlement. Whilst many leaseholders were actively involved, households without legal tenure were less active, or indeed unable, to participate in community-based initiatives. They were also less willing to make spontaneous physical adjustment to their dwelling units because they did not own their plots legally.

(ii) Land use and spatial morphology

Rupsha is surrounded by a wide range of mixed land use such as industrial and commercial establishments, including shrimp processing houses and cold storage, sawmills and retail stores (Figure 5.2). Mixed land use located in relatively higher elevated areas, particularly along Stand Road, provides diversified livelihood opportunities that enable residents to adapt to the adverse disaster impacts on livelihood options. Spatial concentration of diversified land uses in close proximity and in relatively safe places enables the settlement dwellers to get alternative jobs all year round. Study data revealed the prevalence of the following employment patterns:

a)   maintenance of more than one occupation at different locations;
b)   both males, females and children participating in IGAs at different places;
c)   children and male heads of household and immediate neighbours participating in household work and babysitting while the female-head is out for work;
d)   maintenance of long-term social relations with possible employers (e.g. *Sarder* or agent of fish company, owner of company, businesspersons, etc.); and
e)   maintenance of good relations with local political leaders and NGO workers so as to switch to safer jobs during disaster periods.

In terms of spatial morphology, the settlement is highly dense with more than 600 households per acre (approximately 2,589 people per acre). It spreads in a linear rectangular structure along the river bank. The settlement is almost covered with built forms except for a large pond at the rear middle part. This spatial morphology is very distinctive with uniformly distributed single-storey (65 percent) and double-storey (35 percent) row houses (10′ to 18′ height) along narrow (mostly 3′ to 6′ wide pedestrian lanes) circulation spines generated from the main communication line (i.e. Rupsha Stand Road). The houses in the lower

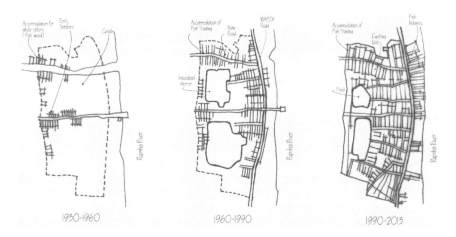

Figure 5.2 Spatial growth of settlement through physical adaptation since the 1930s
Source: Authors' elaboration.

part of the settlement are inundated for hours during heavy rainfall coupled with high tide which prevents fast drainage of rainwater to the river. Nonetheless, this compact settlement morphology adapts to potential negative impacts of extreme weather events in the following ways:

a) The compact form can largely withstand seasonal storms with partial damage.
b) The narrow spines with semi-covered space prevent rain getting into the house and create shade against direct sun and hence reduce heat stress.
c) The pond acts as a natural reservoir and helps reduce waterlogging; however, being highly polluted, it creates a high-risk post-disaster health situation.
d) In a passive way, the narrow paths make door/window shading devices redundant and thus reduce space requirements and construction costs.

(iii) Access to utilities and basic services

Access to utilities and basic services such as road, public transport, drainage, water supply, sanitation, electricity, waste collection, education and health care is highly inadequate in the settlement. This aggravates disaster impacts, which have continuous, multiple effects on the lives and livelihoods of the residents. At the settlement level, community-based adaptation (CBA) strategies concerned with improvements to infrastructure and services included:

a) pre- and post-monsoon repairing and retrofitting of common wall and roofing to protect from storms;
b) cleaning and maintenance (as and when required) of existing drainage systems to ease drainage congestion;

c)   installation of deep tube wells with the help of KCC or NGOs to have access to groundwater with low levels of salinity;
d)   help to build perforated walls and indoor ceiling canopies to ensure maximum natural air ventilation and cool indoor areas during heat waves; and
e)   use of outdoor circulation space such as lanes for household activities and social interaction to relieve heat stress.

Adaptation in the domain of dwelling unit

Rupsha is formed of rows of houses, with some clustered houses at the ends of lanes. Both the row and cluster organisation of dwelling units are built on internal lanes and bi-lanes without any setback from the common pedestrian (and non-motorised vehicles, e.g. van carrying goods) circulation spine or from the adjacent unit on the other three sides of the unit. During tidal flooding, water enters most of the houses situated in the lower part of the settlement. Storms and cyclones cause severe damage to houses followed by inundation due to high tide. Being organised in narrow lanes, there is no scope to consider climatic orientation. Thus, most of the houses (facing west) get very hot during summer. Dwellers cope with these impacts through innovative adjustment in three sub-domains of the built environment as follows.

(i) Built form

The built form of dwelling units in Rupsha settlement are composed of three types – single storey, double storey and stilted (Figure 5.3). The built forms sit mostly on the street level with very low plinths (six inches to a foot). To cope with waterlogging, the residents of single-storey houses place their valuables, such as cooker, food and poultry, on the raised beds. Building two-storey and stilted houses are effective strategies to minimise adverse effects of extreme weather events, particularly flooding and waterlogging. Residents also try to adapt to increasing heat stress by designing large openings without shutters, perforated walls, openings in the roof and ceiling, keeping doors open until midnight, rooftop planting and designing semi-outdoor spaces (verandas) at the upper level for ample air flow.

(ii) Space planning

Configuration of row- and cluster-type housing helps social adaptation through maximising the capacity of dwelling units to accommodate multiple household and neighbourhood activities both during and after weather events. For example, in row houses the circulation spine is used as an extension of the house where residents perform semi-private activities and interact socially with neighbours. In cluster households, on the other hand, the shared space is used for private, semi-private and public use. Again, despite having limited space, individual households have created varied spatial arrangements for different indoor space use.

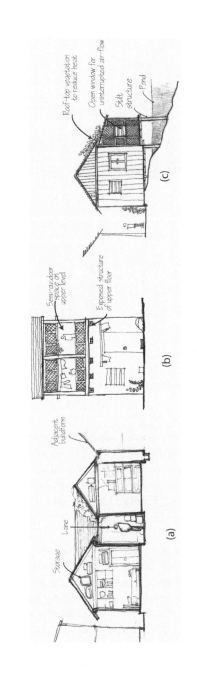

Figure 5.3 Different types of built forms – single storey (a), double storey (b) and built form on stilts (c)

Source: Authors' elaboration.

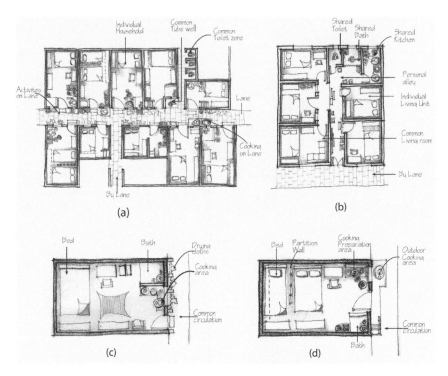

Figure 5.4 Space configuration of row houses (a) and clustered houses (b); kitchen inside the house at the frontal part (c) and kitchen outside at the entry point (d)

Source: Authors' elaboration.

With regard to dwelling entry points, services (kitchen and bathing areas) and bed space, four types of configurations are common in the dwelling units. In single-storey houses, the service space is found mostly in the front part of the house, followed by bed space inside. In some cases, the kitchen is found outside the house in the open air by the side of the lane. Keeping the kitchen outside the house at the entry point allows the female members to cook and clean on their doorstep (Figure 5.4).

In double-storey dwelling units, services (and sometimes beds) are found at the lower level, while the upper levels are comprised of bed and storage spaces with a small semi-outdoor space (veranda). In some cases, the kitchen is also found on the upper storey with bed and storage. These varying configurations are shaped mainly by climatic considerations (to enhance comfort and avoid hazards), and by the preferences of individual households depending on the size of the family, age of family members, values and economic status. Regarding flooding, waterlogging and heat stress, moving the kitchen to the upper level is an effective strategy. Considering heat stress only, having the kitchen near the door or outside at the entry point was found to be effective.

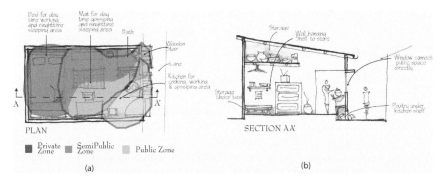

Figure 5.5 Multiple use of single space in plan (a), and in section (b)
Source: Authors' elaboration.

Residents have also developed creative ways to put poultry within the limited domestic space, such as in-built box space under the bed, or pocket space under the kitchen shelf, which is accessible from outside through a hole in the exterior wall. Livestock is also accommodated within the same domain through a low-height extension of the room with semi-permanent materials. This multiple use of space on the ground level helps minimise disruption of living activities during flooding and waterlogging. Heat stress is another determinant of such space use patterns. Adaptation through dynamic space use includes shifting as many things as possible on the bed during flooding and waterlogging, building temporary platforms to put the poultry and livestock on, sending things to a neighbour's house if necessary, use of low-height partition walls to protect from heat from the cooker, keeping children outside in the shaded lane to protect from heat stress, and use of energy-efficient cookers[4] inside the living unit.

Field observations revealed that dwellers are constantly transforming their extremely compact neighbourhood spaces into multilayered social spaces through performing every activity within the constrained built environmental system. Besides pedestrian movement, these circulation spaces are used for cooking, poultry rearing, bathing, washing, child rearing and playing, eating, intimate neighbourhood interaction, watching television, vending and community interaction. They have invented diversified ways to accommodate different household activities within a single indoor space. Some of the households also use the dwelling unit for IGAs, such as tailoring, fish processing, *katha* sewing, carpentry and handicraft (Figure 5.5).

Based on this evidence, Rupsha settlement arguably depicts an extreme example of the multiple use of available space, suggesting the unique capacity of the dwellers to live in an intensely shared socio-spatial environment. These socio-spatial dynamics result in intricate social networks that trigger spontaneous group responses to slow-onset and extreme weather impacts. This network thus enables poor dwellers to cope with adverse situations through mutual self-help, whether through sharing food, water, shelter, money, or helping with house repair.

(iii) Construction materials and techniques

The households use a wide variety of construction materials for building houses, depending on the availability of materials, affordability, climatic hazards and comfort. Most of the dwelling units are a temporary (*katcha*) construction built with organic materials such as bamboo, wood, *golpata*, thatch, mud and waste materials such as plastic sheets, jute sack, cardboard, paper and so forth. Some units are semi-permanent (*semi-pacca*), built with combinations of permanent materials, such as brick, *tali* and concrete, and organic materials. Few dwellings are of permanent (*pacca*) construction with brick and concrete.[5]

In most of the double-storey houses, residents generally extended the upper floor beams over the bi-lanes, or built structures (e.g. platforms) for future extension (Figure 5.6). Anticipating hazard effects, and depending on affordability, households choose durable or temporary building materials. At the lower level of the external wall, they use durable materials such as brick to withstand flood and waterlogging. They also use pitched roofing for better drainage of rainwater. There are also examples of shared gutters built to drain away rainwater from adjacent rooftops. In order to minimise damage and loss of life during storms, they use lightweight materials for overhead construction. Lightweight wooden platforms supported by bamboo or wooden joists are used for intermediate floor construction.

Climate adaptation: big issues, small perspectives

The built environment is an important system through which low-income urban dwellers experience vulnerability from slow-onset and extreme weather events associated with climate change. However, the built environment is also the system through which people, their local alliances and extra-local organisations channel adaptive efforts to reduce vulnerability. Evidently, within Rupsha, residents deploy a range of adaptive strategies in the dwelling and settlement built environment domains. For example, spatial planning, home design, gradual improvements and investments in dwellings and various forms of CBA such as construction of line drainage, community shared water points and toilets, and periodic risk awareness drives. Crucially, these adaptations are highly uneven, with access to opportunities (employment, NGO participation and tenure security) differentiated according to one's social and political networks. Most notably, religious politics were increasingly becoming a force of social division within the settlement, with many of the Christian and Hindu minority fearing eviction by the Muslim majority.

Although detailed analysis of settlement level impacts of (and dwelling or household adaptations to) climate change is useful, it produces only partial knowledge. This is because informal settlements (such as Rupsha) do not exist

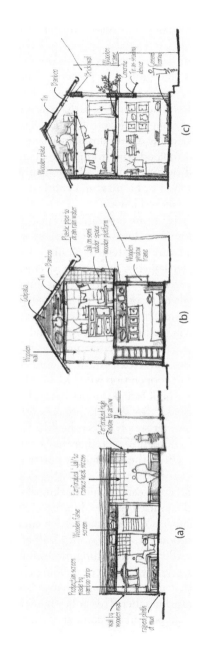

Figure 5.6 Example of construction materials and techniques used in a single-storey dwelling – *pacca* (a), and a double-storey dwelling – *semi pacca* (b) and *pacca* (c)

Source: Authors' elaboration.

in isolation from citywide processes. This is evident in the following two observations. First, although Rupsha residents could access some municipal 'lifeline services' (e.g. water, drainage), and benefited (indirectly) from the construction of the city protection embankment, levels of insecurity remained high, and investment in adaptation could be rendered meaningless if eviction was to occur. Second, whilst some longer term, better connected and financially stable households could get lease holdings (recognition of property ownership), or perhaps negotiate for *in situ* upgrading, and/or rehabilitation with NGOs and local officials, the extent to which Rupsha and these resettlement areas would be more or less prone to climate change impacts (even if infrastructure was improved) remains uncertain. Rupsha, like many other informal settlements, is on low-lying land and remains highly prone to floods and storm surges. Furthermore, rising in economic value and bounded by an economically productive neighbourhood, the land is increasingly sought after by business and political elites who have the muscle power and finances to evict residents.

This study reveals that policies to incorporate informal, low-income settlements with other built environment domains are absent, inadequate or even perverse. Indeed, the urban planning system in Khulna does not address the issues surrounding informal settlements due to an overarching policy constraint – that it does not recognise informality, as this entails illegal housing activities. As such, it is difficult to incorporate physical adaptation of informal settlements within formal planning and development initiatives. Whilst some residents can access support via clientelistic networks and vote-bank politics, the municipal authority (KCC) is mandated to provide basic services for all citizens and therefore recognises the settlement to a limited extent. NGOs can work with approval from (and in cooperation with) KCC. This is why, although limited in scope and coverage, NGOs and donors have played an active role in implementing community-based, small-scale projects for sanitation, housing, solid waste management, water supply, urban health, family planning and micro-credit. It is important to note, however, that the benefits from these projects are distributed unevenly within the community due to hidden power relations between residents.

These findings reinforce earlier research which acknowledges that the way built environment is delivered can itself lead to disasters (Ofori 2002), and the intensity of climate change impacts on informal settlements is determined by the condition of the built environment, which is the result of perverse planning practices in the city (Wamsler 2008). Such findings necessitate a paradigm shift in the policy framework to enable the process of building climate resilient cities as a shared responsibility that includes climate change issues, urban poverty and city planning in an integrated manner. This policy framework needs to conceive urban vulnerability of urban poor in the context of existing unequal social, political, economic and institutional systems that influence health, education, income, building safety and location of work and home – the building blocks of their built environment system.

Notes

1 In this study, 'informal settlements' refers to the dense low-income settlements comprising poor communities housed in dweller-built shelters located on public or private land with or without authoritative permission.
2 According to the 2011 population census, Khulna city's population is recorded as 688,880 (KDA 2012).
3 It is a *Char* land, i.e. the low-lying river bank formed due to siltation. This is a natural process of land formation in deltaic geological conditions, as in Bangladesh. Any land developed through this process is considered *Khas* land. *Khas* land is central-government-owned land intended to be leased for both agricultural and non-agricultural purposes. The most eligible for *Khas* land are: the landless poor (both urban and rural), significant contributors to society and economy, or persons/groups/institutions who wish to use it for public benefit.
4 An energy-efficient cooker is designed and supplied by NGOs at a cheaper rate for the slum dwellers who are members of the community clusters guided by the NGO concerned. The cooker is a closed container with a piped outlet to release fumes in the air outside the indoor space.
5 Floor construction – plinths mostly made of mud, increasingly of brick. Wall construction – mostly made of wood; however, increasing inclination to brick wall for the households who can afford it. Roof construction – mostly thatched, partially with corrugated tin and few with permanent reinforced cement concrete roof. Intermediate floor – wooden platform supported by bamboo or wooden joists. Perforated window '*jali*' and free façade to ensure adequate ventilation.

References

Alam M 2004 *Adverse Impacts of Climate Change on Development of Bangladesh: Integrating Adaptation into Policies and Activities* CLACC Working Paper No. 1 Dhaka: Bangladesh Centre for Advanced Studied (BCAS)

Alam M and Murray 2005 *Facing Up to Climate Change in South Asia* IIED Gatekeeper Series 118 London: IIED

Angeles G Lance P Barden-O'Fallon J Islam N Mahbub A Q and Nazem N 2009 The 2005 census and mapping of settlements in Bangladesh: design, select results and application *International Journal of Health Geographics* 8 32

Asian Development Bank (ADB) 2011 *Adapting to Climate Change: Strengthening the Climate Resilience of the Water Sector Infrastructure in Khulna, Bangladesh* Philippines: ADB

Aziz T A and Shawket I M 2011 New strategy of upgrading slum areas in developing countries using vernacular trends to achieve a sustainable housing development *Energy Procedia* 6 228–235

Bangladesh Centre for Advanced Studies (BCAS) Bangladesh Institute of Development Studies (BIDS) and Bangladesh Unnoyon Parishad (BUP) 1996 *Climate Change Country Study Bangladesh* Climate Change Study Programme US Government. (BCAS) Dhaka

Bangladesh Centre for Advanced Studies (BCAS) and Bangladesh Unnoyon Parishad (BUP) 1994 *Vulnerability of Bangladesh to Climate Change and Sea Level Rise* Dhaka Resource Analysis (RA) / Approtech Ltd with support from the Netherlands Government

Bangladesh Institute of Development Studies (BIDS) 1994 *Country Study on Bangladesh under Regional Study of Global Environmental Issues Project on the Impact of Climate*

Change in Bangladesh: the Available Options for Adaptation and Mitigation Measure and Response Strategies. Dhaka: BIDS and ADB

Bangladesh Unnoyon Parishad (BUP) 1993 *The Greenhouse Effect and Climate Change: An Assessment of the Effects on Bangladesh* BUP Centre for Environmental and Resource Studies, (CEARS) New Zealand and Climate Research Unit (CRU) University of East Anglia, UK

Banks N Roy M and Hulme D 2011 Neglecting the urban poor in Bangladesh: research, policy and action in the context of climate change *Environment & Urbanization* 23(2) 487–502

Centre for Urban Studies (CUS) 2006 *Settlements of Urban Bangladesh: Mapping and Census 2005* Dhaka: CUS

Douglas I 2012 Urban ecology and urban ecosystems: understanding the links to human health and well-being *Current Opinion in Environmental Sustainability* 4 385–392

Gandy M 2008 Landscapes of disaster: water, modernity, and urban fragmentation in Mumbai *Environment and Planning A* 40 108–130

Handy S L Boarnet G B Ewing R and Killingsworth R E 2002 How built environment affects physical activity: views from urban planning *American Journal of Preventive Medicine* 23 64–73

Intergovernmental Panel on Climate Change (IPCC) 2014 *Climate Change 2014: Impacts, Adaptation, and Vulnerability* (Part A: Global and Sectoral Aspects) Cambridge and New York: Cambridge University Press

Institute of Water Modelling (IWM) 2010 *Bangladesh: Strengthening the Resilience of the Water Sector in Khulna to Climate Change* ADB Technical Assistance Consultant's Report (Project No. 42469-01) Dhaka: ADB

Jabeen H and Guy S 2015 Fluid engagements: responding to the co-evolution of poverty and climate change in Dhaka, Bangladesh *Habitat International* 47 307–314

Khulna Development Authority (KDA) 2002 *Structure Plan, Master Plan and Detailed Area Plan (2001–2020) for Khulna City* Khulna: Aqua Sheltech Consortium for Khulna Development Authority (KDA)

Khulna Development Authority (KDA) 2012 *Preparation of Detailed Area Development Plan for Khulna Master Plan Area: Survey Report* Khulna: Development Design Consultant Ltd, Data Expert Private Ltd KDA

Ministry of Environment and Forests (MOEF) 2009 *Bangladesh Climate Change Strategy and Action Plan 2009* Dhaka: Government of the People's Republic of Bangladesh

Ofori G 2002 Construction Industry Development for Disaster Prevention and Response. *International Conference on Post-Disaster Reconstruction: Planning for Reconstruction*, May 23–25 Montreal Canada

Roy M Hulme D and Jahan F 2013 Contrasting adaptation responses by squatters and low income tenants in Khulna, Bangladesh *Environment and Urbanization* 25(1) 157–176

Satterthwaite D Huq S Reid H Pelling M and Lankao P R 2009 Adapting to Climate Change in Urban Areas: The Possibilities and Constraints in Low- and Middle-Income Nations in Bicknell J Dodman D and Satterthwaite D (eds) *Adapting Cities to Climate Change: Understanding and Addressing the Development Challenges* London: Earthscan

Simon D 2010 The challenges of global environmental change for urban Africa *Urban Forum* 21 235–248

Srinivasan S O'Fallon L R and Dearry A 2003 Creating healthy communities, healthy homes, healthy people: initiating a research agenda on the built environment and public health *American Journal of Public Health* 93 1446–1450

Thorn J Thornton T F and Helfgott A 2015 Autonomous adaptation to global environmental change in peri-urban settlements: evidence of a growing culture of innovation and revitalisation in Mathare Valley Slums Nairobi *Global Environmental Change* 31 121–131

Wamsler C 2008 Planning Ahead: Adapting Settlements before Disasters Strike in Bosher L (ed) *Hazards and the Built Environment: Attaining Built-in Resilience* London: Routledge

6 Health implications of climate change for dwellers of low-income settlements in Tanzania

Iddi Mwanyoka, Kelvin Haule, Riziki Shemdoe and Manoj Roy

Introduction

That health burdens are particularly damaging for low-income people, and that climate change risks greatly exacerbate these burdens, consistently appears in development and policy literature. Research in India's urban informal settlements, for example, identifies ill health as a critical trigger in the shift from 'just managing' to 'being in chronic poverty' (Mitlin and Satterthwaite 2013). Earlier, Hulme (2003) observed in Bangladesh that the failure of public health services to provide for poor people's health needs was central to their slide into poverty. Health is one of three core dimensions of the Global Multidimensional Poverty Index 2015 developed by the Oxford Poverty and Human Development Initiative (Alkire et al. 2015). The *State of African Cities* report (UN Habitat 2014) also identifies the diverse health impacts associated with climate change risks in African cities. Finally, in its Fifth Assessment Report (AR5) the Intergovernmental Panel on Climate Change (IPCC) identified 'urban health' as a particularly important element in the differential risk and vulnerabilities within and between urban centres (IPCC 2013).

This existing and emerging scholarship indicates the need for a twin-track examination of the health implications of climate change for the urban poor, namely, how climate change influences health (status) amongst poor urban populations; and the quantity and quality of healthcare services (Sclar et al. 2013). In this chapter, we look at the first dimension, with emphasis on Tanzania in general, and informal, low-income settlements in Dar es Salaam in particular. By focusing on urban health as a characteristic of the population and society in general, we acknowledge the need for incorporating both individual and policy perspectives. Health is one of the most important assets underpinning human wellbeing at the individual *and* household level. Critically for low-income people, ill health among any of their family members – be it the earning member or those who depend on that income – is fatal for the household and sometimes to its extended members. In this sense, health is more a household than individual asset for low-income people.

From a public policy perspective, Sclar et al. (2013) argue that urban population health is an important input into creating a productive urban economy via its contribution to labour force productivity, or it can be viewed as the output of a productive, vibrant and socially equitable urban economy. In low-income cities of the developing world, where the informal economy dominates (see Harriss-White and Rodrigo Chapter 11, this volume) and drives the national and global economy (Olinto et al. 2015), ill health amongst the workforce (that propels the informal economy) is hugely unproductive. Significantly, the vast majority of this workforce lives in informal, low-income settlements, making ill health not just a national but also a global concern.

It must be emphasised that health burdens on poor urban people may be inflicted in different forms and for a variety of reasons. Indeed, urban health issues intersect a broad range of social determinants of health, including decent shelter, safe drinking water, adequate nutrition, good education, as well as the quantity and quality of available healthcare services (McGranahan 2013). Climatic change affects population health both directly and indirectly. Altered temperature and rainfall patterns, for example, directly influences the growth and spread of disease vectors. High variability in flooding and waterlogging also raises the prospect of people being exposed to disease vectors more widely than ever before. Indirectly, as a growing body of literature (e.g. Githeko et al. 2000; Patz et al. 2005; Afrane et al. 2006; Adelekan et al. 2015; Hashemi et al. Chapter 12, this volume) shows, climate change affects all of the social determinants of health noted above.

In this chapter we focus on climate change implications on vector-borne diseases (specifically malaria), given the paucity of research on this issue in general, and urban Tanzania in particular. We draw our motivation from widely reported increases in infectious diseases in urban Africa, notably from Sakijege et al. (2012), as well as Kau et al. (2011) who identify 'environmental enteropathy' – a condition that impairs food absorption in children – as one of the most serious impacts of urban pathogenesis. Although not fatal, the condition stunts children's growth, hinders their cognitive development and gives rise to illness in later life. All of this relates to their childhood exposure to vector-borne diseases. This is and should be preventable.

In deepening our understanding of the climate sensitivity of a range of vector- and water-borne diseases in urban Tanzania, we draw on literature that focuses on the national level, as well as insights from two recent, and one ongoing research project (EcoPoor[1]) on informal settlements in Dar es Salaam, Tanzania's largest city. Our aim is to instigate an intellectual discussion around the need for systematic evidence-gathering on the health status of the urban poor linked to climate change (i.e. the first of the two dimensions noted above), thus providing a basis for targeted public policy to improve the quantity and quality of the required healthcare services (the second dimension).

Climate change and human health: conceptual association

The association between human activities (such as increased use of fossil fuels, land use change and agriculture) and climate change is widely known (IPCC

2014). Temperature increase, in particular, is directly linked to climate change, with recent models indicating much higher temperature increases in 2100 than initially estimated (Stainforth et al. 2005). Despite many international and local initiatives on disaster risk management and advances in scientific knowledge, the social and economic impact of climate change in rural and urban areas in emerging economies is critically underexplored, even though the impacts are potentially severe (CLUVA[2] 2010). Increasingly, fragile economies are unable to absorb the shocks caused by climate change impacts and natural disasters. This, combined with increasing vulnerability of the exposed population due to rapid unplanned urbanisation, weak institutions, low levels of technology and conflict has significant implications in these countries (WHO 2008).

The IPCC (2007; 2014) asserts that extreme temperatures can lead directly to loss of life, while climate-related disturbances in ecological systems can indirectly affect the incidence of infectious diseases. Climate change is also argued to be closely related to the prevalence of some tropical diseases such as Ebola, with significant implications for human health, as demonstrated in the 2014 outbreak (EFSA 2015). The magnitude and nature of climate change impacts on human health vary spatially by region, according to the relative vulnerability of population groups, extent and duration of exposure to climate change and by society's ability to cope with, or adapt to, these changes (IPCC 2014). Climate change can affect human health and wellbeing in a variety of ways. Whilst warm temperatures can increase air and water pollution, harming human health, extreme weather events (e.g. floods, cyclones, high winds) can destroy shelter, contaminate water supplies, cripple crop production, and tear apart existing health and other service infrastructures. This will ultimately increase the existing burden of disease and other non-health needs, particularly for the urban poor (Mboera et al. 2011).

Crucially, the variability of weather associated with climate change is argued to increase the breeding ground for harmful pests and vectors that transmit various tropical diseases. Climate change is also anticipated to increase antibiotic resistance, survivability of vectors and amplify the expansion of diseases. In 2007 for example, the FAO reiterated that changing temperatures and rainfall in drought-prone areas is likely to shift populations of insect pests and other vector-borne diseases in both humans and crops FAO (2007). Whilst extensive evidence reports the impacts of climate change in rural areas, little is known in the context of urban settings. This is highly problematic, as the urban poor are the most at risk to ill health due to existing vulnerabilities within the social, political, economic and built environment, and low adaptive capacity (Sclar et al. 2013).

Climate change and vector-borne disease prevalence in Tanzania: national perspective

Tanzania, a low-income country in East Africa, has been experiencing real and visible impacts of climate change. Severe and recurrent droughts in the past few years have triggered the recent devastating electricity power crisis. There have also been dramatic drops in lake water levels across the country.[3] These impacts have already affected communities in both rural and urban areas, as well as the economic development of the country overall. Furthermore, climate projections indicate that northern and southern parts of the country could experience an increase in rainfall ranging from 5 to 45 percent, and that most other parts of the country might experience a decrease in rainfall of 10 to 15 percent (Mwandosya et al. 1998).

The majority of urban residents in Tanzania (an estimated 50 to 80 percent) live in informal, unplanned settlements that lack adequate infrastructure and services (UN Habitat 2014). In the capital Dar es Salaam, over 70 percent of the five million residents live in informal, unplanned settlements, with over half surviving on roughly one dollar per day (World Bank 2002; Kombe 2005; START Secretariat 2011). These urban areas are increasingly affected by the impacts of climate change, with direct (and indirect) implications for health and healthcare.

Although there are limited studies on health and climate change in urban areas, various studies conducted across the country (e.g. Shemdoe 2011; Shemdoe and Kihila 2012) have shown that communities (especially in livestock-keeping areas, farming communities and those who are dependent on fishing) have linked climate change with health. Pests and diseases in particular have significant impacts on health for humans (Shemdoe 2011). In Lushoto and Mpwapwa regions, for example, various diseases linked to climate variability affected rural dwellers, such as skin disease, stomach problems, cancer, malaria and malnutrition. In both areas, malaria cases were on the rise. Table 6.1 summarises major infectious diseases in Tanzania.

Malaria is by far the most important vector-borne disease causing high rates of illness and mortality across Tanzania. The extent to which malaria is endemic varies with topography, climate, tradition and customs. Malaria has been a common disease in low-altitude rural areas and warm climate regions of Tanzania. However, due to changes in socio-economic, environmental and vector-related factors, the disease is now common in previously malaria-free highland and mountainous areas such as Lushoto in the Tanga region, Njombe in the Iringa region and the Kilimanjaro region where a few years ago malaria was not common (Mboera and Kitua 2001; Mboera 2004). Crucially, the recent trend of malarial expansion indicates that malaria is endemic to almost the whole country (Mboera et al. 2010). This expansion is associated with increases in ambient temperature. Warmer temperatures have affected the rates at which mosquitoes reach sexual maturity, frequency of mosquito blood meals, and rates at which parasites are acquired, as well as shortened incubation time of parasites within mosquitoes (Vora 2008). On the other hand, increased precipitation associated with global warming may result in increases in the number of breeding sites, and hence mosquito populations (Harrus and Baneth 2005).

Studies in north-east Tanzania have shown that ecological changes that occurred in the East and West Usambara mountains played a significant role in the increase of malaria transmission in the area (Matola et al. 1987; Bødker et al. 2003; 2006).

Table 6.1 Major infectious diseases in Tanzania

Disease	How is acquired/transmitted
1. Hepatitis A	Through consumption of food or water contaminated with fecal matter, principally in areas of poor sanitation; victims exhibit fever, jaundice, and diarrhoea.
2. Hepatitis E	Spread through fecal contamination of drinking water; victims exhibit jaundice, fatigue, abdominal pain, and dark-coloured urine.
3. Typhoid fever	Spread through contact with food or water contaminated by fecal matter or sewage.
4. Vector-borne diseases	Acquired through the bite of an infected arthropod.
5. Malaria	Transmitted to humans via the bite of the female *Anopheles* mosquito.
6. Dengue fever	Mosquito-borne (*Aedes aegypti*) viral disease associated with urban environments.
7. Yellow fever	Mosquito-borne viral disease.
8. Japanese encephalitis	Mosquito-borne (*Culex tritaeniorhynchus*) viral disease.
9. African trypanosomiasis	Caused by the parasitic protozoa *Trypanosoma*; transmitted to humans via the bite of bloodsucking tsetse flies.
10. Cutaneous leishmaniasis	Caused by the parasitic protozoa *Leishmania*; transmitted to humans via the bite of sand flies.
11. Plague	Bacterial disease transmitted by fleas normally associated with rats; person-to-person airborne transmission also possible.
12. Crimean–Congo hemorrhagic fever	Tick-borne viral disease; infection may also result from exposure to infected animal blood or tissue.

13. Rift Valley fever	Viral disease affecting domesticated animals and humans; transmission is by mosquito and other biting insects; infection may also occur through handling of infected meat or contact with blood.
14. Chikungunya	Mosquito-borne (*Aedes aegypti*) viral disease associated with urban environments, similar to dengue fever; characterised by sudden onset of fever, rash, and severe joint pain.
15. Water contact diseases	Through swimming or wading in freshwater lakes, streams and rivers.
16. Leptospirosis	Bacterial disease that affects animals and humans; infection occurs through contact with water, food, or soil contaminated by animal urine.
17. Schistosomiasis	Caused by parasitic trematode flatworm *Schistosoma*; freshwater snails act as intermediate host and release larval form of parasite that penetrates the skin of people exposed to contaminated water.
18. Aerosolised dust or soil contact disease	Acquired through inhalation of aerosols contaminated with rodent urine.
19. Respiratory disease	Acquired through close contact with an infectious person.
20. Meningococcal meningitis	Bacterial disease causing an inflammation of the lining of the brain and spinal cord
21. Animal contact disease	Acquired through direct contact with local animals.
22. Rabies	Viral disease of mammals usually transmitted through the bite of an infected animal, most commonly dogs.

Source: Adapted from CIA World Fact Book (2015).

In Mpwapwa district, central Tanzania, the malaria epidemic of 1999 was directly associated with climatic factors, particularly rainfall and temperature. During that year, the district experienced its highest temperatures and a prolonged period of rainfall (Mboera et al. 2005). Mpwapwa district is located in the central plateau of Tanzania and is usually semi-arid with a short period of rainfall occurring between December and April. Further climate-linked malaria epidemics have been reported elsewhere in East Africa, notably in Kenya and Uganda (Matola et al. 1987; Mboera and Kitua 2001).

In the Mbeya Region, Kangalawe (2009; 2012) demonstrated a clear association between temperature trends and malaria incidences as an impact of climate change. A common characteristic of many affected areas prior to the malaria epidemics is that they had suffered a recent period of drought and were recognised as having serious food security problems. Further support for the link between food security and malaria epidemics comes from the study in Mbulu District in 1942 (Clyde 1967) and Muleba District in 1978 (Garay 1998). The risk of mortality from malaria during the Muleba epidemic was observed to be seven times higher in malnourished than well-nourished children, giving support to the view that the consequences of epidemic malaria are most intensely felt in low-income communities where food entitlement is constrained.

The impact of climate change variability on malaria has been outlined in a number of studies in Africa (Lindsay and Birley 1996; Lindsay and Martens 1998; Lindsay et al 2000). The relationship can be explained by the fact that as altitude increases, temperature declines and both the development and survival of the mosquito vector and parasite are critically dependent on the ambient temperature. As the temperature drops, so does the risk of infection, and there is a typical threshold below which transmission ceases. *Anopheles gambiae* complex and *An. funestus* mosquitoes are responsible for transmission of most malaria in Tanzania. These species of mosquitoes are sensitive to temperature changes both as adults and immature stages in the aquatic environment (Rueda et al. 1990). When water temperature rises, the immature stages take a relatively shorter time to mature and consequently there is a greater capacity to produce more offspring during the transmission period (Rueda et al. 1990).

In warmer climates, the gonotrophic cycle of *Anopheles* mosquitoes is shorter, meaning that the adult female mosquitoes digest blood faster and feed more frequently, thus increasing transmission intensity (Gillies 1953). Similarly, malaria parasites complete extrinsic incubation within the female *Anopheles* mosquito in a shorter time as temperature rises, thereby increasing the proportion of infective vectors. The distribution of *Anopheles gambiae* complex siblings is determined by ecological factors. While *Anopheles gambiae* prefers the wet and humid zones, *An. arabiensis* has adapted to drier climates. It has been reported by Lindsay and Martens (1998) that the distribution and relative abundance of these species can be predicted fairly accurately using climate models and could be used to indicate future changes in vector distributions associated with climate change. On the other hand, increased precipitation has the potential to increase the number and quality of breeding sites for mosquitoes.

Rift Valley Fever (RVF) is another climate change related infection. In Tanzania, RVF epidemics were recorded in 1956, 1978–79, 1997–98 and 2007. In January 2007, an outbreak of RVF was detected in the northern districts of Tanzania, but later spread southwards and westwards to affect people in other parts of the country. A total of 511 suspected RVF cases were reported from 10 of the 21 regions of Tanzania, with laboratory confirmation of 186 cases and another 123 probable cases. All RVF cases were located in the north-central and southern regions of the country, with an eventual fatality rate of 28.2 percent ($N = 144$; Mohamed et al. 2010). While the 1997–98 epidemics were confined to the Arusha region in northern Tanzania, the 2007 epidemics spread southwards and westwards to cover a number of regions (Mohamed et al. 2010).

Arguably, climate change will have short- and long-term impacts on disease transmission. For example, a short-term increase in temperature and rainfall (as seen in the 1997–98 El Niño, an example of inter-annual climate variability) caused *Plasmodium falciparum* malaria epidemics and RVF in Kenya. RVF is expected to occur in other regions across and within East Africa, including Tanzania, as changes in temperature and rainfall are expected to magnify the driving causes for the spread of infection.

Along with malaria and RVF, dengue fever is considered to be the most important arbovirus disease throughout the world. Its link to climate change cannot be underestimated. The disease is present throughout the tropics and subtropics, and more prevalent in highly urbanised communities with poorly managed water and solid waste systems. Although the history of dengue in Africa is poorly documented, the disease is known to have been on the continent since the turn of the 20th century. Tanzania recorded the first outbreak of dengue in Dar es Salaam in February 2010. The cases were confirmed by the polymerase chain reaction (PCR) to be dengue fever type 3 virus (DENV-3) infections. Later, in May 2010, more cases of dengue fever were reported from hospitals in Dar es Salaam. Out of 126 samples collected, 46 were positive for dengue (MHSW 2010). Additionally, in a recent study in Mbeya in southwestern Tanzania, a 6 percent seroprevalence of DENV 1–4 was reported in the Mlowo area (Weller et al. 2010). The overall burden of dengue virus infection in Tanzania is uncertain.

Dengue viruses, like all other arboviruses, are transmitted primarily by arthropods to vertebrates. The virus is transmitted to humans by mosquitoes, especially *Aedes aegypti* and *Aedes albopictus*. *Aedes aegypti* is a highly domestic day-biting species that prefers to feed on humans. Generally, small and inconspicuous containers of water, both natural and artificial, such as discarded cans and cups, roof gutters, barrels, flower pots, tree holes, water tanks, or tyres are used as breeding sites for these vectors. With the intensity of climate change, the increased risk and resurgence of dengue in Tanzania is expected to magnify. This relates to temperature (which is known to influence adult survival), length of the gonotrophic cycle, the extrinsic incubation period of the virus in the vector, and vector size, a factor that indirectly influences the biting rate (Jetten and Focks 1997). Moreover, climate change is anticipated to increase breeding grounds and survivability of vectors, especially within low-income urban communities.

The prevalence of Human African trypanosomiasis (HAT; also known as sleeping sickness), caused mainly by *Trypanosoma brucei rhodesiense* and transmitted by tsetse flies of the *Glossina* species can also be associated with climate change in Tanzania. *Glossina morsitans morsitans* have adapted to ecosystems ranging from humid forests to dry savannas, whereas G. *palpalis* is a riverine species preferring to rest under dense vegetation close to river banks. As these ecosystems change, so does the distribution of vector species. Ecosystem change contributes to shifts in the distribution of the disease. Deforestation in the HAT-endemic regions of Tanzania has been associated with drought and decrease in precipitation. In turn, this is likely to affect the survival of immature tsetse, and affect the population and transmission of sleeping sickness. It is important, therefore, to understand how environmental modifications, population dynamics and climate change will impact on the distribution and incidence of the disease. Change in climate and vegetation are factors that have been associated with the re-emergence of HAT.

Leptospirosis is another climate-related disease. Leptospirosis is a globally important zoonotic disease, most commonly found in tropical or subtropical countries. It is prevalent in both urban and rural settings. Although the epidemiological status of human leptospirosis in Tanzania has not been well defined (due to a general lack of awareness of the disease, and difficulties in its diagnosis), some studies in Tanzania have reported a prevalence of 15.1 percent (Schoonman and Swai 2009). Biggs et al. (2011) also found a prevalence of 8.8 percent leptospirosis among admitted patients in two hospitals in Moshi, Tanzania. Its association with climate change is attributed to the fact that the incidence of infection is seasonal, with peak incidence occurring during rainy season.

Plague is a rapidly progressing, serious and highly fatal infectious disease for humans (Gage and Kosoy 2005). In Tanzania, plague is endemic in Lushoto district, with cases generally occurring in seasonal stages (Kilonzo et al. 1997). Environmental factors are suspected to play a role in the complex plague cycle. This may explain (at least partly) the details of its spatial distribution (Neerinckx et al. 2008). Climate is suspected to be a key factor in the alternation between quiescent and active periods of plague (Ari et al. 2011). It has been reported that human plague outbreaks in several African countries are less frequent when the weather is too hot (>27°C) or cold (<15°C), while an increased plague incidence during the hot, dry season followed by a period of high seasonal rainfall has been reported in Vietnam (Pham et al. 2009). This is to say the lifecycle of plague can be linked with climate change.

Climate change also has a significant impact on water-borne diseases. Water-borne diseases are anticipated to be rampant in areas where there is shortage of clean water and sanitation facilities. Among the notable diseases are diarrhoea, cholera and typhoid. Whilst diarrhoea is much more common in higher temperatures (WHO 2009), flooding and unusually low levels of water can also lead to water contamination and bring higher rates of illness and death from cholera and other diarrhoeal diseases (Hashizume 2008). Warming and greater variability in rainfall threatens to increase the burden of these diseases. In turn, warmer surface temperatures increase the abundance of phytoplankton, supporting a large population of zooplankton, which serve as a reservoir for cholera bacteria.

Human health and climate change in urban Tanzania: the case of Dar es Salaam

Whilst there is a good deal of research on climate-related diseases in rural areas (as above), little is known about the impacts of climate change on health in low-income urban settings. This is despite the fact that nearly 26 percent of Tanzania's urban population (4.2 percent of who live in Dar es Salaam and 21.7 percent in other towns and cities) are poor (URT 2013). To shed some light on these neglected contexts, this section takes a closer look at Tanzania's largest city, Dar es Salaam, drawing on EcoPoor data and existing literature.

Dar es Salaam, situated by the Indian Ocean, is one of the fastest-growing urban areas in Sub-Saharan Africa, covering an area of approximately 1,800 square kilometres. Its current population of 4.4 million (URT 2013) grew at 5.8 percent per annum during the last decade (Kiunsi 2013a). UN Habitat (2014) predicts the city will grow at a rate even faster than the previous decade, raising the prospect of it becoming a megacity (of over 10 million people) by 2034. Population growth will exert greater pressure on hard infrastructure (Kiunsi 2013b) but also increase demand for health services. An evident trend is that low-income settlements become progressively more densely populated – an inadvertent result of informal development (Kyessi 2010; Roy et al. forthcoming).

The city has three municipalities – Kinondoni, Ilala and Temeke – which are divided into 73 wards (Penrose et al. 2010; UN Habitat 2010). Despite increasing efforts of municipal and city governments to address informal settlement expansion, the speed of the city's growth and inability to invest adequately in housing and infrastructure have led to the growth of existing settlements and to the development of new ones. As a result, Dar es Salaam now has one of the highest proportions of informal settlement households in East Africa, with 65 percent of households living in informal areas (Penrose et al. 2010). Nearly 80 percent of the population lives in around 43 low-income, informal settlements of different sizes, each with limited access to basic infrastructure and services, such as water supply, sewerage and storm water drainage systems (UN Habitat 2010). This situation makes low-income dwellers in Dar es Salaam highly vulnerable to diseases.

In these informal areas, flooding (as a result of both intense short-burst or prolonged rainfall) is frequent, and a range of non-climatic factors such as dumping of sewage and solid waste into rivers and channels, blockage of storm drains with garbage or illegal construction can exacerbate health impacts. Apart from damage to property, inadequate or absent supply of clean water, poor sanitation provision, widespread use of pit latrines that overflow easily, overcrowding and unhygienic practices render many residents of low-income settlements vulnerable to disease, particularly following flooding. Residents in high-density areas

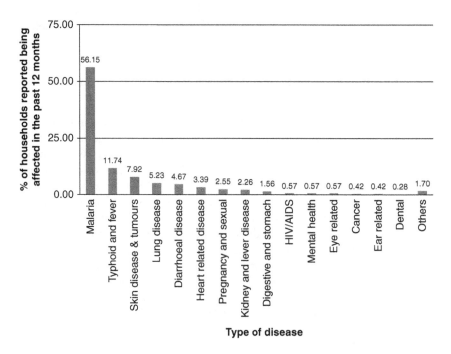

Figure 6.1 Disease type and percentage of households affected (over 12 months)
Source: Authors' elaboration based on EcoPoor household survey (2015).

are also particularly prone to malaria, lymphatic filariasis, cholera, dengue fever and diarrhoea amongst others (START Secretariat 2011).

As Figure 6.1 shows, a staggering 56 percent of over 700 household respondents from four informal settlements in the city (Bonde la Mpunga, Hananasif, Magomeni Suna and Uzuri Manzase) reported that at least one member of their household had malaria in the 12 months prior to July 2015. Close to 20 percent of households also reported being affected by a range of infectious diseases such as typhoid, tumours and skin diseases. Surprisingly, only five percent of respondents reported diarrhoeal disease.

Another recent study (Sakijege et al. 2012) that examined attendance at a local dispensary (known as Tyma dispensary) over a period of three months (March to May in 2009) came out with a similar findings, that malaria is by far the most serious health risk facing poor urban dwellers in the city, followed by urinary tract infection, diarrhoea, schistosomiasis and typhoid. Table 6.2 shows the trends of climate change diseases reported in this study.

Further, in an assessment of the 2006–2010 municipal council records, Sakijege et al. (2012) differentiate disease prevalence of children under five from the population above five years old. Once again, the author identifies malaria to be the most serious health issue, followed by respiratory (coughing, pneumonia

Table 6.2 Trends in selected water-related diseases (March–May 2009)

Diagnosis	March	April	May	Total
Malaria	31	52	39	122
Urinary tract infection	33	44	30	107
Diarrhoea	11	22	20	53
Schistosomiasis	5	9	7	21
Typhoid	4	7	6	17
Total	84	134	102	320

Source: Sakijege et al. (2012: 6).

and tuberculosis) and water-borne diseases (diarrhoea, cholera and typhoid) – see Table 6.3. Although the sampling and methodologies underpinning the three studies referred to above are not compatible (so we may not generalise the findings), one could easily spot that malaria prevalence is rocketing in low-income settlements of Dar es Salaam. This finding is consistent with the national picture presented above.

Evidently, climate and environmental change may alter the context within which pathogens, vectors and their hosts interact, resulting in greater intensity and expansion of various diseases (Vora 2008). Human-driven ecological changes such as deforestation, agriculture and animal husbandry, water control projects, urbanisation, loss of biodiversity and introduction of alien species are also argued to contribute to increases in diseases (Vora 2008). Vector-borne and water-borne diseases are the most important climate-sensitive diseases reported in Tanzania. In turn, food- and water-borne diseases such as diarrhoea, cholera, hepatitis A and typhoid fever, as well as vector-borne diseases such as malaria, dengue fever and schistosomiasis, are widespread in Dar es Salaam (WHO 2008). Whilst many of these diseases indicate poor environmental conditions (URT 2013), it is important to note that climate change – in altering humidity and rainfall – could increase the spread of both vector- and water-borne diseases in this context.

In particular, the increased frequency of droughts and flooding is likely to increase the frequency and magnitude of epidemics of water-borne diseases, as well as influence the incidence of vector-borne diseases. Warming will also aggravate the impacts of air pollution on respiratory illnesses (McMichael et al. 1996; Githeko et al. 2000; Patz et et al. 2005; Afrane et al. 2006). Low-income settlements in Dar es Salaam are at the forefront of these impacts. Drought, flooding, increased heat and cyclones have particular implications for the health of low-income people. For a number of years, heavy rainfall in Dar es Salaam has been followed by cholera outbreaks, especially in areas with a relatively low water table (Mayala et al. 2003). Flooded areas and ditches, latrines and septic tanks are key reservoirs that perpetuate cholera in Dar es Salaam.[4] Furthermore, residents of low-income settlements are indirectly affected by drought that occurs in the

Table 6.3 Diseases prevalent in Dar es Salaam city by municipality (2006–2010)

Kinondoni 2006–Sept 2010		Ilala 2006–2009		Temeke 2007–Sept 2010	
Above 5	Under 5	Above 5	Under 5	Above 5	Under 5
Malaria	Malaria	Malaria	Malaria	Malaria	Malaria
Acute respiratory infection	Acute respiratory infection	Acute respiratory infection	Pneumonia	Urinary tract infection	Acute respiratory infection
Skin infections	Skin infections	Diarrhoea	Gastroenteritis	Acute respiratory infection	Diarrhoea
Anaemia	Anaemia	Nutritional disorders	Acute respiratory infection	Pneumonia	Urinary tract infection
Diarrhoea	Pneumonia	Pneumonia	Ski infections	Diarrhoea	Pneumonia
Urinary tract infection	Diarrhoea	Urinary tract infection	Urinary tract infection	Skin infection	Skin infection
Pneumonia	Protein energy malnutrition	Skin infection	Anaemia	Intestinal worms	Ear infection
Non-infectious gastro	Eye infections	Skin infection, non-fungal	Worms	Anaemia	Eye infection
Skin infection, non-fungal	Skin infection, non-fungal	Tuberculosis	Minor surgery	Ear infection	Dysentery
Intestinal worm	Nutritional deficiencies	Anaemia	Diarrhoea	–	–

Source: START Secretariat (2011: 41–42).

freshwater source areas of the country. EcoPoor household interviews revealed that during drought, supply of water is restricted and increasingly irregular, especially for low-income households who, as a result of scarcity and low-income, resort to using unclean water. This, in turn, links to the regular eruption of cholera and diarrhoea. There is a clear relationship, therefore, between drought, water scarcity and disease.

Concluding remarks: implications for research and policy

Studies on climatechange-related diseases in Tanzania, especially in low-income settlements of Dar es Salaam, are limited. This chapter attempted to address this gap by providing a general overview of the health implications of climate change in Tanzania, especially for communities in low-income settlements. These unequal impacts can be attributed to short- and long-term processes (e.g. floods and droughts) that are affecting all rural and urban dwellers, but especially low-income people. In terms of comprehensiveness, the evidence presented may not be representative of even one (albeit the largest) city in the country. Nevertheless, the evidence highlights how the prevalence of particular forms of infectious disease like malaria is rising sharply amongst poor urban people. The social cost of this increased disease prevalence, if unattended, could be catastrophic. If young children are repeatedly affected by malaria, those children may not reach their development potential for themselves, their family or country.

While efforts to address malnutrition and food insecurity are gaining momentum (Kau et al. 2011; Ahmed et al. 2012), intervention based on food supplements is generally preferred over disease preventive measures. Based on the evidence presented here, however, we would argue that side-stepping prevention of infectious diseases would be catastrophic. Climate change and health researchers have a duty to gather robust evidence (in the form of longitudinal studies with appropriate geographical coverage) and disseminate the information so that the health sector and municipalities are prepared to tackle health problems related to climate change induced impacts, not only in low-income settlements, but across the whole country.

Notes

1 EcoPoor is acronym for a three-year (2013–2016) research project on 'Institutions for the urban poor's access to ecosystem services: A comparison of green and water structures in Bangladesh and Tanzania'. It is funded by the UK government's ESPA (Ecosystem Services for Poverty Alleviation) programme (www.espa.com). Visit the EcoPoor website (www.ecopoor.com) to learn more about the project.

2 The EU Commission-funded CLUVA project (2010 to 2013) assessed the vulnerability of urban systems, populations and goods in relation to natural and man-made disasters in five cities in Africa, including Dar es Salaam, Tanzania. The project objective was to 'develop methods and knowledge to be applied to African cities to manage climate risks, reduce vulnerabilities and improve their coping capacity

and resilience towards climate changes' (CLUVA 2010). For more information visit http://www.cluva.eu/.
3 Lake Victoria, for example, dropped by 2.57 metres between 1965 and 2006.
4 This said, analysis of annual cholera trends indicates an irregular cyclical pattern, with a general increase in cases and a reduction in the interval between peaks. Recent analysis has shown that the five coastal regions in Tanzania are among the top eight regions by number of cases per capita (Taylor 2009).

References

Adelekan I Johnson C Manda M Matyas D Mberu B U Parnell S Pelling M Satterthwaite D and Vivekananda J 2015 Disaster risk and its reduction: an agenda for urban Africa *International Development Planning Review* 37(1) 33–43

Afrane Y A Zhou G Lawson B W Githeko A K and Yan G 2006 Effects of microclimatic changes caused by deforestation on the survivorship and reproductive fitness of *Anopheles gambiae* in Western Kenya Highlands. *American Journal of Tropical Medicine and Hygiene* 74 772–778

Ahmed T Michaelsen K F Frem J C and Tumvine J 2012 Malnutrition: report of the FISPGHAN working group *Journal of Pediatric Gastroenterology and Nutrition* 55(5) 626–631

Alkire S Jindra C Aguilar G R Seth S and Vaz A 2015 *Global Multidimensional Poverty Index 2015* Oxford: Poverty and Human Development Initiative, UK

Ari T B Neerinckx S Gage K L Kreppel K Laudisoit A Leirs H and Stenseth N C 2011 Plague and climate: scales matter *PLOS Pathogens* 7(9)

Biggs H M Bui D M Galloway R L Stoddard R A Shadomy S V Morrissey A B Bartlett J A Onyango J J Maro V P Kinabo G D Saganda W and Crump J A 2011 Leptospirosis among hospitalized febrile patients in northern Tanzania *American Journal of Tropical Medicine and Hygiene* 88 275–281

Bødker R Akida J Shayo D Kisinza W Msangeni H A Pedersen E M and Lindsay S W 2003 Relationship between altitude and intensity of malaria transmission in the Usambara Mountains, Tanzania. *Journal of Medical Entomology* 40 706–717

Bødker R Msangeni H A Kisinza W N and Lindsay S W 2006 Relationship between the intensity of exposure to malaria parasites and infection in the Usambara Mountains Tanzania *American Journal of Tropical Medicine and Hygiene* 74 716–723

CIA World Fact Book (2015) Major Infectious Diseases in Tanzania Central Intelligence Agency Fact Book Washington DC Available from: https://www.cia.gov/library/publications/the-world-factbook/fields/2193.html#tz [Accessed: 5/11/15]

Clyde D F 1967 *Malaria in Tanzania* London: Oxford University Press

Climate Change and Urban Vulnerability in Africa (CLUVA) 2010 *Objectives* Available from http://www.cluva.eu/ [Accessed: 21/10/15]

European Food Safety Authority (EFSA) 2015 *Drivers for occasional spillover event of Ebola virus* EJ EFSA Journal Available from: http://www.efsa.europa.eu/en/efsajournal/pub/4161 [Accessed: 15/10/15]

Food and Agriculture Organisation (FAO) 2007 *Adaptation to Climate Change in Agriculture, Forestry and Fisheries: Perspective, Frameworks and Priorities.* Rome: FAO

Gage K L and Kosoy M Y 2005 Natural history of plague: perspectives from more than a century of research *Annual Review of Entomology* 50 505–528

Garay J 1998 *Epidemiological Survey and Situation Analysis: Malaria Epidemic in Nshamba Division Muleba District Tanzania* Spain: MSF

Gillies M T 1953 The duration of the gonotrophic cycle in *Anopheles gambiae* and *An. funestus* with a note on the efficiency of hand catching *East African Medical Journal* 30 129–135

Githeko A K Lindsay S W Confalonieri U E and Patz J A 2000 Climate change and vector-borne diseases: a regional analysis *Bulletin of the World Health Organisation* 78(9) 1136–1147

Harrus S and Baneth G 2005 Drivers for the emergence and re-emergence of vector-borne protozoal and bacterial diseases *International Journal Parasitology* 35 1309–1318

Hashizume M 2008 The effect of rainfall on the incidence of cholera in Bangladesh *Epidemiology* 19 103–110

Hulme D 2003 *Why Does Poverty Endure? Maymana and Mofizul's Story* CPRC Working Paper Vol 22 University of Manchester, UK

Intergovernmental Panel on Climate Change (IPCC) 2007 *Climate Change 2007: Impacts Adaptation and Vulnerability Contributions of Working Group II to the Fourth Assessment Report of the Intergovernmental Panel on Climate Change* Cambridge, UK: Cambridge University Press

Intergovernmental Panel on Climate Change (IPCC) 2013 *The Physical Science Basis 2013: Working Group I Contribution to AR5 Fifth Assessment Report of the Intergovernmental Panel on Climate Change* Cambridge, UK: Cambridge University Press

Intergovernmental Panel on Climate Change (IPCC) 2014 *Climate Change 2014: Impacts, Adaptation, and Vulnerability* (Part A: Global and Sectoral Aspects) Cambridge and New York: Cambridge University Press

Jetten T H and Focks D A 1997 Potential changes in the distribution of dengue transmission under climate warming *American Journal of Tropical Medicine and Hygiene* 57 285–297

Kangalawe R Y M 2009 *Impact of Climate Change on Human Health: Example of Highland Malaria – Mbeya Region* Study report submitted to the Division of Environment Vice President's Office Dar es Salaam Tanzania

Kangalawe R Y M 2012 Food security and health in the southern highlands of Tanzania: a multidisciplinary approach to evaluate the impact of climate change and other stress factors *African Journal of Environmental Science and Technology* 6 50–66

Kau A L Ahern P P Griffin N W Goodman A L and Gordon J I 2011 Human nutrition, the gut microbiome and the immune system *Nature* 474 327–336.

Kilonzo B S Mvena Z S Machangu R S and Mbise T J 1997 Preliminary observations on factors responsible for long persistence and continued outbreaks of plague in Lushoto district Tanzania *Acta Tropica* 68 215 227

Kiunsi R B 2013a A review of traffic congestion in Dar es Salaam city from the physical planning perspective *Journal of Sustainable Development* 6(2) 94–103

Kiunsi R B 2013b The constraints on climate change adaptation in a city with large development deficits: the case of Dar es Salaam city *Environment and Urbanization* 25(2) 321–337

Kombe W J 2005 Land use dynamics in peri-urban areas and their implications on the urban growth and form: the case of Dar es Salaam, Tanzania *Habitat International* 29 113–135

Kyessi A 2010 Enhancing security of land tenure in informal settlements: the case of WAT Human Settlements Trust in Hanna Nassif Settlement, Dar es Salaam, Tanzania *Utafiti Journal* 8(1) 87–104

Lindsay S W and Birley M H 1996 Climate change and malaria transmission *Annals of Tropical Medicine and Parasitology* 90 573–588

Lindsay S W and Martens W J 1998 Malaria in the African highlands: past, present and future *Bulletin of the World Health Organisation* 76 33–45

Lindsay S W Bødker R Malima R Msangeni H A and Kisinza W 2000 Effect of 1997–8 El Niño on highland malaria in Tanzania *The Lancet* 355 989–990

Matola Y G White G B and Magayuka S A 1987 The changed pattern of malaria endemicity and transmission at Amani in the eastern Usambara mountains north-eastern Tanzania *Journal of Tropical Medicine and Hygiene* 90 127–134

Mayala B K Mboera L E G and Gwacha F 2003 Mapping cholera risks using geographical information system in Ilala District Tanzania *Tanzania Health Research Bulletin* 5 8–12

Mboera L E and Kitua A Y 2001 Malaria epidemics in Tanzania: an overview *Tanzania African Journal of Health Sciences* 8(1–2) 17–23

Mboera L E Mayala B K Kweka E J and Mazigo H D 2011 Impact of climate change on human health and health systems in Tanzania: a review *Tanzania Journal of Health Research* 13(5) 1–23

Mboera L E G 2004 Environmental and socio-economic determinants of malaria epidemics in the highlands of Tanzania *Tanzania Health Research Bulletin* 6 11–17

Mboera L E G Massaga J J Munga M A Mayala B K Kahwa A M Msovela J Shija A Mushi A K and Kilale A M 2010 *Current Status of the Service Availability at Various Levels Health System in Tanzania* Dar es Salaam Tanzania: National Institute for Medical Research

Mboera L E G Molteni F Nyange A and Thomas E G 2005 Using retrospective epidemiological data to determine malaria epidemic prone areas and development of an epidemic early warning system in Mpwapwa District, central Tanzania *Tanzania Health Research Bulletin* 7 73–78

McGranahan 2013 Evolving Urban Health Risks: Housing, Water and Sanitation, and Climate Change in E D Sclar N Volavka-Close and P Brown (eds) 2013 *The Urban Transportation: Health, Shelter and Climate Change* Chapter 2 15–41 London: Routledge

McMichael A J Haines A Slooff R and Kovats S 1996 *Climate Change and Human Health* Geneva: World Health Organisation

Ministry of Health and Social Welfare (MHSW) 2010 *Baseline Survey on Quality of Paediatric Care in Tanzania* Dar es Salaam: The United Republic of Tanzania

Mitlin D and Satterthwaite D 2013 *Urban Poverty in the Global South: Scale and Nature* London and New York: Routledge

Mohamed M Mosha F Mghamba J Zaki S R Shieh W J Paweska J Omulo S Gikundi S Mmbuji P Bloland P Zeidner N Kalinga R Breiman R F and Njenga M K 2010 Epidemiologic and clinical aspects of a Rift Valley fever outbreak in humans in Tanzania 2007 *American Journal of Tropical Medicine and Hygiene* 83 22–27

Mwandosya M J Nyenzi B S and Luhanga M L 1998 *The Assessment of Vulnerability and Adaptation to Climate Change Impacts in Tanzania* Dar es Salaam Centre for Energy Environment Science and Technology (CEEST)

Neerinckx S B Peterson A T Gulinck H Deckers J and Leirs H 2008 Geographic distribution and ecological niche of plague in sub-Saharan Africa *International Journal of Health Geographics* 7 54

Olinto P Beegle K Sobrado C and Uematsu H 2015 The State of the Poor: Where are the Poor, Where is extreme poverty harder to end, and what is the current profile of the world's Poor? *The World Bank Economic Premier* 125 Available from: http://siteresources. worldbank.org/EXTPREMNET/Resources/EP125.pdf [Accessed: 28/10/15]

Patz J A Campbell-Lendrum D Holloway T and Folley J A 2005 Impact of regional climate change on human health *Nature* 438 310–317

Penrose K Castro M C Werema J and Ryan E T 2010 Informal urban settlements and cholera risk in Dar es Salaam Tanzania *PLOS Neglected Tropical Diseases* 4(3)

Pham H V Dang D T Minh N N T Nguyen N D and Nguyen T V 2009 Correlates of environmental factors and human plague: an ecological study in Vietnam *International Journal of Epidemiology* 38(6) 1634–1641

Rueda L M Patel K J Axtell R C and Stinner R E 1990 Temperature-dependent development and survival rates of *Culex quinquefasciatus* and *Aedes aegypti* (Diptera: Culicidae) *Journal of Medical Entomology* 27 892–898

Roy M Riziki S Hulme D Mwageni N and Gough A forthcoming Climate change and declining levels of green structures: life in informal settlements of Dar es Salaam, Tanzania *Landscape and Urban Planning*

Sakijege T Lupala J and Sheya S 2012 Flooding flood risks and coping strategies in urban informal residential areas: the case of Keko Machungwa Dar es Salaam Tanzania *Jàmbá: Journal of Disaster Risk Studies* 4(1) 1–10

Schoonman L and Swai E S 2009 Risk factors associated with the seroprevalence of leptospirosis amongst at-risk groups in and around Tanga city Tanzania *Annals of Tropical Medicine and Parasitology* 103 711–718

Sclar E D Volavka-Close N and Brown P (eds) 2013 *The Urban Transportation: Health, Shelter and Climate Change* London: Routledge

Shemdoe R S 2011 *Tracking Effective Indigenous Adaptation Strategies on Impacts of Climate Variability on Food Security and Health of Subsistence Farmers in Tanzania* Working paper published by African Technology Policy Studies (ATPS) Network Available from: http://www.atpsnet.org/Files/wps51.pdf [Accessed: 10/10/15]

Shemdoe R S and Kihila J 2012 Understanding community-based adaptation strategies to climate variability in fishing communities of Rufiji River Basin in Tanzania *African Journal of History and Culture* 4(2) 17–26

Stainforth D A Aina T Christensen C Collins M Faull N Frame D J Kettleborough J A Knight S Martin A Murphy J M Piani C Sexton D Smith L A Spicer R A Thorpe A J and Allen M R 2005 Uncertainty in predictions of the climate response to rising levels of greenhouse gases *Nature* 433 403–406

START Secretariat 2011 *Urban Poverty and Climate Change in Dar es Salaam, Tanzania: A Case Study* START Secretariat Available from: http://start.org/download/2011/dar-case-study.pdf [Accessed: 1/11/15]

Taylor B 2009 *Situation Analysis of Women, Children and the Water, Sanitation and Hygiene Sector in Tanzania* Draft Report for the Joint Water Sector Review 2009, Joint Annual Health Sector Review 2009, Joint Education Sector Review 2009 and MKUKUTA Review

UN Habitat 2014 *The State of African Cities 2012: Re-imagining Sustainable Urban Transitions* Nairobi: UN Habitat

UN Habitat 2010 *Citywide Action Plan for Upgrading Unplanned and Un-serviced Settlements in Dar es Salaam* Nairobi: UN Habitat

The United Republic of Tanzania (URT) 2013 *2012 Population and Housing Census: Population Distribution by Administrative Areas* Dar es Salaam: National Bureau of Statistics

Vora N 2008 Impact of anthropogenic environmental alterations on vector-borne diseases *Medscape Journal of Medicine* 10(10) 238–248

Weller N Elias N Dobler G Clowes P Kroidl I Saathoff E Maboko L Hoelscher M and Heinrich N 2010 Epidemiology of neglected arthropod-borne viral diseases in the

Mbeya Region, south-west Tanzania *Proceedings of the 24th Annual Joint Scientific Conference, Arusha,Tanzania*, March 15–18

World Health Organization (WHO) 2008 *Report on the Review of Primary Health Care in the African Region* Geneva, Switzerland: WHO

World Health Organization (WHO) 2009 *Protecting Health from Climate Change: Connecting Science, Policy and People* Geneva, Switzerland: WHO Available from: http://apps.who.int/iris/bitstream/10665/44246/1/9789241598880_eng.pdf [Accessed: 1/11/15]

World Bank 2002 *Upgrading Low Income Urban Settlements: Country Assessment Report Tanzania* Africa Technical Unit (AFTU 1&2)

Part III

Understanding change and adaptation

From institutional interface to co-production

7 Urban livelihoods in an era of climate change

Household adaptations and their limitations in Dhaka, Bangladesh

Nicola Banks

Introduction

Large increases in urban poverty have accompanied Bangladesh's urbanisation. Its poor population is expected to become predominantly urban within this generation, whilst climate change impacts are likely to accelerate Bangladesh's ongoing urbanisation and deepen the scale and severity of urban poverty (Banks et al. 2011). This chapter explores how social hierarchies within low-income settlements reinforce household vulnerabilities and limit the ability of most households to cope with, or adapt to, climate change impacts.

The following section illustrates a framework for understanding social hierarchies and the vulnerabilities this accords to different households within a low-income settlement (or *bustee*) setting, keeping resources and opportunities for household improvement confined to a small elite. The chapter then goes on to explore the livelihood strategies of Dhaka's urban poor, whether and how these enable them to adapt to the current and anticipated impacts of climate change. In doing so, we distinguish between two groups within Dhaka's low-income settlements: those who are connected to informal systems of governance that dominate resource allocation and ownership of productive resources within the settlement, and the majority of households who are dependent on this small elite for access to shelter, services and security. These social and economic differences influence whether households can adapt to climate change impacts, as well as who benefits from adaptation. The analysis, based on research in four low-income settlements in central and peripheral Dhaka,[1] highlights the limitations of viewing household livelihoods as the central focus of climate change interventions and adaptations. Doing so overlooks urban poverty's social and political roots which place significant constraints on household livelihoods.

Understanding urban poverty in Bangladesh in an era of climate change

We cannot begin to understand the additional vulnerabilities that low-income urban households will face in an era of climate change without an understanding of the nature and dynamics of urban poverty in Bangladesh. Low-income settlements in Dhaka are places where physical, social, economic and political vulnerabilities collide (Banks 2012). Existing frameworks, however, tend to overlook the social and political vulnerabilities of urban poverty which, as we will see, have implications on household and community resilience to climate change impacts.

Urban poverty is largely conceptualised as an accumulation of asset deprivations (e.g. Moser 1998; Farrington et al. 2002; Baud et al. 2009). Similar to sustainable livelihoods frameworks, existing frameworks highlight urban poverty as a result of: limited, irregular and insecure incomes (a lack of financial capital); unsanitary and environmentally hazardous environments (a lack of natural capital); sub-standard and poorly serviced housing with insecure tenure, often as rental tenants (a lack of physical capital); limited skills and education, and chronic illness, malnutrition and routine health shocks (a lack of human capital); and limited social networks for support and assistance (a lack of social capital).

Banks (2014) highlights the importance of situating an analysis of household assets, resources and livelihoods strategies within the local political economy that controls access (and terms of access) to different resources. Figure 7.1 illustrates the social and political hierarchies that dominate resource distribution within Dhaka's low-income settlements, allowing *bustee* elite to keep opportunities for household improvements confined to powerful groups. Those in the top level of the hierarchy access lucrative resources and opportunities through their connections outside the settlement. Those in the middle tier (the family and kinship networks of local leaders, active political supporters and house owners) can access these resources and opportunities indirectly through their connections to *bustee* leadership. The majority of low-income households find themselves at the bottom of these hierarchies, dependent on the elite for their access to shelter, services and security. Returns from their own social networks are limited by similar resource constraints of households, or the exploitative terms of patron–client relationships. The vulnerability of the urban poor, therefore, goes beyond low incomes and asset bases. It is exacerbated by a hostile political economy that gives low-income urban households in Dhaka little room for manoeuvre when it comes to devising and deploying effective livelihoods strategies (Wood and Salway 2000).

Our understanding of urban poverty must centre on employment, the primary form of income generation for most urban households (Amis 1995; Moser 1998; Mitlin and Satterthwaite 2013). Three main categories of employment are available to the urban poor in Bangladesh: unskilled labour (rickshaw-pulling and unskilled day labour), small business, and formal sector or skilled work that requires some level of qualifications, skills and experience (Banks 2012). Urban livelihoods can be distinguished by these occupational categories in terms of security, stability and prospects for advancement (Pryer 2003), as can a household's ability to cope with or adapt to the impacts of climate change (as we will see in the next section).

Unskilled labour dominates employment opportunities for the urban poor. One in three household heads find employment in this sector. Despite generating

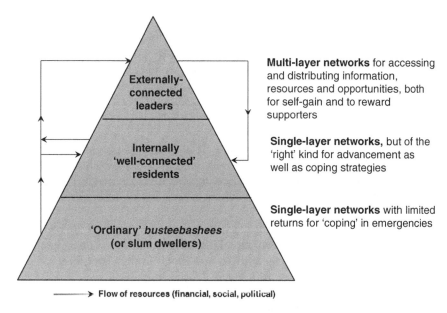

Figure 7.1 Social hierarchies and patron–client relationships in a *bustee* setting
Source: Banks (2014: 14).

daily income (making it easier to balance incomes and expenditures), unskilled labour offers few benefits. Low incomes and work irregularity provide little scope for household advancement, generating uncertainty, risk and a high probability of ill health due to dependence on physical labour. Many day labourers report securing only 10 to 15 days work each month. Only seven percent of households were headed by a day labourer, illustrating that this is unviable as a household's core economic support (Banks 2012). Likewise, for rickshaw pullers, Begum and Sen (2005) highlight that their physical exertion dampens long-term prospects for mobility because of their poverty and malnutrition.

For those who can accumulate capital, starting a small business is preferable. However, difficulties accumulating capital prevent the majority of workers from pursuing this dream. Only one in five household heads support their households through small business. They vary considerably in size and profitability, highlighting the dangerous misconception that small business is a viable route out of poverty for all. Only one in four households supported by small businesses report household improvements, and the research revealed many households struggling to recover from failed business (Banks 2012). Most businesses start with small amounts of capital and run with low management capacities. Businessmen and women struggle to separate business and household cash flows, so when businesses struggle, so too do household incomes (and vice versa).

The third option for low-income workers is to gain skills or qualifications and move towards formal sector employment. Most workers, however, lack the qualifications and social contacts for this. Perceptions of formal sector jobs may suggest relative stability and job prestige, but the majority of workers access informal 'temporary' contracts that offer low salaries, long working hours and job insecurity. Those able to access formal contracts that provide high salaries, job security and scope for promotion are those with the 'right' social contacts. As one respondent explained:

> There are high-profile jobs available. The problem is people cannot find them [...] You need a *mamu* (uncle) to connect you to jobs. This person can be inside or outside the *bustee*, they can be relatives or friends, political or non-political. I don't know of any way you can get a job without this.

While some jobs can seemingly offer a pathway out of poverty, these are confined to households with the 'right' contacts. This limits the jobs that offer the most stable platform for household mobility to households in the upper levels of the settlement's social hierarchies, as in Figure 7.1. Local leaders have connections with businessmen, politicians and other powerful actors outside the settlement, using these connections to secure jobs for themselves and their networks. Most households cannot access better jobs on terms conducive to household mobility and their livelihoods remain precarious. It is against this backdrop that we must assess the impacts and effects of climate change on urban livelihoods.

Struggling for security: livelihoods strategies of the urban poor in Dhaka

Low-income urban households deploy several strategies to cope with and reduce their vulnerability. These are limited in effectiveness even in day-to-day lives, let alone when the additional threats of climate change are in question. This is strikingly evident when we look at household incomes and expenditures. Fifty-five percent of households experience significant budget deficits each month. Only one percent break even (Figure 7.2). If we take average monthly costs on healthcare into account, only one in three households experience a budget surplus each month, highlighting how ill-prepared the urban poor are to cope with chronic ill health, health shocks and seasonal fluctuations in employment and income. Households describe their economic position as *tanatani*, a term synonymous with 'coping' that highlights a financial tug-of-war in which incomes and expenditures pull in opposite directions. Budgets may fluctuate in either direction if a household has additional expenditures or has earned a higher income through more regular work.

Figure 7.2 highlights a small proportion (less than one in five) of households with significant income surpluses. Several channels contribute to these higher incomes among the *bustee* elite. Owning rental rooms offers the most

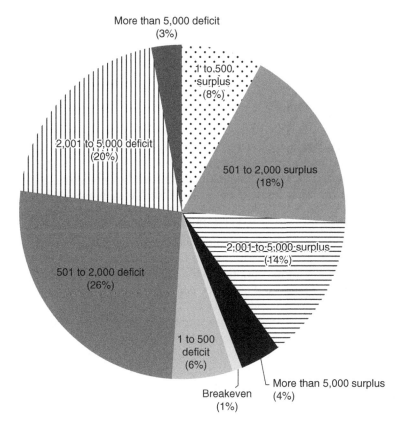

Figure 7.2 Size of budget surplus and deficit (percentage of households, in Bangladesh taka)*
* This includes monthly expenditure for food, rent, electricity, water and firewood but excludes spending on education and healthcare (*n* = 420 households).
Source: Banks (2012: 25).

lucrative income-generating opportunity. Some house owners own up to 22 rooms. Landlords earn between 47 and 200 percent higher incomes than tenants due to this additional income stream (Banks 2012). Those connected to local leaders can also access informal rights to service provision across the *bustee*, offering another substantial source of income generation. Lastly, as we have discussed, those with the 'right' social connections can access the best forms and terms of employment. These three sources of income, however, are inaccessible to households at the bottom of the social hierarchy, for whom opportunities for house ownership are negligible, who are not linked to distribution networks by family ties or political affiliation and for whom economic insecurity forces risk-averse households to focus on employment rather than investing time and income in extending social networks (Banks 2014).

Where they are outside these networks, households devise multiple strategies for balancing incomes and expenditures, including labour mobilisation, asset ownership and managing portfolios of savings and loans. As we will see, however, these strategies cannot provide day-to-day security, let alone help households cope in the face of crises such as flooding, heat stress or ill health.

Household labour mobilisation

Given the difficult conditions and uncertain terms under which the urban poor secure employment, households can rarely survive on one income, making labour mobilisation integral to household security, let alone advancement. Engaging in two jobs simultaneously is one strategy through which household heads can reduce or overcome the obstacles that limit working hours (e.g. work irregularity, old age or physical weakness). Unable to work full-time as a rickshaw puller due to physical constraints, some household heads maximise the hours they work by pulling a rickshaw in the morning and running small businesses in the afternoon.[2] However, incomes from both activities remain low, preventing their transition into small business as a full-time option, and forcing households to supplement this with labour of other household members. Around 60 percent of households mobilise additional members to work (Banks 2012).

Female employment is central to these strategies, but under conditions of endemic insecurity, female employment is critical to survival and stability, let alone advancement (Gonzalez de la Rocha 2007; Kantor 2009). That the female labour force is subject to regular disruptions due to pregnancy, childcare, harassment at work, or after daughters leave the household at marriage, acts as a strong limitation on the ability of labour mobilisation strategies to provide the stability necessary for household improvement (Banks 2013). That only one in four household heads reporting household improvements have mobilised their wife's labour also indicates that it is not female income contributions that play the primary role in household strategies for improvement. In fact, this brings the additional risk that female employment displaces longer-term prospects of household advancement, because the status, prestige and social networks most conducive to household mobility require households to uphold patriarchal norms that forbid women from working (Banks 2013).

Asset ownership

Accumulating productive assets is another strategy through which households minimise risk, diversify livelihoods opportunities, increase household resilience and prepare for future crises (Jabeen et al. 2010). The ownership of productive assets is low, however, and largely limited to house owners. Less than one third of households own their own house and 30 percent own at least one productive asset, such as rental rooms, shops and equipment for small businesses, rickshaws, agricultural land or sewing machines. Nearly 70 percent of house owners have productive assets, in comparison with only 12 percent of tenants (Banks 2012). With the exception of rental rooms, assets owned tend to be associated with the employment of the household head (e.g. a rickshaw, or equipment for a small business) rather than constituting a separate, diversified flow of income. Asset ownership, too, therefore, may increase incomes but is limited in its ability to provide additional income support to the household head's employment. The assets that do provide significant alternative income streams (predominantly rental rooms) are limited to the *bustee* elite.

Managing financial portfolios

As we have seen in Figure 7.2, incomes are insufficient despite efforts to diversify economic activities. Households must find alternative ways to bridge regular (and often severe), income deficits. Dhaka's urban poor have devised a number of strategies for coping with income shortfalls, including buying in small quantities (at higher prices), skipping meals and purchasing foods of lower nutritional value (Zingel et al. 2011). But the depth of income shortfalls often means these are insufficient. The need for alternative means of consumption-smoothing has led to the search for loans becoming the most common livelihoods strategy. Nearly three-quarters (72 percent) of households have at least one loan or debt (Banks 2012). Many households seek loans on a monthly basis to bridge income deficits and repay previous loans.

Loans play different roles, ranging from assisting with daily struggles of survival and coping in emergencies, to aiding investment and facilitating prospects for household improvement. Where loans are sourced (which dictates the interest and terms of the loan) and how they are spent differentiate between consumption-smoothing loans and those taken for productive purposes. It also dictates a household's ability to repay them without exacerbating financial pressures. Formal microfinance loans offer fixed interest and repayment schedules across a finite term. Where loans are invested productively, returns to the investment can cover repayment, returning to the household as income when fully repaid. Informal loans sourced from relatives or friends offer low- or zero-interest and flexible repayment terms, enabling households to invest funds or access good terms for consumption-smoothing or emergency finance. However, this requires having connections with better-off households that can give sizeable loans, or good relationships with formal employers who may offer cash advances against future salaries. In contrast, the reciprocal networks of most households are limited by their similar resource constraints.[3]

The most devastating loans are those from moneylenders, or *mohajons*. They play an important part in survival strategies since they are available quickly or when other funding sources are exhausted. However, they are accompanied by onerous terms, including high monthly interest (up to 30 percent of the capital borrowed *per month*) and strict repayment criteria. Together, these trap borrowers into unending interest payments, capturing large proportions of a household's monthly income and maintaining pressures on income long after the crisis is over. *Mohajons* are portrayed as menacing and unyielding

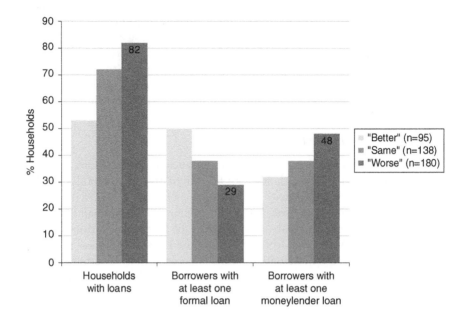

Figure 7.3 Loan prevalence across households by coping status*

* 'Households with loans' shows the percentage of *all* households with loans. For formal and moneylender loans, this shows the percentage of *borrowers* within each category.

Source: Banks (2012: 28).

businessmen, described through illustrative terms such as 'they are catching our blood' or 'cutting our throats'. As one household head illustrates, 'I'm only paying interest, and sometimes I can't even manage this. I'm working hard and trying hard not to take more loans, but with the interest my struggles just keep increasing'.

Coping and deteriorating households are characterised by their dependence on multiple loans. Between 70 and 80 percent of households reporting their status as 'the same' or 'worse than' five years ago have at least one loan, dropping to around 50 percent of those experiencing household improvements (Banks 2012). Not only are improving households less likely to have taken loans, they are also more likely to have accessed formal loans offering investment potential or loans from friends and relatives on preferable terms (see Figure 7.3). In contrast, half of coping households have resorted to moneylenders. This is both a cause and consequence of household deterioration.

If households have liquid savings this can provide investment capital or a buffer for meeting consumption-smoothing needs or emergency costs. The experiences of 'improving' households demonstrate the importance of both these 'prevention' and 'promotion' roles. Savings prevented health shocks from reversing household improvements and allowed households to consolidate capital and assets, leading to better jobs or higher incomes. Again, those able to save tend to be the house-owning elite with lower costs of living (through not paying rent) and high and stable monthly incomes (through their rental properties). Over half (54 percent) of house owners have savings in comparison with just over a quarter (27 percent) of tenants. The constraints to urban livelihoods we have discussed vastly restrict savings abilities.[4] Households also lack places to save, with bank accounts requiring a legal address and official recommendation. These in turn require connections to local politicians, which are confined to the settlement's better-connected residents.

Household livelihoods in an era of climate change: coping or adapting?

This section asks whether, given these multiple vulnerabilities, low-income urban households in Dhaka are coping with, or adapting to, the additional challenges that climate change brings. 'Coping' focuses on survival today, a strategy that may deal with immediate insecurity but is likely to be accompanied by higher future costs, such as high interest payments from an exploitative moneylender. A preferable solution is improving the adaptive capacity of households so that they can undertake actions that help them to avoid loss and speed recovery from climate change impacts in the short term, as well as reduce vulnerability and enhance resilience in the medium to long term (Satterthwaite et al. 2007).

Climate change is exacerbating an already complex and vulnerable livelihood context in Bangladesh (Banks et al. 2011; Roy et al. 2012; 2013). Two major processes are increasing the scale and exacerbating the severity of urban poverty. First, in rural areas climate change is leading to the loss of land and livelihoods, leading to poverty and destitution and pushing migrants to the city (Opel 2000; GoB 2009). Furthermore, more frequent, severe and prolonged weather events add additional stresses to urban households by decreasing work opportunities and increasing environmental and health hazards (Tanner et al. 2009; Jabeen et al. 2010; Banks et al. 2011; Roy et al. 2012; 2013). Dhaka is particularly affected given its size and nature as an unplanned city in an environmentally vulnerable country prone to flooding and cyclones. Climate-induced hazards affect the urban poor on a near-annual basis, destroying houses and belongings, increasing exposure to disease through flooding and the inundation of sanitation facilities, and disrupting employment, amongst others (Rashid 2000; Rashid et al. 2007; Braun and Abheuer 2011; Haque et al. 2012).

These impacts will affect the poorest urban residents disproportionately, but are not necessarily distributed evenly. Some impacts, such as increased heat stress or food prices, will be universal, while others, such as flooding, will be more localised with physical, tenure-related, socio-political and institutional factors making them more significant in some settlements (or even corners of settlements) than others (Jabeen et al. 2010; Banks et al. 2011).[5] While these impacts are neither the only nor the primary challenges the urban poor face, they will (and do) compound and exacerbate the risks and challenges faced. Here we look in more detail, given the centrality of employment to urban livelihoods, at how households are affected by (and cope with) the work disruptions brought by the challenges of increased rainfall and heat stress.

Increased rainfall and heat stress have severe implications on the working lives of unskilled labourers and small businessmen. Unskilled labourers face direct disruptions given that their work is dependent on physical labour unsheltered from bad conditions. Even where work is available, all unskilled labourers face gruelling conditions throughout the rainy season and the hottest parts of the year, reducing work hours. For day labourers, work availability grinds to a complete halt in the rainy season, increasing demand for rickshaw pulling, the closest substitute. Physical labour under extremely high temperatures or excessive rainfall has severe health implications. To some extent, rickshaw pullers can cope with the highest temperatures by working fewer hours, choosing not to work throughout the hottest hours of the day or taking advantage of higher fares during those hours and resting afterwards. Options are limited during rainy season. Rickshaw pullers try to prevent falling ill by not working in torrential rains, but this strategy is limited in time frame, because households require a minimum income to meet rent, food and loan obligations. At some point, these costs force rickshaw pullers to work despite adverse conditions, making it nearly impossible to avoid illness. As one group of rickshaw pullers illustrated, 'For the rain, if I go to work one day, then for three days I am suffering from fever. But I have to work at least two days a week to meet household costs'. Higher fares during rainy season are not enough to make up for income losses, especially when combined with the additional burden of medical costs.

Households devise other strategies for dealing with reduced incomes, but these are detrimental to the ability of the household's recovery after rainy season. One strategy is to rely upon credit and other forms of borrowing, but this creates further obstacles for the household when rains stop. As another group of rickshaw-pullers explained, 'We rely on taking goods on credit in rainy season or by borrowing money, usually on interest. After that, when the good times come, we have to earn double our usual incomes so we can repay debts and loans. Otherwise we have to take even more loans just to repay them'. Seasonal vulnerabilities, therefore, add an additional layer of stress to household efforts to secure livelihoods. Few households can prepare for these periods by saving money or food given the difficulties of balancing household budgets throughout the rest of the year.

While small businesses do not face these same direct impacts of seasonal work disruptions, they are indirectly affected through their customer base, the majority of whom are unskilled labourers. Restricted incomes during rainy season means that customer demand for non-essential items drops, as does their ability to pay cash. Purchasing goods on credit may offer an important coping mechanism during periods of crisis, but leads to struggles for businesses in maintaining cash flow, slowly depleting profits and draining the business's capital.[6] As one businessman explained, 'When people are taking goods without paying money […] the shop's daily income needs to be spent on my household, so I am constantly losing capital for my shop'. Businessmen and women face a similar problem to that of rickshaw pullers. They require a minimum income to meet obligations of rent, food and loan repayments, and where incomes are vastly reduced have to find other means of bridging this gap. Unlike rickshaw pullers, they have one other option to exhaust before turning to costly moneylender loans for this purpose, withdrawing capital from their business to meet income needs. This means, however, that businessmen and women emerge from rainy season weaker than before, having less capital invested in and lower profits from their business.

We see therefore, that persistent economic vulnerabilities are central constraints on urban livelihoods, and that these are and will continue to be exacerbated by seasonal fluctuations in heat and rainfall that are predicted to get longer and more extreme. Households have little means of coping, let alone adapting to these changes. Insecurity throughout the year leaves them poorly prepared and the co-variant nature of this vulnerability reduces the ability of networks of reciprocity to be an additional source of support. As one household member explained, 'If we can save a little one month, it is quickly destroyed the next when we have illness costs. So when it comes to rainy season, we have no financial back-up'.

Crucially, a small number of *bustee* elite remain relatively insulated from the economic vulnerabilities faced by most households. The elite are comprised of house owners and long-term residents of the *bustee* that share political affiliation or kinship networks with local leaders. These hierarchies have two important implications for NGO or donor programmes in an era of climate change, one on adaptive capacities at the community level, and one on the limitations to household agency in the face of this structural environment. Programmes that do not consider the implications of these power hierarchies may overestimate the potential of asset-building at the household level, or have unintended consequences in terms of exacerbating inequality at the community level.

Adaptations to the built environment: who adapts and who benefits?

Possibilities for climate change adaptation are restricted to the upper levels of the social hierarchy. The high and stable incomes that house owners benefit from gives them greater adaptive capacity for themselves and their tenants. While there is little incentive for tenants to invest in physical adaptations that reduce risk and losses, for house owners there are a number of structural improvements that can be made to the built environment, including upgrading wall materials from wood or bamboo sheeting to corrugated iron, building windows for ventilation, and building a concrete floor with a raised lip at the entrance (Jabeen et al. 2010; Roy et al. 2013).

Household repairs and upgrades are the landlord's responsibility, and it is in the house owner's interests to carry out adaptations when they can afford them, as this minimises property damage and avoids recurrent repair costs after the rainy season. Improvements to the built environment also offer a financial incentive. With rents varying by housing quality and location, these adaptations allow the landlord to charge higher rents. While this benefits the house owner *and* tenants in terms of improved resilience to climate change impacts, it has an adverse impact on the poorest households. This means that the poorest (and least-equipped) households are also those most likely to face the brunt of climate change impacts and its repercussions on their health and employment. Searching for the lowest rent means they tend to live both in vulnerable areas (e.g. those in closest proximity to or above water bodies) and in the poorer quality housing less able to withstand extreme weather.

House owners and community leaders have also helped to improve the built environment through their role in NGO community upgrading and service provision programmes. NGOs tend to operate through existing community leadership and institutions, otherwise facing resistance from local leadership. Providing services, selecting participants or distributing resources through these channels further increases the community's dependence on the *bustee* elite, consolidating their power and income. As one NGO participant joked, 'At least some are happy [with our programmes] – we have legalised the position of *mastaans'* (local leaders, or musclemen). Programme benefits are not necessarily distributed equally, and *mastaans* are viewed as a 'necessary evil' that may be able to bring services into the *bustee*, but who often use extortion or threats of violence to control the community (Banks 2008; Hackenbroch and Hossain 2012; Hackenbroch 2013; Hossain 2013). They have reason to fiercely protect their power given the resources they can accumulate through their leadership in terms of income from housing and informal service provision.

Similar to the effect of household improvements, community upgrading increases rental prices across the settlement, particularly where legal access to water and electricity is negotiated. This has twofold financial benefits for house owners. Not only do rental incomes increase because of infrastructure and service improvements, but legalisation of service provision reduces the costs of providing services to tenants. Of the two neighbouring communities in peripheral Dhaka, for example, one had recently secured legal water supply. Average rental costs here (including water supply) were 1,000 BDT per month, in comparison with around 700 BDT in the neighbouring community. Not only were house owners benefiting from increased rental incomes, legal water connections had greatly reduced the water costs that house owners paid for their tenants. Monthly water bills were between 200 and 300 taka for up to 14 households where previously they had cost around 100 taka per household. Cost savings were not passed on to tenants and this was a visible source of tension for tenants, for whom there was no prospect for house ownership and who were spending large proportions of their monthly incomes on rent and utilities.

What we see, therefore, is that while local leaders and their networks of associates have been integral to the community's development and adaptive capacity, benefits are not spread equally and come at the cost of increasing inequality within the *bustee*. Improvements have increased the monthly incomes (and reduced monthly expenditures) for landlords, but have increased living costs for their tenants, who constitute the majority of residents. We must not overlook the impact NGO programmes have had in improving living environments, but we must also recognise how such programmes may unwittingly reinforce and exacerbate existing power hierarchies and inequalities. While infrastructure improvements and better access to services undeniably improves the ability of communities to withstand extreme weather events, such investments have also had a negative impact in terms of increasing the living costs of those facing the most insecure livelihoods. Those worst off in this situation are the poorest households, who may get pushed out of better-quality housing or better-serviced communities due to increasing rental costs.

Limitations to household agency – no scope for moving from survival to advancement

There is one further danger of overlooking these informal systems of governance and resource distribution by focusing too narrowly on households and their livelihoods strategies. The asset-based frameworks with which urban poverty is commonly conceptualised and that view urban poverty as a result of an accumulation of asset deprivations, have within them an implicit assumption that the correct strategy for urban poverty reduction is the expansion or protection of natural, physical, human, financial or social capital at the household level, better equipping the household to devise strategies for household stability and advancement. These perspectives may give an accurate understanding of how urban poverty is *experienced*, but by solely focusing on the household as the unit of analysis, they overlook these social and political inequalities that drive inequality, exacerbate the vulnerability of the poorest urban households, and limit the autonomy that they have in devising more effective livelihoods strategies (Banks 2014).

The opportunities and obstacles facing the urban poor as they struggle to secure their livelihoods and cope with or adapt to the increased threats they face as a result of climate change are not only influenced by their ownership or lack of different assets. Critically, they are also shaped by social and political processes and institutions at the community level. As we have seen, the local political economy that dominates resource distribution within Dhaka's low-income settlements is closed to those outside the upper two tiers of the social hierarchy (as seen in Figure 7.1). This means that there is little that the majority of households who find themselves at the bottom of the hierarchy can do to overcome the need for the 'right' social networks for advancement. Assessing livelihoods strategies with the bigger picture of a community's stock of social capital gives an incomplete picture of the ability of households to capitalise on their existing resources. Asset-based livelihoods frameworks have, therefore, been argued to overestimate an urban household's 'room for manoeuvre' when it comes to designing and deploying their livelihood strategies (Wood and Salway 2000).

In a political economy in which access to information, resources and opportunities is dependent on a household's social networks, household heads also struggle to balance an incompatible trade-off, namely the need to balance the household's immediate economic needs with its long-term strategic interests. Amidst endemic insecurity, this means that for the majority, economic necessity takes priority, regardless of the long-term sacrifice this entails. In terms of female employment, for example, while the majority of households need women's work to survive, the subsequent erosion of their social status and networks ensures that they are, in the process, excluding themselves from the social networks that provide the most effective means of mobility (Banks 2013). Social obstacles can in fact make longer-term investments irrational, such as household investment in costly skill development.

Without a close relation to externally connected local leaders, skills and qualifications are not enough to secure the forms and terms of employment that are associated with skilled positions. Some household heads making such investments are left worse off having depleted their savings and taken loans to undergo unpaid apprenticeships, only to find themselves unable to realise the expected returns they had associated with the investment (Banks 2014). There is little they can do to overcome the need for the 'right' social connections for accessing the best jobs and they find themselves in insecure and low-paid employment despite the investments they have made.

Conclusions

This research indicates that urban poor households have few weapons in their arsenal for coping, let alone adapting to the threat of climate change. Their day-to-day lives are a constant struggle, leaving few resources to cope in the face of emergencies. Labour mobilisation, asset ownership, patterns of savings and loans, and social support networks all play a role in helping households to cope and to reduce their future vulnerability. What is important to emphasise, however, is the limitations to their effectiveness. They may offer some potential to contribute to adaptive strategies, but the reality is that households use these to cope in the short term, rather than to advance their interests in the medium to long term. Crucially, ongoing insecurity reduces the ability of households to build and consolidate upon their assets, making any household improvements incremental and vulnerable to reversal, and leaving households ill-equipped to deal with the additional financial pressures and health disruptions caused by seasonal fluctuations and extreme weather events.

While this situation characterises the livelihoods of most low-income urban households in Dhaka, there is a small group of *bustee* elite who are in a stronger position, controlling the power, resources and opportunities within the settlement and receiving high and stable incomes from this position. It is within these closed circles that opportunities for adaptation to livelihoods and the built environment are concentrated, both at the household and community level. While improvements to the built environment at the community level have a positive impact on the community via improved living environments and access to services, they also push up rental prices. While increasing incomes for house owners, this simultaneously increases pressure on the incomes of tenants, who are already struggling to balance incomes and expenditures. The poorest households are worst off, who (in the search for the lowest rents) are pushed out to poorer quality housing in more environmentally vulnerable areas.

A climate change lens on urban poverty offers both strengths and dangers. On the one hand, it brings urgency and attention to the increasingly pressing priority of urban poverty in Bangladesh. The problems that the urban poor already face on a day-to-day basis are becoming more frequent and severe, and the urban poor are ill-equipped given the endemic insecurity of their urban livelihoods to cope with these changes. At the same time, however, a climate change lens can also serve to reinforce existing perspectives that urban poverty is driven and realised at the household level, and that the current predominant focus on asset-based frameworks for understanding urban poverty and building resilience and adaptation are the most appropriate means for responding to these issues. In doing so, it overlooks the important role played by social and political institutions and processes within the *bustee* setting, which act as a significant constraint on household agency and create, reproduce and exacerbate inequality at the community level. If programmes for urban poverty reduction or climate change adaptation do not take these structural obstacles into account in programme design, they run the risk of further consolidating the power of the *bustee* elite, while reproducing and further embedding vulnerability for the large number of tenant households outside these social networks.

Notes

1 Banks (2014) gives a full overview of this research. It used a variety of methods, including 22 focus group discussions, community surveys covering 420 households and 77 in-depth interviews with 'coping', 'deteriorating' and 'improving' households.
2 Capital limitations prevent them from running businesses full-time as they would prefer.
3 Borrowing through unpaid debt or credit in local grocery shops was another avenue for consumption-smoothing that does not necessarily constrain future household finances.
4 Around one in five households headed by unskilled labourers, one in four headed by small businessmen and one in three headed by formal sector workers have savings. These figures exclude compulsory savings attached to NGO loans, which are usually used to repay the loan at the end of the cycle rather than returned to the household.
5 Geographic factors increasing environmental vulnerability include proximity to water bodies and houses built on low-lying ground subject to subsidence and soil erosion (Jabeen et al. 2010; Roy et al. 2012; 2013).
6 Only businesses able to offset falls in demand could cope throughout rainy season. These were the businesses serving non-poor clientele outside the *bustee*. Such businesses are rare among *bustee* residents, however, given the amount of capital they require.

References

Amis P 1995 Making sense of urban poverty *Environment and Urbanization* 7(1) 145–158
Banks N 2014 *Livelihoods Limitations: The Political Economy of Urban Poverty in Bangladesh* Brooks World Poverty Institute Working Paper No. 199 University of Manchester, UK
Banks N 2013 Female employment in Dhaka, Bangladesh: participation, perceptions and pressures *Environment and Urbanization* 25(1) 95–109
Banks N 2012 *Urban Poverty in Bangladesh: Causes, Consequences and Coping Strategies* BWPI Working Paper No. 178 Manchester, University of Manchester, UK

Banks, N 2008 A tale of two wards: political participation and the urban poor in Dhaka city *Environment and Urbanization* 20(2) 361–376

Banks N Roy M and Hulme D 2011 Neglecting the urban poor in Bangladesh: research, policy and action in a context of climate change *Environment and Urbanization* 23(2) 487–502

Bashar T and Rashid S 2012 Urban microfinance and urban poverty in Bangladesh *Journal of the Asia Pacific Economy* 17(1) 151–170

Baud I S A Pfeffer K Sridhharan N and Nainan N 2009 Matching deprivation mapping to urban governance in three Indian mega-cities *Habitat International* 33(4) 365–377

Begum S and Sen B 2005 Pulling rickshaws in Dhaka: a way out of poverty? *Environment and Urbanization* 17(2) 11–25

Braun B and Abheuer T 2011 Floods in megacity environments: vulnerability and coping strategies of slum dwellers in Dhaka/Bangladesh *Natural Hazards* 58 771–787

Farrington J Ramasut T and Walker J 2002 *Sustainable Livelihoods Approaches in Urban Areas: General Lessons, with Illustrations from Indian Cases* ODI Working Paper No. 162 London: Overseas Development Institute

Gonzalez de la Rocha M 2007 The construction of the myth of survival *Development and Change* 38(1) 45–66

Government of the People's Republic of Bangladesh (GoB) 2009 *Bangladesh Climate Change Strategy and Action Plan 2009* Dhaka Bangladesh

Hackenbroch K 2013 Negotiating public space for livelihoods: about risks, uncertainty and power in the urban poor's everyday life *Erdkunde* 67(1) 37–47

Hackenbroch K and S Hossain 2012 'The organised encroachment of the powerful' Everyday practices of public space and water supply in Dhaka, Bangladesh *Planning Theory and Practice* 13(3) 397–420

Haque A N Grafakos S and Huijsman M 2012 Participatory integrated assessment of flood protection measures for climate adaptation in Dhaka *Environment and Urbanization* 24(1) 197–213

Hossain S 2013 The informal practice of appropriation and social control – experience from a *bosti* in Dhaka *Environment and Urbanization* 25(1) 209–224

Jabeen H Johnson C and Allen A 2010 Built-in resilience: learning from grassroots coping strategies for climate variability *Environment and Urbanization* 22(2) 415–431

Kantor P 2009 Women's exclusion and unfavourable inclusion in informal employment in Lucknow, India: barriers to voice and livelihood security *World Development* 37(1) 194–207

Mitlin D and Satterthwaite D 2013 *Urban Poverty in the Global South: Scale and Nature* London and New York: Routledge

Moser C O N 1998 The asset vulnerability framework: reassessing urban poverty reduction strategies *World Development* 26(1) 1–19

Opel A 2000 The social content of labor markets in Dhaka slums *Journal of International Development* 12(5) 735–750

Pryer J A 2003 *Poverty and Vulnerability in Dhaka Slums: The Urban Livelihoods Study* Aldershot: Ashgate Publishing Limited

Rashid S F 2000 The urban poor in Dhaka city: their struggles and coping strategies during the floods of 1998 *Disasters* 24(3) 240–253

Rashid H Hunt L M and Haider W 2007 Urban flood problems in Dhaka, Bangladesh: slum residents' choices for relocation to flood-free areas *Environmental Management* 40(1) 95–104

Roy M Hulme D and Jahan F 2013 Contrasting adaptation responses by squatters and low-income tenants in Khulna, Bangladesh *Environment and Urbanization* 25(1) 157–176

Roy M Jahan F and Hulme D 2012 *Community and Institutional Responses to the Challenges Facing Poor Urban People in Khulna, Bangladesh in an Era of Climate Change* BWPI Working Paper 163 Manchester: Brooks World Poverty Institute

Satterthwaite D Huq S Reid H Pelling M and Lankao P R 2007 *Adapting to Climate Change in Urban Areas: The Possibilities and Constraints in Low- and Middle-Income Nations* Human Settlements Discussion Paper Series: Climate Change and Cities 1 London: IIED

Tanner T Mitchell T Polack E and Guenther B 2009 *Urban Governance for Adaptation: Assessing Climate Change Resilience in Ten Asian Cities* IDS Working Paper 315 Brighton: Institute of Development Studies

Wood G and Salway S 2000 Introduction: securing livelihoods in Dhaka slums *Journal of International Development* 12(5) 669–688

Zingel W P Keck M Etzold B and Bohle H G 2011 Urban Food Security and Health Status of the Poor in Dhaka, Bangladesh in Kramer A Khan M H and Kraas F (eds) *Health in Megacities and Urban Areas* Berlin: Physica-Verlag pp301–319

8 Facing the floods

Community responses to increased rainfall in Guarulhos, Brazil and Arequipa, Peru

Michaela Hordijk, Francine van den Brandeler and María Evangelina Filippi

Introduction

In January 2011 record floods killed over 800 people and made thousands homeless in Southeast Brazil (Viana 2011). The residents of the neighbourhood of Jardim Guaracy in Guarulhos, a municipality neighbouring the São Paulo megalopolis, lived in muddy and polluted waters for over a month without receiving assistance. It was the third time in five years that the neighbourhood had flooded. In February 2012 the inhabitants of the Andean city Arequipa in Peru also experienced heavy floods due to unprecedented rainfall, followed by even more intense and heavy rains in March 2013. The rains in Arequipa were the heaviest since rainfall has been systematically recorded (from 1949; Alegria 2013). These events seem to confirm the predicted effects of anthropogenic climate change in the region (Hordijk et al. 2013). Although predictions are uncertain, increasing intensity and volume of rain is predicted for Guarulhos, as well as more frequent heat spells and periods of drought. In 2013–2015, the São Paulo Metropolitan region experienced the most intense drought in more than 80 years. For Arequipa, predictions are even more uncertain. There might be more intense rainfall and tropicalisation, more intense drought, or a combination of both (Hordijk et al. 2013).

Although the flood risks in the two case study communities presented in this chapter are unique to their locations (exposure to fluvial flooding at the banks of the Brazilian river Tietê versus pluvial flooding and the resulting mudslides on the hill-slopes of the Peruvian Andes), residents' experiences are similar to those facing many urban poor, 'now weather is getting crazy' (Interview with resident in Arequipa 2012). What binds the cases together is that they are both placed within formal institutional settings that (at least on paper) foster so-called 'soft resilience' through increasing participation and deliberation of local people in water governance.

Whereas hard resilience refers to making physical systems (dykes, parks, drainage systems, etc.) more resistant to the consequences of extreme weather events, soft resilience refers to the ability of communities to reduce risks, and respond effectively to climate variability (Godschalk 2003: 137). Soft resilience requires preparation, coordination and collaboration among actors based on information sharing, communication, relationships and trust (Miao and Banister 2012). Without underestimating the importance of strengthening 'hard resilience' in flood-prone communities, this contribution focuses on the capacities that could strengthen communities' soft resilience.

Framing the co-creation of knowledge as 'soft resilience'

Although 'resilience' became a popular term much later than 'vulnerability', its definitional ambiguity has already reached a similar level of popularity. Vulnerability and resilience are often discussed together: as the two ends of a continuum (Manyena et al. 2011), as two sides of the same coin (Twigg 2007), or an oxymoron (Füssel 2007). In turn, 'vulnerability' has been defined in many different ways, notably varying in the relative importance given to internal (either socio-economic or biophysical) and/or external vulnerability factors (either socio-economic or biophysical). These approaches differ further by adopting an 'end point' interpretation on vulnerability (focusing on the expected net impacts of climate change), or starting point interpretation (focusing on reducing internal socio-economic vulnerability to climatic hazards). Whereas the end point interpretation identifies climate change as the issue to be tackled, the starting point interpretation focuses on social vulnerability (Füssel 2007). This chapter is written from the latter perspective, arguing that strengthening links between communities and actors or organisations external to the community can strengthen residents' capacities to deal with climatic variability.

'Community resilience' can be defined as 'a *process* linking sets of *networked capacities* to a positive trajectory of functioning and adaptation' (Norris et al. 2008: 131, emphasis added), encompassing both biophysical/hard infrastructure and 'soft' aspects of resilience. Whereas the absence of certain capacities results in vulnerability, their presence can enhance resilience. Importantly, resilience does not protect a community from risk, dysfunction or distress. A community is never 'free' of risk (Twigg 2007), and distress and dysfunction are normal to an abnormal event. The priority is the extent to which a community is able to adapt to an altering environment. In the best-case scenario, a community is able to 'bounce forward' (Manyena et al. 2011), showing potential for renewal and innovation in the face of rapid transformation and crises (Berkes et al. 2003), resulting in a better quality of life than before. Yet, resilience is to be understood as a *process* (not an outcome), in which the sets of networked capacities are in constant interaction and often reinforce or erode each other. A clear example of this is the link between community ties, trust, and capacity for collective action. Community ties (bonding social capital[1]) and trust are often considered a pre-condition for community collective action. However, whilst 'successful' collective action fosters trust and community ties, collective action with limited/no result can erode trust and weaken ties in a community. Given that community resilience is a process, it should be actively maintained (Hordijk and Baud 2011; Miao and Banister

2012). That said, such cooperation is difficult in more heterogeneous communities (Mansuri and Rao 2004). In general, we can argue that collective action becomes more difficult in consolidated urban neighbourhoods where access to, and installation of, basic services is largely secured, so collective action is no longer required (Hordijk 2000).

The set of capacities that refer to biophysical and infrastructural (or hard) community resilience encompass access to (safe) land, security of tenure, housing, sanitary infrastructure, but also access to health, education and employment opportunities. A second set of capacities refer to a community's social capital, including bonding and linking ties, but also perceived (expected), received (enacted) social support, and trust among community members. A third set of capacities refers to a community's ability to act collectively: a willingness to work together for the common good, the capacity to identify problems, achieve working consensus on goals and priorities, and implement the required actions. This is greatly enhanced by attachment to place. It also requires proactive community leadership and the possibility to link with actors outside the community when external assistance is required. This builds on a fourth set of capacities, namely, ability to access (and interpret) information, communication, and the capacity to reflect and learn. This encompasses the capacity to learn from past experience, assess the current situation and imagine potential futures to enable anticipatory action to prepare for surprises and discontinuities (Nelson et al. 2007; Norris et al. 2008).

Social learning, or the co-creation of knowledge, is increasingly highlighted in climate change adaptation (Ensor and Berger 2009; Ensor and Harvey 2015), including in community-based adaptation (Reid et al. 2009; Forsyth 2013), community resilience (Hordijk and Baud 2011) or adaptation as social learning (Collins and Ison 2009). Learning emerges from collaborative processes that enable a shared sense of meaning within the community (Ensor and Harvey 2015: 510). What is known and experienced locally can, however, differ considerably from the technocratic, science-based assessments of climate change risks. This disparity can constrain adaptation (Fraser Chapter 13, this volume). The co-creation of knowledge offers the potential to integrate local knowledge with different sets of knowledge from other actors external to the community. For example, scientific, long-term climate change predictions can be combined with local knowledge based on specific trends experienced in communities, which then produce a more localised understanding (Reid et al. 2009).

Integrating and re-contextualising 'disparate knowledges' can generate new social learning (Perry and May 2010: 18). The co-creation of knowledge is socially embedded, and therefore, through information and knowledge exchange, a shared understanding can be built and trust can be fostered. This in turn creates ties that can be utilised when swift action is needed in times of crisis. This is another example of how different sets of networked capacities can reinforce each other, namely, social learning fostering community trust and strengthening competence for collective action. For this to happen, however, the co-creation of knowledge must be a continuous and iterative process.

Methodology

This chapter is based on fieldwork carried out in Guarulhos, Brazil and Arequipa, Peru, as part of the EU-funded research project Chance2Sustain[2] (2010–2014). In both cities we combined research at neighbourhood level with citywide interviews of key actors involved in water governance and/or climate change programmes. In Guarulhos, 27 key actors, as well as 16 respondents in the case study neighbourhood of Jardim Guaracy were interviewed. In Arequipa, 23 key actors, and 26 residents in the case study neighbourhood of Villa Ecológica, were interviewed. Both residents and key actors were asked about the main water-related risks they identified in their city and neighbourhood, and the extent to which they expected climate change to affect these in the future. Participatory mapping exercises were undertaken in both cities. The results of these exercises were discussed in focus groups with residents, though this proved difficult to organise (especially in Jardim Guaracy).

With 1.2 million inhabitants, Guarulhos is the second city in the state of São Paulo in terms of gross domestic product (GDP) and population. It functions as a satellite city for São Paulo, hosting its international airport and many industries. The case study neighbourhood Jardim Guaracy has approximately three to four thousand residents, and has existed since the early 1990s. It is located along (and even within) the Tietê riverbed, which marks the border between São Paulo and Guarulhos (Figure 8.1). Jardim Guaracy is (and will be) increasingly affected by the creation of a linear park along 70 kilometres of the Tietê River. Although most of the households have tenure security, houses on the floodplains do not. Around 500 households were told they will be evicted and relocated in order to make space for the park. Although these households had a number painted on their house by governmental officials in 2011, they have not heard from them since, and in 2015 still lived in great uncertainty about their future.[3] A peculiarity of the neighbourhood is its relative isolation – locked between a major highway and the Tietê River. These are significant obstacles to the mobility of residents and access to work opportunities. In fact, many residents of Guarulhos do not know of the existence of this area (van den Brandeler et al. 2014).

With 844,000 residents, Arequipa is the second largest city of Peru, situated in the Andean mountains at 2,330 metres above sea level (Figure 8.2). In Arequipa, the neighbourhood Villa Ecológica was selected as a case study. It is part of the district Alto Selva Alegre which has historically been exposed to three types of risk: volcanic, seismic and pluvial flood risks, the latter being the most frequent. Villa Ecológica, one of the last legally recognised neighbourhoods of the district, existing since the early 2000s, is one of the most vulnerable areas. The uneven topography of the neighbourhood and the district in general is characterised by dry stream beds (known as *torrenteras*) that cross the area from east to west and eventually discharge in the Chili river. These *torrenteras* have an irregular discharge, dependent on the precipitation levels, and go through densely populated zones. Moreover, in Villa Ecológica, some of the *torrenteras* have been filled with soil and other materials to allow for the expansion of the neighbourhood, thus blocking the

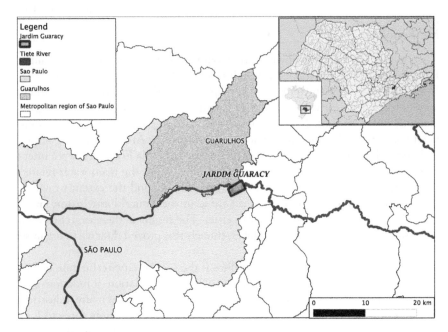

Figure 8.1 Location of Guarulhos and Jardim Guaracy
Source: Authors' elaboration.

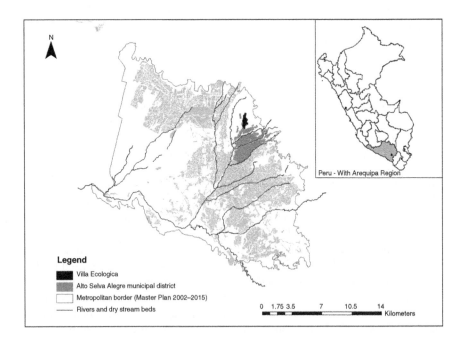

Figure 8.2 Location of Villa Ecológico in Arequipa (metropolitan area)
Source: Authors' elaboration.

Table 8.1 Characteristics of the case study neighbourhoods

	Jardim Guaracy, Guarulhos	*Villa Ecológica, Arequipa*
Age of neighbourhood	25 years (approx)	12 years
Population	3,000 to 4,000	3,000 (approx.)
Population's origin	Immigrants from the northeast	Immigrants from neighbouring regions (Apurímac, Cusco and Puno)
Number of floods 2007–2013	3	2
Location of the houses at risk	–Houses by the square –Houses by the river	–Houses located on top of artificially closed *torrenteras* –Houses by the naturally preserved *torrenteras*
Prevention of flood risks by	–Raising furniture –Building flood barriers (metal or brick walls) –Removing garbage and unclogging drains	–Building flood barriers (small brick walls)
Adjustment measures	–Blocking the drains so that floodwaters cannot come out of them –Sandbags –Evacuation –Cleaning the house and saving as much as possible	–Sandbags given by civil defence –Digging a path around the house for the water to evacuate –Cleaning the house and saving as much as possible

Source: Authors' elaboration based on fieldwork.

natural paths of rainwater. Villa Ecológica has a population of approximately 3,000 residents, most of them immigrants from the neighbouring regions – Apurímac, Cusco and Puno. Almost 90% of the households have tenure security. Table 8.1 summarises the key characteristics of both case study neighbourhoods.

Flood exposure and (bio)physical vulnerability

In both neighbourhoods, residents settled in risky lands exposed to floods because they lack access to housing in safer areas. Despite this important detriment, they have been able to build liveable housing units (though frequently flooded) and have found employment opportunities. This was easier in Villa Ecológica, which is well connected to the city when not cut off by floods, than in isolated Jardim Guaracy. In socio-economic terms, the residents are poor in both neighbourhoods, but not destitute, and have established a foothold and livelihood in the city. Most have a formal land title and houses made from durable materials, and send their children to school. In both neighbourhoods, male household heads are mainly employed in civil construction, while women either work in grocery shops or stay at home.

Figure 8.3 Informal occupations of the floodplain, Jardim Guaracy
Source: Photo – van den Brandeler (2012).

The major vulnerability to floods is a consequence of two sets of (bio)physical factors in both neighbourhoods. The first is a consequence of risky location, whilst the second relates to a lack, or low quality, of infrastructure. In Jardim Guaracy, informal households on the riverbeds are vulnerable to flooding (Figure 8.3), but floods are often more severe and frequent in the formalised main square of the neighbourhood (approximately 100 metres away from the river), due to the lower altitude and dysfunctional drainage and sewerage systems.

Floods frequently occur during the rainy summer season. On average, affected residents reported that their houses had been flooded three times between 2007 and 2013. Whilst most people reported material loss and damage to homes, the water entering homes was also extremely polluted, causing various diseases.[4] In addition, residents from Jardim Guaracy explained that as the outlets of sewage pipes in the river were too low, sewage flowed back out of drains in the streets and domestic drains when the river level rose. Importantly, the risks of flooding and reflux are very unequally distributed amongst the residents of Jardim Guaracy. There is a divide in the neighbourhood between 'those downhill who experience floods' (Interview with residents 2012) and those who do not. The residents most exposed to floods are often the ones with the least socio-economic resources (e.g. lower incomes and/or insecure tenure), especially those living along and within the riverbed.

In Villa Ecológica, dry stream beds would fillup in the rainy season, leading to pluvial flooding and mud slides (known as *huaycos*). Residents identified two types of dry stream beds: naturally preserved and artificially filled. In the second case, these *torrenteras* can be hardly visible, as they have filledup with soil and other materials. Whilst most houses had not been severely affected, major problems were associated with the consequences of heavy rains on the built environment and infrastructure. In 2012 rains were heavier and more frequent than respondents had ever experienced, with many stating that it was the first time it rained with such intensity, for such a long time. All major natural *torrenteras* filled up, isolating the upper part of the district from the rest of Alto Selva Alegre, because there was no bridge, and local transport could no longer pass.

The artificial filling of *torrenteras* meant that houses had been constructed where there used to be dry stream beds. Yet, when it rained water ran downhill through its former paths, sweeping away everything in its way. '*El agua busca su camino*' (the water seeks its course) was one of the most reiterated phrases among residents. Because the natural water paths had been blocked, it spread across the neighbourhood, severely affecting the main road. This was a problem not only for transportation but also for water supply. Most of the public taps and wells were located alongside the main road, which coincided with the path rainwater and mudslides followed, destroying the provisional water connections and pipelines linked to the reservoir. In addition, heavy rains increased the amount of water in the Chili River, as well as the sediment loading, overwhelming the pumping capacity of the water treatment plant that supplied the reservoirs in the upper northeast. As a result, residents suffered from power cuts over a period of two to four weeks during the rainy season.

Resilience to floods in Jardim Guaracy and Villa Ecológico

Individual resilience

Residents took various actions to address floods In Jardim Guaracy. The most common adjustment taken by exposed households was raising their furniture when flooding occurred.[5] Several residents mentioned pouring caustic soda into drains to eliminate the foul smell,[6] and during severe flood, households evacuated, taking essential items such as documents and a few clothes.[7]

Preventive measures in Jardim Guaracy were largely structural. For instance, respondents reported that they placed sandbags in front of doors and to have built permanent flood barriers (Figure 8.4). Other households located near the river raised their floors with mud and concrete. However, since the floods are partially caused by the reflux of wastewater through the house drains, the effectiveness of these measures was relatively limited. This helplessness caused households to focus on minimising the damage. Other measures that could increase household resilience, such as insurance, savings and income diversification, were rare.

In 2011 and 2012, Villa Ecológica residents experienced an extraordinary rainy season, resulting in severe flooding for the first time. Most adaptation strategies were therefore adjustment measures during this time. They started to construct dykes and put sandbags to guide water away from the households and the main road. The most severely affected households evacuated if they could. At the individual household level, some containment walls were constructed. For the settlement as a whole, much emphasis was placed on the need for a proper drainage system. Prevention strategies, however, were acknowledged as necessary future steps.

Figure 8.4 Flood barrier constructed in Jardim Guaracy
Source: Photo – van den Brandeler (2012).

Neighbourhood social capital

In both neighbourhoods, residents expressed a strong sense of attachment to place. On average, respondents lived in Jardim Guaracy for 19 years and in Villa Ecológica for 8 years, during which time they had struggled to build their houses. Attachment to place was expressed as resistance to possible relocation: imminent in Jardim Guaracy because of the planned park, and a latent risk for informal residents in Villa Ecológica, living on exceedingly risky lands. The sense of community was stronger in Villa Ecológica than in Jardim Guaracy, arguably due to a range of divisive factors in the latter. First, some residents in Jardim Guaracy were directly threatened with eviction, while others could potentially benefit from the planned park through higher property values. Second, residents experienced that solidarity and help during flooding came mostly from neighbours who were also affected, whereas the non-affected households higher up neglected, or even mocked, them. Many respondents said '*Aqui é cada um por si*' (here it's every man for himself). One resident of the floodplains in Jardim Guaracy explained how 'there are a lot of thugs here, who don't help. There are people who laugh off our situation. But between neighbours we help each other'. It was a very different story in Villa Ecológica. As noted, Villa Ecológica is a considerably younger settlement, and thus the collective history of settlement consolidation is still omnipresent, resulting in both expectations of, and experiences with, mutual help.

Community competence

The differences in social capital between the two neighbourhoods are linked to the differences in community competence. In Jardim Guaracy, there was no functioning grassroots organisation, the neighbourhood leader was inactive, and partly because of their physical (and psychological) isolation from the city, they also lacked functioning ties with external actors. Moreover, there was a high level of mistrust of the authorities. While some residents collectively unclogged drains and picked up street waste, all collaboration seemed mostly limited to a few immediate neighbours, demonstrating bonding (over bridging) social capital.

In Villa Ecológica, on the other hand, participation in communal work in the neighbourhood was high, such as in the maintenance of a water reservoir, the construction of public wells or repair of the informal water network destroyed by flooding. Residents actively participated in neighbourhood meetings, and in various collective efforts to claim formalisation and services. Through these community efforts, they realised important improvements in the neighbourhood: 90 percent of the plots were legalised, water provision through yard taps was provided, and sewerage connections were foreseen in the near future. This progress could also be attributed to a functional (although quite authoritarian) leadership and strong ties to external actors. This shows once more how social capital and community competence overlap and reinforce each other. The neighbourhood leader was also a leader in the Front for the Defence of Sector IV, an organisation that negotiates with the authorities for water and sanitation. The Front has been successful on a number of issues.

Community information, communication and knowledge

In both neighbourhoods, residents were very aware of the risks: 'We have seen it live, what is happening and what has happened in the past. Where we live we have good knowledge of the neighbourhood' (Interview with Jardim Guaracy resident 2012). Knowledge in Jardim Guaracy was, however, noticeably more extensive and precise amongst residents who lived downhill and had experienced floods directly. In terms of differential knowledge, there was not only a contrast between those exposed to floods (in the riverbanks and along the main square) and those who were not, but also between people living in streets connected by side streets (who could describe what happened in the neighbouring street) and people living in unconnected streets, who rarely knew what happened in the parallel streets. For respondents living near the low-lying square, the sewage reflux was by far the most pressing problem. Several respondents in the unconnected streets were aware of the flooding problem in general, and mentioned the problem of clogged drains (Miranda Sara et al. 2014: 44).

Residents in Jardim Guaracy felt disconnected from Guarulhos and invisible to the authorities. Rare communication with civil defence mainly consisted of warnings that floodgates were to be opened in times of heavy rain, and that floods were expected to increase in the future. More importantly, the fact that residents had received no information on the pending relocation had seriously eroded trust in the authorities. Those residents who were threatened with relocation also perceived flood risks to be relatively unimportant in comparison.

In Villa Ecológica, residents' knowledge of pluvial flooding was mainly based on their personal experiences. Due to their rural origin, residents were familiar with seasonal cycles: rainfall season (December–March), followed by windy season (May–September). When this was disrupted by the extraordinary rains that extended throughout April, the vast majority of respondents linked the events to climate change. Indeed, one of the most common expressions was: 'The weather is crazy'. Respondents associated climate change with changes in temperatures, dangerous solar radiation and risk of cancer, and/or extraordinary rainfall or alteration in the normal pattern of rains and frost.[8] Residents' lived experience of risk could also be traced in their spatial knowledge. They were able to locate the main hazardous areas and vulnerable houses precisely on a map of the neighbourhood, and indicated where water infrastructure was at risk. In Villa Ecológica we were able to develop and validate a map of the water-related risks in the neighbourhood in a participatory manner (Figure 8.5), something that turned out to be much more difficult, and with more limited participation, in Jardim Guaracy due to mistrust and lack of willingness to work together.

Besides personal experience, communication between residents proved to be an effective source of information in Villa Ecológica. Although residents usually claimed they did not interact much with each other, there were spaces that allowed for the exchange of information. Usually held once every two weeks, neighbourhood meetings were the main formal communication channel. At first glance they seemed not to offer a real space for the exchange of ideas, as it was usually the neighbourhood leader unilaterally talking. However, these meetings did bring all residents together, allowing them to interact and share their daily problems and anecdotes. Finally, there was also a more informal communication channel indirectly triggered by the existing water provision system. Water supply was organised in a network, where each public tap/well had a certain number of affiliates coordinated by a person in charge.

As for communication with external actors and organisations, most respondents shared the feeling that government and non-governmental organisations (NGOs) had neglected them during the floods. The local civil defence officials contacted the most affected residents only after the damage was done. However, outside times of crisis, communication with local authorities seemed to be flexible and open. Many respondents acknowledged that the mayor of the district was always keen to meet them and listen to their requests about jobs, water, bridge building and so forth. Furthermore, meetings had been held in the municipality between residents and the mayor,[9] and the mayor joined a neighbourhood

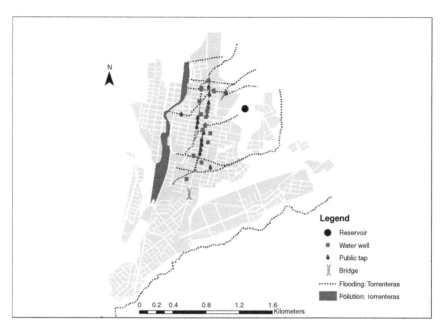

Figure 8.5 Flood risks mapped by residents in Villa Ecológico
Source: Authors' elaboration based on participatory workshop (2012).

meeting in May 2012. Again, the neighbourhood leader played a central role in linking the residents and local authorities.

Community resilience and the co-creation of knowledge in Guarulhos and Arequipa

As stated, community resilience should be considered as a continuous and iterative process, fostered through different sets of networked capacities. We can not therefore conclude that one community is more resilient than the other, but can assess the different sets of networked capacities that enable or erode resilience. The comparison of Jardim Guaracy and Villa Ecológica clearly indicates that capacities are considerably stronger in Villa Ecológica, where strong bonding social capital was on a par with a willingness to work together, identify problems and solutions, agree on goals and undertake collective action. Although these actions (such as provisional dykes) only reduced flood risks to a very limited extent, it is a sign of their competence and capacity for collective action. Comparing the cases also illustrates the interrelation between capacities. For example, the combination of a functioning leader, the willingness to work together and resulting collective action has enabled better information sharing and community knowledge creation (e.g. community risk map) in Villa Ecológica. On the other

Table 8.2 Capacities in Jardim Guaracy and Villa Ecológica*

	Jardim Guaracy (Guarulhos)	Villa Ecológica (Arequipa)
Neighbourhood social capital		
Bonding ties	–	+
Enacted social support	+/–	+
Expected social support	– –	+
Linking ties	– –	++
Trust	– –	+
Competence for collective action		
Attachment to place	++	++
Willingness to work together	–	++
Shared problem identification	– –	+
Shared goals	– –	+
Functional leadership	– –	+
Information, communication & knowledge		
Access to information (external)	– –	–
Information exchange (internal)	– –	+
Communication with external actors and organisations	– –	+

* ++ very strong, + strong, +/– neutral, – weak, – – very weak
Source: Authors' elaboration based on fieldwork.

hand, the absence of leadership, grassroots organisation and willingness to work together, as well as the differential spatial layout of the neighbourhood, impeded the sharing of information in Jardim Guaracy. Distrust of authorities, and lack of information with respect to the foreseen relocation, also aggravated the feelings of isolation and abandonment. Table 8.2 provides a summary of the community capacities in Jardim Guaracy and Villa Ecológica.

The conclusion that community capacities in Villa Ecológica were stronger than in Jardim Guaracy should not be taken in a judgemental sense. At the time of the research, Villa Ecológica was in a phase of consolidation where collective action was still required to realise important infrastructural improvements, fostering community competence. The threat of relocation experienced in Jardim Guaracy could unite residents, but this is less likely when only a few households in the community are affected. Arguably, this created heterogeneity of interests that undermined the competence of collective action. Finally, lack of trust among community members and in authorities, feelings of abandonment, lack of information and communication on the planned relocation exemplifies what many urban poor experience around the world – exclusion, lack of representation and neglect.

Official expert-led assessments of flood risks also differed substantially from residents' assessments in both Guarulhos and Arequipa. Jardim Guaracy is marked as a zone at risk of flooding in the official plans (Prefeitura de Guarulhos in Miranda Sara et al. 2014: 83), but officials and residents differ on what they identify as causes. Whilst government officials mainly blame proximity to the river, and therewith legitimise the relocation of the households to make room for the linear park, residents point at the lack of drainage, blocked drains and soil-sealing. The construction of the park will not solve the flood risks faced by the residents around the low-lying square. They do not know whether the construction will also imply that the inadequate drainage will be improved and reflux addressed. In the official risk maps of the municipality, Villa Ecológica is not even marked as at risk from flooding (Miranda Sara et al. 2014: 46).

On paper, both countries have a water governance framework that enables co-creation of knowledge. In 1991, the state of São Paulo adopted a law that integrated water management '*avant la lettre*' of the Integrated Water Resource Management (IWRM) principles of decentralisation and participation. This Water Act also sets the example for the National Water Act in Brazil (adopted in 1997), which is in turn echoed in the Peruvian Water Act of 2009. The legal framework in Brazil stipulates that water resources should be managed at the basin level by river basin councils composed of an equal number of state, municipal and civil society representatives. Crucially, decisions on water governance in the river basin councils are supposedly (at least on paper) based on participation and deliberation, the key components of co-creation. Indeed, one state engineer explicitly acknowledged the relevance of including community knowledge in water governance deliberation (Interview 2012):

> When we saw that there was erosion, we would first talk to local residents and ask them how this erosion appeared, because they experience it. I know technically how erosion is formed, but they can provide a few details that will help me in the elaboration of the project, details that if I had not asked this question I would not have included.[10]

Civil society organisation (CSO) representatives in the basin committees consisted of NGOs, and members of user, neighbourhood, business or industry associations,[11] thus representing diverse yet fragmented interests. For the CSOs, there are numerous strict rules in terms of who is eligible to participate. Whilst this is to prevent 'non-qualified' individuals from joining the debate, it can also create obstacles for those interested stakeholders who belong to organisations lacking the necessary structure. For residents of Jardim Guaracy it was, for instance, impossible to participate because of their lack of a formal organisation. Indeed, many residents did not even know of the basin committees.

The CSO representatives that do participate come from more formalised organisations (outside of Jardim Guaracy), but many reported that the excess of technical jargon impeded their understanding of the discussions. Scientific/ expert knowledge is still recognised as the most legitimate form of knowledge, shifting power relations towards those in possession of this type of knowledge. The River Basin Plan is, for instance, produced through workshops and discussions and thereafter submitted to the plenary of the basin committee for approval. A former president of the Alto-Tietê basin committee suggested, however, that although the documents are developed through a participatory process, they are almost entirely created by technical experts based on their technical knowledge.

The existing participatory channels mainly serve, therefore, to transmit expert knowledge to non-experts. This 'one-way' communication runs counter to what is needed for the co-creation of knowledge. There are few channels through which non-experts can share their knowledge and use it to influence decision-making processes. Consequently, community knowledge (e.g. that inadequate drainage is a more important factor in floods than proximity to the river) is not taken up in disaster prevention.

In Peru, the new water law was adopted in 2009, and also requires the formation of river basin councils. An important objective of the law was to decentralise water governance to the basin level, and bring together all key actors in a formal space so that they could design the Water Resources Management Plan in a participatory manner. An important difference with the Brazilian system is that the law explicitly stipulates that community-based organisations *cannot* be part of the basin councils, though NGOs and other CSOs may be invited to participate in working groups where the council considers this appropriate.

Agrarian and non-agrarian user associations, peasant communities, native communities, professional associations and universities can participate in the councils. Interestingly, in Arequipa, Civil Defence is not represented in the river basin council (Filippi et al. 2014). Regarding Arequipa's water governance, there is an urgent need to improve information sharing and co-creation of knowledge among key actors. Virtually all respondents pointed to the dispersion and/or unavailability of up-to-date information. There is little scientific knowledge on water-related risks produced by knowledge institutions or other actors. Whatever is produced (such as hydro-meteorological knowledge) is not shared. Much more knowledge is produced 'on the job', but is neither shared nor integrated. The local water authorities have recognised the problems related to their fragmented knowledge base and have recently started a process of building a joint diagnosis of the water basin they are responsible for, inviting many actors to 'working groups'. However, it might require much more than these relatively recent reforms to meaningfully incorporate community knowledge (Filippi et al. 2014).

Conclusions

This chapter has shown that residents have relevant and important knowledge of their street and neighbourhood, the levels they are most able to represent. Co-creation of knowledge should therefore start at these levels. However, even in countries with progressive water governance systems that emphasise participation and deliberation, such as Brazil and Peru, the incorporation of lay knowledge in policy formulation and decision-making remains a major challenge. Much more is needed than inviting CSO members to meetings. The co-creation of knowledge emerges when a shared sense of meaning is developed in a collaborative process (Ensor and Harvey 2015). This first and foremost requires a willingness to share information. Moreover, it requires the recognition of the value of diverging sets of knowledge, plus a willingness to engage in two-way communication using accessible language.

This chapter also shows that not every low-income neighbourhood will have the capacities needed to engage in co-creation. In Jardim Guaracy, low levels of social capital, fragmented local knowledge on flood risks, and mistrust of authorities (resulting from a continuous lack of information) seriously impedes the possibility of co-creation. This is not to say that strengthening soft resilience in Jardim Guaracy is irrelevant or impossible. Indeed, psychological isolation, feeling invisible and being physically cut off are issues that could be addressed through sustained engagement with key actors and organisations. Continuous information provision on the construction of the park and foreseen relocation is the highest priority. By means of two-way communication, residents' knowledge on houses at risk of flooding outside the floodplains (i.e. the main square) and on problems caused by inadequate infrastructure could be collected by civil defence and the water company. If done in a participatory manner, this could reduce such feelings of isolation. However, low levels of community capacities (i.e. ability and willingness to work together, level of organisation) indicate that long-term involvement is necessary to achieve results.

Community capacities in Villa Ecológica are at a substantially higher level than Jardin Guaracy. We found more potential for participatory knowledge generation at community level (especially in the form of participatory mapping exercises). Linking capital to actors and organisations external to the community was much more present in Villa Ecológica. It is clear that Villa Ecológica also requires investments in infrastructure (hard resilience), such as the construction of an adequate drainage system and bridge over the major *torrentera*. If these measures are planned and implemented through co-creation, community knowledge on areas most affected by floods and courses taken by the water in covered stream beds could be incorporated. This can strengthen links with external actors, fostering a positive feedback loop between community social capital and community competence, as well as strengthening links with civil defence. This is an important asset in times of crisis. Effective community adaptation requires links with external actors, as communities cannot adequately adapt to flood risks on their own. Including representatives of civil defence in overall water governance systems to ensure that disaster prevention and climate change adaptation measures are considered together could lead to win–win situations.

Notes

1 Bonding social capital refers to ties of similar people within a community; linking social ties refers to ties with higher-placed actors external to the community (Woolcock 2001: 13–14).
2 This chapter is part of the research project Chance2Sustain: 'Urban Chances – City growth and the sustainability challenge'. For more information see the acknowledgements and preface of this book, and the Chance2Sustain website: http://www.chance-2sustain.eu/.
3 Residents were originally told that the evictions were planned for 2012, but as of August 2015 residents were still waiting in uncertainty.

4 Examples include outbreaks of cold and flu, diarrhoea and in some cases people mentioned leptospirosis and dengue as possible consequences.
5 They would do this either by carrying furniture to upper floors, or by piling them up one on top of the other, sometimes using bricks at the bottom.
6 They explained that even when their houses were not flooded the 'unbearable' smell of the river would enter their houses through pipes.
7 Out of the sample, all respondents had been able to stay with relatives or friends for the necessary time.
8 The most elaborated answers were given by those who distinguished climate change in terms of its causes: climate change was either caused by changes in the climate of other countries (e.g. Brazil), or it was triggered by pollution or La Niña. Finally, a few respondents related climate change with the end of the world, an idea mostly spread out by the Evangelical church in the neighbourhood.
9 One of the residents recorded several of these meetings with his camera and shared the videos with us.
10 He afterwards pointed out the importance of talking to the longer-term residents of an area, as residents who moved there recently could be ill-informed on risks.
11 Concerned individuals can also attend meetings but have no voting rights.

References

Alegria J 2013 Lluvias que afectó Arequipa podria repetirse Peru sin riesgos de desastres Available from: http://www.perusinriesgodedesastres.com/materiales-foro-regional/notas-pasadas/lluvias-que-afect%C3%B3-arequipa-podr%C3%ADan-repetirse-y-con-mayor-severidad [Accessed: 15/10/15]

Berkes F Colding J and Folke C (eds) 2003 *Navigating Social-Ecological Systems: Building Resilience for Complexity and Change* Cambridge, UK: Cambridge University Press

Brandeler van den F Hordijk M A Von Schönfeld K and Sydenstricker Neto J 2014 Decentralization, participation and deliberation in water governance: a case study of the implications for Guarulhos Brazil *Environment and Urbanization* 26(2) 489–504

Collins K and Ison R 2009 Jumping off Arnstein's ladder: social learning as a new policy paradigm for climate change adaptation *Environmental Policy and Governance* 19(6) 358–373.

Ensor J and Berger R 2009 Community-Based Adaptation and Culture in Theory and Practice in Adger W N Lorenzoni I and O'Brien K *Adapting to Climate Change: Thresholds, Values, Governance* 227–239 Cambridge, UK: Cambridge University Press

Ensor J and Harvey B 2015 Social learning and climate change adaptation: evidence for international development practice *Wiley Interdisciplinary Reviews: Climate Change* 6(5) 509–522

Filippi M E Hordijk M A Alegría J and Rojas J D 2014 Knowledge integration: a step forward? Continuities and changes in Arequipa's water governance system *Environment and Urbanization* 26(2) 525–546

Forsyth T 2013 Community-based adaptation: a review of past and future challenges *Wiley Interdisciplinary Reviews: Climate Change* 4(5) 439–446

Füssel H M 2007 Vulnerability: a generally applicable conceptual framework for climate change research *Natural Hazards Review* 4(3) 136–143

Godschalk D R 2003 Urban hazard mitigation: creating resilient cities *Natural Hazards Review* 4(3) 136–143

Hordijk M 2000 *Of Dreams and Deeds: The Role of Local Initiatives for Community-Based Environmental Management in Lima, Peru* PhD thesis University of Amsterdam

Hordijk M A and Baud I S A 2011 Inclusive Adaptation: Linking Participatory Learning and Knowledge Management to Urban Resilience in Otto-Zimmermann K (ed) *Resilient Cities: Cities and Adaptation to Climate Change – Proceedings of the Global Forum 2010* 111–122 Dordrecht: Springer

Hordijk M A Miranda Sara L Sutherland C Sydenstricker-Neto J Jo Noles A and Rodrigues Batata A G 2013 *Water Governance in Times of Uncertainty: Complexity, Fragmentation, Innovation* WP-4 Fieldwork Report Bonn: EADI

Mansuri G and Rao V 2004 Community-based and -driven development: a critical review *The World Bank Research Observer* 19(1) 1–39

Manyena S B O'Brien G O'Keefe P and Rose J 2011 Disaster resilience: a bounce back or bounce forward ability? *Local Environment* 16(5) 417–424

Miao X and Banister D 2012 *Coping with Natural Disasters through Resilience* Working Paper No. 1059 Transport Studies Unit School of Geography and the Environment Oxford University

Miranda Sara L Hordijk M A and Khan S 2014 *Actors' Capacities to Address Water Vulnerabilities in Metropolitan Cities Facing Climate Change* Chance2sustain WP4 Final Report p 90 Bonn: EADI

Nelson D R Adger W N and Brown K 2007 Adaptation to environmental change: contributions of a resilience framework *Annual Review of Environment and Resources* 32(1) 395–419

Norris F H Stevens S P Pfefferbaum B Wyche K F and Pfefferbaum R L 2008 Community resilience as a metaphor, theory, set of capacities, and strategy for disaster readiness *American Journal of Community Psychology* 41(1–2) 127–150

Perry B and May T 2010 Urban knowledge exchange: devilish dichotomies and active intermediation *International Journal of Knowledge-Based Development* 1(1) 6–24

Reid H Alam M Berger R Cannon T Huq S and Milligan A 2009 Community-based adaptation to climate change: an overview *Participatory Learning and Action* 60 11–34

Twigg J 2007 *Characteristics of a Disaster-Resilient Community: A Guidance Note* DFID Disaster Risk Reduction Interagency Coordination Group DFID

Viana N 2011 *Floods in Brazil Are a Result of Short-Term Planning* Available from: http://www.guardian.co.uk/global-development/poverty-matters/2011/feb/02/brazil-floods-urban-planning [Accessed: 12/10/15]

Woolcock M 2001 The place of social capital in understanding social and economic outcomes *Isuma: Canadian Journal of Policy Research* 2(1) 1–17

9 From asset vulnerability to asset planning

Negotiating climate change
adaptation solutions in an
informal settlement in Cartagena,
Colombia[1]

Alfredo Stein and Caroline Moser

Introduction

In the last decade, climate change modelling projections have been incorporated into urban planning agendas in order to determine regional- and local-scale vulnerabilities alongside future global impacts (Blanco and Alberti 2009; IPCC 2012). With their primary objective to influence local policy and planning, the majority of methodologies for such urban vulnerability assessments and climate change adaptation planning consist of a diagnosis of vulnerable areas, groups or types of hazards that impact a city. While some identify vulnerability 'hot spots' using climate data scenarios and downscaling methods to the city level (ICLEI 2007; World Bank 2011), others combine scientific vulnerability mapping with city-level policy and institutional mapping in order to assess the capacity of local authorities to deal with projected hazards (Cavan and Kingston 2012).

Although most vulnerability assessments are based either on potential climate disasters associated with extreme and severe weather, or on slower incremental changes with less immediate impacts, to date, few appraisals engage directly with urban poor communities, even though such groups usually live in the most hazardous areas of a city and are generally most vulnerable to adverse weather (Bicknell et al. 2009). This means that planners remain largely uninformed about local people's perspectives concerning the effects of climate variability on their households and communities. In addition, current assessment methodologies are more likely to focus on physical and institutional vulnerability at the local government level rather than consider other local vulnerabilities, or sources of resilience, at household and community level. Given the increasing size of urban poor populations that will be most affected by severe weather, it is particularly important to 'capture' their perceptions of the impacts of climate change as well as to identify the ways in which their adaptive strategies can be integrated collaboratively into planning procedures with local partners.

This chapter illustrates how 'bottom-up' community asset planning can help to address this gap, by designing feasible local solutions that can be mainstreamed into 'top-down' citywide strategic planning. The chapter draws on the experience of implementing participatory diagnostic and planning tools in an informal settlement located in the city of Cartagena, Colombia, and is divided into three sections. The first outlines the conceptual and operational rationale of the Asset Planning for Climate Change Adaptation (APCA) framework; the second section describes the main climate change issues in the city of Cartagena as well as the tools used in the APCA process; and the third section analyses the results of the asset adaptation planning process and identifies the challenges this climate change planning framework faces.

Conceptual and operational rationale

The APCA framework builds on previous applied studies on asset accumulation for urban poverty reduction (Moser 2009), as well as on studies of the erosion of assets resulting from violence, insecurity and urban poverty in Jamaica (Moser and Holland 1997) and in different cities in Colombia and Guatemala (Moser and McIlwain 1999). It also draws on the participatory planning approaches used by the Foundation for the Promotion of Local Development (PRODEL) in Nicaragua for housing improvement and the provision of basic services and infrastructure in mid-size cities for the period 1994–2008 (Stein 2010), as well as a long tradition of community action planning in different cities of the world (Hamdi and Goethert 1997; Hamdi 2004). Finally, the framework is the outcome of two applied research projects implemented by the Global Urban Research Centre (GURC), the first supported by the Social Development Department of the World Bank and the second by the Ford Foundation, both of which provided important inputs to the Cartagena asset planning process.

The objective of the World Bank project was to better understand how poor households, small businesses and communities in the cities of Mombasa, Kenya, and Estelí, Nicaragua, were coping with the impacts of climate change, and to identify how policy and institutional systems could best build on local realities to develop pro-poor urban climate change adaptation actions to build resilience (Moser et al. 2010).[2] The Ford Foundation-supported project took the methodology to the next stage and developed an operational framework intended to identify how asset planning for climate change adaptation could be mainstreamed into city planning. The project was undertaken in Cartagena, Colombia, during 2011, and then in Pondicherry, India, in 2012 – in this case, with an emphasis on the climate change impacts on health and environmental hazards in informal settlements.[3]

The conceptual and operational approach that underpins APCA seeks to contribute to identifying the impacts that climate change has in cities, and specifically in urban locations where the poor live. The APCA assumes that people in local communities – despite their urban location – know about weather and environmental hazards, perceive variations in weather patterns and have reasonable

Feasibility phase   Diagnostic phase   Planning phase

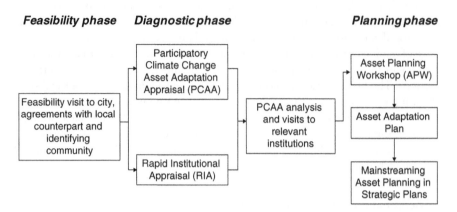

Figure 9.1 Connections between different elements of Asset Planning for Climate Change
         Adaptation (APCA)
Source: Authors' elaboration.

knowledge as to how this affects their assets and wellbeing at household, community and business levels, and that they can identify what needs to be done. The
APCA also seeks to integrate assessments of vulnerability and planning for climate change adaptation processes, first at the scale of an urban poor community,
then to link such assessments with broader strategic and operational planning
at city level. It therewith addresses the limitation of so-called community-based
adaptation (CBA) initiatives that remain too localised and confined to community initiatives (Dodman and Mitlin 2013). Finally, by developing a series of
participatory methods and tools, it seeks to contribute to the debates on the best
ways to involve different stakeholders in planning practices taking into account
the uncertainties associated with climate change (see Blanco and Alberti 2009).

The implementation of the APCA

The APCA has different implementation phases, each with a set of participatory
tools (Figure 9.1). The methods summarised in this section were used by GURC
and the Universidad Tecnológica de Bolivar (UTB) in the APCA process in
Cartagena.

Feasibility and preparation phase

This consists of exploratory visits to a city to understand its characteristics
and climate-related issues. These visits allow for the identification of potential
partner institutions as well as potential sites (urban poor communities) within
which to undertake the planning process. Meetings also take place with different
stakeholders from national agencies as well as local government, to explain the

APCA's conceptual and operational framework. The outcome of this phase is agreement among the different stakeholders regarding the components, activities and responsibilities required for the implementation of the APCA.

Diagnostic phase

This consists of two main components: a Participatory Climate Change Asset Adaptation Appraisal (PCAA) and a Rapid Institutional Appraisal (RIA). The PCAA identifies the vulnerability of urban poor households, small businesses and communities to climate change, as well as their adaptive capacity and sources of resilience before, during and after the onset of severe and extreme weather events. Using various participatory tools, the PCAA starts directly with weather issues to ascertain how communities list and rank severe weather events. It also identifies what main type of weather events affect specific assets and how different assets are affected by specific weather phenomena. For each of these phases, adaptation strategies are identified along with associated institutions that support or undermine these actions at household, community and small business levels. The PCAA methodology is based on purposive sampling from a range of focus groups that are representative of community members by age, gender, ethnicity, economic activities and other socially and culturally specific variables (Moser and Stein 2011).

The RIA identifies relevant national policies, programmes and projects taking place in the country and the city relating to climate change adaptation or indirectly dealing with environmental, basic infrastructure, housing and economic issues. This includes documentation of national and municipal legal frameworks, public and private institutions working nationally, sub-nationally and at city level on climate change adaptation and disaster risk management. It summarises the main city-level projects and associated budgetary resources, and seeks to provide city-level historical data on weather variables (mean wind speed, humidity, precipitation amounts, mean temperatures among others), information on hydrodynamic variables (including the rise in rivers and sea levels) for the same period, as well as watershed problems that affect the surroundings of the communities where the asset planning process is being implemented (Moser et al. 2010). Finally, the profiles of local poor communities where the PCAA will take place are generated, based mainly on secondary information regarding their socio-economic characteristics, pre-identification of key actors working in the communities and other environmental conditions.

Planning phase

This consists of two main components: an Asset Adaptation Planning Workshop (APW) and a process of mainstreaming asset adaptation into strategic planning.

The workshop builds on the results of the PCAA and the RIA, and usually takes place in the community with the participation of community members and representatives of local government, NGOs, the private sector and other agencies working in the city. To ensure that the results of the workshop are feasible, a thorough process of dialogue and negotiation takes place before the workshop with members of public and private institutions that have resources and decision-making powers. The same dialogue process also takes place with community leaders to ensure the wide participation of different sectors of the community. During the workshop, participants are divided according to themes that have been prioritised during the PCAA by the different focus groups. The outcome is an asset adaptation plan, which is negotiated and agreed among the participants. The prioritised strategies identified can later be transformed into short project profiles.

The mainstreaming process requires close follow-up and monitoring of the agreements reached during the planning workshop. A distinction between the roles that the community and the local authorities and other agencies play is crucial, and the local counterpart who helps implement the PCAA and the RIA can provide this. The mainstream process requires providing technical assistance to the different partners so they have the capacity to transform the ideas and short profiles generated and agreed during the planning workshop into viable projects that are socially, financially and technically feasible. These also need to be approved and incorporated into the operational and strategic plans of different institutions and organisations, especially local governments.

The implementation of the APCA in Cartagena

The APCA process in Cartagena was implemented between January and September 2011. In January, a feasibility mission from GURC visited the city and a roadmap for implementing the APCA was agreed with the local counterpart. The RIA was conducted between February and June 2011, resulting in three background documents: an overview of the socio-economic conditions of the city and an appraisal of the main policies addressing climate change adaptation and environmental issues in Colombia and in Cartagena, a summary of historical weather and hydrodynamic data for Cartagena for the last 50 years, and a profile of Barrio Policarpa, where the PCAA was to take place.

The PCAA was carried out between 28 June and 9 July and included training the UTB facilitators in participatory tools, implementation of 22 focus groups in the *barrio*, and systematisation of the focus group findings. These focus group reports, together with the findings of the RIA, served as the backbone for the analysis presented to the APW that took place on 9 July 2011 in the elementary school located in the *barrio*. Under GURC guidance, the local counterpart team facilitated the workshop group discussions and plenary meetings in which 51 representatives (23 from the community and 28 from different public and private agencies) prioritised and assessed different solutions according to the following criteria: urgency, cost, technical feasibility, legal and administrative feasibility. The outcome was an asset adaptation plan that was later mainstreamed by the local counterpart institution and the *barrio* community leaders in different departments of the Municipality of Cartagena and other private institutions. The following sub-sections present the main findings from the different diagnostic and asset planning tools used during the APCA in Cartagena.

Cartagena

Cartagena de Indias is the most important port of Colombia in the Caribbean. Tourism, port activities and chemical, oil and plastics industries constitute the main economic activities. In 2006, the District of Cartagena had an overall population of one million, of which 95 percent lived in the city (Perez and Salazar Mejia 2007). Poverty and income inequality have increased significantly (the Gini coefficient increased from 0.38 in 2000 to 0.48 in 2012; Rueda and Espinosa 2010; *El Heraldo* 2014) and the city is marked by patterns of spatial and ethnic segregation; the urban poor live primarily in the north and southeast of the city, which have the highest proportions of low incomes, low educational levels and informal workers, and the highest unemployment and crime rates.

Over the last 40 years, a gradual and sustained increase in mean temperatures has been documented, providing important climate science data for the APCA. Due to its geographical location, Cartagena has experienced significant and frequent flooding caused by extreme rainfall events and sea level rise. A historical analysis of the annual monthly average rain in Cartagena shows a lineal trend between the years 1942 and 1999, with increases of 78 millimetres every 10 years – double that observed in other cities in the Caribbean region. The monthly average values for rains registered in the years 1945, 1962, 1979 and 1986 were significantly high. Moreover, in 2004 and 2010 there were unprecedented levels of precipitation, which generated flooding in different parts of the city (CIOH 2011). Finally, in the last 50 years there has been an increase in the sea level on the coast of Cartagena of approximately 22 centimetres, the result of recurrent and combined weather events caused by wind, surf and sea storm surges.

Barrio Policarpa[4]

The Policarpa Salavarrieta neighbourhood (known as Barrio Policarpa) is located in the southwest of Cartagena on swampy terrain (due to its proximity to Cartagena Bay) and is part of the Mamonal industrial area. Policarpa's topography is relatively flat, with a slight ascending slope that goes from east to west. Two open rainwater drainage canals run in the same direction. The topography in the south of the *barrio* has been modified by land-filling in the adjacent industrial area, which has diverted the course of the waterways and created a dam.

The settlement was established in 1975, with the steady arrival of families from rural areas of the Caribbean and Andean regions and other areas of Cartagena. Less than a year after the first land occupation, there were 100 families living on boggy plots of land. According to community leaders, as more people arrived the landowner brought in the police to evict them. However, because of the tenacity

Table 9.1 Weather phenomena affecting Barrio Policarpa

Type of weather	Number of votes	Percentage
Rain and flood	322	40.9
Heat	231	29.4
Dust (summer)	107	13.6
Bad odours	44	5.6
Wind	41	5.2
Contamination	19	2.4
Mud	16	2.0
Thunderstorms	4	0.5
Other	3	0.4
TOTAL	787	100

Source: Based on 22 focus group reports, Barrio Policarpa (author's elaboration).

of the leaders, this did not happen – 'Policarpa' was the name of an important leader and the *barrio* was named in her honour.[5] Ever since then, residents have tried to legalise the neighbourhood but the problem has not been resolved. More than 35 years later, 7,200 people live in the *barrio* in 972 houses (an average of 7.4 people per house), but only one family has a land title; the rest do not have any legal recognition of their land rights.

According to the sequence of land occupation, the *barrio* today is divided into four sectors: Las Flores, Central, El 13 and El Chino. In spite of its proximity to Cartagena's most important industrial area, more than 70 percent of the *barrio*'s labour force works in informal activities. In recent years, water, waste collection, gas, electricity (although the majority have illegal power connections), telephone and internet services have gradually been introduced.

Asset vulnerability to severe weather

The *barrio* is exposed to adverse severe weather events during both the rainy season (winter) and the dry season (summer). The Mamonal area, which includes Policarpa, is affected by rainfall in the neighbouring Municipality of Turbaco because the rain there creates runoffs that run through this area. This means that the *barrio* can be affected by rain falling in neighbouring Turbaco even when it is not raining in Cartagena Bay. The open drainage canals that cross the *barrio* drain into the bay, where the rising sea level acts as a plug in the estuary, preventing rainwater runoff and thus increasing the intensity and severity of the floods.

The PCAA identified the most important weather events affecting the *barrio* based on the experiences and historical memories of the citizens (Table 9.1). Rain and flooding were recalled as the main events affecting their assets (about 41 percent), but also heat (29.4 percent) as well as a variety of environmental problems associated with wind (for example, dust and bad odours) which together made up 24.4 percent.

The poor condition of the roads and streets meant that rain caused major transport problems, while the lack of adequate drainage infrastructure caused floods and streets to be covered with mud. Bad odours and wind were also identified as factors affecting small businesses, in addition to the impacts caused, which included humidity and increased mud, oil and grease on the streets.[6] A causal flow diagram created by participants in a focus group of women from the Central and Las Flores sectors shows the effects of rain on different assets, including septic tanks, electricity and health, as well as on the streets and houses (Figure 9.2). Although the direction of some of the arrows in Figure 9.2 might not seem logical, these represent the perceptions of the focus group members who drew the causal flow diagram.

Asset adaptation strategies

The PCAA used matrices to identify adaptation strategies implemented by households, small businesses and the community before, during and after severe weather events to protect and rebuild their assets. Causal flow diagrams highlighted the links between the impacts of severe weather and asset adaptation strategies. Listing and ranking of proposed solutions within focus groups facilitated the identification of more concrete solutions that went beyond general strategies. One focus group, for instance, identified specific strategies to protect community nursery houses (*hogares comunitarios*) used for child care in the *barrio* (Table 9.2).

Finally, the PCAA listed those institutions with a presence in the *barrio*, identifying those that supported the community to build resilience or responded to severe weather events. Institutional maps and matrices were used for this purpose. Interestingly, a significant number of organisations worked in the community, with a total of 27 identified. More than 50 percent highlighted the company Syngenta Agro S.A. (which borders the *barrio*), the two Policarpa schools, the Municipality of Cartagena and the Mamonal Foundation (a social foundation funded by a private company) as those most relevant. About 30 percent recognised 20 other organisations, such as the police and the armed forces, the Red Cross, various official district and national entities and private companies; these, as well as helping during the occurrence of extreme weather, carry out programmes that support training in small business for the population. The third group of institutions are those based in the settlement, including the Committee of Leaders, Fundación Planeta y Vida and the Junta de Acción Comunal (JAC), the last of which was not considered particularly important by community members.

Asset adaptation planning workshop in Policarpa

During preparations for the planning workshop, members of the local counterpart team and GURC visited different public and private institutions previously identified as important during the RIA and the PCAA.[7] Some were working on climate change adaptation, others on environmental issues, while others supported

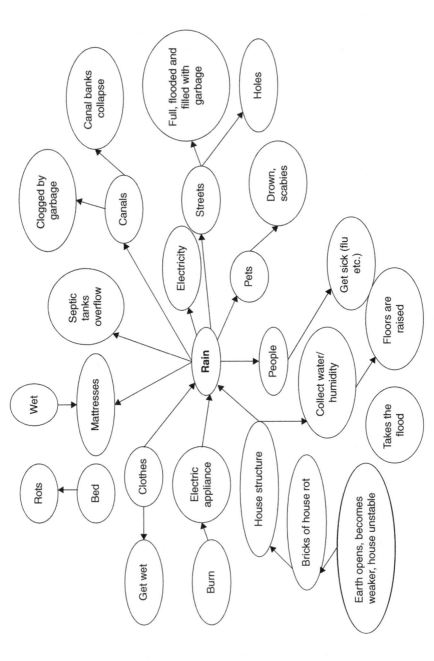

Figure 9.2 Causal flow diagram of vulnerabilities produced by rain, Policarpa, Cartagena

Source: Focus group of eight women from Las Flores and Central Sector (Authors' elaboration).

Table 9.2 Listing and prioritisation of solutions to impacts on community nursery houses caused by rain

Solution	Votes by focus group participants
Raising the foundations of the house	12
Study land conditions	–
Improve high voltage cables	5
Increase house space	1
Improve bathrooms, floors and walls	19
Build multiple activity spaces	1
Improve septic tanks	2

Source: Focus group of eight community mothers aged between 30 and 48 from different sectors, 4 July 2011 (author's elaboration).

different poverty reduction initiatives in the Mamonal industrial area, including Barrio Policarpa. In these meetings, the researchers described the PCAA participatory process in the community as well as the conceptual and operational rationale that would guide the workshop.

During the meetings, representatives were asked if their organisation would be interested in supporting the asset adaptation planning process in Barrio Policarpa and if so, what specific policies, programmes, projects and resources could be allocated to the process. They were also asked to identify any legal, technical, financial and administrative constraints facing them that could impede or interfere with their ability to support this climate change adaptation process. These meetings clarified that the lack of land regularisation and the risk of recurrent flooding in the *barrio* were the main factors that could constrain them from contributing to the process. Some representatives also expressed that the lack of cooperation between public institutions and private companies also diminished the impact of their interventions, and therefore it was important to find ways by which both sectors could cooperate with the community. Given the sensitivity of the land regularisation issue, assurances were given that the workshop was not intended to put public officials or private sector representatives 'against the wall' in terms of public opinion scrutiny. The consultations ended with representatives being invited to participate in the planning workshop and asked to identify how many representatives from their organisation they could send.

The local counterpart focus group facilitators also had discussions with community leaders, in order to identify *barrio* representatives beyond those in the 22 focus groups who could participate in the workshop. Selection criteria included the following: a balance between women and men, different age groups, participants from the four different sectors of the *barrio* as well as from small businesses and, finally, representatives of different community organisations. The APW took place on 9 July 2011 with 51 participants (not including GURC and local facilitators), of which 23 represented the *barrio* and 28 came from different public and private organisations. Participants were divided into groups, with different stakeholders equally represented in each. Each group addressed one of five themes identified as critical by the focus groups during the PCAA analysis:

- housing improvements for families living near the open drainage canals and in other places,
- small businesses (both those located in the *barrio* and motorcycle taxis),
- health (especially respiratory diseases and diarrhoea, and pests such as mosquitoes and rats),
- infrastructure (including open drainage, streets, gutters and kerbs), and
- community facilities and services (including sport facilities, community centres and illegal electricity connections).

In each group, facilitators introduced the analysed PCAA results relevant to the group's theme. With this input, each group discussed possible solutions to the main problems identified. They used a matrix to do this, with participants each ranking and prioritising solutions. The prioritised solutions were then analysed and weighted according to four criteria: urgency (which solution was the most urgent of all), cost (which solution was the least expensive of all), technical feasibility (which solution was technically most feasible in terms of implementation), and legal and administrative feasibility (which solutions did not require complicated legal changes and administrative decisions).[8] For example, the housing group listed, ranked and prioritised different solutions (Table 9.3). They then decided to weight and prioritise the four solutions with the highest votes according to the predefined criteria. As Table 9.4 shows, the topographical and pluviometric survey came first in spite of not being priority one, dredging and widening of drainage canals came second, improvements to the community nursery houses third, and housing improvements fourth.

The asset adaptation plan

Once each group had identified and prioritised solutions, these were presented in a plenary session so that all participants could share their most important solutions. Participants then returned to their groups and started to build an asset adaptation plan, which specifically identified what needed to be done to start implementing the prioritised solution, when each activity should take place, and who should be responsible for it (with emphasis on the actions the community and the Municipality of the District of Cartagena would have to undertake). Again, the plan for housing adaptation developed by the Housing Group provides an interesting example (Table 9.5). A similar plan was elaborated by each of the other four groups, presented in turn to the plenary. The first two priorities of each group's asset plan were then merged into a plan for the entire *barrio*, and this asset plan became the starting point for negotiations with the Municipality of the District of Cartagena, as well as other private institutions and NGOs.

Table 9.3 Listing and ranking of solutions to housing vulnerability, Barrio Policarpa

Housing	Listing of solutions	Ranking of solutions by number of votes
Improvements near the drainage canals	• Dredging and widening of drainage canals	1st (20 votes)
	• Housing census on banks of drainage canals, for relocation	
	• Training and awareness-raising for people, including youth	
	• Control measures to stop people throwing rubbish into drainage canals	
	• Courses for households to define minimum improvements	
Improvements in other places	• Improvements to the bridge to Mamonal	
	• Topographical and pluviometric survey of the *barrio*	2nd (17 votes)
	• Raising houses using gravel fill	5th (5 votes)
	• Healthy Houses Minimum Improvement Programme*	3rd (13 votes)
	• Sewage system	6th (5 votes)
	• Construction and improvement of septic tanks	
	• Improvements to the community nursery houses (*hogares comunitarios*) (floors, walls, roofs) and raising the foundations	4th (7 votes)

Note: * This programme, managed by the Housing Department of the District of Cartagena, provides building materials for the improvement of floors, roofs and bathrooms, but not walls.
Source: Housing Group, Asset Planning Workshop, Barrio Policarpa, 9 July 2011 (author's elaboration).

During the RIA, the local authorities had clarified publicly that they were not permitted to invest public resources in the *barrio* because of its location in a high-risk area subject to recurrent flooding. Therefore, the *barrio* could not be included in the District of Cartagena's operative and investment plans despite the fact that the majority of people had lived there for more than 30 years, during which they had improved their houses and infrastructure. Despite these constraints, the APW showed that there were a number of potential project solutions that could be undertaken without having to approve the process of land regularisation and titling. These included environmental health campaigns, improvement of infrastructure, housing and basic services, and microcredit for economic activities. In one APW group, the private electricity company insisted that all it required was for the municipality to categorise Policarpa as *sub normalidad* (a Colombian planning concept that defines informal status in terms of land tenure, allowing for the recognition of the rights of occupancy, although not necessarily

Table 9.4 Weighting and ranking of some of the proposed housing solutions, Barrio Policarpa

Criteria	Dredging and widening of drainage canals	Topographical and pluviometric survey of neighbourhood	Healthy Housing Minimum Improvement Programme	Improvements to the nursery community houses
Urgency	3	3	2	2
Cost	2	3	1	2
Technical feasibility	3	3	3	3
Legal and administrative feasibility	3	3	3	3
TOTAL	11	12	9	10
Ranking	2	1	4	3

Note: Weighting grading – urgency: 3 = more urgent / 1 = less urgent; cost: 3 = less expensive / 1 = more expensive; technical feasibility: 3 = more feasible / 1 = less feasible; legal and administrative feasibility: 3 = more feasible / 1 = less feasible.

Source: AWP Housing Group, representatives from the neighbourhood and from public and private institutions, 9 July 2011 (author's elaboration).

Table 9.5 Action plan matrix on housing vulnerability to weather, Barrio Policarpa, 9 July 2011

Priorities	What must be done?	When?	By whom?		
			Community	District	Other
Topographical and pluviometric survey of *barrio*	* Community organisations Junta de Acción Comunal (JAC) (or other organisations) ask for support from Corvivienda (Housing Department) * Coordination between Corvivienda and neighbours * Socio-economic study * Survey * Coordinate with the planning, infrastructure and community development departments to share results of Asset Planning Workshop	August–September (2011)	JAC; other organisations; neighbours from each street	Corvivienda; Planning Department; Infrastructure Department	
Dredging and widening of drainage canals	* Community asks the Valuation Department for costs to dredge and widen canals * Census of houses situated on the banks of drainage canals to classify and resettle if necessary * Land Value Department starts works with support from the Infrastructure Department * Community Development Department prepares for community participation about best management * Awareness-raising campaigns and checks on rubbish with local Town Hall 3 * Clearing and cleaning of drainage canals	Application in July 2011	JAC; other organisations	Planning Department; Local Town Hall 3; Land Value Department; Community Development Department	

Table 9.5 (cont.)

Priorities	What must be done?	When?	By whom?			
			Community	District	Other
Healthy Housing Minimum Improvement Programme	* Application by community organisation (JAC or another) to Corvivienda * Survey of houses * Identify houses to be included in the programme * Socio-economic and technical study of houses * Programme implementation according to budget (pilot plan)	August–7 October 2011 December 2011	JAC; other organisations	Corvivienda; Planning Department; Local Town Hall 3	Argos; Syngenta; Reficar; Ecopetrol; Cemex;
Improvements to the community nursery houses (*hogares comunitarios*)	Include *hogares comunitarios* in the Minimum Housing Improvement Programme; manage support from private businesses	August 2011 – December 2011	JAC; *hogares comunitarios*; Fundación Planeta y Vida; other organisations	Planning Department; Corvivienda; Participation Department; PES; Local Town Hall 3; association of *hogares comunitarios*	Argos Syngenta; Fundacion Mamonal; Reficar; Ecopetrol; Cemex; Hermana Efrida; IESFA

Source: Adapted from Moser, Stein and Acosta (2011).

of land titling) for it to start investing resources to ensure house connections to the main power lines. The Universidad Tecnológica de Bolivar and the community leaders followed up on these agreements in September and October 2011.

At the end of October 2011, elections in the municipal authority in Cartagena took place. The elected mayor was keen to formulate the city's development plan (including climate change adaptation) through consultation and active citizen participation processes. However, one year later, the mayor left office and it was unclear the implications this would have for implementing the plans elaborated through participatory processes (Campos Perez 2012).

Lessons from the asset planning for climate change adaptation in Cartagena

The APCA in Cartagena provides important lessons and highlights future challenges that the process faces. First, it shows that climate change can be used as an entry point for planning for the upgrading of marginal, vulnerable urban poor settlements in cities of the Global South. By identifying the impacts of climate change both in the city more generally and in locations where the poor live, the APCA process seeks to identify whether the increasing intensity and frequency of severe and extreme weather events exacerbate existing housing, infrastructure and other problems, or whether it creates specific new problems and conditions that did not exist previously. This demonstrates to decision-makers and planners that climate change adaptation should not be seen as an additional burden but, rather, as part of a process of transformation that addresses some of the roots of vulnerability (Pelling 2010) and deals with core development and urban poverty deficits faced by poor households and communities (World Bank 2011).

Second, the APCA succeeds in challenging conceptions of urban poverty that reproduce images of the poor as destitute, lacking knowledge, resources and capabilities, and therefore unable to confront the challenges posed by severe and extreme weather (Moser and Satterthwaite 2008). In contrast, it clearly shows that the urban poor know about weather and have reasonable knowledge of how extreme and severe weather events affect their assets and well-being at the household, community and business levels.

Third, the APCA process identifies vulnerability not only as a function of exposure, sensitivity and adaptive capacity but also, more importantly, it identifies what people are already doing to cope and adapt their assets in response to the ongoing climate extremes. In this sense, the APCA recognises that the urban poor are not passive vulnerable victims of adverse climate change; they are themselves already actively involved in 'autonomous adaptation' measures that, if strengthened by investment and technical assistance from national and local institutions, can allow them to build long-term resilience. The participatory diagnostic and planning tools used in Policarpa demonstrate the scale and size of resources that households, small businesses and the community are already investing to address climate-related impacts and, more importantly, that the solutions required for strengthening their asset adaptation strategies do not require huge resource investments. In the context of recent legislation enacted by the Colombian government in 2012 which calls on municipalities and local communities to adopt disaster risk management strategies through participatory approaches (Campos Perez 2012), the APCA can become a complementary tool to strengthen the adaptation strategies that urban poor communities are already undertaking to face climate-change-related hazards.

Fourth, since the APCA is not based on multiple, limitless problems and needs manifest in urban poor communities, but is grounded in the specific strategies that they are already implementing to adapt their assets, there are very real possibilities of finding points of agreement between the urban poor and local government – despite legal and technical constraints that may prevent public authorities from investing in this type of settlement. This is especially true in the context of an informal settlement like Policarpa. On the one hand, it lacks secure land tenure and is located in high-risk areas prone to flooding, which has impeded the investment of fiscal resources by Cartagena's municipality for the last decades. On the other hand, it occupies valuable land coveted by local and transnational industry. The adaptation strategies that the urban poor develop allow them, as Sen (1997) suggests, to negotiate with (and even confront) the institutions that govern the control and use of their assets.

The key question, however, is whether the external institutions involved in the APCA process act upon this knowledge, and deliver according to the needs and priorities of the community members. The answer requires sustained and critical engagement, and the necessary resources to implement participatory climate change adaptation in towns and cities of the global South. The biggest challenge that remains is to convince local institutions to allocate resources to this process.

Notes

1 A first version of this chapter was presented by the authors at the ClimUrb conference in September 2013, and subsequently published in April 2014 in the journal *Environment and Urbanization* 26(1) 166–183. The authors wish to acknowledge the journal for allowing its reproduction in this book.
2 The Mombasa study was conducted by Caroline Moser in collaboration with Eco Build Africa Trust, four Mombasa community-based organisations (Licodep, Alishe Trust, CODETI and CRF) and a team of local researchers. In Estelí, Alfredo Stein collaborated with NITLAPAN, Central American University and a research team from FAREM, Autonomous University of Nicaragua, together with the Municipality of Estelí and PRODEL.
3 In Cartagena, Moser and Stein collaborated with Alberto Abello and his team from the Universidad Tecnológica de Bolívar, with training support from Angelica Acosta. In Pondicherry the collaborating counterpart was the French Institute of Pondicherry. In both studies, Elizabeth McKeon from the Ford Foundation provided important guidance.
4 This section draws from UTB and GURC (2011).

5 Information obtained from the timeline tool applied to the focus group of members of Fundación Planeta y Vida, 4 July 2011, and the matrix on general data applied to the focus group of community leaders, 2 July 2011.
6 Focus group of restaurant owners in the Central sector.
7 In the Municipality of Cartagena, meetings were held with representatives of the Secretariats of planning, the environment, housing, infrastructure, social investment, community participation and development, and members of Sector 3 Cartagena. Private institutions visited were Fundación Mamonal, Reficar (oil refinery), Argos (cement plant), Syngenta and Electricaribe (electricity). NGOs included Cemprende (promotion of small businesses) and Actuar por Bolivar (microfinance institution).
8 The weighting and ranking used in the workshop was adapted from similar methodologies used in microplanning processes in Asia and Latin America (see Hamdi and Goethert 1997; Stein 2010).

References

Bicknell J Dodman D and Satterthwaite D (eds) 2009 *Adapting Cities to Climate Change: Understanding and Addressing the Development Challenges* London and Sterling, VA: Earthscan

Blanco H and Alberti M 2009 Building capacity to adapt to climate change through planning *Progress in Planning* 71(4) 158–169

Campos Perez J E 2012 Planning for climate change in Cartagena, Colombia: institutionalizing alternative approaches *Economia & Region* 6(2) 53–85

Cavan G and Kingston R 2012 Development of a climate change risk and vulnerability assessment tool for urban areas *International Journal of Disaster Resilience in the Built Environment* 3(3) 253–269

Centro de Investigaciones Oceanográficas e Hidrográficas del Caribe (CIOH) 2011 *Boletín meteomarino mensual del Caribe Colombiano* Available from: http://www. cioh.org.co/ meteorologia/ ResumenClimatologico.php [Accessed: 10/07/11]

Dodman D and Mitlin D 2013 Challenges for community-based adaptation: discovering the potential for transformation *Journal of International Development* 25(5) 640–659

El Heraldo 2014 *Pobreza, Pobreza Extrema y Gini por ciudades 2012–2013* Sábado 22 de marzo 2014 en base a Departamento Administrativo Nacional de Estadísticas (DANE) Available from: http://www.elheraldo.co/infografias/pobreza-pobreza-extrema-y-gini-por-ciudades-2012-2013-146907 [Accessed: 30/03/14]

Hamdi N 2004 *Small Change: About the Art of Practice and the Limits of Planning in Cities* London: Earthscan

Hamdi N and Goethert R 1997 *Action Planning for Cities: A Guide to Community Practice* Chichester: Wiley

ICLEI 2007 *Preparing for Climate Change: A Guidebook for Local, Regional and State Governments* Available from: http://www.cses.washington. edu/db/pdf/snoveretalgb574 .pdf [Accessed: 24/03/10]

Intergovernmental Panel on Climate Change (IPCC) 2012 Summary for Policy Makers in C B Field V Barros T F Stocker D Qin D J Dokken K L Ebi M D Mastrandrea K J Mach G-K Plattner S K Allen M Tignor and P M Midgley (eds) *Managing the Risks of Extreme Events and Disasters to Advance Climate Change Adaptation* Special Report of Working Groups I and II of the Intergovernmental Panel on Climate Change, Cambridge and New York: Cambridge University Press

Moser C 2009 *Ordinary Families, Extraordinary Lives: Assets and Poverty Reduction in Guayaquil 1978–2004* Washington DC: Brookings Institution

Moser C and Holland J 1997 *Urban Poverty and Violence in Jamaica* World Bank Latin American and Caribbean Studies Viewpoints Washington DC

Moser C and McIlwaine C 1999 Participatory urban appraisal and its application for research on violence *Environment and Urbanization* 11(2) 203–226

Moser C Norton A Stein A and Georgieva S 2010 *Pro-poor Adaptation to Climate Change in Urban Centres: Case Studies of Vulnerability and Resilience in Kenya and Nicaragua* Report No 5494 Washington DC: World Bank

Moser C and Satterthwaite D 2008 *Towards Pro-poor Adaptation to Climate Change in the Urban Centres of Low- and Middle-Income Countries* Climate Change and Cities Discussion Paper 3 London: IIED

Moser C and Stein A 2011 Implementing urban participatory climate change adaptation appraisals: a methodological guideline *Environment and Urbanization* 23(2) 463–486

Moser C Stein A and Acosta A 2011 *Urban Asset Planning in Cities of the South; Sourcebook: Conceptual, Methodological and Operative Framework for Participatory Asset Appraisal and Asset Planning Workshop. Examples from Cartagena* Draft Working Paper Global Urban Research Centre, University of Manchester

Pelling M 2010 *Adaptation to Climate Change: From Resilience to Transformation* London: Routledge

Perez V G J and Salazar Mejia I 2007 *La pobreza en Cartagena: Un análisis por barrios, Documentos de trabajo sobre economía regional* Documento de trabajo sobre economía regional No. 94 Centro de Estudios Económicos Regionales Banco de la Republica (CEUR) Cartagena

Rueda F and Espinosa A 2010 Will the poor of today be the poor of tomorrow? The determinants of poverty and vulnerability in Cartagena, Colombia *Economía & Región* 4(1) 47–71

Sen A 1997 Editorial: human capital and human capability *World Development* 25(12) 1959–1961

Stein A 2010 *Urban Poverty, Social Exclusion and Social Housing Finance. The Case of PRODEL in Nicaragua* Housing Development and Management PhD Thesis No 7 Lund University Sweden

Universidad Tecnológica de Bolívar (UTB) and Global Urban Research Centre (GURC) 2011 *Perfil de la comunidad y planificación de activos; proyecto piloto en el Barrio Policarpa* internal document, UTB and GURC, Cartagena de Indias

World Bank 2011 *Guide to Climate Change Adaptation in Cities* Washington DC: World Bank

10 Climate change and water scarcity

Implications for the urban poor in coastal Bangladesh

Aftab Opel

Introduction

A growing body of research indicates that climate change can have significant effects on the availability of fresh water resources (Bates et al. 2008; Nicol and Kaur 2009; Calow et al. 2011; World Bank 2013). The effects are usually worst felt in urban areas, where changing patterns of precipitation (due to global warming) along with increased contamination of ground and surface water (due to saline intrusion) result in a declining supply of safe water. At the same time, rapid urbanisation and overcrowding in cities results in increasing demand for water by urban dwellers. Past research has shown that as cities grow in population, the total water needed for adequate municipal supply grows as well (Bradley et al. 2002). This increase in total municipal water demand is driven not just by the increase in urban population, but also by a tendency for economic development to increase the fraction of the urban population that use municipal supply rather than other sources such as local wells or private water vendors (McDonald et al. 2014). Moreover, the economic development that generally goes along with urbanisation increases *per capita* water use, as new technologies such as showers and flush toilets increase residential use of water (McDonald et al. 2011). In order to meet increasing levels of water demand, cities tend to rely more and more on groundwater withdrawal, a practice that usually coincides with a declining recharge capacity of the urban aquifer because of the high degree of imperviousness of urban landscapes. This ultimately contributes to the depletion of the overall availability of fresh water in cities (Foley et al. 2005; Lankao 2008; World Bank 2013).

The situation is aggravated by a rapidly growing urban population. Currently, around 60 million people are added to the urban population every year, a figure which is expected to rise. It is estimated that six out of every ten people will be living in cities by 2030, rising to seven out of ten by 2050 (WHO and UN Habitat 2010). This projection may change, however, as recent evidence suggests that climatic events have accelerated, with profound effects on rural to urban displacement. An Asian Development Bank (ADB) report suggests that 10.7 million people in Asia were displaced due to climatic events between 2009 and 2011, of which 3.5 million were from South Asia (ADB 2012). Large proportions of these people move and settle in urban areas for their livelihoods (Brown 2008; ADB 2012). Thus, alongside non-climatic drivers, accelerated migration from vulnerable rural areas to towns and cities further aggravates the pressure on already exhausted freshwater resources in urban areas. Poverty is also highly concentrated within towns and cities, compared to rural areas. Indeed, approximately one third of all global urban residents and one quarter of the total poor in developing countries are extremely poor (i.e. living on less than US$1.25 a day; Ravallion et al. 2007; Baker 2008). Climate change disproportionately affects the urban poor, exacerbating their multiple, interlocking vulnerabilities (Satterthwaite et al. 2007; Banks et al. 2011).

The impacts are also spatially variable. Most notably, coastal urban areas face a dual pressure of climatic (e.g. slow-onset and extreme weather) and non-climatic (e.g. population growth) stresses. Drawing on research from WaterAid Bangladesh,[1] this chapter explores how urban poor households in two small coastal towns in Bangladesh – Paikgacha and Kalaroa – are affected by these processes. Three main arguments are outlined. First, that low-income households are worst affected by water scarcity in coastal towns and cities, and that they are effectively 'priced out' of safe drinking water alternatives, such as filtered or bottled water. Secondly, that the findings presented here raise significant questions about the long-term future of dwelling and livelihoods for all urban dwellers in coastal towns and cities. If safe water is not accessible or affordable, then serious questions must be asked about the feasibility of alternatives, and inevitability of involuntary displacement and/or relocation as a result of water scarcity. Thirdly, that these questions must be addressed through ongoing discussion about loss and damage in Bangladesh, and other coastal towns and cities at the forefront of climate change.

The following section discusses the relationship between climate change and water scarcity in greater depth. The next section then explores the implications of climate change for Bangladesh, an 'impact hotspot' (World Bank 2013) and the subsequent sections expose the tensions around urbanisation and water scarcity in two coastal towns, before conclusions are drawn.

Climate change and water scarcity

Climate change and freshwater systems are interconnected in complex ways (Doll and Zhang 2010). Any change in one system directly or indirectly influences the other (Kundzewicz et al. 2007; Millar 2007). The Intergovernmental Panel on Climate Change (IPCC) Fifth Assessment Report (AR5) also confirmed that the impacts of climate change on freshwater systems and their management is (and will be) very high (IPCC 2014). Fresh water availability, as well as demand, is directly or indirectly affected by various elements of climate change. Decreasing availability of and increasing demand for fresh water has already made the situation uninhabitable in some parts of the world, and increases the vulnerability of a large number of people (World Bank 2013). Observed and projected increase of temperature, sea level rise and precipitation variability due to climate change are the key driving factors of this changing situation (Kundzewicz et al. 2007; Bates et al. 2008; Calow et al. 2011).

Whilst there have been many models and projections about climate change and its potential impacts, almost all have concluded that the sea level has risen, and will rise further as a result of global warming (Bates et al. 2008; Nicholls and Cazenave 2010; Christensen et al. 2011; Nicholls et al. 2011). This has a range of impacts on coastal areas, including submergence, increased land erosion, eco-system changes and increased salinisation (World Bank 2013). Increased salinisation significantly affects fresh water availability from surface water sources, as well as groundwater aquifers. The effects of climate change on surface water resources are more visible and widely studied compared to the impacts on groundwater (Franssen 2009). Changes in air temperature and rainfall variability affect river flow, which in turn affects the mobility and dilution of contaminants. Increased air temperature also results in increased water temperatures which affect chemical reaction kinetics and deteriorates water quality and ecology (Delpla et al. 2009; Whitehead et al. 2009). Thus, higher water temperatures, precipitation variability and longer periods of low flow exacerbate different forms of water pollution, including sediments, nutrients, dissolved organic carbon, pathogens, pesticides and thermal pollution (Murdoch et al. 2000; Bates et al. 2008). Sea level rise and higher frequency of storm surges also causes saline intrusion in the surface water sources in coastal areas. All these factors significantly reduce the availability of safe water for human consumption (Delpla et al. 2009).

The impact of climate change on groundwater is less visible, because aquifers react slowly, compared to surface water (Franssen 2009). However, the long-term implication for drinking water supply is catastrophic because groundwater is the major source of drinking water for most people in the world (Wijnen 2012). The groundwater recharge rate largely depends on precipitation. However, volume, timing and intensity of precipitation is heavily influenced by climate change (Bates et al. 2008; Ng et al. 2010). Temperature increase results in increasing evaporation of available surface water and vegetation transpiration, which influences precipitation amounts, timings and intensity rates, and indirectly impacts the storage of water in surface and subsurface aquifers (Kumar 2012). Thus, groundwater recharge rates and groundwater tables are severely affected by climate change (Bates et al. 2008; Rodell et al. 2009; Doll and Zhang 2010; Ng et al. 2010; Green et al. 2011; Taylor et al. 2013; World Bank 2013).

In coastal areas, the effect of climate change on both fresh water and groundwater availability is particularly devastating. Reduction of groundwater recharge rates in the coastal areas due to precipitation variability, as well as sea level rise, inevitably results in saline intrusion in the shallow and deep aquifers, affecting the availability of fresh water from groundwater sources (Al-Gamal and Dodo 2009). Surface water sources are also affected by climatic factors like tidal surge, floods and temperature variability, and non-climatic factors such as increased demand for agriculture, aquaculture and so on (World Bank 2013). These factors result in severe scarcity of fresh water which, in turn, increases the struggle for water collection, and forces people to employ detrimental coping strategies, such as lower consumption and use of unsafe drinking water. Ultimately, long-term and short-term health problems associated with water scarcity disproportionately affect the poorest and most vulnerable in society (Haines et al. 2006; Bates et al. 2008; Khan et al. 2011).

Bangladesh: The 'worst victim' of climate change

Bangladesh is considered to be an 'impact hotspot' (Wold Bank 2013) and the most vulnerable country to climate change (Maplecroft 2011). Two-thirds of the nation lives less than five metres above sea level, whilst the country is susceptible to frequent river and rainwater flooding, particularly during the monsoon (World Bank 2010). Climate change is exacerbating existing extreme weather events experienced in Bangladesh (World Bank 2013). Sea level rise, storm surges and saline intrusion have significant implications for the contamination of fresh water and groundwater supplies. Bangladesh is also considered to be the most vulnerable country to tropical cyclones (UNDP 2004), facing severe cyclones every three years (GoB 2009), most recently Sidr in 2007 and Aila in 2009. Projections suggest that the frequency and intensity of cyclones will increase over time (IPCC 2007; 2014; World Bank 2013). Murty and El Sabh (1992) estimate that coastal areas of Bangladesh receive nearly 40 percent of the impact of total storm surges in the world. Inundation due to storm surges generated by severe cyclones poses a great threat to lives and the availability of fresh water sources in the coastal region (Dasgupta et al. 2010; World Bank 2013).

Sea level rise leading to the submergence of low-lying coastal areas and saline intrusion in coastal rivers (and subsequently groundwater aquifers) also significantly reduces fresh water availability in the region (Parry et al. 2007; GoB 2009; World Bank 2013). Whilst at the national level, use of improved water sources (as per World Health Organisation [WHO] and UNICEF's Joint Monitoring Program [JMP] definition[2]) is around 97.8 percent, reducing to 80 percent in the 19 coastal districts (BBS and UNICEF 2010). Problematically, a recent baseline study suggests that 57.7 percent of these improved water sources do not actually produce safe water, and total thermotolerant choliform (TTC), arsenic, iron and salinity was found to be higher than the acceptable limits set by the WHO (Water Aid 2012). The study also implies that a large part of the population is being affected. Indeed, one estimate suggested that over 5.5 million people in Bangladesh were exposed to problems associated with climate change (Parry et al. 2007). Using 2011 population census data (BBS 2012), the estimated population to be affected by climate change now stands at around 20 million, over 13 percent of the total population of the country (World Bank 2013).

Climate change impacts not only exacerbate poverty in the coastal regions, but also becomes one of the dominant push factors of internal population displacement and migration in Bangladesh. A comparative analysis of two census reports suggests that although the overall population growth rate of

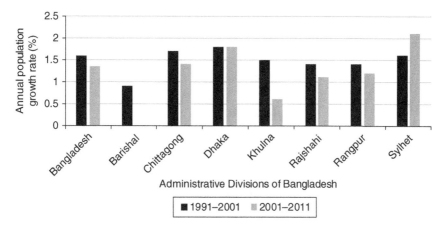

Figure 10.1 Population growth rates in different divisions of Bangladesh
Source: Author's elaboration based on Bangladesh Bureau of Statistics [BBS] (2012).

the country has declined by 0.24 percent between two census periods (from 1.58 percent in 1991–2001 to 1.34 percent in 2001–2011), the two coastal regions Barishal and Khulna show zero and 0.6 percent population growth respectively (Figure 10.1).

Detailed analysis of one of the coastal districts (Khulna), which has a current population of over 2.3 million, suggests that population growth rate has reduced from 1.70 percent in 2001 to −0.25 percent in 2011 (Figure 10.2). Out of 14 sub-districts of Khulna district, 5 rural sub-districts and 3 urban sub-districts show negative population growth rates. The other sub-districts also show very marginal population growth. Not surprisingly, all the rural sub-districts which show negative growth rates (such as Khalishpur and Khanjahan Ali) are closest to the coast, and worst affected by saline intrusion in surface water and groundwater. Other coastal districts in the region show similar patterns, reconfirming that many areas are becoming uninhabitable, and people are moving away from coastal regions. Whilst there are multiple processes affecting movement of people, lack of safe water is arguably one of the key factors of this out-migration.

In Bangladesh, this internal migration has huge social and economic implications. One study on economic loss from disaster due to climate change suggests that the average annual economic cost for damage to infrastructure, livelihoods and losses from forgone production due to natural disasters is estimated to be 0.5 to 1 percent of the GDP of Bangladesh (World Bank 2010). This would be much higher if other implications, such as health impacts due to the intake of saline water, unsafe water or other social impacts due to the scarcity of fresh water, were added to costs.

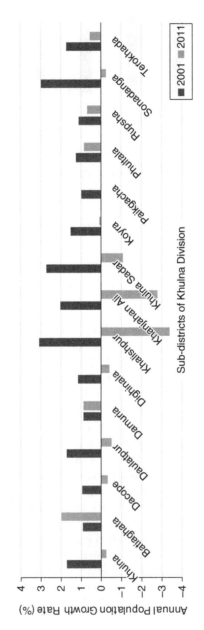

Figure 10.2 Population growth rate in Khulna district

Source: Author's elaboration based on Bangladesh Bureau of Statistics [BBS] (2012).

Urbanisation in coastal Bangladesh and water scarcity in secondary cities

Bangladesh is a rapidly urbanising country. High rural to urban migration and natural growth rates are resulting in the physical expansion of towns and cities. The urban population reached close to 30 percent in 2013, and is projected to outnumber the rural by 2050 (Banks et al. 2011; UN 2011). The urban space of Bangladesh has exceptionally high population density. Excluding city-states and small islands, it has the highest population density in the world with 1,015 people living per square kilometre (Muzzini and Aparicio 2013). The tremendous pace of urbanisation has also given rise to unregulated growth of small and medium-sized towns in Bangladesh (Nazem 2011; BBS 2012). In turn, the urban service sector is under tremendous pressure to meet the increasing demands of this rapidly growing population, and has not grown commensurate with urban growth (Jahan and Rouf 2011; Nazem 2011). As a result, a large number of low-income people remain excluded from essential state services in towns and cities across the country (WaterAid 2012).

In the water sector, this has inevitably resulted in a declining coverage trend. Between 1990 and 2011, urban population had grown by eight percent while the use of improved water sources declined by two percent. Consequently, use of unimproved (or inadequate) water sources in the urban areas has increased by three percent during the same period. Piped water supply into households, which is mainly provided by the government service provider, only increased by three percent during this period, but the other types of improved water supply (i.e. shallow tube-well, deep tube-well) have declined by six percent. However, between 2008 and 2011, access to piped water in households had increased by seven percent, while use of other improved sources had declined by seven percent. This scenario strongly suggests that low-income people living in the slums and squatter settlements in urban areas are the worst affected by declining water service coverage (Opel and Islam 2015).

Figure 10.3 demonstrates the declining access to improved water sources for a rising number of urban centres in Bangladesh. Crucially, measuring progress by considering only the people who use an improved water source provides a very partial picture (Opel and Islam 2013). For example, if service level, in terms of reliability, accessibility, quality and quantity of water available to households is considered, the scenario becomes somewhat different, highlighting the struggle to access safe water, especially for the urban poor (WaterAid 2012).

Extent of water scarcity in two coastal towns in Bangladesh

The experience of water scarcity among the urban poor – 21.3 percent of the total urban population of Bangladesh (World Bank 2013a) – is very high. As shown in Figure 10.3, with growing urban population, the real coverage of safe water in cities is declining. Climate change exacerbates the situation for the urban poor, increasing their struggle for water. Water scarcity relating to climate

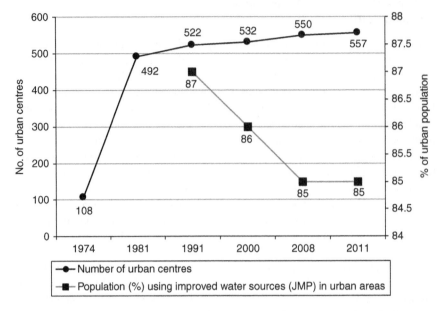

Figure 10.3 Declining access to improved water sources for a rising number of urban centres in Bangladesh

Source: Author's elaboration based on Bangladesh Bureau of Statistics [BBS] (2012) and WHO/UNICEF JMP (2015).

change impacts and its consequences on low-income households is examined in two small coastal towns below. The two towns – Kalaroa in Satkhira district and Paikgacha in Khulna district – are situated in the southern parts of Bangladesh, in the exposed coastal area (Figure 10.4).

Paikgacha: a town with no safe water resources

Paikgacha is a small town situated in the southwest of Bangladesh under Paikgacha sub-district in Khulna district. The total area of the town is 2.52 square kilometres and the total population is around 17,000 (Thames Water 2013[3]). The larger Paikgacha sub-district shows a declining population growth rate, which reduced from 0.98 percent in 2001 to −0.01 percent in 2011. However, the rate of urbanisation has increased from 5.73 percent in 2001 to 6.46 percent in 2011 (BBS 2012a). Paikgacha is a ruralised town with most people engaged in the agricultural sector or fisheries. The poorer section of the population is engaged in wage labour, small business or in the small service sector (Thames Water 2013a). Over 42 percent of people live below the poverty line in Paikgacha, over 16 percent of whom are extremely poor.

Safe water is extremely scarce in this town. Out of its nine administrative wards, four wards are fully, and two wards are partly affected by salinity. The presence of

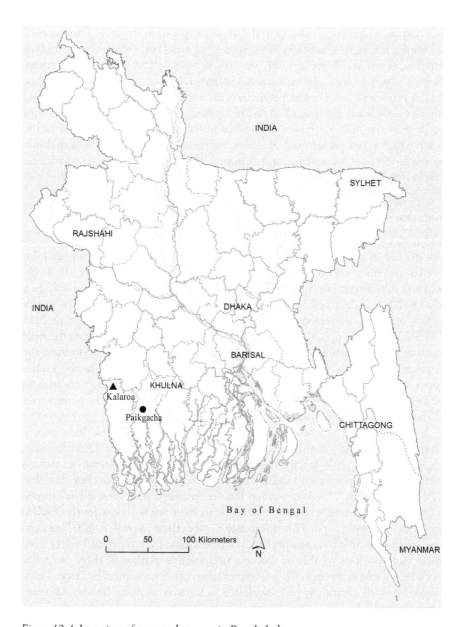

Figure 10.4 Location of case study towns in Bangladesh

Source: Adapted from mapsopensource.com and licensed by Creative Commons 3.0 Unported Licence (http://creativecommons.org/licenses/by/3.0/deed.en_US). The original version is attributed to mapopensource.com and can be found here: http://www.mapsopensource.com/bangladesh-political-map-black-and-white.html.

salinity is much higher than the tolerable limit for human consumption in shallow and deep aquifers, as well as in the available ponds in the area. The presence of salinity is comparatively less in the remaining areas but, unfortunately, shallow aquifers in the wards are seriously affected by arsenic and iron contamination. Recently, two arsenic and iron removal plants have been installed in the town by the private sector. They run commercially and have already developed a good client base. However, these plants do not have a piped network, but supply door to door in ten litre bottles to paying customers. Whilst there is a pond in the town which is not yet affected by arsenic and iron, the water is not safe to drink, as residents use it for washing and cleaning. Thus, Paikgacha is a town with no safe water sources.

Kalaroa: a town where water comes from a nearby city

Kalaroa is a small town situated in the southwest of Bangladesh under Kalaroa sub-district in Satkhira district. The total area of the town is 15.07 square kilometres and the total population was 27,250 in 2011. Like Paikgacha, the larger Kalaroa sub-district also has a declining population growth rate, from 1.51 percent in 2001, to 0.71 percent in 2011. However, similar to Paikgacha, the rate of urbanisation has increased from 11.74 percent in 2001 to 12.3 percent in 2011 (BBS 2012b). This means that people are moving towards the city from the rural areas of the sub-district. Agriculture, fishing and the service sector dominate the economy of Kalaroa. Small business, wage labour and the service sector are the main sources of income for poorer residents. Poverty rates are also very high in Kalaroa, with over 49 percent of people living below the poverty level, and over 20 percent of this group being extremely poor.

Safe water is also a scarce resource for the residents of Kalaroa. Most people in the town use shallow tube-wells as their main source of water. Unfortunately, the presence of arsenic and iron is very high in the shallow aquifer. Even though residents are aware of this, most people still use these sources, as they have few viable alternatives. The deep aquifers have increasingly been affected by salinity. There are few deep tube-wells still working in the town with low levels of salinity, so many people depend on this source to meet their water demand. However, there is a high risk that salinity levels will increase over time, and water from these deep aquifers would also become undrinkable. Although there are a few ponds available in the city, the use of pond water is not common practice. There is also no water treatment plant available in Kalaroa, so many households regularly buy bottled water supplied from a nearby city (Satkhira), 18 kilometres away from Kalaroa.

Implications of water scarcity in climate-vulnerable small towns

The implications of groundwater contamination by salinity have inevitably resulted in more people depending upon alternative sources of water. While over

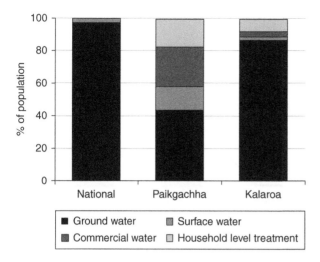

Figure 10.5 Change in the use of water sources
Source: Author's elaboration based on fieldwork.

97 percent of people use groundwater at the national level, only 43.5 percent of people in Paikgacha use groundwater sources due to the spread of saline intrusion, and high levels of salinity in this area, as well as the presence of arsenic and iron in the shallow aquifers. Whilst the situation in Kalaroa is not as severe, the use of groundwater is less (87.1 percent) than the national average (97.9 percent). Figure 10.5 demonstrates water usage in the two towns, compared to the national average. Paikgacha has notably different usage patterns compared to Kalaroa. For example, use of surface water in Paikgacha (14.8 percent) is much higher than that of the national average, and the average use in Kalaroa (2 percent). This is mainly because certain NGO programmes promote and support household-based rainwater harvesting systems. However, this option is not very reliable because of precipitation variability, and is not very accessible to extreme-poor households. Rather, the poor and extreme poor use pond water which is neither suitable nor safe for drinking purposes.

Household-level water treatment is also an option increasingly used by the people in Paikgacha and Kalaroa, 17.2 and 8 percent of households respectively. However, these filters cannot remove salinity from the water, but can only remove arsenic and iron. Installation and maintenance costs of these filters are usually beyond the affordability of the poorest people, thus, this option is only used by better-off households. The increase of saline intrusion in these two towns also means that household-level water filtration may not be a feasible option in the longer run due to unavailability of saline-free treatable water in the area, with implications for the health and well-being of all urban residents.

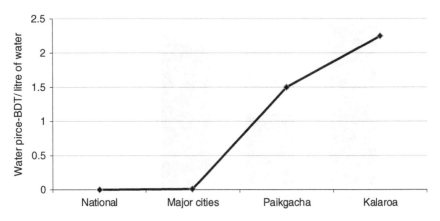

Figure 10.6 Comparison of water prices in different conditions
Source: Author's elaboration based on fieldwork.

The situation of water scarcity in these two small towns has attracted the private sector to enter into the water purification business. As mentioned, two water treatment plants installed in Paikgacha have already achieved a large client-base because of relatively high water scarcity in the city. Although there is no such treatment plant in Kalaroa, the town has been covered by another treatment plant in Satkhira. Nearly a quarter of the households (24.5 percent in Paikgacha and 3 percent in Kalaroa) now use water from these commercial sources. This clearly has financial implications, raising questions of affordability for poor and extreme-poor households. A comparison shown in Figure 10.6 suggests that while water is a free commodity in Bangladesh, those who are fortunate to have piped water connections in their dwellings in big cities (8.1 percent of the total population of Bangladesh) pay much less compared to the people who buy water in these climate-affected coastal towns. Those who have a piped water connection from government service providers in the big cities pay only Tk 0.007 per litre of water, whereas in Paikgacha, the cost of water per litre is 142 to 214 times higher – Tk 1 to Tk 1.5, including transport cost. The cost of water is even higher in Kalaroa because the supply comes from a different city. Here, water is Tk 2.25 per litre, which is 321 times more than the cost of piped water in the big cities.

This not only implies that people have to spend more money on water, but also that the price of water is beyond affordability of the poorest residents. A very conservative estimate suggests that if these areas are considered as 'areas of emergency', and basic requirement of water for 'drinking purposes' (only) is considered as per the standard set by WHO (Reed and Reed 2011), people have to spend 9.36 and 12.3 percent of their monthly income on water in Paikgacha and Kalaroa respectively (Table 10.1). However, these people are not in emergency and require a lot more water for drinking, cooking and hygiene management purposes. As per the Millennium Development Goal (MDG) standard set by WHO

Table 10.1 Percentage of monthly income required to meet drinking water needs

Item	Paikgacha	Kalaroa
Average household size	4.16	4.10
Average monthly household income (BDT)	6000.00	6750.00
Average monthly drinking water needs in emergency (litre/household)*	374.40	369
Average cost of monthly water needs (BDT)	561.60	830.25
Percentage of monthly income required to meet the water needs	9.36	12.30
Average monthly basic water needs (litre/household)**	2496	2460
Monthly cost of basic water needs (BDT)	3744	5535
Percentage of monthly income required for basic water needs	62.40	82.00

Source: Author's calculation based on * 3 litres/day/person basic drinking water needs in emergency (Reed and Reed 2011); ** 20 litres/day/person basic water requirement as per WHO standard (WHO 2015).

(2015): 'Access to drinking water means that the source is less than 1 kilometre away from its place of use and that it is possible to reliably obtain at least 20 litres per member of a household per day' to meet the basic needs of drinking, cooking and personal hygiene. Households in Paikgacha have to spend 62.4 percent of their total monthly income if they want to meet this basic requirement. The situation is even worse in Kalaroa where households have to spend 82 percent of their monthly income to meet this requirement (Table 10.1).

The scarcity of water leading to price hikes in these two cities ultimately implies that although there is some supply from the private sector, poor people do not have access to safe water at an affordable price. This is a violation of human rights since it goes against the standard set by the United Nations, which states that 'water and sanitation facilities and services must be available and affordable for everyone, even the poorest. The cost for water and sanitation services should not exceed 5% of a household's income, meaning services must not affect peoples' capacity to acquire other essential goods and services, including food, housing, health services and education' (United Nations 2011a: 6).

Poor residents of these towns remain excluded and are forced to drink and use unsafe water for their survival. The health and economic implications of this are severe. Whilst there is a lack of data available, one study suggests the estimated salt intake from drinking water by the population in the coastal region in Bangladesh exceeds the recommended limit, and is associated with maternal health problems. This is a cause of serious public health concern for the people living in the coastal areas in Bangladesh (Khan et al. 2011).

Conclusions

Climate change puts additional stress on the already scarce safe water resources globally, and this affects the poor disproportionately. Rapid urbanisation aggravates the situation further. As one of the countries in the world worst affected by climate change, and with its rapid pace of urban growth, Bangladesh faces dual climatic and non-climatic pressures. The rise of private sector providers, as seen in the two case study towns and other neighbouring districts, brings some solutions; however, poor people remain excluded and reliant upon unsafe water sources. Water scarcity and high costs affect the poorest people negatively, forcing them to consume less and use unsafe water for hygiene management as a short-term coping measure, with serious health implications.

Unfortunately, the issue of drinking water has received little attention in the national-level climate change mitigation agenda or global-level climate financing agenda. Current emphasis is mainly on local-level adaptation, but this chapter demonstrates the importance of recognising that without safe drinking water, there cannot be any adaptation. Rather, relocation or displacement from high-risk areas may be the only option. Lower consumption, drinking and using unsafe water cannot be adopted as long-term strategies as health costs would be extremely high. It is therefore crucially important to invest in viable and affordable water treatment technologies that can address the water scarcity problem in the highly affected coastal areas, as well as long-term solutions that can keep the costs affordable for poorer residents. Ongoing discussion about loss and damage in Bangladesh, and other coastal towns and cities at the forefront of climate change, is therefore crucial, to ensure that the poorest are not 'priced out' of viable alternatives for water security.

Notes

1   WaterAid Bangladesh is the country programme of the international non-governmental organisation (INGO) WaterAid.
2   In 2015, an estimated 663 million people worldwide still used unimproved drinking water sources, including unprotected wells and springs and surface water. The WHO/UNICEF JMP for Water Supply and Sanitation began monitoring the sector in 1990 and has provided regular estimates of progress towards the Millennium Development Goal targets, tracking changes over the 25 years to 2015 (WHO and UNICEF 2015: 2). For more information on the WHO and UNICEF JMP see http://www.wssinfo.org/.
3   WaterAid partnered with Thames Water (a private water company in the UK) as part of the 'Small Towns Water and Sanitation Delivery Programme'. The programme targeted numerous small towns in Bangladesh, including Paikgacha and Kalaroa (WaterAid 2010; WaterAid 2011). For more information visit www.small-towns.org.

References

Asian Development Bank (ADB) 2012 *Addressing Climate Change and Migration in Asia and the Pacific* Philippines: Asian Development Bank
Al-Gamal S and Dodo A K 2009 Impacts of climate changes on water resources in Africa with emphasis on groundwater *Journal of Environmental Hydrology* 17 1–11
Baker J L 2008 *Urban Poverty: A Global View* Urban papers (UP 5) Washington DC: The World Bank Group

Bangladesh Bureau of Statistics (BBS) 2012 *Population and Housing Census 2011 Socio-Economic and Demographic Report National Series Volume 4* BBS Dhaka: Ministry of Planning Government of Bangladesh

Bangladesh Bureau of Statistics (BBS) 2012a *Community Report Khulna Zila June 2012 Population and Housing Census 2011* BBS Dhaka: Ministry of Planning Government of Bangladesh

Bangladesh Bureau of Statistics (BBS) 2012b *Community Report Satkhira Zila June 2012 Population and Housing Census 2011* BBS Dhaka: Ministry of Planning Government of Bangladesh

Bangladesh Bureau of Statistics (BBS) and UNICEF 2010 *Progotir Pathey: Multiple Indicator Cluster Survey (MICS 2009)*. Dhaka: Statistical Division Ministry of Planning Government of Bangladesh and UNICEF

Banks N Roy M and Hulme D 2011 Neglecting the urban poor in Bangladesh: research, policy and action in the context of climate change. *Environment and Urbanization* 23(2) 487–502

Bates B C Kundzewicz Z W Wu S and Palutikof J P (eds) 2008 *Climate Change and Water* Technical Paper of the Intergovernmental Panel on Climate Change Geneva: IPCC Secretariat

Bradley R M Weeraratne S and Mediwake T M M 2002 Water use projections in developing countries *Journal American Water Works Association* 94(8) 52–63

Brown O 2008 *Migration and Climate Change* IOM Migration Research Series No 31 Geneva Switzerland: International Organisation of Migration

Calow R Bonsor H Jones L O'Meally S MacDonald A and Kaur N 2011 *Climate Change, Water Resources and WASH: A Scoping Study* Working paper 337 ODI and British Geological Survey

Christensen O B Goodess C M Harris I and Watkiss P 2011 European and Global Climate Change Projections: Discussion of Climate Change Model Outputs, Scenarios and Uncertainty in the EC RTD ClimateCost Project in Watkiss P (ed) *The Climate Cost Project Final Report Volume 1: Europe* Sweden: Stockholm Environment Institute

Dasgupta S Huq M Khan H Z Ahmed Z M M Mukherjee N Khan F M Pandey K 2010 *Vulnerability of Bangladesh to Cyclones in a Changing Climate: Potential Damages and Adaptation Cost* Policy Research Working Paper (5280) Development Research Group Washington DC: The World Bank

Delpla I Jung A V Baures E Clement M Thomas O 2009 Impacts of climate change on surface water quality in relation to drinking water production. *Environment International* 35(8) 1225–1233

Doll P and Zhang J 2010 Impact of climate change on freshwater ecosystems: a global-scale analysis of ecologically relevant river flow alterations *Hydrology and Earth System Sciences* 14 783–799

Foley J A DeFries R Asner G Barford C Bonan G Carpenter S R Chapin F S Coe T M Daily C G Gibbs K H Helkowski H J Holloway T Howard A E Kucharik J C Monfreda C Patz A J Prentice C Ramankutty N and Snyder K P 2005 Global consequences of land use *Science* 309 570–574

Franssen H H 2009 The impact of climate change on groundwater resources *International Journal of Climate Change Strategies and Management* 1(3) 241–254

Government of the People's Republic of Bangladesh (GoB) 2009 *Bangladesh Climate Change Strategy and Action Plan 2009* Dhaka, Bangladesh: Ministry of Environment and Forests

Green T R Taniguchi M Kooi H Gurdak J Allen D Hiscock K Treidel H Aureli A 2011 Beneath the surface of global change: impacts of climate change on groundwater *Journal of Hydrology* 405 532–560

Haines A Kovats R S Campbell-Lendrum D Corvalan C 2006 Climate change and human health: impacts, vulnerability and public health *Public Health* 120(7) 585–596

Intergovernmental Panel on Climate Change (IPCC) 2007 *Climate Change 2007: The Physical Science Basic: Summary for Policymakers.* Working Group II contribution to the Intergovernmental Panel on Climate Change Fourth Assessment Report

Intergovernmental Panel on Climate Change (IPCC) 2014 *Climate Change 2014: Impacts, Adaptation, and Vulnerability* (Part A: Global and Sectoral Aspects) Cambridge and New York: Cambridge University Press

Jahan S and Rouf A M 2011 *Growth of Urban Centres in Bangladesh Urban Futures of Bangladesh: Making Cities and Towns Work for All* Special publication of the 1st Bangladesh Urban Forum December 2011 10–17 Dhaka: Bangladesh

Khan A E Ireson A Kovats S Mojumder S K Khusru A Rahman A Vineis P 2011 Drinking water salinity and maternal health in coastal Bangladesh: implications of climate change *Environmental Health Perspectives* 119(9) 1328–1332

Kumar C P 2012 Climate change and its impact on groundwater resources *International Journal of Engineering and Science* 1(5) 43–60

Kundzewicz Z W Mata L J Arnell N W Döll P Kabat P Jiménez B Miller K A Oki T Sen Z and Shiklomanov I. A 2007 Freshwater Resources and their Management in Parry M L Canziani O F Palutikof J P van der Linden P J and Hanson C E (eds) *Climate Change 2007: Impacts, Adaptation and Vulnerability. Contribution of Working Group II to the Fourth Assessment Report of the Intergovernmental Panel on Climate Change* 173–210 Cambridge UK: Cambridge University Press

Lankao P R 2008 *Urban Areas and Climate Change: Review of Current Issues and Trends* Institute for the Study of Society and Environment Issue paper for 2011 Global Report on Human Settlements National Centre for Atmospheric Research USA

Maplecroft 2011 *Climate Change Vulnerability Index (CCVI)* Available from: http://maplecroft.com/about/news/ccvi.html [Accessed: 30/10/15]

McDonald R I Douglas I Grimm N B Hale R Revenga C Gronwall J and Fekete B 2011 Implications of fast urban growth for freshwater provision *Ambio* 40 437–447

McDonald R Weber K Padowski J Flörke M Schneider C Green P A Gleeson T Eckman S Lehner B Balk D Boucher T Grill G and Montgomery M 2014 Water on an urban planet: urbanization and the reach of urban water infrastructure *Global Environmental Change* 27 96–105

Millar I 2007 *Water Pressure: Climate Change and Adaptation in the Niger River Basin* International Institute for Environment and Development (IIED) UK

Murdoch P S Baron J S and Miller T L 2000 Potential effects of climate change on surface-water quality in North America *Journal of the American Water Resources Association* 36(2) 34–366

Murty T S and El-Sabh M I 1992 Mitigating the effects of storm surges generated by tropical cyclones: a proposal *Natural Hazards* 6(3) 251–273

Muzzini E and Aparicio G 2013 *Bangladesh: The Path to Middle-Income Status from an Urban Perspective* Washington DC: The World Bank.

Nazem N I 2011 Urbanisation in Bangladesh: Pattern and Process in *Urban Future of Bangladesh: Making Cities and Towns Work for All* Dhaka Bangladesh: Bangladesh Urban Forum

Ng G H McLaughlin C D Entekhabi D and Scanlon B R 2010 Probabilistic analysis of the effects of climate change on groundwater recharge *Water Resources Research* 46(7)

Nicholls R J and Cazenave A 2010 Sea-level rise and its impact on coastal cones *Science* 328(5985) 1517–1520

Nicholls R J Marinova N Lowe J A Brown S Vellinga P de Gusmão Hinkel J Tol R 2011 Sea-level rise and its possible impacts given a 'beyond 4°C world' in the twenty-first century *Philosophical Transactions* A 369(1934)

Nicol A and Kaur N 2009 *Adapting to Climate Change in the Water Sector* Background Note London Overseas Development Institute (ODI)

Opel A and Islam K 2013 *Faecal Sludge Management: An Emerging Challenge for the Cities in Developing Countries* Dhaka: Bangladesh WaterAid

Opel A and Islam K 2015 Water, Sanitation and Hygiene: The Urban Realities in Ahmed M S Islam K K and Bhuiya A *Urban Health Scenario: Looking Beyond 2015* 31–43 Dhaka: Bangladesh Health Watch BRAC University

Parry M L Canziani O F Palutikof J P van der Linden P J and Hanson C E (eds) 2007 *Climate Change 2007: Impacts, Adaptation and Vulnerability. Contribution of Working Group II to the Fourth Assessment Report of the Intergovernmental Panel on Climate Change* Cambridge UK: Cambridge University Press

Ravallion M Chen S and Sangraula P 2007 *New Evidence on the Urbanization of Global Poverty* Policy Research Paper No 4199 Washington DC: World Bank

Reed B and Reed B 2011 *How Much Water Is Needed in Emergencies* Technical notes on drinking water, sanitation and hygiene in emergencies Switzerland: World Health Organisation

Rodell M Velicogna I and Famiglietti J 2009 Satellite-based estimates of groundwater depletion in India *Nature* 460 999–1002

Satterthwaite D Huq S Reid H Pelling M and Lankao R P 2007 *Adapting to Climate Change in Urban Areas: The Possibilities and Constraints in Low- and Middle-Income Nations* Human settlements discussion paper serious Climate change and cities (1) London International Institute for Environment and Development (IIED)

Taylor R G Scanlon B Doll P Rodell M van Beek R Wada Y Longuevergne L Leblanc M Famiglietti J Edmunds M Konikow L Green T Chen J Taniguchi M Bierkens M MacDonald A Fan Y Maxwel R Yechieli Y Gurdak J Allen D Shamsudduha M Hiscock K Yeh P Holman I and Treidel H 2013 Ground water and climate change *Nature Climate Change* 3 322–329

Thames Water 2013 *Paikgacha* Available from: http://www.thameswater.co.uk/about-us/14260.htm [Accessed: 29/10/15]

Thames Water 2013a *'We're half way there' Team Thames in Bangladesh* Thames 4 Bangladesh End of Year 2 Review Available from: http://www.thameswater.co.uk/aboutus/Thames4 Bangladesh-May-2013.pdf [Accessed: 29/10/15]

United Nations (UN) 2011 *World Urbanization Prospects: The 2011 Revision* Department of Economic and Social Affairs United Nations

United Nations (UN) 2011a *The Human Right to Water and Sanitation Media Brief* Available from: http://www.un.org/waterforlifedecade/pdf/human_right_to_water_and_sanitation_media_brief.pdf [Accessed: 23/10/15]

United Nations Development Programme (UNDP) 2004 *A Global Report: Reducing Disaster Risk: A Challenge for Development* Bureau for Crisis Prevention and Recovery UNDP

WaterAid 2010 *Small Town Water and Sanitation Delivery: Taking a Wider View* WaterAid (Online)

WaterAid 2011 *Small Town Learning Review: The Synthesis Report of a Four Country Study* WaterAid (Online)

WaterAid 2012 *State of Water, Sanitation and Hygiene in Hard-to-Reach Areas of Bangladesh: A Baseline Study* Internal Report Dhaka: Bangladesh WaterAid Available from: http://www.wateraid.org/~/media/Publications/Small-towns-learning-review-synthesis-report.pdf. [Accessed: 16/2/2016]

Whitehead P G Wilby L R Battarbee R W Kernan M and Wade A J 2009 A review of the potential impacts of climate change on surface water quality *Hydrological Sciences* 54(1) 101–123

World Health Organization (WHO) 2015 *Health Through Safe Drinking Water and Basic Sanitation* Available from: http://www.who.int/water_sanitation_health/mdg1/en/ [Accessed: 23/10/15]

World Health Organization (WHO) and UN Habitat 2010 *Hidden Cities: Unmasking and Overcoming Health Inequities in Urban Settings* Switzerland: World Health Organization and United Nations Human Settlements Programme

World Health Organization (WHO) and UNICEF 2015 *25 Years Progress on Sanitation and Drinking Water 2015 Update and MDG Assessment Report* Available from: http://www.wssinfo.org/fileadmin/user_upload/resources/JMP-Update-report-2015_English.pdf [Accessed: 29/10/15]

Wijnen M 2012 *Managing the Invisible: Understanding and Improving Groundwater Governance* Water Partnership Programme Washington DC: The World Bank

World Bank 2010 *Bangladesh: Economics of Adaptation to Climate Change* Washington DC: The World Bank

World Bank 2013 *Turn Down the Heat: Climate Extremes, Regional Impacts, and the Case for Resilience* International Bank for Reconstruction and Development Washington DC: The World Bank

World Bank 2013a *Bangladesh Poverty Assessment: Assessing a Decade of Progress in Reducing Poverty 2000–2010* Bangladesh Development Series Paper No. 31 Dhaka Bangladesh

Part IV

From learning to knowledge, innovation to action

11 Innovation in the context of climate change

What is happening in India's informal economy?[1]

Barbara Harriss-White and Gilbert Rodrigo

Introduction

This chapter draws on research from an Indo-British scientific project on 'Resources, Greenhouse Gases, Technology and Jobs in India's Informal Economy'.[2] It is important to note that unlike other chapters in this volume, this research did *not* examine the everyday lived experiences of urban poverty and climate change in low-income settlements. Neither did it focus exclusively on the urban context. Rather, the research examines whether innovations emerging from India's vibrant and growing informal economy could play a role in a 'low(er) carbon' (low-C hereafter) future. This is an important issue for this volume, as the informal economy is where the vast majority of people living in low-income settlements are employed.

Commonly, informal enterprises – whether of products, technologies or organisational processes – are not seen as being innovative. This chapter challenges this misconception by arguing that the informal economy is a primary source of innovation. It must be noted that while wealth is created by (and within) this sector – some of it legal and some illegal – India's poverty is largely located in the informal economy. However, it also offers opportunities for institutional hybridity, connecting agents and interests at different spatial, administrative and operational levels, of which residents of low-income settlements are an important part.

In the context of global climate change, a low-carbon/low-matter industrial and agricultural revolution is urgently needed (World Bank 2010). Despite the fact that the informal economy accounts for more than 60 percent of gross national product (GNP) and 90 percent of employment (GoI 2012), the informal economy in India seems absent from almost all discussions of any kind of low-C revolution. While cities are accepted as strategic sites for global integration, and key drivers of economic growth and innovation, most of India's population lives in villages and small towns dominated by the informal economy – firms and markets that are not regulated by the state but by local business associations and forms of authority mediated through institutions of identity. The literature on 'mofussil towns' and 'subaltern urbanisation' records huge and persistent deficits in infrastructural provision which evokes stagnation, relative underdevelopment and lack of innovation (Harriss-White 2015).

The research initially posed the question: *If India were to embark on a low-carbon transition, would the informal economy in which nine-tenths of all jobs and two-thirds of GDP are located be a barrier to the innovation needed?* Despite an institutional architecture for renewable energy and energy efficiency (Harriss-White et al. 2009; 2011), and since a low-carbon transition is precisely the opposite direction to India's current development trajectory, there was no direct way of discovering the answer. The question was therefore reframed: *Does India's informal economy innovate?* The research finds that the informal economy in a small Indian town is highly innovative (in many different ways), yet the forms that this innovation takes increase carbon emissions rather than stabilise/reduce them. This apparent dilemma is explored in sections three and four below.

The chapter is broken into four main sections. The first attempts to clarify complex and 'fuzzy' concepts within the informal economy and introduces the research site, the second welds together the fieldwork material and key concepts (innovation and institutional hybridity), the third outlines the diversity of innovative institutions and the fourth highlights key messages and recommendations in response to the questions above.

Unpacking 'fuzzy concepts': innovation and enterprise in the informal economy

In addressing the question of innovation in the informal economy, some points about concepts, discourse and epistemology require clarification at the outset. The terms 'innovation' and 'informal economy' are typical of contemporary social science in generating a repertoire of 'fuzzy concepts' – ones with multiple meanings and many associated thematic subfields. Innovation denotes novelty, but novelty can be relative and is always socially grounded. For every act of invention, there is novelty attached to local economic and social adaptations and adoption. The concept of an innovation system – all the institutions in place to develop, protect, finance, disseminate and commercialise (adapt and adopt) innovation[3] – presupposes the process of invention can be routinised once institutions are in place inside a corporation or a state. That assumption has been widely questioned.

India has a distinctive set of terms for innovation: Indovation, Frugal Innovation, *Jugaad*, Bottom of the Pyramid innovation and marketing (see Prahalad 2004; 2011; Radjou et al. 2012; Birtchnell 2013). However, although low-cost, incremental, corner-cutting bricolage may be incentivised outside research labs, the context is always the corporation and its adaptation to India's low-income mass market. This conceptual family is far from Anil Gupta's 'honey bee' data bank of rural innovation, where rural development is seen as embodying constant adaptive innovations emerging from an indigenous capacity to innovate, far removed from labs (Gupta 2012). Problematically, neither approach ('innovation system' or 'honey bee' data bank) examines the urban informal economy, or the regulation of innovation.

A further distinctively Indian concept is 'enterprise', this time focused on the individual. The noun 'enterprise' is widely used to denote an individual firm – regardless of its capacity to innovate. Generalised to an 'enterprise culture', innovation inside and outside work loses its original Schumpeterian meaning and instead glosses the conformity of subjects to the totalising neo-liberal era (see Gooptu 2009).[4] Clearly, this use of 'enterprise' does not actually mean entrepreneurship. Meanwhile, political anthropologists of knowledge have shown how new practices rest on a base of skilled (but routine) knowledge and physical competence. They show how much innovation is incremental rather than disruptive, and that it is not only the technological researcher (or the manager) but also the labour force that is capable of innovation. Taking note, the question of informal innovation can be unpacked to include:

i) the type and scope of innovation (invention, adaptation and adoption/disruptive versus incremental/sites, products, processes, organisation, technological repertoires);
ii) the question of the state's role in informal innovation and institutional hybrid vigour; and
iii) the extent to which institutions existing in the informal economy parallel those of the 'innovation system'.

Learning from the field: the informal economy in a small Indian town

Based on the assumption that place-specific history can produce insights about more general processes, and responding to calls for research on smaller secondary towns, a single site was selected to investigate the informal economy in India – a small town with a population of one lakh (100,000). This is a town that has been studied through repeat visits since 1972, providing a historical profile and longitudinal analysis of its spatial, economic, social and political transformations. Respecting the request of the research participants, and since the town has very few low-income settlements, the town will remain anonymous and the name replaced by a pseudonym (Town A).

Town A's economic base consists of administrative activity, agricultural marketing, general retail and transport, plus small industrial clusters of food processing, craft textiles, gold ornaments and (recently) an education hub of private colleges. In the town, over two-thirds of livelihoods take the form of self-employment (Srinivasan 2015). The local economy is regulated through business associations rooted in aspects of identity ('town unity', occupation, caste and gender). Half of the 67 presidents of business associations and trade unions first surveyed in 1997 were re-interviewed in 2012, together with focus group discussions (FGDs) with 74 respondents. Presidents were assumed to have been elected to represent their sectors, being knowledgeable, experienced and able to present a third-person account of the sector, rather than an individualised business history. The following discussion outlines some key conclusions from the research.[5] The innovations presented here are then discussed in the context of climate change mitigation, of which the informal sector could play a central role.

Innovation and institutional hybridity

Town A is full of innovative activity, as high aggregate growth is transformed into innovativeness and institutional churning on the ground. These innovations take multiple interlinking forms but can be broken down into inventions, adaptive and adoptive innovation.

Inventive, adaptive and adoptive innovation

Examples of *inventions* were provided by electricians – over 700 of them, mostly rural-urban migrants or commuters, of whom only 20 had any formal educational qualification. Inventions rested on a substrate of 'learning by doing' as electricians are informally formalising their skills through certification from their trade association based on years of work experience. The trigger for innovation has been state failure: in this case wild voltage fluctuations and power cuts which raise the maintenance costs of electrical equipment, most notably irrigation pump-sets. Customers were used as 'research labs', with risk and physical danger being insured in an *ad hoc* way by the trade association. The development and dissemination of innovations adapting three-phase equipment for two-phase power supply were not hampered by lack of property rights. Indeed they were incentivised through a collective culture of collegiality.

Adaptive innovation was common, exemplified in Town A by a 'computer centre' which combined novel forms of collective ownership and part-time management, instalment payment systems, process innovation (3D software), capacity building for product innovation (computer-aided design), capacity building in the English language for poorly educated rural clients and informal/formal certification of competence. This demonstrates a novel adaptive organisational response to lack of adequate capital or adequate demand in which formal educational skills were diffused in to the informal language economy in return for an informal formalisation through certification.

Adoptive innovation was by far the most common form of innovation in Town A. Recalling the wave of innovation adoption characterising the green revolution, this is far from a new process. Yet, the dizzy pace and wide scope of adoption of products, processes/technologies and forms of organisation are without precedent. In the explosion of new products and processes, new knowledge and media, new packaging, branding and competition to defend market shares and forge loyalty, innovation adoption frequently requires the destruction of products and exchange relations for which there are new substitutes. Examples range from local alcohol (which has yielded to mass-manufactured liquor) to shell crushing for paint, hand-washing of clothes, hand crafting of stainless steel and aluminium vessels. Practically all the contemporary replacements require increases in energy and material content. Interestingly, innovations in the formal sector, particularly for finance and exchange were found to be preconditions for informal adoptive innovation. For example, grain sales in the Regulated Market (after decades of failure) triggering new village-level bulking, transport and new sites of quality checking using newly assembled labour forces. In turn, automated teller machines (ATMs) and National Electronic Fund Transfers (NEFT) challenge informal credit, enable new scales of trade and transport, and frequently substitute fixed prices for haggling.

The innovations of *capital* have had ambivalent impacts on labour: informal certification empowers workers and enables them to exit from local relations of control. Local labour markets are becoming increasingly segmented as workers acquire new skills and specialisation. Within a given sector (say construction), contradictory processes emerge, for instance outsourcing versus vertical integration, and elsewhere low-caste female workers are simultaneously displaced in one sector (e.g. rice milling) but then allowed to enter others (e.g. fruit retailing/ tailoring). A comprehensive labour shortage incentivises mechanisation, feminisation and the in-migration of labourers from less-developed states of India. Migrants have then to be taught elementary language skills, as well as the competences of 'unskilled' work. The transformations to apprenticeships necessary for most self-employment also have ambivalent outcomes. On the one hand, increased velocities of skilling, informal certification and gender-specific training versus on the other, increased drop-outs prior to completion of apprenticeships and intensified undercutting with a lowering of standards. Local market spatiality is being transformed through de-spatialised electronic transactions, but the entry of women into artisan services (such as tailoring) also leads to newly segmented markets according to gender, sited in domestic as well as public space.

Town A's wage labour force is also exerting new kinds of agency, demonstrated by simultaneous but class-specific in-migration (for informal wage work in the bazaar) and out-migration (for formal wage work requiring certified education and children for education). This emphasises the complex linkages between spatial and social mobility. *Labour* itself is also capable of innovation, notably at the design stage under the putting-out system for handloom weaving. Supplementary interviews with the town's sanitary labour, transport workers, loading, unloading and portering workforces revealed a fault line between the abundant innovative activity among self-employed workers and owners of small family firms on the one hand, and low-caste wage labour on the other, in which there was a marked absence of change in technologies and work conditions.

Arguably, the small family business (the building block of the Indian economy) has expanded rapidly in the last two decades of 'domestic liberalisation' (Harriss-White 2015). Indeed, the economy is expanding through the multiplication of tiny/small firms which rarely accumulate – Town A is no exception. Not only are all sectors expanding in numerical terms, but new skills generate increasingly specialised firms – the former general-purpose 'hardware' shop (which sold everything from screws and rope to irrigation equipment) has spawned specialised machine tools, white goods, ironmongery and electrical goods, for example. Alongside such incremental change, a new phase of ruptural change is likely to begin. When sons (whose economic socialisation had been kept within a tight circle of kin) have at last started to be educated from a young age to high standards in English-medium schools, they prove less willing than ever to submit to patriarchal authority. When sons, daughters and nephews exit from their hometown, either the family firms collapse or they are replaced by wage labour, and sensitive tasks (such as negotiating credit/haggling over prices which cannot be subcontracted) are replaced 'innovatively' by fixed prices and cash or NEFT payments. The next stage of ruptural innovation is likely to see the family firm replaced by formal branches, franchises and agencies aligned to new scales of sub-national capital.

Institutional hybridity and hybrid informality

While the concept of the informal economy is of lasting value in drawing attention to the limits to existing regulative law, it must not be considered as a blanket category. These days, a firm will typically be registered with the local authority – and perhaps even with the Commercial Tax Authority – but will likely flout the labour laws, transact on verbal contracts, pay local taxes with utmost reluctance and ignore environmental law and rules regulating construction. At the same time, formal and informal institutions are increasingly interdependent – exemplified by the hybridity of education in Town A.

Education doesn't directly increase productivity but enhances access to finance, infrastructure and the state, thus indirectly contributing to productivity. What about innovation? As the powers of family, caste and gender are slowly and unevenly dissolving as barriers to entry, education is emerging both as a labour market requirement and as an indispensable pre-condition to running a small firm. Recent years have witnessed a vast increase in private, 'English-medium' education. Town A has 25 pre-school nurseries, around 100 private schools (some with swimming pools and websites) and 7 private colleges, for example. All have their own bus services. Private education is now part of the town's economic base. Regarded by some as 'private businessmen's playthings', these schools are formally registered, regulated and state-inspected. However, this process is flawed and vulnerable to informal practices such as low and individualised pay, capitation fees (bribes for entry), unregulated teaching standards, even the corruption of examinations. In addition, they are manned by teachers and patronised by students from outside the immediate locality.

The underfunded state system acts as a skills safety net when it receives drop-outs from the private system. At the same time, much innovation is happening in state education. From smaller class sizes, new curricula and the prohibition of physical punishment, to the introduction of activity-based learning-state education and teaching practice is increasingly receptive to (and reflective of) innovation. The research also encountered informal invention in formal education. For example, for children forced to drop out for weeks at a time due to parental sickness and/or the peaked compulsions of work,[6] state-school Parent–Teacher Associations (PTAs) innovatively organised evening classes to help these children catch up. One non-governmental organisation (NGO) was working with local state schools to expand this initiative. However, innovative change is sometimes constrained by the very same state system: party politics swinging between a freeze on teacher recruitment and a failure to allocate recruited teachers to positions, resulting in dysfunctional class sizes, wrecking the capacity of the public system to respond to the legal requirement of 100 percent enrolment and forcing surplus teachers into the private and informal sectors.

Demand for education has generated an explosion of informal tuition centres, which, set alongside apprenticeships, informal training centres, learning by doing, and the trade-assisted dissemination of media messages, complicates the hybrid institutional ecosystem. By 2012, there were over 100 tuition centres in Town A, mostly manned by fresh graduates (often women) or retired teachers, with classes ranging from 15 to 20 at the low end up to 200 at the high extreme. Regular state teachers are not allowed to moonlight (though a few seasonally break the rules). Competition in the parallel informal education system of 'tuitioning' is fierce, with some misleading advertisements of success crowding the advertising hoardings in the town centre. However, an 'education paradox' is at work, for the positions requiring high education in banks, corporation branches and state agencies were seen to require conformity, *not* innovation. In this small town, education is for exit, not for innovation.

Informal innovation in the state

The state is normally assumed to be inefficient and un-entrepreneurial. As with the case of education, and more generally, however, our discussions with the business association presidents, an Electricity Board director, representative of Town A's lawyers, and the leader of the transport workers disclosed the existence of a constant stream of *adoptive innovation*. Along with the education paradox noted above, an 'informality paradox' is at work whereby the state can regulate innovation outside its political reach in the informal economy. Generally such effects fall into the category of unintended consequences which operate at a range of scales. Macro-level reforms to trade policy (reducing direct protection) has led to the scoping of new raw material sources requiring adoptive innovation in mechanisation (for example in yarn). At the state level, indirect support to informal transactions is given by the provision of infrastructure (lowering its transaction costs and facilitating, for instance, new scales of networked specialisation in gold ornaments, processed food, etc.)

At the same time, municipal development can tolerate informal activity (providing sites in municipal marketplaces), or it can forcibly destroy the informal economy, for example when urban beautification and new roads put roadside sites out of bounds, generating new hybrid practices (such as the overnight storing of verge-side stock and small stalls in formally registered, glass-fronted, secure shops). Nevertheless, it may also sustain the informal economy both through social safety net/rudimentary social protection outside work and through supplying a practical alternative wage floor nearby. The Mahatma Gandhi Rural Employment Guarantee Act (MGNREGA) is one example which reduces the impact of risk factors. Thus, the state regulates the informal economy indirectly, selectively and without coherence.

The role of institutions in innovation

Over and above the threats to, and transformations of, the *family firm* (working as self-employed, with or without other family members and wage workers), the hybrid public/private–formal/informal *education system*, and the indirect interventions of the *state* (summarised above), four other kinds of institutions stand out from the research. Two are formally registered but affect informal innovation: banks and business associations (the latter is hardly surprising since we interviewed their presidents). The third is the gold sector and fourth, informal institutions of identity (such as caste and gender) clearly matter to agency and innovation. Each is discussed below.

Banks and finance

The effects of the influx of formally registered national banks cannot be overestimated. First, they encourage innovation in new scales of technology, with subsidised loans encouraging capital bias, which in turn demands physical logistics for high capacity utilisation. Banks also allow working capital loans for pure commerce (forbidden until the late 1990s). There is also no onwards lending into informal money markets. 'As long as we repay the instalments, the bank doesn't interfere at all' was a common phrase among interviewees.

By virtue of their collateral requirements (title deeds, etc.) banks may play a role in formalising the informal economy along the lines advocated so influentially by De Soto (2000). Loans for education and housing have rapidly increased in size and frequency. Formal property may secure (multiple) loans from (multiple) formal accounts that are subsequently invested in the informal economy or lent onwards to others. These are impossible for banks to monitor (reported one bank manager). Title may be vested in a collective (the family) under the customary laws embedded in the constitution, and hard to associate exclusively with an individual. And yet, according to some interviewees, 'there have been problems with duplicate (forged) title deeds'. Certain banks do not require collateral to lend to some occupation groups (e.g. tailors and sanitary workers). Yet the 'new' banks are far from routing the big informal financiers in Town A who remain businessmen (traders and agents), landlords and 'finance corporations' (in which a group of savers, including government employees, invest).

Business associations

Beyond the state's reach, informal economic activity is regulated either as though the law was being enforced, through authority based on identity, or through decisions of business associations. These organisations span the entire spectrum from the formal and nationally federated to the local and non-registered (Basile 2013). Caste remains a crucial element in a corporatist system of economic regulation in which caste ideology is secularised and increasingly internally differentiated, while the institutions of caste move from the domain of culture to that of the economy and are loosely mapped onto business associations. These define economic behaviour, co-opting members across class and thwarting the development of class consciousness. Their regulative roles may include screening entry, apprenticeship, defining contractual measures and types, credit, price control in the 'market' (especially for the labour and derived markets such as portering and transport), working conditions, the guarantee of livelihoods, mobilisation to compensate for accidents and premature death, poverty and social distress. The state also shapes business association activity, with the need to limit the state's intrusiveness (e.g. from the Labour Act; the Packaging of Commodities Act and VAT), to protect members from the police, or to appeal against discrimination, while campaigning (often using bribes) for preferment and for infrastructure, for social rights and contracts. How have business associations themselves innovated?

Many associations exist reactively, spurred by threats. But federation is one innovation that has gathered strength over the last 15 years in Town A. A second is business association support for informal training and the provision of accreditation for skills, a human 'collateral' permitting the development of de-personalised transactions and migration for work. A third is the circulation of trade information, essential for the adoption of innovations from elsewhere. A fourth is the diversification of membership, such that the alignment between caste and trade associations is increasingly weak and acquired skills replace ascribed merit.

Risk protection and the gold economy

Innovation requires risk-taking. For electricians and construction workers this risk may be physical, but for the most part it is financial. We have no direct evidence about the equivalent in the informal economy of venture capital but, since no one mentioned it, conclude that lack of it is not a constraint on most incremental or adoptive innovation. Risk, however, permeates the informal economy, with the labour force facing multiple shocks. Sickness, marriage allowances (despite the downward drift and increasing optionality of dowries), and private school and college education costs are as 'shocking' to the small firm budget as are weather-related downturns or business losses. For shock-absorption purposes, bank interest is not high enough to compete with returns from property and gold, which can be cashed or mortgaged easily. In response to the demand for gold, a large jewellery company is setting up in Town A. And yet, the biggest savers (and lenders) are widely said to be government officials with the least shock-prone work conditions and contracts.

Identity

The informal economy is still deeply embedded in institutions of identity, and their intersection affects agency and innovation.[7] These identities include gender, caste and religious minorities.

- Gender: While women are well represented among classes of workers enduring chronically oppressive conditions, and have entered the labour market as home-workers, no woman was mentioned as an 'entrepreneur' during the research. Educated girls and women aspire to salaried jobs, an educated groom and reduced dowries.
- Caste: Modestly educated Dalits work in fruit and veg, sanitation and recycling, portering, 'rooftop work', blacksmithing, lorry driving and, lately, informal finance. Though one Dalit is the administrator of Town A's municipal bureaucracy, and another is a high-ranking teacher, the well-known role models for Dalits are three illegal moneylenders with large houses, compounds and swimming pools (an innovation in Town A) whose financial careers emerged from portering and fruit and vegetable selling. While most economically active people hanker for exit, Dalit aspirations are different from those mentioned by the 'purer' castes: the police, the army, chauffeuring.
- Religious minorities: For Muslims and Christians, innovative reservations, each at 3.5 percent, have been carved out in state employment but access is reportedly dominated by Christians. Muslim children are educated in Urdu until 6th standard, after which they go to government schools where they are reported 'not always to perform well'. Muslim girls are also starting to obtain education but 'do not transform it into work afterwards' commented one teacher.

Despite the town being a 'low-caste place', it is clear that being a Dalit, belonging to a religious minority and being a woman confine work possibilities for roughly two-thirds of its population to positions where it is much harder to innovate in the informal economy. Ultimately, formal and informal institutions, state, market and pervasive social institutions are intertwined and dynamically unstable. But the institutional nutrient base for innovation spans the bounds of formal and informal regulation in idiosyncratic ways and seems to operate with few interlinkages – even informal ones. The combination of the family firm, education, the (informalised) state, banks and gold, business associations and institutions of identity does not form a coherent structure of innovation.

Low(er)-carbon transition and innovation in informal economy?

This section summarises the relationship between high growth rates and local innovation in the informal economy. It outlines some of the environmental challenges for the town, before offering key insights in a question-and-answer format. Reflections are then drawn about the implications of this research for the question about low-carbon transitions in the informal economy.

New scales of environmental predation

Like everywhere else, Town A is heavily and increasingly dependent on energy from fossil fuel consumption. Competition to control energy flows is conducted outside the arena of the town. For example, the number of petrol stations doubled from 6 to 12 between 2007 and 2012; demand for diesel and petrol tripled and continues to rise, currently averaging around 300 tonnes per station, per week. Fuel is not only used for lorries and cars (neither of which can negotiate the central maze of narrow alleys) in the region in and around Town A, but motorbike ownership is expanding at an estimated rate of 1,000 per month. In turn, demand for diesel power generators is rocketing to substitute for (and complement) the deteriorating electricity supply.

The bourgeois western suburb is said to be mining the water table as unsustainably as if paddy were being cultivated there. The appetite of the fully automated rice mill paddy driers requires wood and husk for firing – up to 30–50 tonnes per month, per rice mill. Some wood comes from farms in a radius of 50 kilometres from the town but some is also hacked from common land – 'I know this is destructive' said one innovating miller. 'Wood cutting' is a further serious problem for the construction industry, for which sand is also mined illegally from the beds of the now permanently dry local rivers (Rajasekharan 2015). Over wide tracts of land, agricultural topsoil is also lifted to provide clay for bricks. Much of this activity is not just informal but illegal. None of this depredation appears to be regulated in practice by the state.

Key questions and answers

1. **Is the informal economy an obstacle to innovation?** Not in Town A. The town can be regarded as an 'innovation crucible'.
2. **What kinds of innovation happen in the informal economy?** All kinds, but mostly adoptive (both incremental and ruptural), for profit but also for other motives: livelihood and the standard of living; the problem-solving mentality celebrated by *Jugaad*; the need to respond to selective state failures in provision, regulation and enforcement; risk minimisation; pre-emptive reactions to threatened change; collegiality/collective advancement and nurture; by labour as well as capital; relying on continuity of knowledge plus new forms of knowledge; involving exit, exodus and destruction.

3. How important is institutional hybridity? Institutions of the state, market and 'civil' society are intertwined. Laws may be selectively ignored, captured or transformed beyond recognition in implementation. Interests in the state create illegal markets and then benefit privately through rent from them. The meshing of formal and informal institutions counters the idea that they are discrete epistemological universes but this does not mean that the formal–informal distinction should be abandoned or that this hybrid 'ecosystem' works in a coordinated systematic way, or that it is immune from contradictions. Institutions serving useful roles in the structure of accumulation (gender for instance) may be barriers to agency and innovation.

4. Is there an institutional cradle like the 'innovation system'? The key institutions mentioned in the narratives of Business Association Presidents were: the family firm (self-employment), education, manifestations of the state, banks and gold, business associations and institutions of identity. However, a coherent informal structure of innovation has yet to emerge and may never do so. Many development processes are interacting in concatenations to produce innovations. English-medium education interacts with local jobless growth to incentivise exit from the family firm at a time when new scales of subnational and national capital are waiting to displace bazaar arrangements with franchises, agencies and branches. Branding/packaging and innovations in electronic banking combine to replace price haggling with fixed prices. Together with the replacement of family labour by wage work, discretionary retail credit is also compromised. While some wisdom stresses the stagnation of mofussil towns (HPEC 2011), this new research shows the informal economy is not resistant to change, but is the dynamic manifestation of India's comparatively high growth rates and the site of all kinds of relatively low-cost innovation. While the developmental synergy between public and private investment has long been stressed, this research also reveals that small-scale private investment is not inconsistent with backwardness in public infrastructure.

5. What are the implications of these findings about innovation for the evolution of new low-carbon technologies and processes? Although this is not an Indian problem but a global one, the scope of informality is distinctively Indian, and the informal economy is *moving in the opposite direction to a low-carbon economy*. For each example of energy efficiency, there are many more requiring energy from fossil fuels and/or the unsustainable plundering of local natural resources.

That the direction of travel is negative is not the product of the informal economy *per se*. It reflects the entire post-independence thrust of industrialisation. A low-carbon economy is a radical novelty, as yet far from being accepted discursively as 'development'. Indeed, advocates of development often resist the idea that carbon emissions must be reduced. Appropriate and superior technology exists that can reduce carbon emissions, obstructed not by patent law but, if at all, by licensing. It is currently designed for a scale above that of the small-town informal economy. One challenge is therefore to scale down (the size of new technology) while scaling up (industrial output). However, the difference in capital intensity between the bazaar and current low-C innovation is further accentuated because many new renewable energy technologies have high capital costs relative to variable ('running') costs – and up-front investment costs are rarely available to informal enterprises (Harriss-White et al. 2009).

In the policy literature on informality, the argument that institutions of property rights and finance must counter pre-emptive informal development is attributed to De Soto (2000). But property rights were rarely mentioned to us as problems in the informal economy: the impossibility of protecting innovation rents promotes rapid diffusion of innovations. Even when products and processes are protected by patents, ingenious attempts are made to reverse-engineer products and technology in the informal economy. Lack of access to formal investment finance is indeed an impediment to those lacking formal titles to property. But bank credit does not always require collateral[8] and once obtained it is easily wired into informal activity. The scale of capital requirements can also be an impediment to innovation, where it tends at present to be relatively small-scale and labour-intensive in small towns, but there is evidence of novel forms of collective organisation to scale up collective venture capital (Rohra 2012, personal communication).[9]

Lack of knowledge is an other obstacle, but there is an insatiable thirst for knowledge and evidence of informal institutions which exist to provide it. The energy sector is where low-carbon transitions must start, and some of the most vibrant capabilities are to be found among informally qualified electricians and engineers. The embedding of the informal economy in institutions of identity might even privilege Dalits, the most socially underprivileged workers, for, despite the chronically oppressive conditions in which they work and despite their eagerness to leave such conditions, many have great practical expertise in energy, and in the management of waste (Harriss-White and Rodrigo forthcoming).

A significant change in political capabilities would be needed, however, to address the two problems of the sluggish transition to low-C technology and the pervasive nature of India's informal economy whose innovative capabilities are not harnessed by the state. There is no indication from our fieldwork as to how it might emerge. However, a *new research agenda* could make progress in the search for a low-C transition. This would include:

a) the material stock and flow accounts of a small town, including its energy economy and construction sector;
b) the waste economy (solid, liquid and gaseous waste from economic activity), its social relations and livelihoods, technologies and regulative institutions;
c) the roles of Dalits (and other 'waste-pickers') in the management of solid and liquid waste, the question whether their potential as leaders in the management of *gaseous* waste should be incentivised, or whether Dalit aspirations to exit the waste sector should not be resisted;

d)   green innovation in the informal economy (exceptionally difficult to locate);
e)   private college education and informality in the privatising knowledge economy; and finally,
f)   the motors and effects of formalisation (the effects on the informal economy of banks, of corporate capital and of the state).

Ultimately, national policy for climate change cannot avoid a confrontation with technological/innovation systems already constructed by specific political interests, vested in existing arrangements, path-dependent and dense in their demands for fossil fuel. This is reflected not in policy statements – for India is committed discursively to solar energy – but in a knot of poorly coordinated regulations – subsidies, tariffs, practices of bank lending, profit extraction and asset ownership – which together lock India into the fossil fuel use that dominates the subsidy bill for infrastructure and other public sector support (WISE 2008). Low-C development is currently conceived as the product of a research, development and diffusion process which cannot do without planning and is assumed to be state regulated (Harriss-White et al. 2009; Ma 2015). (Formal) market forces alone cannot create the new institutions and destroy the old ones in ways appropriate for a new (low-C) industrial revolution.

Notes

1 This chapter is adapted from an earlier version – Harriss-White and Rodrigo (2013).
2 See http://www.southasia.ox.ac.uk/resources-greenhouse-gases-technology-and-jobs-indias-informal-economy-case-rice.
3 A multitude of potential actors, such as producer organisations, research organisations, extension and advisory services, universities and educational bodies, governments and civil society organisations, co-coordinating bodies, individual farmers and farm labourers, and the private sector (including traders, processors, supermarkets, etc.)
4 For an overeducated segment of the labour force even mundane work for a wage in a supermarket is relabelled as 'enterprise' (Gooptu 2009).
5 For the detailed working paper see Harriss-White and Rodrigo (2013).
6 See Roman and Harriss-White (2003).
7 While women are 50 percent of the population, Dalits are around 15 percent and Muslims and Christians about 10 percent.
8 It may rely on collective guarantees, on reputation or on stable income flows.
9 See also http://www.ceew.in/blog/.

References

Basile E 2013 *Capitalist Development in India's Informal Economy* London: Routledge
Birtchnell T 2013 *Indovation: Innovation and a Global Knowledge Economy in India* Basingstoke: Palgrave Macmillan
De Soto H 2000 *The Mystery of Capital: Why Capitalism Triumph's in the West and Fails Everywhere Else* London: Basic Black Swan
Gooptu N 2009 Neoliberal subjectivity, enterprise culture and new workplaces: organised retail and shopping malls in India *Economic & Political Weekly* XLIV(22) 45–54

Government of India (GoI) 2012 *Report of the Committee on Unorganised Sector Statistics* National Statistical Commission Available from: http://mospi.nic.in/Mospi_New/upload/nsc_report_un_sec_14mar12.pdf [Accessed: 28/10/15]

Gupta A K 2012 Innovations for the poor by the poor *International Journal of Technological Learning, Innovation and Development* 5(1/2) 28–39

Harriss-White B 2015 Introduction: The Economic Dynamism of Middle India in Harriss-White B (ed) *Middle India and Urban-Rural Development: Four Decades of Change* 1–28 Heidelberg and New Delhi: Springer

Harriss-White B and Rodrigo G 2013 '*Pudumai*' – *Innovation and Institutional Churning in India's Informal Economy: A Report from the Field* Working Paper available from: http://www.southasia.ox.ac.uk/working-papers-resources-greenhouse-gases-technology-and-jobs-indias-informal-economy-case-rice [Accessed 28/10/15]

Harriss-White and Rodrigo G forthcoming Discrimination in the waste economy: narratives from the waste-workers of a small town *Journal of Social Inclusion Studies* Decennial Volume of the IIDS

Harriss-White B Rohra S and Singh N 2009 The political architecture of India's technology system for solar energy *Economic and Political Weekly* XLIV(47) 49–60

Harriss-White B Rohra S and Singh N 2011 Revisiting Technology and Under-development: Climate Change, Politics and the 'D' of Solar Energy Technology in Contemporary India in Fitzgerald V Heyer J and Thorp R (eds) *Overcoming the Persistence of Inequality and Poverty* Basingstoke: Palgrave Macmillan

High Powered Expert Committee (HPEC) 2011 *Report on Indian Urban Infrastructure and Services Ministry of Urban Development* New Delhi: Government of India

Ma Y 2015 *The Emergence of Low Carbon Development in China and India: Energy Efficiency as a Lens* PhD thesis Oxford University

Prahalad C K 2004 *The Fortune at the Bottom of the Pyramid: Eradicating Poverty with Profits* Philadelphia, PA: Wharton Business Publishing

Prahalad C K 2011 Bottom of the pyramid as a source of breakthrough innovations *Journal of Product Innovation Management* 29(1) 6–12

Radjou N Prabhu J Ahuja S and Roberts K 2012 *Jugaad Innovation: Think Frugal, Be Flexible, Generate Breakthrough* San Francisco, CA: Jossey-Bass

Rajasekharan I 2015 A requiem for rivers *Frontline* July 24 Available from: http://www.frontline.in/cover-story/a-requiem-for-rivers/article7391540.ece [Accessed: 28/10/15]

Roman C and Harriss-White 2003 Behind the looms: on the insecure lives of Tamil Nadu's silk-weaving families *Frontline* 20(24)

Srinivasan M V 2015 [Town 'A's] Workforce: Segmentation Processes and Labour Market Mobility, Self-employment and Caste in Harriss-White B (ed) *Middle India and its Dynamism: Four Decades of Rural–Urban Development in Tamil Nadu* 65–97 New York: Springer

World Bank 2010 *Cities and Climate Change: An Urgent Agenda* Urban Development Series Knowledge Paper 10 Available from: http://siteresources.worldbank.org/INTUWM/Resources/340232-1205330656272/CitiesandClimateChange.pdf [Accessed: 27/10/15]

World Institute for Sustainable Energy (WISE) 2008 *Power Drain: Hidden Subsidies to Conventional Power* A WISE Research Report, Pune India

12 Can asset transfer promote adaptation amongst the extreme urban poor?

Lessons from the DSK-Shiree programme in Dhaka, Bangladesh

Syed Hashemi, Sally Cawood, Noara Razzak, Mamun Ur Rashid and Manoj Roy

Introduction

One in seven of the world's population lives in poverty in urban areas, mostly within the Global South, with limited access to basic services, livelihood opportunities, food security and voice (Mitlin and Satterthwaite 2013). Amongst the urban poor are the extreme poor,[1] largely excluded from poverty estimates and development programmes. According to the World Bank (2013), over 1.2 billion people globally are extremely poor (living below US$1.25 per day). Whilst definitions vary according to country context, official estimates often overlook the poorest within this group – those with an income of less than US$0.50 per day (IFPRI 2007),[2] who suffer from chronic hunger and malnutrition, have inadequate shelter, are highly prone to disease, deprived of [quality] education, and vulnerable to recurring natural disasters (BRAC 2013).

Mainstream adaptation and poverty reduction initiatives arguably remain unsuited to the daily realities and needs of the poorest. This is highly problematic given that the extreme poor live at the front line of climate change impacts in cities – affected both by everyday slow-onset processes and extreme weather events. Bangladesh is a case in point, where the effects of climate variability and change, such as a significant increase in mean temperatures, and extreme rainfall events are already experienced (Shahid et al. 2015). Consequently, the extreme urban poor experience exacerbated levels of (existing) risk and insecurity towards employment, food, dwelling and health.

The mismatch between lived experience, policy and practice reflects the challenges locating, reaching and organising this group. It also reflects social and political apathy, a particular problem in Bangladesh, where the urban poor face 'a double whammy of neglect – both in climate change and poverty policy' (Banks et al. 2011: 17). In Bangladesh, lack of political will to assist this group has resulted in a service delivery gap, filled by non-governmental organisations (NGOs) and donors, with implications for mainstreaming adaptation, urban development and social protection.

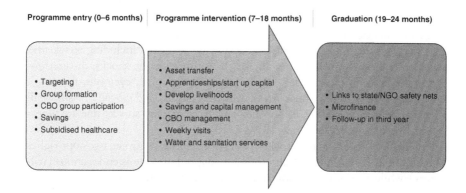

Programme entry (0–6 months)	Programme intervention (7–18 months)	Graduation (19–24 months)
• Targeting • Group formation • CBO group participation • Savings • Subsidised healthcare	• Asset transfer • Apprenticeships/start up capital • Develop livelihoods • Savings and capital management • CBO management • Weekly visits • Water and sanitation services	• Links to state/NGO safety nets • Microfinance • Follow-up in third year

Figure 12.1 Steps towards graduation from extreme poverty
Source: Adapted from DSK (2012).

Against this vacuum of interest, action and policy, the DSK-Shiree project[3] represents an interesting experimental intervention. A donor-funded and NGO-implemented project, DSK-Shiree ran in two phases (April 2009 to March 2012 and April 2012 to 2015), targeting a total of 25,000 extreme poor households in Dhaka city, the capital of Bangladesh (DSK 2012). DSK-Shiree targeted those normally excluded by NGO and donor projects, and whose livelihoods are highly sensitive to extreme weather events. The DSK-Shiree 24-month 'Graduation Model' (Figure 12.1) included a grant (promoting wealth redistribution) of 14,000 BDT (approx. US$180) and/or asset transfer, livelihoods training, healthcare, and collective savings and loan schemes to graduate beneficiaries out of extreme poverty. Additionally, community-based organisations (CBOs) were created with beneficiaries to encourage group savings and learning.

By investigating the DSK-Shiree project, this chapter offers an opportunity to examine the adaptation and/or risk reduction benefits of a development project. It serves to reinforce the argument that in an urban poverty context, adaption money should add to or underpin (not replace) development funds. It also helps to argue why and how wealth redistribution mechanisms (e.g. social protection) should reach the extreme urban poor. These arguments are an essential part of the concept of adaptive development which 'highlights the need for development policy to address existing and anticipated [adaptation] deficits by accounting for risks directly and insistently' (Agrawal and Lemos 2015: 2).

From risk prone to risk averse: adaptation pathways for the extreme poor

Urban climate change risks are conventionally interpreted in terms of environmental risk and physical hazards associated with extreme weather events, but should also consider risk exposure, perceived and actual risks endured by a household or community due to climate variability (Jasanoff 1998; Dickson et al. 2012). The extreme urban poor are exposed to a multitude of hazards across a range of climatic and non-climatic shocks and stressors, such as extreme weather events, infectious and parasitic diseases or accidents including shack fires and road collisions (Adelekan et al. 2015). Within climatic shocks, distinctions are made between rapid-onset events (e.g. heavy rainfall, cyclones, flooding), slow-onset processes (e.g. heat stress, saline intrusion) and cascade or snowball effects (one shock leading to another), such as income shocks due to illness caused by working in heavy rain (IOM 2010).

Risk theory (Shrogen and Crocker 1991) distinguishes between two approaches to handling risk and vulnerability through adaptation. One is endogenous (voluntary) while the other is exogenous (involuntary). Endogenous behaviour is regarded as a preventive measure of adaptation, where individuals, households or communities employ a wide range of steps such as waterproofing of housing or insurance. For the purpose of this study, households practising these behaviours are regarded as 'risk averse'. Exogenous behaviour, on the other hand, is understood as a recovery measure of adaptation, whereby individuals or communities are forced to deal with the after-effects of an extreme weather event. This study regards households practising these behaviours as 'risk prone'. Adaptive capacity of individuals and households is not, therefore, limited to perceived risks of extreme weather events, but also their approach towards, and understanding of, risk and vulnerability, which is informed by their social interactions and cultural context (McNeeley and Lazrus 2014).

This line of thinking assumes that for the extreme urban poor, being risk averse is preferable to being risk prone, underpinning the following core hypothesis to examine the DSK-Shiree project – that extreme poor households who became programme beneficiaries are likely to have become 'risk averse', from a state of being predominantly 'risk prone' before receiving programme support. In operational terms, risk prone households are likely to have fewer resources (i.e. poor quality housing, lower income) and adopt fewer recovery strategies (i.e. mitigating the effects of extreme weather events), whereas risk averse households have access to more resources, and adopt preventative strategies (i.e. savings, repair and self-builds).

Research context and methods

Context

The DSK-Shiree project targeted 10,000 extreme poor slum dwellers in Dhaka between 2009 and 2012, and a further 15,000 from 2012 to 2015 (DSK 2012). It must be acknowledged that in terms of coverage, the project is a mere scratch on the surface in a city where over 35 percent of the 16 million urban inhabitants live in slums (CUS, 2006; Angeles et al. 2009). By concentrating in Dhaka, it also excluded other large metropolitan areas such as Chittagong and Khulna, with slum populations of 35.4 and 19.5 percent respectively

(Angeles et al. 2009), as well as over 300 secondary cities and smaller towns (CLGF 2014).

DSK-Shiree targets the bottom 10 percent of the extreme urban poor population (earning below 5,000 BDT per month), particularly women (who comprise over 90 percent of the membership) living in slum settlements (DSK 2012). It defines 'extreme poor' according to the following criteria: those who work in the informal sector as day labourers, beggars, rickshaw pullers, push-cart drivers, house maids and vegetable vendors, who eat less than three meals per day, and remain beyond the scope of any existing government safety net support (DSK 2012). The primary identification criteria for selecting the target group is based on those paying below 1,500 BDT in rent per month, and not involved in a microfinance institution.

This chapter focuses on the first phase of DSK-Shiree intervention (2009 to 2012) in three project sites in Dhaka – Korail and Kamrangir Char 1 and 3 (Figure 12.2). Key characteristics of the case study settlements are as follows:

- Kamrangir Char 1 and 3 are located on low-lying land in the southern outskirts of Dhaka (near the Buriganga River). An estimated 400,000 people live in this area – the highest concentration of slums in Dhaka city. Average living standards in the area are poor, with many living in temporary bamboo, wood or tin housing. Many households are built on the edges of the river, on raised bamboo platforms. Several leather, textile and pet-food factories lie in close proximity, making the air heavy and pungent, whilst toxic waste flows into the river, contaminating water and soil.
- Korail is the single largest slum in Dhaka, with a population of around 72,000 people, located in northern Dhaka. Its location on the bank of Gulshan Lake makes it extremely vulnerable to rising water levels during times of heavy and extended monsoon. Residents living on the outer edges of the slums have adapted by building their houses on raised platforms.

There is very little government presence in these settlements. The few social safety nets that are provided are extremely limited. Within the slums, healthcare, school facilities, stipend or asset transfer programmes are organised by NGOs such as BRAC, DSK and Proshika, amongst others. Residents in both settlements suffer from poor water, electricity, gas infrastructure and supply crises. Whilst most residents in Kamrangir Char resort to unreliable and expensive illegal utility supply, residents in Korail can now access legal water supply from the Dhaka Water and Sewerage Authority (DWASA).

Methods

Findings are based on in-depth interviews of graduates or beneficiaries (the 'treatment' group) and entrants or non-beneficiaries (the 'control' group), as well as focus group discussions (FGDs), key informant interviews and

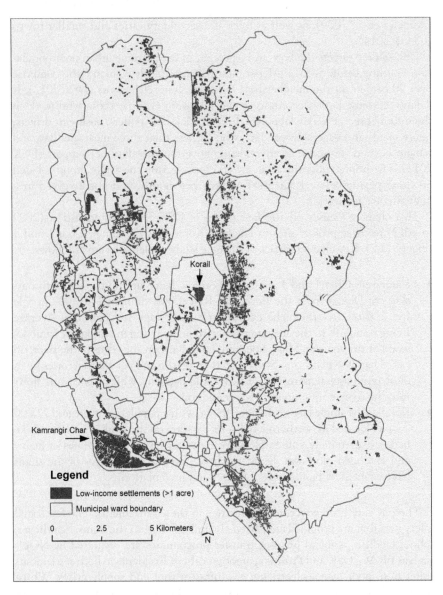

Figure 12.2 Map showing case study settlements within the Dhaka City Corporation

Source: Adapted from Gruebner et al. (2014), who dedicated the dataset to the public domain using the CC0 (Creative Commons) waiver.

observations conducted across the field sites.[4] While the 'control' group were also DSK-Shiree participants, they were early entrants who had not received training or assets at the time of research. The 'treatment' group, on the other hand, had gone through the two-year Graduation Model (Figure 12.1), receiving both training and assets. The methodology was designed so that extreme poor households could be compared prior to and post DSK-Shiree intervention, capturing programme-related effects on household resilience to vulnerability and climate variability.

In total, 27 FGDs and 21 in-depth interviews (seven per site) were conducted with treatment and control groups in each site (KC 1, KC 3 and Korail). Interviews were divided among programme beneficiaries performing very well, medium, or poor, and DSK-Shiree field staff. FDGs were carried out in three phases. In the first phase, field staff and programme participants were asked about the various programme components such as targeting, training, asset transfer, healthcare, monitoring and so forth. In the second phase, field staff and programme participants were asked about their experiences with weather variability, as well as their coping mechanisms for slow-onset and extreme weather changes. Finally, in the third phase, programme entrants were interviewed. One limitation with the sampling procedure was that interviews were conducted only among programme participants. As a result, the extreme poor *not* included in DSK-Shiree were excluded from analysis. The findings therefore reflect DSK members only, and cannot be generalised to other (non-DSK) households.

Understanding how seasonal variation leads to increased insecurity for extreme poor

Bangladesh experiences three main seasons: winter, summer and monsoon, with significant variability in weather. The weather is characterised by a period of light monsoon and extreme heat in summer (March to June), followed by the heavier monsoon season (June to October) and cool winter (October to March). The data revealed the participants' awareness of the changes in weather patterns, and how their everyday lives are affected by this change. For example, one participant noted how: 'weather has become very unpredictable, sometimes there is a storm with very few previous signs and at other times, there is heavy thunder and roaring from clouds but no storms and rain'. Another participant stated that: 'before, winter, summer and rain used to come in the designated seasons ... now heat, rain, cold are all mixed up and erratic'. Participants also noted how, compared to the past, heat waves had increased in frequency and intensity. These changes have implications for the lives and livelihoods of the extreme poor in Dhaka, and support the notion that climate change has already affected weather patterns in Bangladesh (Shahid et al. 2015). Table 12.1 outlines four insecurities of the extreme poor which are exacerbated by seasonal variation in weather.

Table 12.1 Impact of weather variability on insecurity type*

Main seasons	Weather patterns	Impact on employment insecurity		Impact on food insecurity		Impact on dwelling insecurity		Impact on health insecurity	
		Type	Details	Type	Details	Type	Details	Type	Details
Summer	Extreme heat and dry	–	Excessive lethargy, perished/stale shop goods	–	Lack of refrigeration, stale food, lack of gas supply to cook and reheat food, lower food intake, water scarcity	–	Electricity power cuts, frequent fire hazards, sleep outside on ground as houses absorb heat	– –	Sleep deprivation, prevalence of diarrhoea and headaches, heat stroke and water shortage
		+	Longer working (daylight) hours	+	Variety of food available	+	Limited flood damage	+	*None identified*
Monsoon	Heavy rainfall and humid	– –	Reduced working hours, customers and mobility, debt from shop credit. Damage and destruction of shop goods	– –	Lack of fuel (firewood), decreased food intake and poor diet. Less (quality) food available	– –	Roof leaks, flooding in households, destruction of belongings, water pipe leakages and contamination, pests	–	Poor hygiene, contaminated water, (overflowing) latrines, water-borne and skin diseases
		+	*None identified*	+	*None identified*	+	*None identified*	+	*None identified*

Winter	Cold and dry	–	Increased mugging incidents, ill health (colds, coughs) leading to income loss	–	Higher cost of firewood and gas	–	Cold spells, tin shacks not insulated	–	Colds, fever, flu, joint problems, coughs and pneumonia
		++	Longer working hours, more customers resulting in higher earnings	++	Food higher quality (not stale), greater availability of harvested crops and higher earnings to buy food	++	Higher earnings used for house repair/paying due rent and bills. Limited/no flood damage.	++	Greater mobility to/from healthcare facilities. Higher earnings so medicines more affordable

*++ indicates very positive impact, + positive impact – negative impact and – – very negative impact

Source: Authors' elaboration based on FGDs and interviews in field sites.

Employment insecurity

Most of the extreme poor in Dhaka work in the informal sector, running small income-generating activities such as stationery and vegetable shops, tea stalls, rickshaw pulling, domestic work and day labour. The hours they work and amount they earn are heavily dependent on the prevailing weather. As indicated in Table 12.1, monsoon season poses a particular threat to the economic livelihood of the extreme poor, as physical mobility becomes restricted due to heavy rainfall, flooding, storms or blustery winds. In turn, the tendency to borrow from shopkeepers increases dramatically in periods of heavy and prolonged rainfall, resulting in ongoing debt.

For people who have small *tongs* (mobile shops) and work under the open sky (such as fruit or vegetable vendors), it becomes near to impossible to work in times of monsoon rain. There are also fewer customers, as buyers have less disposable income. Construction workers and mud-cutters could not find work in the rainy season. Interviewees whose husbands were rickshaw pullers said that they could not work when it rained, as they would fall sick. Domestic workers complained that they could not go to work in days of heavy rain, and sometimes would lose their jobs, or have their monthly payments slashed. 'We have to show up for work every day, even when it pours and we get sick in the rain, my employer does not pay me on the days I do not show up' complains one FGD participant.

Most interviewees said they fared better in the summer months. The days started earlier and people stayed in the streets later into the night, boosting business. Street vendors, mobile cloth sellers, domestic workers and tea-stall owners earned much more than they did during months of frequent and heavy rain. However, rickshaw pullers and day labourers found it difficult to work for longer hours during extreme heat, returning home early. Some participants mentioned that they could not sleep in the summer, and as a result could not wake up and work early in the morning. Others said that the heat caused headaches and nausea and it was difficult to keep working when someone fell sick. Those who sold food materials found that their food went stale. This demonstrates the unequal experience (according to employment type) in summer. In general, almost every interviewee mentioned that he/she earned most in times of Ramadan, Eid and during winter. The cool temperature and lack of rain meant that people could work longer hours.

Food insecurity

Food insecurity is directly linked with income. Therefore, by default, many interviewees mentioned that they were more food insecure during the monsoon season, when their income was the lowest. This relates to two factors. First, that food prices increase when vast rural areas are flooded, shrinking supply to urban areas. People also have less disposable income, because they work fewer hours during extreme rain, or family members suffer from water-borne diseases such as typhoid, diarrhoea, jaundice and fever. Most interviewees mentioned that they decreased the quality of food, and bought more grains but less fish, eggs or poultry. Secondly, when individual households flood during rainy season, residents have to consume low-quality food like dry bread or husk rice from the shops, as most people cannot cook in their houses. When rain leaks or floods households, the *lakri* (firewood) and mud-stoves get wet, making it impossible to cook. Availability of clean drinking water is also threatened in monsoon, as floodwater contaminates water stored in the households.

Although food security generally improved in the summer, many interviewees said that the food they cooked went stale from the heat, causing diarrhoea. Since gas supply is scarce and other fuel alternatives are expensive, cooked food could not be reheated regularly. Finally, winter months ensured that almost all interviewees had greater food security. Vegetables and newly harvested crops meant that food prices were lower than the summer and monsoon months, and cooked food did not go stale as easily. However, prices of *lakri* and kerosene went up in winter and gas supply dwindled, forcing households to switch to expensive alternatives. As Nazma Begum aptly states: 'People dream about their own houses, and we dream about *lakri*. In times of shortages, we don't worry about rice but about *lakri*!'

Dwelling insecurity

Dwelling insecurity relates to all risk associated with the household (i.e. physical structure, fire and lack of secure tenure). The poor structural quality of housing in slums means that inhabitants face severe dwelling risks due to unpredictable extreme weather events. A vast majority of the houses are either *kutcha* (flimsy and temporary) or *semi-pacca* (mixed building materials and temporary). Most houses have mud floors which sink and collapse during floods in the monsoon season. Rain also leaks into the *kutcha* and *semi-pacca* houses during extreme rainfall, damaging furniture and personal belongings. Many interviewees said that they could not sleep in their houses during flood, as they would suffer from skin diseases if they walked through dirty flood water.

Pests such as millipedes, frogs, rats and snakes could also enter flooded households. Fatema, who lives in Korail in a tin house, said that even though the floor is cemented, rats have gnawed through:

> We can't keep anything inside the house because of rats. I bought some cereals yesterday and the rats took it. Rats make our lives extremely difficult and their numbers increase in the monsoon season. They have dug holes all over the floor, and we can't even afford pesticides to kill the rats. I blocked the rat holes with mud.

Controlling pests is not only expensive but also time consuming, resulting in apathy towards the problem. On the contrary, instances of extreme heat waves in summer caused many residents to leave their houses and spend the day (and night) in the open. The tin houses absorb heat, making it unbearable to stay

Table 12.2 Achievement of DSK-Shiree: impact of programme components on sensitivities by type*

Sensitivity type	DSK-Shiree programme component					
	Grant or asset transfer	Training	Healthcare	Water and sanitation services	Savings	CBO participation
Employment	●●	●●●	●●	●	●●●	●●
Food	●●	●●	●	●●	●●●	–
Dwelling	●	–	–	●●	●●	–
Health	●	●●	●●	●●	●●	●●

* ●●● (very effective), ●● (moderately effective), ● (average) and – (no effect)
Source: Authors' elaboration based on FGDs, interviews and observations. Criteria adapted from Sen (2013).

inside. Summer months are also dogged by frequent power outages, disrupting the use of electric fans and leading to water shortages as electric motor tanks fail.

Another dwelling insecurity was frequent fire caused by electric circuits, mosquito coils, cigarette stubs and even arson. Fire spreads quickly in the densely populated slums, especially in the dry summer months. During the FGDs, many participants said they live in constant fear of fire. This fear translates into a perennial insecurity of life and livelihoods, as homes or businesses may be destroyed in an instant. As a result, most participants felt reluctant to make improvements to their dwellings.

Health insecurity

As extreme poor households are typically involved in labour-intensive activities (e.g. rickshaw pulling and domestic work) to earn a living, health risks during summer directly affects income and diet. For programme participants, extreme heat during this period brought a number of health risks such as heat stroke, acute dehydration, nausea and physical weakness. Stale food, linked to increased humidity and higher temperatures, caused stomach problems, whereas longer working hours under the sun led to heat exhaustion. On the other hand, during monsoon, the common diseases were cold, fever, diarrhoea, stomach problems, skin allergies and water-borne diseases. Working under pouring rain meant that people suffered from sore throats, colds and fevers with constant headaches and breathing problems. In times of heavy rainfall, shared latrines would also overflow. Wastewater from the latrines mixed with rubbish on the street and residents would have to walk through the dirty water, posing serious health risks, especially to small children and the elderly.

Siddika Khatun, 66, faced several ailments, and felt physically weaker in the summer months: 'My hands and feet shiver, I think this is because of the heat. I don't feel hungry in the summer months, I usually have one meal a day, I don't feel like eating, I lose taste of food. Winter is better, I can eat twice daily'. In the winter months, people faced joint problems, colds and coughs, fever, sore throats, breathing problems and pneumonia associated with extreme cold spells. The lack of adequate healthcare facilities had significant implications for addressing these insecurities. In turn, many households faced financial crisis associated with the high cost of medicines, transport to/from medical facilities and treatment.

Achievements of DSK-Shiree to reduce vulnerability

This section analyses the extent to which the DSK-Shiree project has reduced the four types of insecurity for the extreme poor in Kamrangir Char (1 and 3) and Korail. During the analysis, the treatment and control groups were assessed in terms of how they coped or 'adapted' to the risks posed by weather variability. The initial findings indicated that (as outlined in the hypothesis) extreme poor households (prior to receiving support from DSK-Shiree) mostly took recovery measures and were therefore 'risk prone'. Importantly, after receiving assets, the participants used more preventative measures, and hence portrayed more 'risk averse' behaviour. Table 12.2 provides an overview of the achievements in relation to the four insecurities.

Investigation revealed that the enterprise training, savings and asset transfer programme had the most significant and immediate impact in reducing participants' employment and food insecurity. This is because both the training and asset transfer components helped to diversify income opportunities in a matter of weeks. This in turn translated to greater food security, as the beneficiaries not only earned more in a given month, but were left with extra savings. These savings acted as a backup in months of lower income, ensuring that they could pay their rent and bills, and could be assured minimum food security.

Improved economic security

Interviews with the treatment group revealed that with more diversified income and sufficient assets, they could save regularly in times of higher income, and use savings as insurance (avoiding debt) in months of lower income. Mossamot Alo, a female beneficiary, explains: 'Savings [are] important because I can keep it, [it] will be useful during a crisis. With whatever [is] saved at home, I'll buy raw materials. But I won't use up the DSK savings; I am planning to open my own store.' Crucially, by diversifying her income, Mossamot did not necessarily reduce her exposure to an extreme weather event, but reduced the probability of her income being adversely affected by climatic shocks and stressors.

As indicated in Table 12.2, training sessions were found to be particularly helpful to beneficiaries who were concerned with seasonal low income. DSK staff advised participants that any business will have both profit and loss, and as a result, they needed to save capital in times of high income, which could be used during times of low income. During the monsoon, they advised participants to use raincoats, umbrellas and other waterproof materials to protect their assets and person. DSK staff encouraged participants to conduct market surveys, take loans and do business (e.g. buy raw materials) in groups to lower cost, and cope collectively in times of financial crisis. Overall, the treatment group were better equipped in coping with seasonal dips in income, and took preventive measures for the monsoon season.

On the other hand, interviews with the control group revealed that they took mostly recovery measures, such as borrowing money from neighbours or relatives, and reducing the number of meals per day. The control group also had difficulty obtaining loans, as they could not offer anything as collateral and NGO field staff, friends, relatives or neighbours would not trust them to repay. In terms of both economic and food insecurity, the treatment group demonstrated risk averse behaviour, compared to the risk prone control group.

Improved food security

Increase in income security (due to savings) quickly translated into an increase in food security. The association between savings and food security is evident in Table 12.2. Crucially, coping strategies between the treatment and the control group differed. Whilst the treatment group spent carefully in the monsoon months, and saved a little money for days with limited/no income, the control group borrowed heavily from shopkeepers and paid them back during times of higher income. The coping strategies of the treatment group were preventative (as savings enabled them to be prepare for difficult days), whilst they were reactive in the control group. Many in the control group had to live on one meal per day. However, not all in the treatment groups managed to save and use preventative measures.

Notwithstanding this variability, food security was (generally) higher for project beneficiaries. For example, Asma Begum expanded her catering business and now serves about 35–40 people per day, previously only 7–10: 'My profits have increased a lot. In the past, I could not have three meals every day. But now I can save between 2000–2500 Tk every month, after all expenses are accounted for.' Asma changed her menu in different seasons, in accordance with the availability and affordability of different food products, ensuring a constant profit margin. Again, by having a significant profit margin and savings, Asma did not necessarily reduce her exposure to an extreme weather event, but greatly reduced the probability of her food security being adversely affected.

Improved dwelling security

Reducing dwelling and health risks proved to be harder for the participants. As indicated in Table 12.2, DSK training procedures did not enable them to cope with most of the dwelling risks. However, the treatment group with higher assets and income were generally able to take more preventive measures than the control group by moving into better-quality housing, for example. Assets from DSK diversified income and enabled some beneficiaries to pay higher rent. For example, in the past Mossamot Alo paid 1,000 Tk per month, and now pays around 1,500 Tk:

> My previous house had water shortages and rat infestation. The new house still has rats, but the latrine is secure, and we get water three or four times a day. In my previous house, we were constantly in fear of fire [as] there was a polythene depository nearby. It also got flooded and I once suffered from extreme diarrhoea as a result. In this house I drink water from the tap [and] have not faced any problems yet.

Mossamot ultimately reduced her chances of being struck by an extreme weather event, such as flooding, by moving into better-quality housing, with further amenities.

On the contrary, participants in the control group tended to choose lower-quality housing in low-lying areas which was cheaper but also more hazardous. Shahinur Begum, a non-beneficiary in Kamrangir Char, said:

> We have recently moved into this house. Water from the latrine has nowhere to go except for on the streets. The dirty water clogs the street. Walking on the street becomes a strain. Another problem is the houses are low-lying. My neighbours tell me the rooms get flooded during the monsoon season. I have nowhere to go. Rent is cheap, we have to stay here.

Like Shahinur Begum, many others have no choice but to stay where they are and employ recovery measures. These decisions, prompted by low incomes, ensure that the probability of being struck by an extreme weather event, such as flooding, remained high. In turn, the likelihood of being affected by the adverse effects of flooding such as business loss, damage to or destruction of furniture, household materials, skin diseases and stomach problems also remained high.

Improved health security

Whilst DSK-Shiree staff provided *phitkhiri* (water purification tablets) to treat dirty water, and advised programme participants to boil drinking water, many participants in the treatment group could not always boil the water due to limited gas supply (or firewood) throughout the year. Experiences also varied significantly within and between the control and treatment groups. For example, Mujibur Rahman installed his own water filter (worth 3,000 Tk), whilst Nazma Begum, also a beneficiary, saved money from her small shop selling hardware and umbrellas and combined this with the salaries of her two daughters who work in garments to build a two-floored house made of wood with a secure latrine and independent water supply. On the other hand, Rashida Begum, a non-beneficiary, lives in a cluster of 68 households that share six latrines and two water taps.

Ill health caused by poor sanitation and water quality was one of the primary risks that the participants faced in Kamrangir Char and Korail. However, there were significant differences in how the treatment and control groups adopted coping strategies against health risks brought about by these structural inadequacies. We emphasise that health risks (due to weather variability) were further aggravated by a lack of civic amenities. The control group were more likely to follow recovery measures and deal with the aftermath of these health insecurities, whereas the treatment group adopted preventive measures. In cases when health problems were not treatable at home, many participants went to the DSK satellite clinic where they could buy medicines at half the cost to treat illness. Problematically however, many of the treatment group shared how they did not know where the DSK medical team met every week, and that if they did go, their condition did not improve.

DSK-Shiree experiment and everyday risks for the extreme poor

Overall, DSK-Shiree had a positive effect on the extreme urban poor households in all field sites. Among the programme participants, the treatment group were better able to adopt preventative measures to avoid economic, food, dwelling and health insecurities, exacerbated by weather variability linked to climate change. However, the effectiveness of DSK-Shiree cannot be assessed without understanding the broader *context* in which the extreme poor live. This discussion focuses on two underlying issues in particular – tenure insecurity and socio-political exclusion.

Arguably, tenure insecurity is the most persistent and overarching insecurity for the extreme poor in Bangladesh (Rahman 2001; Ahammed 2011) and indeed across the developing world (UN-OHCHR 2013). Many participants from the control and treatment groups voiced their fear of both political and market-led evictions (e.g. being priced-out by real estate projects, increased rent and service costs). Indeed, a vast majority of those interviewed lived in rented dwellings built on private as well as government land, with little/no tenure security. Many interviewees hoped that they would receive some form of tenure security from DSK or government agencies in the future. In reality, however, a small-scale NGO intervention such as DSK-Shiree could not (and did not), at least directly, improve tenure security. Whilst some beneficiaries were able to move to more secure dwellings (paying higher rent or purchasing land/dwellings informally), lack of formal land title meant that fear of eviction persisted.

A second fundamental daily insecurity faced by respondents was social and political exclusion. This and other research (e.g. Banks et al. 2011; Chapter 7, this volume), shows that extreme poor households are heavily reliant on NGOs, landlords, friends, neighbours, local moneylenders and political elites to survive. These relationships can be exploitative. The threat of violence by political elite and local *mastaans* (musclemen/women) perpetuates the silencing and manipulation of the extreme poor. This emerged in many interviews. For example, Mosammot Alo shared how drug dealers sat on the street she used to commute: 'Those drug peddlers always stare at me when I'm returning home. I think they wonder how much money I'm carrying in my bag'. Mosammot did not inform DSK, because she thought any interference would provoke the men. In other cases, DSK beneficiaries were targeted by muggers (who knew they carried money) and local *mastaans* who controlled the area demanded payments or free items from their businesses. In some cases, DSK beneficiaries had their tea stalls or roadside shops vandalised. DSK advised members how to avoid these risks (e.g. move in groups, avoid carrying large sums of money) but this did not address the deeper threat.

Apart from physical threats, many of the female DSK members faced social discrimination. Rahima Begum, who was abandoned by her husband, explains: 'My husband did not divorce me nor did he let me live with him. I am constantly teased by the women in my neighbourhood. They also torment my parents.' Rahima and her family are not invited to any social events, which aggravates their vulnerability. In times of need, they have no one to rely on. Crucially, the strength of social networks among and between households greatly influences community resilience to climate variability.

The creation of CBOs served to address some of the social and political insecurities mentioned above. CBOs were assigned as 'problem solvers', with questions and concerns voiced in monthly meetings. They resolved conflicts among beneficiaries and between beneficiaries and outsiders. CBOs were also used as savings and training hubs, with members meeting weekly to deposit savings and for training sessions. Whilst the CBOs provided support to beneficiaries throughout the 24-month period, they became less active once DSK-Shiree staff withdrew activities in the project sites. They were not federated across the city. Being wholly local, they struggled to earn their legitimacy to represent the community. This reflects a fundamental challenge for NGO- and donor-led (time-bound) projects, and broader trends in Bangladesh towards an unfederated CBO model.

Arguably, DSK-Shiree operates on two problematic assumptions – that all participants are entrepreneurs, and that CBOs entail equal participation. It is important to recognise that not all members have the desire or the skills to run a small business (often they spend the money elsewhere on household items and rent). Internal and external household dynamics also have a significant impact on the success of small businesses and savings. For example, many female participants passed on the grant or asset to their husbands. The selection of beneficiaries and CBO members also reflected hierarchies within the project sites, with local influential, relatively solvent and well-connected individuals manipulating the selection of certain households, ensuring self-selection, and grabbing leadership positions within CBOs.

Conclusion

This chapter concludes with two main points. First, DSK-Shiree is ultimately an NGO–donor project, which has both positive and negative implications. In positive terms, it is an experimental approach which has proven to be generally effective in reducing the multidimensional and interrelated insecurities faced by the extreme poor, a hard-to-reach group. The various components of the Graduation Model (especially the grant) acted to redistribute wealth from the global and national level to the local. This marks a departure from the prevailing rural bias in redistributing national wealth to assisting the extreme poor in Bangladesh. For example, an estimated 17.5 percent of the population in Bangladesh are extremely poor but only 9.42 percent of extreme poor *urban* households have been covered by a social safety net, compared to a 24.57 percent national average (BBS 2010).

In negative terms, sustainability is a major challenge. This is evident in the creation and subsequent demise of the CBOs, a classic problem with short-term donor-funded projects. It also relates to the extent to which project beneficiaries can maintain long-term employment, food, dwelling and health security in a context of tenure insecurity and socio-political exclusion. Also, the model has not been mainstreamed with national or municipal fiscal policy, meaning that support for the extreme poor ceases when funding (or interest) ceases.

Secondly, weather variability (linked to climate change) clearly has significant impacts on the existing insecurities faced by the extreme urban poor. This was especially the case during monsoon season, but also linked to slow-onset (e.g. intense heat waves) and cascade processes (e.g. extreme heat leading to illness and income loss). The comparison between the treatment and control groups indicated how savings, training, asset and grant transfers enabled project beneficiaries to diversify their income, increase food security, relocate households and avoid ill health. Non-beneficiaries, on the other hand, could not prepare for or overcome these interrelated insecurities. In other words, the treatment group was increasingly risk averse following DSK support, whilst the control group remained risk prone.

Although DSK-Shiree is not a project focusing on resilience or adaptation to weather variability, the programme enabled beneficiaries to better cope with, and prepare for, various climate and non-climatic shocks. Whether this is short-term resilience, or longer-term adaptation, remains to be seen. Arguably, though, this study reflects a need to incorporate development (i.e. infrastructure improvement) *and* adaptation (i.e. damage-resilient livelihoods) into NGO, donor and government policy, planning and practice. The challenge remains how to include the extreme poor in meaningful processes of adaptive development.

Notes

1 The terminology of 'extreme' and 'ultra' poor is often used interchangeably (with ultra poverty being a category *within* extreme poverty, e.g. IFPRI 2007). When poverty is

intergenerational and long term, it is also regarded as chronic poverty (CPAN 2014). Extreme poor is used here to refer to the 'poorest of the poor', whether chronic or not.
2 According to this definition, an estimated 162 million people lived in *extreme* poverty worldwide in 2007 (IFPRI 2007).
3 *Dushtha Shasthya Kendra* (DSK) is a development NGO registered with the Government of Bangladesh Social Welfare Ministry and NGO Affairs Bureau in Bangladesh. Shiree is a UK (DFID) funded livelihoods project.
4 Findings are also validated by insight from PhD work, the EcoPoor Project [www. ecopoor.com] and the ClimUrb Project [http://www.bwpi.manchester.ac.uk/research/ researchprogrammemes/climurb/].

References

Adelekan I Johnson C Manda M Matyas D Mberu B U Parnell S Pelling M Satterthwaite D and Vivekananda J 2015 Disaster risk and its reduction: an agenda for urban Africa *International Development Planning Review* 37(1) 33–43
Agrawal A and Lemos M C 2015 Commentary: adaptive development *Nature Climate Change* 5 185–187
Ahammed R 2011 Constraints of pro-poor climate change adaptation in Chittagong city *Environment and Urbanization* 23(2) 503–515
Angeles G Lance P Barden-O'Fallon J Islam N Mahbub A Q M Nazem N I 2009 The 2005 census and mapping of slums in Bangladesh: design, select results and application *International Journal of Health and Geography* 8(1) 1–32
Bangladesh Bureau of Statistics (BBS) 2010 *Survey on Social Safety Nets Programmes (SSNP) in Bangladesh* National Household Survey Dhaka: Bangladesh Bureau of Statistics
Banks N Roy M and Hulme D 2011 Neglecting the urban poor in Bangladesh: research, policy and action in the context of climate change *Environment and Urbanization* 23(2) 487–502
BRAC 2013 *Targeting Ultra Poor Programme* Available from: http://tup.brac.net/ [Accessed: 10/5/15]
Centre for Urban Studies (CUS) 2006 *Slums of Urban Bangladesh: Mapping and Census* CUS and National Institute of Population Research and Training [NIPORT] Dhaka
Chronic Poverty Advisory Network (CPAN) 2014 *The Chronic Poverty Report 2014–2015: The Road to Zero Extreme Poverty* Overseas Development Institute Available from: http://www.odi.org/sites/odi.org.uk/files/odi-assets/publications-opinion-files/8834.pdf [Accessed: 10/05/15]
Commonwealth Local Government Forum (CLGF) 2014 *The Local Government System in Bangladesh Country Profile Bangladesh* CLGF Available from: http://www.clgf.org. uk/userfiles/1/files/Bangladesh%20local%20government%20profile%202011–12.pdf [Accessed: 01/05/14]
Dickson E Baker J L Hoornweg D and Tiwari A 2012 *Urban Risk Assessments: Understanding Disaster and Climate Risk in Cities* Washington DC: The World Bank
DSK 2012 *Evidence of Eradication of Extreme Poverty in the Slums of Dhaka* Project Evaluation 2009–2012 Dhaka: DSK
Gruebner O Sachs J Nockert A Frings M Khan M M H Lakes T and Hostert P 2014 Mapping the slums of Dhaka from 2006 to 2010 *Dataset Papers in Science* 2014(1) 1–7
International Food Policy Research Institute (IFPRI) 2007 *The World's Most Deprived: Characteristics and Causes of Extreme Poverty and Hunger* IFPRI 2020 Discussion Paper 43

International Organisation for Migration (IOM) 2010 *Assessing the Evidence: Environment, Climate Change and Migration in Bangladesh* Dhaka: IOM

Jasanoff S 1998 The political science of risk perception *Reliability Engineering and System Safer* 59 91–99

McNeely S M and Lazrus H 2014 The cultural theory of risk for climate change adaptation *Weather Climate and Society* 6 506–519

Mitlin D and Satterthwaite D 2013 *Urban Poverty in the Global South: Scale and Nature* London: Routledge

Rahman M 2001 Bastee eviction and housing rights: a case study of Dhaka, Bangladesh *Habitat International* 25(1) 49–67

Sen B 2013 *Breaking the Cycle of Urban Extreme Poverty? Insights from the Mid-Term Evaluation of DSK-Shiree Project* Dhaka: DSK

Shahid S Wang X J Harun S Shamsudin S B Tarmizi I and Minhans A 2015 Climate variability and changes in the major cities of Bangladesh: observations, possible impacts and adaptation *Regional Environmental Change* 1–13

Shrogen J F and Crocker T 1991 Risk, self-protection and ex ante economic value *Journal of Environmental Economics and Management* 20(1) 1–15

United Nations Office of the High Commissioner for Human Rights (UN-OHCHR) 2013 *Secure Housing for Millions Remains a Global Challenge* Available from: http://www.ohchr.org/EN/NewsEvents/Pages/SecureHousing.aspx [Accessed: 25/10/15]

World Bank 2013 *Global Monitoring Report Rural-Urban Dynamics and the Millennium Development Goals* Available from: http://siteresources.worldbank.org/INTPROSPECTS/Resources/334934-1327948020811/8401693-1355753354515/8980448-1366123749799/GMR_2013_Full_Report.pdf [Accessed: 19/10/14]

13 The politics of knowledge and production of vulnerability in urban informal settlements

Learning from Bogota, Colombia

Arabella Fraser

Introduction

Concern that 'poverty is urbanising and needs different thinking on development' (Haddad 2012) continues to make news headlines. There are two key dimensions to this concern in the context of global climate change. First, that the numbers of poor people living in towns and cities of developing countries are growing rapidly. Second, that poor people in urban areas experience hazards differently to those in rural areas, often having weaker social ties (Chatterjee 2011), concentrating in risky locations (McFarlane 2012) and lacking access to formal risk reduction mechanisms (Christoplos et al. 2009). Understanding and addressing the risk of urban hazards for low-income people is therefore a policy relevant area of research within climate change adaptation.

A great deal of work has already been devoted to explore urban risk (Dickson et al. 2012) and inform adaptation (Adelekan et al. 2015). However, urban risk remains a deeply contested concept. The 'actual' risk as measured by experts rarely matches the 'perceived' risk as experienced by laypersons (Jasanoff 1998). Urban policies and actions are often guided by expert-measured risks, with little or no regard of how risk is experienced by people on the ground. This in turn constrains rather than supports adaptation to urban risks by dwellers of low-income settlements.

This chapter examines the construction of urban risk as an entry point to urban adaptation, with emphasis on the '*what, who* and *how*' questions of adaptation. Forsyth and Evans (2013) offer the following rationale for this particular framing of 'adaptation science': that development planning should not predefine the nature of risk and adaptive responses arising from environmental changes or scarcity. Rather, it should ask 'what' is being adapted to (the experience of risk), 'who' adapts (what are the socio-economic barriers to adaptation) and 'how' (how do these actions, adopted by certain groups, reduce vulnerability to environmental change).

Romero Lankao and Qin (2011) outline three paradigms for understanding these aspects of adaptation. First, impact-based approaches rely on knowing future climate conditions to specify what is to be adapted to, but are weak on how people cope and adapt, and who adapts (Ford 2002). As such, a second paradigm is needed, one focused on the vulnerability of social actors and groups, in order to understand the 'who and why' of adaptation. However, this reading of social vulnerability neglects the point that vulnerability approaches can (and should) highlight what local experiences of risk can tell us about what is being adapted to (Forsyth and Evans 2013). Finally, a third paradigm of urban adaptation as resilience stresses the capacities of the urban system (as a socio-ecological entity) to respond to risk. The resilience concept increasingly focuses on actors and power relations key to urban resilience (Pelling 2011; Béné et al. 2012) and engages with how competing understandings of climate risk by different urban actors may affect social learning for adaptation (Boyd et al. 2014).

Several authors have emerged in support of incorporating the 'what, who and how' questions of adaptation, justifying its adoption in this study to analyse a specific urban risk – landslide. The following questions are asked: *What* aspects of landslide risks do poor urban dwellers experience? *Who* constructs these risks and who (re)acts? *How* do these actions contribute to reducing actual and constructed (or perceived) landslide risks? These questions help reveal the role of meaning and identity in shaping responses to risk by poor urban groups, often in contrast to the dominant meanings of risk deployed by more powerful actors. In doing so, this chapter contributes to the urban risks debate in three main ways:

- First, it questions whether official/expert-led risk measurements actually invalidate some forms of urban adaptation such as asset-based adaptation examined by Moser and Satterthwaite (2008). When, for example, people find tenure over their homes (their most important asset) is subject to externally constructed risk, they are likely to prioritise contestation and political routes over investing in their homes to address such risks. This arguably undermines asset-based adaptation.
- Secondly, the research questions if there is a limit to what people can do by using their agency (Bebbington 1999) in contexts where urban risks are constructed externally. In order to properly manage externally constructed urban risks, this chapter shows how people might need to go beyond their individual agency to build networks and forge partnerships with institutions and economic and political elites, indicating supremacy of bridging over bonding social capital in urban risk reduction.
- Thirdly, echoing Williams et al. (2015), people must possess and make use of knowledge. They must know who is constructing the risk and how to influence that construction. Knowledge is not merely the possession of information. Rather, producing knowledge requires interpreting information and organising it into a set of evidence-based beliefs about a particular phenomenon (Williams et al. 2015).

The theoretical foundations of these three core arguments are elaborated in the next section. The subsequent sections are devoted to examining, empirically, three case study communities with differential exposure and vulnerability to landslide risk in Bogota, Colombia. The chapter then concludes with reflections on the implications for understanding urban adaptation.

Conceptualising urban risk and adaptation

Reframing the asset-based approach

Livelihoods approaches can be considered as both a conceptual vehicle and operational framework for understanding social vulnerability to climate risk. This is demonstrated by Moser and Satterthwaite's (2008) assets-based adaptation framework, which seeks to support the protection and accumulation of household assets by different actors at different phases of a disaster cycle (both pre and post), and participatory climate change adaptation appraisals (through which communities diagnose the impacts of climate-related events on household assets and strategies) (Moser 2011). As Moser and Satterthwaite (2008) have noted, however, there is also a need for analysis that moves beyond understanding how vulnerability relates to well-established categories of capital assets, to understanding how other, less tangible aspects of livelihoods affect vulnerability and coping.

Although insights into these less visible dimensions of urban livelihoods (i.e. meaning, identity and cultural practice) are found in anthropological studies of urban life (Holston 1991), this has received little attention in scholarship that takes a livelihoods perspective of urban risk. However, analysis of the less visible dimensions of people's activities does have a relatively long pedigree in livelihoods-oriented research overall (Bebbington 1999). Arguably, a reframing of asset-based approaches to better account for the role of meaning, identity and cultural practice in the agency of households links to debates about the use of livelihoods approaches to illustrate how environmental risks are experienced in context (the 'what' of risk). Here, Forsyth critiques approaches that 'add' a discussion of livelihoods 'on top of pre-existing notions of environmental risk, rather than being a way to specify this risk using the perspectives of vulnerable people' (Forsyth 2007: 95).

In the context of urban climate change risk, it could be argued that this tendency is evident in livelihoods studies which, although rooted in local social contexts, use external (climate or hazard) models as the only way of specifying what risks might be, and/or measure people's experience of risk solely against their recognition of risks as derived from these models. While this data is of course important for the design of adaptation strategies, Forsyth draws attention to the potential of livelihoods approaches to define the localised causes and effects of environmental risks, and highlights how local adaptations might mitigate environmental risk in ways that could be obscured by externally defined, universalistic explanations of biophysical change (Forsyth 2007).

Beyond agency: the role of institutions, networks, power and meaning in adaptation

Building on livelihoods and entitlements approaches to vulnerability, which highlight the importance of social networks in the capacity of households to protect themselves against risk (Pelling 2003; Moser and Satterthwaite 2008), recent scholarship on local-level urban adaptation stresses not only the physical modifications low-income dwellers make to their environment, but also their use of social and political networks to leverage resources, emphasising bridging over bonding social capital (Wamsler 2007; Douglas et al. 2008; Jabeen et al. 2010; Braun and Abheuer 2011).

The nature of the institutional context, and people's access to institutional resources, is particularly important in the context of urban informality (as a critical feature of many low-income settlements), where the 'politico-legal' domain structures key aspects of vulnerability, such as tenure rights and entitlements to infrastructure and services (Roy et al. 2013). Crucially, the ability to leverage resources through collective action is unevenly distributed across households, as urban households with very low asset levels are often unable to spare the time or resources to participate or reciprocate (Moser and Satterthwaite 2008). Beyond seeing the barriers to participation simply as a function of asset constraints, Pelling (2003) highlights how the formation of social capital is historically and contextually contingent, and how the politics of different government regimes can build or erode patterns of social association in ways that affect vulnerability. For example, social organisations may be co-opted or maintained in dependent and clientilistic relationships by political regimes in ways that limit the engagement and flow of opportunities for the most vulnerable households in particular communities (Pelling 2003).

Ultimately, this ties in with the view that livelihoods-based work should re-emphasise the structural factors that influence livelihoods practices and outcomes, away from fully agent-centred applications of assets approaches, which assume households have total control over the allocation and exchange of assets (Haan and Zoomers 2005). This demands that adaptation analysts give greater weight to the role of institutional access and entitlements alongside assets, in ways that recognise how power distributions and political marginalisation shapes the vulnerability of certain groups (Devereux 2001; Keen 2008).

The environmental entitlements approach developed at the Institute of Development Studies (IDS) in the late 1990s further allows us to recognise debates about social meaning, as well as material resources in negotiations over entitlements (Leach et al. 1997). Certain sets of claims may be contested by counter-claims made by other actors, for example when hunters are banned from hunting in a nature reserve by state law but continue on the basis of customary rights they regard as legitimate (Leach et al. 1997). By analysing the meanings held by different actors in different relationships of power, this analysis prompts us to ask about the role of knowledge held by particular actors and, in the context of debates about climate risk, the reception and use of science-based knowledge in poor urban contexts.

Contests over risk: the politics of knowledge and urban vulnerability

Numerous authors writing about urban disaster risk note the potential for societal contestation versus dominant knowledge actors around the causes, nature of and possible solutions to disaster-related risks (Pelling 1999; Mustafa 2005; Aragon-Durand 2007; Rebotier 2012). Perhaps because of its roots in political ecology, this theorisation leans towards an emphasis on struggles over resources and societal resistance to dominant framings. To give one example from Rebotier (2012: 392): 'understanding [the] meanings [of risk] to different social groupings highlights the differences in interest that are part of the struggle to claim rights and resources within the very territories at risk'. The meanings that underpin such struggles are discussed in order to show the dissonance between official and lay understandings.[1]

In his analysis of how conflicting local and state knowledge affects groundwater resource management, Birkenholtz (2008) illustrates how this tension is conditioned by the ways in which people 'see' and encounter the state itself. In stressing the ways in which societal responses work against the state, however, we miss the possible influence of state interpretations of risk on local understandings and actions. Here, Zeiderman's (2013) analysis of urban risk management highlights how new forms of risk governance give rise to new sets of state entitlements, and new discursive frames around which individuals and groups mobilise and negotiate.

There is a need in all of these treatments of the politics of meaning and knowledge to avoid essentialising local and contextual knowledge, or attribute it to social groups without exploring the possible differences in conceptions held by these groups (Robbins 2000; Agrawal 2005). Such differences may in fact be the basis on which people resist the state, as simplifying their social experience (Birkenholtz 2008). Societal agency may also take multiple forms, reflecting multiple positioning vis à vis the state (Li 2007). Given what Roy (2009) describes as the 'inevitable heterogeneity' of informal urban areas, this is a critical point in context. Scholars have certainly suggested that there are differences within informal settlements in how newer and older settlers, and those with different tenure statuses, view and manage risk (Baker 2012), yet, we do not know how this relates to public attitudes towards the state and expert knowledge production. The following section links these conceptual debates with empirical research in Bogota, Colombia.

Research background and methods

The research used a case study of the disaster risk management system in Bogota, Colombia, and in particular the *ladera* or hill-slopes programme, which has a long history of operation in some of the poorest areas of the city. While not a 'climate adaptation' programme, the case study was used as a potential 'analogue' for climate change research into adaptation in informal urban communities.

The *ladera* programme reflects a risk assessment approach reminiscent of an ongoing 'geophysical/technocratic paradigm' in disaster research and management (Varley 1994; Pelling 2003), through which spatial boundaries of high-, medium- and low-level risk are mapped (and then governed) according to physical criteria. Engineers from the disasters agency evaluate the likelihood of physical threat according to the geological and slope characteristics of the area, hydrology (rainfall and ground filtration such as public service networks) and seismic activity. This is overlain with a Physical Vulnerability Index based on assessment of the quality of the housing infrastructure, and therefore the likelihood of damage. On the basis of the identification and prediction of physical risk, physical hazards can be controlled (through infrastructure) and people's exposure reduced. The aim of the programme has been to project (even enforce) the results of these risk assessments, with no active involvement of those affected, both in the assessment process, or programme design.

The research sites for this study were three government designated landslide risk zones in the district of Ciudad Bolivar with a common history of unplanned development. The first zone, known as Altos de Estancia, is reported to be the largest urban landslide zone in Latin America. By contrast, the other two zones – Brisas de Volador and Caracolí – constituted partial areas of a single neighbourhood.

Field research included 85 household surveys, in-depth interviews with individuals and families in the three risk zones and government resettlement sites, as well as interviews with community leaders and key informants. Interviews were conducted with as many different types of inhabitants as possible according to their geographical spread, classified level of risk (high or medium), housing type, political status and activities (e.g. newly displaced communities and older community groups). In addition, 33 detailed interviews were conducted with current and former local government officials. Collectively, the data helps to generate a rich understanding of how responses to landslide risk are framed by individuals and communities in informal settlements in the context of socially embedded meanings and identities, which are in part shaped by the institutional relationships between state and citizen in the risk management programmes being undertaken by the local government.

The 'what' of adaptation: interpretations of landslide risk assessment in the informal settlements of Ciudad Bolivar, Bogota, Colombia

Despite nearly two decades of state intervention in the three sites through infrastructure works, resettlement of communities away from high-risk areas, community education projects and new land use policies, a large number of families still remain vulnerable, and illegal settlements continue to grow (Dickson et al. 2010). Landslide disasters are an ongoing occurrence, particularly during

Table 13.1 Characterisation of state and local responses to landslide risk

	Areas of divergence between perspectives	Areas of convergence between perspectives	Areas of absorption
State perspective	1. Probabilistic/futuristic 2. Universal to a given area 3. Given risk levels based on technical assessment of causes and possible solutions 4. Physically given risk assessment 5. Causes of risk often attributed to individual and community processes of urbanisation	Recognition of localised causes of risk in technical assessments (e.g. poor drainage)	Local perspectives acted on only in emergency situations (when people call to report disasters)
Local actors' perspective	1. Historical/presentist 2. Highly localised/ specific to particular social groups 3. Risk appraisal based on daily experience 4. Risks experienced in the social context of the threat to livelihood and broader sets of social risks (e.g. vandalism) 5. Causes of risk often attributed to state	Role of localised causes (and state failure to act upon them) emphasised in local discourses	Risk assessments integrated into community perspectives at particular moments (e.g. emergencies), in highly localised spaces and among particular social groups

Source: Author's elaboration based on fieldwork.

the biannual rainy seasons. Resettlement has certainly enabled some groups to move away from the zones, but others have remained. The process has also been marked by long delays, reflecting significant tension between state and communities. Table 13.1 summarises the ways in which the knowledge generated through state-based risk assessment relates to the views and attitudes expressed across the three risk zones. It summarises how these viewpoints diverge, converge or integrate/absorb each other.

Interviews across the three risk zones indicated that differing social groups articulated concerns about risk and risk management differently in the context of mixed livelihood aspirations and identities. The majority group were home owners and 'long-term settlers', in that they arrived within the main wave of urbanisation of the zones from the 1990s. For those eligible for resettlement, their main concern was to defend the houses they occupied (at least in value if not

Figure 13.1 High asset home owner's house in the San Rafael barrio, Altos de Estancia
Source: Author's own (2010).

in possession) and ensure that new housing they were offered was suitable. In
Altos de Estancia, an area undergoing resettlement, some inhabitants described
how the biggest implication of being in a high-risk zone was not necessarily the
risks they faced, but the fact that they hadn't been able to carry on building their
houses, as house modifications were no longer permitted (Interview with home
owners 2010).

Some households of higher socio-economic status contested the value of compensation for their existing homes, in cases which reflected the huge financial
and emotional investment of home-building. As one original inhabitant in Altos
de Estancia described: 'All that we were sacrificing (to put into the house) meant
that sometimes we didn't even have money to give a soft drink to the children,
or for their toys, we were putting it all into the house to have what we have
today'. New state-built houses were commonly described as *jaulas* [or cages], in
which extended families would struggle to fit. Most people preferred the option to
take 'used housing' rather than the new builds. However, with strict state stipula-
tions attached to the type of used housing that could be approved for use with
a state subsidy, this process could take years. Furthermore, rental accommodation (offered by risk management agencies if new state housing projects were
unavailable) was deeply stigmatised. Many settlers moved into the zones to own

Figure 13.2 Medium asset home owner's house in the former barrio of Santo Domingo, Altos de Estancia

Source: Author's own (2010).

property, and avoid the problems and cost of renting in the city. Examples of the housing in Altos de Estancia are shown in Figures 13.1 and 13.2.

The desire to leave the zones if one could better one's life, but to leave on one's own terms, led to deeply ambivalent attitudes. One home owning family interviewed in Brisas de Volador had been affected repeatedly by landslides, but had declined the rental option because (until they were offered a full housing subsidy for new state housing) they feared they would 'lose what we have'. Such was the value of one's house that it was common practice to leave a family member in the house, even when the rest of the family moved out, to ensure empty houses were not vandalised.

The critical point for home owning groups was to establish a context of certainty in which they could make decisions. However, decisions about the risk status of particular areas could take time, while restrictions on house building and public service provision applied to risk zones. The tension this created was encapsulated in an interview with one resident of Altos de Estancia who was awaiting news of whether his house was to be included in the high-risk zone. The only solution, he explained, lay with making visits to state offices: 'To see what resolution they give us ... If it's true that we are in a high-risk zone, then they should give us the solution and if not we can finish making good our home'.

For groups of newer settlers, however, and in particular groups of *deplazados* or people formally recognised by the state as having been displaced by the country's political conflict, their classification as illegal settlers (because they had settled after resettlement zones were cleared) meant that the same options were not available to them. For these people, risk zones offered shelter and a foothold in the city from which to establish a livelihood. Their discourses about risk were markedly different to those of home owners, with concerns about landslide risk muted by the immediate demands on their livelihoods. The case of Manuel, a displaced settler who had been living for two years in a cleared area of Altos de Estancia, exemplified this: 'Yes, I knew [about it being a high-risk zone], but it didn't matter to me because what was more important to me was being there in the street with the children, I didn't want that so I made this lot …'.

Household experience of landslide risks also varied, even in areas that were classified as uniformly 'high risk' or 'medium risk' by engineers. Among home owners, household responses were in part based on historical experience and highly localised understandings of where landslides did and could occur within the zones, and in part based on people's ability to take measures to mitigate even the lowest-level effects of living in a landslide zone. To give two contrasting examples, in the barrio of Brisas de Volador, a group of around 50 households were classified as medium risk on the grounds that the effects could be mitigated, but petitioned to be included in the high-risk zone on the basis of the impacts they felt (i.e. humidity causing ill health, attracting mosquitoes and other pests, and leading to cracked walls and housing materials). Crucially, the coping measures they were advised to take by state engineers (such as strengthening contention walls and housing structures), did not mitigate these effects and involved too much time and expense for some households (and had to be re-done after each rainy season). Risk as a social phenomenon had not been factored in.

On the other hand, some households were classified as high risk, but discounted that they were at risk, even if they then left for resettlement projects. Ultimately then, risk as constructed in the state's field of vision (based on probability into the future) wasn't always visible in the landscape for people to 'see'. In the Altos de Estancia risk zone, interviewees would describe their situation relative either to where landslides had occurred in space or in time (as being a specific number of blocks away and more or less recently). These tensions fed into the sense of arbitrariness that people expressed in their analysis of state actions.

Furthermore, many inhabitants perceived that the state agencies would only act to resettle when there was an 'emergency', resulting in either loss of life or property, usually during the winter, or rainiest seasons. This perception also reflected the fact that for some groups, the experience of landslide risk was a constant experience punctuated by moments of 'emergency', with negative repercussions for livelihoods that were ignored by the state. Secondly, the way in which risk levels and prioritisations were set was not comprehensible to inhabitants. Although engineers operated at the plot scale to avoid splitting properties across risk boundaries, neighbours could still find themselves classified differently. 'How is it,' one community leader asked, 'that some houses [in the barrio] are low, some medium or some high?'

Reflecting the dynamism of landslide phenomena, levels and prioritisations also changed over time, while official emergencies in 'medium-risk' zones (which occurred in all three of the zones in 2010) illustrated to people that state risk assessments were unreliable guides for action. The critical point for the house-holds concerned was that this process was poorly understood and created huge uncertainty for their livelihoods. However, there was also deep ambivalence as the dependency on the state to define one's livelihoods through risk assessment meant that, through all the critique of state practices, many inhabitants looked to state assessors to stabilise risk boundaries and levels.

Finally, across all three risk zones, existing inhabitants contested state inter-pretations of the causes of and responsibility for landslides. In particular, they raised questions about whether the state was tackling drainage and water man-agement as a perceived critical cause of landslide, and pointed to the state's role in disaster creation. In the Brisas high-risk zone, the official line that cut the zone into high- and medium-risk areas, in which all those in the upper part were to be resettled, and those below it not, rested on judgements by engineers about slope stability, or whether the ground was firm. Inhabitants, however, reported that the problem lay with water filtration – both from the barrio above and due to problems with broken water pipes and tubes within their sector (as people were resettled, houses demolished and as working tubes were managed informally by groups of neighbours). In the Altos de Estancia zone, a significant amount of urban development was permitted before the area was declared a high-risk zone, and existing and former inhabitants described how there had been excavation to put in new roads, and explosives had been used by the water company when putting in new drainage, which destabilised some areas (Interviews with home owners 2010).

Implications for vulnerability: 'who' adapts and 'how'

The aspiration to establish a home in the city, local experiences of risk as a social phenomenon and lack of trust in state institutions shaped the responses of dif-ferent social groups to the state's presentation of risk. The state constructed risk as a dynamic (but therefore uncertain) *physical* phenomenon to be controlled by altering human exposure. The approach ultimately embeds certain values about how urban citizens should live, and who should be entitled to do so, which are felt as 'identity risk' by residents (Wynne 1996).

While access to housing through risk-related resettlement was a key route through which some groups in high-risk zones were able to reduce their exposure and fulfil their livelihoods aspirations, other groups were excluded, even though they too felt the social impacts of living in a landslide risk zone. Both included and excluded groups contested their risk status and the options proposed by the state. This social ambivalence and contestation was central to understand-ing the social challenges of risk management in the three zones, and ultimately shaped the vulnerability of inhabitants. It affected patterns of exposure to risk, where households remained even when they had the opportunity to leave, and expressed a desire to leave. It also affected the sensitivity of inhabitants remaining in high-risk zones, as the prohibition on building modification and curtailed rights to improved public services (measures designed to deter habitation) exacerbated the nature of risk for residents. For example, provisional and community systems of water and drainage, which could not be upgraded in a risk zone, aggravated erosion (DPAE 2006).

To fully understand how patterns of vulnerability were produced in the risk zones, it is necessary to understand how the agency of inhabitants – embedded in the politics of knowledge discussed above – was shaped by the socio-economic and institutional context. This ultimately influenced the possibilities for households to redefine their livelihoods and their vulnerability through securing alternative housing autonomously or through the state. A central point here is the importance of social and political networks to the exercise of agency.

Employers (particularly permanent employers) and social contacts were central to securing loans and work to pay for alternative accommodation and the down payments required for the resettlement programme. Furthermore, inhabitants used multiple forms of political practice to secure or negotiate state housing (either directly or through local power brokers) from verbal and written petitions against risk management agencies, to court cases, community organising and street protest. Here, political connections could be instrumental, and enable the resources to undertake such activities (which required both time and money).

The research confirmed findings elsewhere, however, that horizontal ties with contacts of the same status could be fragile and easily exhausted (Cleaver 2005). One family in Brisas de Volador reported staying with friends or relatives overnight when landslides occurred, but that this was only possible until the friends or relatives got tired of it (Interview 2010). The importance of gaining access to more powerful networks was exemplified by two contrasting cases from the barrio of Caracolí (Box 13.1) where higher-status political connections facilitated entry into the resettlement programme.

Arguably, the broader institutional context framed what adaptive strategies were available to inhabitants, as well as who could undertake them. The politics of meaning and knowledge around who should be classified as 'at risk' and how risks should be addressed played out particularly in the judicial arena, where people brought cases often with the support of civil defence bodies. These were created with the advent of political and constitutional change in the 1990s, such as the 1991 landmark constitution providing an avenue for redress through the act of 'Tutela', a petition based on the violation of constitutional rights (which was used to defend rights to housing and livelihoods).

However, this political 'space' opened up through broader state reform was often undercut by more proximate state actions in the risk zones. For example,

---

Box 13.1 Contrasting cases from Caracolí

One woman's case illustrated the importance of higher-status connections. This woman, an elderly home owner of 65 living in the top part of the barrio, had secured the support of the community leader through her brother's involvement in the junta, and the support of a local politician through her son, to try and advance her progress in the resettlement programme. With this support and that of a law-yer (paid for thanks to the employment of both sons, in particular the permanent job the eldest son held as an electrician), she had written the previous year to the Personaria and Defensoria as well as the Local Mayor. She said she had been prom-ised a place in a housing project due to be completed in 2011 (the following year).

The case above contrasted starkly with that of a 37-year-old woman living in the lower part of the barrio with her husband, five children and one grandchild. Also a home owner of ten years, she was still waiting to find out if they were to be included in the resettlement programme. In her sector, she said '*no hay junta*' [there is no junta, or community organisation], referring to the lack of interest by the junta in the exclusion of her block from the programme. With her husband out of work due to an accident and responsibility for a disabled son, which limited her capacity to take permanent work outside the zone, she supported a family of eight working by the day in a nearby barrio. Although she had visited the Caja de Vivienda's local office once to enquire about their status, 'there are no resources', she said, 'we just have to wait'.

Source: Based on author interviews with home owners (2010).

---

renting in high-risk zones was a crime and although renters described in inter-views many of the same issues as owner occupiers, they did not engage with the state due to their illegal status. When major disasters did occur, any opportunity for agency was also closed down as (faced with the loss of their homes) people were left with little choice but to be evacuated, often resulting in the breakup of communities.

Conclusion

In the informal urban context, people's experience of risk is framed by their own concerns around housing, shelter, access to services, security, and the possibilities opened up and closed off for them in the arenas of risk management and housing policy (more influential than their ability to engage in short-term coping actions, which most residents recognised as extremely limited in effectiveness). In addi-tion, local responses to risk are affected by trust in the legitimacy and accuracy of state-produced knowledge, the institutions that generate it, and judgements about the causes of and responsibility for those risks (echoing Jasanoff and Wynne 1998; Birkenholtz 2008).

In-depth research in Bogota illustrates the role of meaning, identity and knowledge in determining responses to risk. In particular, it illustrates how low-income urban groups mobilise around risk as experienced in the context of their livelihood claims, needs, values and aspirations, and in relationships with the state and state expertise. These may be highly divergent even within a low-income neighbourhood. State failure to engage with the nature of local knowledge drives resistance and ambivalence to government-led risk reduction programmes, which impacts upon vulnerability. However, the possibilities for low-income groups to redefine their livelihoods – including the risks they face – are enabled and constrained by the social and political networks in which households are embedded. These are both formal and informal, and shaped by relationships of power. Building on these findings to reflect on the implications for urban adaptation, the chapter suggests the need for both vulnerability and resilience theorists to interrogate more closely what risks are being adapted to, how and by whom they are defined. This suggests that there is no singular adaptation pathway in a city but multiple possible pathways pursued by different actors at different scales, which play out in the contested political arenas of urbanisation and urban governance.

In policy terms, the research suggests, as others have for rural areas (Forsyth and Evans 2013), that adaptation planners need to move from a focus on controlling physical hazard to improving access to adaptation options that support local livelihoods. It also points to the importance of integrating knowledge for effective adaptation, and, in particular, building partnerships for learning between local governments and low-income groups. Recommendations to this effect are becoming well enshrined in the broader literature on urban adaptation (see Revi et al. 2014). However, a growing body of empirical literature illustrates the challenges to doing so (Ensor et al. 2013). In Bogota, as for other urban areas, knowledge sharing is challenged by unequal power relations, and the ways in which state power is mediated through formal and informal channels.

Finally, this research touches upon the use of particular policy measures advocated as urban 'adaptation measures', such as resettlement, land use zoning and building control. We must understand how risks are defined as the basis for these measures and by whom, and how this legitimises action by particular actors in particular ways. In the case of resettlement policies in the face of environmental risks, the literature stresses the (valid) need to accommodate people's livelihoods and ensure proper consent (World Bank 2011). However, a further important question is who is defined as 'at risk' and included in resettlement programmes, how they are defined and by whom, and how this affects efforts to manage risk and vulnerability.

Note

1 The authors situate lay understandings in differing psychologies of disaster, the meanings of place for people (Rebotier 2012), experience of multiple and interrelated environmental hazards (Pelling 1999; Mustafa 2005) and disputes over the causes of disasters, including the role of the state (Aragon-Durand 2007), the livelihoods options offered by the state, and behaviour of the state itself (Mustafa 2005).

References

Adelekan I Johnson C Manda M Matyas D Mberu B U Parnell S Pelling M Satterthwaite D and Vivekananda J 2015 Disaster risk and its reduction: an agenda for urban Africa *International Development Planning Review* 37(1) 33–43

Agrawal A 2005 *Environmentality: Technologies of Government and the Making of Subjects* Durham NC: Duke University Press

Aragon-Durand F 2007 Urbanization and flood vulnerability in the peri-urban interface of Mexico City *Disasters* 31(4) 477–494

Baker J L 2012 *Climate Change, Disaster Risk, and the Urban Poor: Cities Building Resilience for a Changing World* Washington DC:World Bank Publications

Bebbington A 1999 Capitals and capabilities: a framework for analysing peasant viability, rural livelihoods and poverty *World Development* 27(12) 2021–2044

Béné C Godfrey Wood R Newsham A and Davies M 2012 *Resilience: New Utopia or New Tyranny? Reflection about the Potentials and Limits of the Concept of Resilience in Relation to Vulnerability Reduction Programmes* IDS Working Paper 405 Brighton: Centre for Social Protection

Birkenholtz T 2008 Contesting expertise: the politics of environmental knowledge in northern Indian groundwater practices *Geoforum* 39 466–482

Boyd E Ensor J Castan-Broto V and Juhola S 2014 Environmentalities of urban climate governance in Maputo, Mozambique *Global Environmental Change* 26 140–151

Braun B and Abheuer T 2011 Floods in megacity environments: vulnerability and coping strategies of slum dwellers in Dhaka/Bangladesh *Natural Hazards* 58 771–787

Chatterjee M 2011 The Flood Loss Redistribution in a Third World Megacity: The Case of Mumbai in Brauch H G Oswald Spring Ú Mesjasz C Grin J Kameri-Mbote P Chourou B Dunay P and Birkmann J (eds) *Coping with Global Environmental Change: Disasters and Security* Hexagon Series on Human and Environmental Security and Peach 5 603–612 Berlin and Heidelberg: Springer-Verlag

Christoplos I Anderson S Arnold M Galaz V Hedger M Klein R.J.T Goulven K L 2009 *The Human Dimension of Climate Adaptation: The Importance of Local and Institutional Issues* Stockholm: Commission on Climate Change and Development

Cleaver F 2005 The inequality of social capital and the reproduction of chronic poverty *World Development* 33(6) 893–906

Devereux S 2001 Sen's entitlement approach: critiques and counter-critiques *Oxford Development Studies* 29(3) 245–263

Dickson E Tiwari A Baker J and Hoornweg D 2010 *Understanding Urban Risk: An Approach for Assessing Disaster and Climate Risk in Cities* Washington DC: World Bank Urban Development and Local Government Unit

Dickson E Baker J L Hoornweg D and Tiwari A 2012 *Urban Risk Assessments: Understanding Disaster and Climate Risk in Cities* Washington DC: The World Bank

Douglas I Alam K Maghenda M Mcdonnell Y Mclean L and Campbell J 2008 Unjust waters: climate change, flooding and the urban poor in Africa *Environment and Urbanization* 20(1) 187–205

DPAE 2006 Technical Concept No. 4426 (Caracolí)

Ensor J Boyd E Juhola S and Castan-Broto V 2013 Building Adaptive Capacity in the Informal Settlements of Maputo: Lessons for Development from a Resilience Perspective in Inderberg T H Eriksen S O'Brien K and Synga L (eds) *Social Adaptation to Climate Change in Developing Countries: Development as Usual Is Not Enough* London: Routledge

Ford J 2002 *Vulnerability: Concepts and Issues* University of Guelph

Forsyth T 2007 Sustainable livelihoods approaches and soil erosion risks: who is to judge? *International Journal of Social Economics* 34(1/2) 88–102

Forsyth T and Evans N 2013 What is autonomous adaptation? Smallholder agency and resource scarcity in Thailand *World Development* 43 56–66

Haan L de and Zoomers A 2005 Exploring the frontier of livelihoods research *Development and Change* 36(1) 27–47

Haddad L 2012 Poverty is Urbanising and Needs Different Thinking on Development *The Guardian* 5 October Available from: http://www.theguardian.com/global-development/poverty-matters/2012/oct/05/poverty-urbanising-different-thinking-development [Accessed: 18/09/15]

Holston J 1991 Autoconstruction in working-class Brazil *Cultural Anthropology* 6(4) 447–465

Jabeen H Johnson C and Allen A 2010 Built-in resilience: learning from grassroots coping strategies for climate variability *Environment and Urbanization* 22(2) 415–431

Jasanoff S 1998 The political science of risk perception *Reliability Engineering and System Safer* 59 91–99

Jasanoff S and Wynne B 1998 Science and Decision Making in Rayner S and Malone E (eds) *Human Choice and Climate Change: The Societal Framework* Vol 1 Columbus OH: Battelle Press

Keen D 2008 *The Benefits of Famine* Athens OH: Ohio University Press

Leach M Mearns R and Scoones I 1997 *Environmental Entitlements: A Framework for Understanding the Institutional Dynamics of Environmental Change* IDS Discussion Paper 359 Institute of Development Studies Brighton UK

Li T M 2007 *The Will to Improve: Governmentality, Development, and the Practice of Politics* Durham NC: Duke University Press

McFarlane C 2012 Rethinking informality: politics, crisis and the city *Planning Theory & Practice* 13(1) 89–108

Moser C 2011 A Conceptual and Operational Framework for pro-Poor Asset Adaptation to Urban Climate Change in *Cities and Climate Change: Responding to an Urgent Agenda* Washington DC: World Bank Publications

Moser C and Satterthwaite D 2008 *Towards Pro-Poor Adaptation to Climate Change in the Urban Centres of Low and Middle Income Countries* Human Settlements Discussion Paper 3 Climate Change and Cities London: IIED

Mustafa D 2005 The production of an urban hazardscape in Pakistan: modernity, vulnerability and the range of choice *Annals of the Association of American Geographers* 95(3) 566–586

Pelling M 1999 The political ecology of flood hazard in urban Guyana *Geoforum* 30 249–261

Pelling M 2003 *The Vulnerability of Cities: Natural Disasters and Social Resilience* 1st ed London: Routledge

Pelling M 2011 *Adaptation to Climate Change: From Resilience to Transformation* London: Routledge

Rebotier J 2012 Vulnerability conditions and risk representations in Latin-America: framing the territorializing urban risk *Global Environmental Change* 22 391–398

Revi A Satterthwaite D Aragon-Durand F Coffee-Morlot J Kiunsi R Pelling M Roberts D and Solecki W 2014 Urban Areas in *Climate Change 2014: Impacts, Adaptation and Vulnerability* Assessment Report 5 IPCC

Robbins P 2000 The practical politics of knowing: state environmental knowledge and local political economy *Economic Geography* 76(2) 126–144

Romero Lankao P and Qin H 2011 Conceptualizing urban vulnerability to global climate and environmental change *Current Opinion in Environmental Sustainability* 3(3) 142–149

Roy A 2009 Why India cannot plan its cities: informality, insurgence and the idiom of urbanization *Planning Theory* 8(1) 76–87

Roy A Hulme D and Jahan F 2013 Contrasting adaptation responses by squatters and low-income tenants in Khulna, Bangladesh *Environment and Urbanization* 25(1) 157–176

Varley A 1994 The Exceptional and the Everyday in Varley A (ed) *Disasters, Development and the Environment* Chichester: Wiley

Wamsler C 2007 Bridging the gaps: stakeholder-based strategies for risk reduction and financing for the urban poor *Environment and Urbanization* 19(1) 115–142

Williams C Fenton A and Huq S 2015 Knowledge and adaptive capacity *Nature Climate Change* 5 82–83

World Bank 2011 *Climate Change, Disaster Risk and the Urban Poor: Cities Building Resilience for a Changing World* Washington DC: The World Bank

Wynne B 1996 May the Sheep Safely Graze? A Reflexive View of the Expert–Lay Knowledge Divide in Lash S Szerszynski B and Wynne B (eds) *Risk, Environment and Modernity: Towards a New Ecology* Thousand Oaks London and New Delhi: Sage

Zeiderman A 2013 Living dangerously: biopolitics and urban citizenship in Bogota, Colombia *American Ethnologist* 40(1) 71–87

14 Mobilising adaptation

Community knowledge and urban governance innovations in Indore, India

Eric K. Chu

Introduction

Indore, a rapidly urbanising secondary city of over 2.2 million people in the central state of Madhya Pradesh, India, has been a pilot city for the Rockefeller Foundation's Asian Cities Climate Change Resilience Network (ACCCRN)[1] since 2009. Approximately 27 percent of Indore's population lives in designated slum settlements that are at the forefront of climate impacts (ICRS 2012). With ACCCRN support, Indore embarked upon a comprehensive climate risk and vulnerability assessment process, conducted community workshops, visioning exercises and implemented several public service delivery pilot projects. These projects focused on increasing community knowledge of climate impacts, finding more effective management approaches for the city's scarce natural resources, and building new local water and sanitation infrastructures in slum settlements across the city. This represents a broader trend in India, where different transnational institutions are increasingly supporting urban climate adaptation programmes that bridge sectoral divides between sustainability, water and sanitation infrastructure, disaster risk reduction, and connects decision-makers across local, state and national levels of government (Sharma and Tomar 2010; Anguelovski et al. 2014; Karanth and Archer 2014).

This chapter chronicles the emergence and subsequent reconstitution of community-level institutions for climate adaptation during and after ACCCRN engagement in Indore. Consistent with current scholarship, local communities are increasingly recognising the need to adapt to climate impacts. However, in addition to this, communities are *actively* fusing actions for furthering adaptation goals with mobilisations against historic developmental injustices. Communities are doing so through creatively framing emerging adaptation needs that are nested in (but also synergistic to) pre-existing development interests, while also building new alliances between municipal and non-governmental actors. This apparent dialectical relationship between municipality and community catalyses governance innovations and reasserts the role of local knowledge in urban adaptation.

Theories of local knowledge in urban climate adaptation

This chapter sheds light on the emerging role of community-level knowledge for implementing adaptation projects on the ground. The following section jux-taposes existing understandings of community-based adaptation (CBA), urban governance and inclusive approaches to adaptation to highlight gaps in theoris-ing the role of local community processes in spurring governance change and innovation around adaptation.

Scholars are increasingly documenting the unequal distribution of climate impacts at the local level, including the justice and equity implications of differ-ing structural and institutional capacities to adapt to such impacts (Aylett 2010; Hodson and Marvin 2010; Barrett 2013; Hughes 2013; Bulkeley et al. 2014). This literature argues that poor and marginalised groups have fewer resources to prepare for, cope with and recover from impacts (Roberts 2009; IPCC 2014), creating situations where climate injustices exacerbate existing local inequities (Barrett 2012; Ciplet et al. 2013). These studies highlight the difficult balance between planning long-term economic development programmes while simul-taneously attending to most urgent local poverty alleviation and environmental needs (Roberts and O'Donoghue 2013). For communities in the Global South, climate actions are often framed within a sustainable development agenda, where solutions are considered inseparable from larger discourses of poverty, globalisa-tion and social justice (Pettit 2004).

Adaptation strategies are often more effective if implemented at the urban scale. Many cities oversee responsibility for managing infrastructure and services that are essential for good living standards, inclusiveness and the reduction of climate vulnerability (Dodman and Satterthwaite 2009). City governments tend to formalise adaptation planning in the form of line departments or laws and legislations in order to strengthen legitimacy and facilitate implementation and coordination across sectors (Anguelovski and Carmin 2011; Carmin et al. 2013). Urban adaptation plans are often motivated by internal incentives, available cli-mate science, and opportunities to link adaptation to ongoing programs (Aylett 2010; Carmin et al. 2012; Hughes and Romero-Lankao 2014; Uittenbroek et al. 2014). Due to uncertainties associated with different methodologies, processes of experimentation have characterised the ways in which cities engage in adapta-tion on the ground (Bulkeley and Castán Broto 2013; Anguelovski et al. 2014; Chu 2015).

For resource- and capacity-constrained cities, the ability to integrate adap-tation into existing development, poverty reduction and disaster management agendas is a cost-effective strategy (Huq and Reid 2004; Sharma and Tomar 2010; Solecki et al. 2011). In these cases, the framing of 'co-beneficial' projects becomes an important guiding principle for planning (Puppim de Oliveira 2013), where the effectiveness of such strategies is often dependent on local participa-tion (Archer et al. 2014; Chu et al. 2015). Involvement of local actors in the design, implementation and monitoring of adaptation interventions is important because climate impacts are ultimately interwoven with specific populations and spatial vulnerabilities (Dodman and Mitlin 2011; Bulkeley and Tuts 2013; Friend and Moench 2013).

Although city authorities increasingly recognise that local actors play a key role in legitimising adaptation practices (Forsyth 2013; Reid and Huq 2014), such participatory processes do not always lead to more inclusive outcomes (Cooke and Kothari 2001; Few et al. 2007). Indeed, participation can be an item on donor checklists rather than a genuine social learning process that builds local awareness and capacities (Ensor and Harvey 2015). In response, growing scholarship on CBA argues that improvements in local adaptive capacity can be tied to efforts to redress socio-economic inequalities experienced by poor communities (Ensor and Berger 2009; Forsyth 2013; Bulkeley et al. 2014). Examples of CBA include the formation of community water supply collectives, local credit mechanisms and the strengthening of social safety nets (Ayers and Forsyth 2009; Magee 2013).

In practice, many CBA initiatives pursue co-learning approaches where local and external scientific knowledge is shared between communities, scientists and development workers (Collins and Ison 2009; Forsyth 2013; Nay et al. 2014). However, CBA projects are largely funded by external donors that assume community coherence, which is often not the case. These critiques highlight the difficulties of elite capture and of sustaining CBA over time. While CBA is a contested concept and practice, the examples from Indore demonstrate that the accumulation of knowledge and practice through CBA initiatives has a legacy that *can* be sustained and *can* be mainstreamed into municipal plans through social learning, with positive implications for different local stakeholders.

As one can see, existing theories of urban adaptation and community engagement emphasise how local ownership over integrating adaptation into local development can facilitate the effectiveness of these programmes (Ebi 2009) and provide opportunities for local innovation (Rodima-Taylor 2012). However, there remains a gap in our understanding of how urban adaptation planning programmes shape (and are reshaped by) local knowledge used to redress pre-existing developmental inequalities. In response, this chapter examines Indore's experience with adaptation, and highlights the role of community knowledge in spurring governance innovations that take into account both development and adaptation needs of the urban poor. While community mobilisations around climate adaptation are a relatively new phenomenon in India, state and local governments are beginning to recognise issues of justice and equity as part of their adaptation efforts (Paavola and Adger 2006; Bulkeley et al. 2013). The experiences from Indore serve as an important example of knowledge co-creation in urban adaptation.

Community development and climate adaptation in Indore

Indore is urbanising at a rate of 40 percent per decade. Approximately 27 percent of the rising population lives in 599 designated slum settlements across the city, at risk from climate-induced water scarcity, urban heat and waterlogging (ICRS 2012). While not all slum residents are 'poor', most of Indore's poorest residents live in these settlements, which lack access to basic services, infrastructure and livelihood opportunities. This chapter focuses on Rahul Gandhinagar, a slum settlement of five thousand residents in southern Indore. Most residents of Rahul Gandhinagar lack formal land tenure and inhabit dwellings without access to municipal water and sewage pipelines. The community is highly vulnerable to water scarcity during dry season and waterlogging during monsoon.

In response to growing climate risks, Indore began adaptation planning in 2009. With support from ACCCRN, the city embarked upon a comprehensive climate risk and vulnerability assessment process, culminating in the release of the *Indore City Resilience Strategy* (ICRS 2012), which identified water, public health and human settlements as sectors most vulnerable to climate impacts.

Using 30 semi-structured interviews (conducted in 2013 and 2014), as well as document analysis, this chapter presents findings on Indore's adaptation planning process to show how urban poor communities are increasingly knowledgeable of changes in their local climate, and are beginning to mobilise to protect their development interests in the context of these changes. Through building a historical narrative supported by illustrative quotes from actors on the ground, this chapter highlights the different local projects that rely on reconstituting old knowledge networks between municipal and community actors, which in turn facilitate the integration of community development needs with emerging climate adaptation priorities. The chapter concludes by arguing that the role of urban authorities in adaptation is not based on the centricity of policy making, but on its role in creating a knowledge-based infrastructure that is synergistic to the developmental needs and adaptation priorities of the urban poor.

Prior to the emergence of climate adaptation as an agenda, however, development policies across Indian cities focused on poverty alleviation, governance reform, economic growth and environmental quality. In Indore, since the early 1980s, different international and multilateral organisations have been supporting these priorities. But because Indore, like all other municipalities in India, is not allowed to directly receive donor funds, this money was first given to relevant state authorities and then dispersed to cities. Community beneficiaries subsequently built upon these external knowledge networks, institutional linkages and funding streams to reframe development programmes according to emerging local needs, as in the case of climate adaptation.

One of the first externally supported interventions to improve general urban infrastructure in the city was the Indore Habitat Improvement Project from 1990 to 1997. With a budget of more than US$15 million supplied by the UK Department for International Development (DFID) to the Madhya Pradesh Department of Urban Development, the project funded road construction, extension of sewage pipelines and treatment plants, and housing up-gradation in low-income communities across the state (Verma 2000). The community development component, in particular, included the creation of neighbourhood groups, vocational training collectives (especially for women) and non-formal education programmes (Verma 2000).

During the 1990s and 2000s, Indore received attention from a number of urban poverty alleviation programmes supported by different national and state institutions. For example, the 1997 *Swarna Jayanti Shahari Rozgar Yojana*[2] programme tackled urban poverty by supporting different household savings groups and credit assistance programmes for micro-enterprises. Similarly, again under a partnership with DFID, the Madhya Pradesh Urban Services for the Poor Programme (2006 to 2012) and subsequent Madhya Pradesh Urban Infrastructure Investment Programme (or Project Utthan; 2013 to 2015) were both designed to promote equitable access to basic water and sanitation infrastructure in low-income communities across the state. Many of these urban upgrading and poverty alleviation priorities were included in the *Indore City Development Plan* (2006) and later financed by the Jawaharlal Nehru National Urban Renewal Mission (JNNURM).[3] Lastly, the *Rajiv Awas Yojana*, launched in 2011, built on these previous programmes to rehabilitate informal settlers and provide property rights to urban poor residents (Government of India 2013).

Indore's recent experience with rapid urbanisation not only necessitated the rise of these different urban poverty alleviation programmes, but also catalysed the emergence of environmental and climate change agendas as part of the city's larger urban development discourse. Water accessibility and distribution are Indore's most critical environmental stressors (Dipak and Arti 2011). Nearly 80 percent of its water supply comes from the Narmada River located 70 kilometers away (UN Habitat 2006). Many of Indore's slum settlements are located along creeks and are prone to flooding, waterlogging and vector-borne diseases (ICRS 2012). Furthermore, rapid urbanisation has accelerated loss of green space and contributed to water pollution, high rates of waste generation, and general inadequacy of public services (Gupta et al. 2006).

In response to the convergence of urban development and climate change priorities in the city, the municipality partnered with the Rockefeller Foundation in 2009 to begin planning for climate impacts. The Rockefeller Foundation hired a local implementation agency, TARU-Leading Edge, to assist with organising public meetings, working groups and scientific assessments to quantify climate vulnerabilities and risks (ICRS 2012). These processes involved municipal officials, technical consultants, NGO leaders and community representatives from different pilot project sites, and culminated in the publication of the *Indore City Resilience Strategy* (ICRS 2012) – see Table 14.1 for details on Indore's climate risks and vulnerabilities.

Since Indore has a long history of external engagement, many of the climate adaptation projects proposed by ACCCRN built upon pre-existing capacities of local actors and institutions for implementation. However, early on, local awareness of specific climate impacts was limited (Interview with technical consultant 2013), so these pre-existing institutions were gradually reconstituted in response to the rising knowledge of emerging adaptation priorities, as well as to incorporate other municipal actors. The reconstitution of existing local institutions

Table 14.1 A selection of adaptation needs and options in Indore

Sector	Adaptation need	Short-term adaptation interventions	Long-term adaptation interventions
Water resources	Ensure water availability and adequate supply in the face of increasing water scarcity associated with climate change	Develop comprehensive water management of local and Narmada resources; demand-side management, including leak detection and retrofitting; water literacy modules and citizen engagement and reporting system	Improve redundancy of the water supply system; near real-time water monitoring system; interlink water supply projects; urban user groups for conjunctive water management
Natural disasters	Reduce hazard risk exposure and disaster preparedness of urban residents, especially for the poor	Strengthen warning and forecasting components for severe weather events in city disaster management plan; city-level storm water drainage master plan; improve disaster response plans; disease monitoring system	Community-based flood preparedness programme in high-risk areas; GIS-based disease surveillance system
Urban services and economy	Improve access to urban services, improve urban infrastructure, and reduce economic losses in the face of climate impacts	Benchmark vulnerabilities of existing infrastructure; develop framework for continuously monitoring existing urban service deficiencies; increase livelihood options through informal skill building	Harden infrastructure; improve efficiency of services to better attract business and investment growth
Social equity	Empower local citizens to manage own resources and services at the ward level	Ward-level planning; form and facilitate community-based groups for community action and managing local assets; empower poor communities	Community planning and service provision through a revenue model; training and skills development; launch social safety net programmes

Source: Author's elaboration adapted from ICRS (2012) and Bhat et al. (2013).

relied on a process of experimentation that allowed for the creative reframing of adaptation needs that are nested in community development interests.

Towards community knowledge and adaptation action in Indore

For many of Indore's urban poor, climate change puts additional stresses on their already limited access to reliable freshwater wells and pipelines. Many development programmes in the past (and more recent adaptation initiatives) have focused on this issue of water scarcity. As one municipal engineer remarked:

> Indore has the costliest water management system [in India], operation and maintenance of the water supply system is very expensive. For all the projects … communities are the main stakeholders. In Indore, all the projects are related to ground-level implementation, so community-level is very important.

Even though municipal authorities acknowledge the importance of community actors in supporting the early formulation and implementation of adaptation priorities, these initiatives were often hindered by lack of awareness and resources (Interview with town planner 2013). To bridge these deficits, between 2010 and 2013, TARU-Leading Edge (the local ACCCRN implementation agency) partnered with several community-based organisations to develop adaptation pilot projects (Karanth and Archer 2014). These projects were all framed around issues of poverty alleviation within slum settlements, with a particular focus on experimenting with locally appropriate water harvesting technologies and decentralised wastewater management models (Chu 2015).

In Rahul Gandhinagar, ACCCRN partners constructed a reverse osmosis facility with a daily capacity to treat 7,000 litres of groundwater and grey water. Since its inauguration in March 2013, the reverse osmosis facility has improved the overall reliability of drinking water supply and reduced gastrointestinal disease infection rates within the community, particularly during extreme climate events (Interview with women's group member 2013). However, the reverse osmosis facility is not an entirely novel intervention, but rather a culmination of many years of water supply management interventions in the community. Notably, in 2006, a partnership between Madhya Pradesh Urban Services for the Poor (partly funded by DFID) and the Asian Development Bank's (ADB) Uday Programme[4] first distributed water testing kits in Rahul Gandhinagar in response to high levels of faecal matter detected in the drinking water. The reverse osmosis facility, therefore, builds on these earlier community health and development interventions.

Similarly, the day-to-day management of the reverse osmosis facility in Rahul Gandhinagar relies on pre-existing community groups for knowledge dissemination, social legitimacy and financial accountability. In this case, the *basti vikas samiti* (slum development committee), composed of 26 women representatives from across the community, is responsible for raising awareness and championing the benefits of the facility. Originally created as a community collective to promote microfinance and community health interventions in the early 2000s (supported by DFID and ADB), the *basti vikas samiti*'s role has since been expanded to include overseeing the reverse osmosis facility due to the group's prior experience with financial and personnel management. One group member remarked:

> There is a community leader ... that lady manages the entire water source for the community and she was given some amount [of money] from the community, like twenty rupees or ten rupees from house to house, to manage the existing water source. After the establishing of the reverse osmosis plant, that lady and some other ladies are also managing this water and [the] reverse osmosis plant.

Additionally, each member of the *basti vikas samiti* is responsible for going house to house (or conducting small focus groups meetings) within their neighbourhood to educate others about the health benefits of reverse-osmosis-treated water. The women are motivated by reputational gains rather than financial benefits. As one group member described:

> Climate change is a very big word for the communities. Many are not literate, but they are facing the issue of climate change in their day-to-day life. With our help, people are beginning to use the word climate change – '*global warming ho rahi hai, paani zyada girta hai* (global warming is happening, rain is increasing).' So they are saying that climate change is happening and is multiplying their problems. Awareness is increasing day by day.

The major impact of the *basti vikas samiti*, therefore, is the reconstitution of necessary knowledge infrastructures, social networks and local champions to disseminate knowledge of climate adaptation needs. The success of the reverse osmosis facility ultimately relies on the legitimacy of the women's group itself in championing the collective developmental interests of the community – a role that is strengthened by the group's prior experience in interacting with external and multilateral actors. Under climate change, the *basti vikas samiti* has charted a new mandate of promoting CBA actions.

Finally, the ongoing work of community groups such as the *basti vikas samiti* is supported by advocacy from NGOs. In the case of Rahul Gandhinagar, the Association for the Advancement of Society (AAS) has been working in the community for the past 15 years, and has been instrumental in numerous community development programmes (Interview with NGO leader 2014). In partnership with different ACCCRN members and the *basti vikas samiti*, the AAS not only conducted additional community education campaigns, but also built new coalitions and partnerships between community and municipal actors to implement adaptation interventions. As one AAS staff member noted:

[We] are going to our communities to mobilise more people, to advocate for the reverse osmosis water. [O]ur basic role is implementation in the community, like awareness generation, discussions with community members, training and capacity building, and liaison with the municipal government.

The role of AAS, therefore, entails juxtaposing the community's experiential knowledge of changing climatic conditions against their own development priorities. The urban poor in Rahul Gandhinagar are increasingly acknowledging projected climate impacts. In response, different community actors (such as the *basti vikas samiti*) have joined together to advocate for adaptation actions that not only address locally specific climate impacts, but also build on institutions, programmes, and networks that were created as a result of previous engagements with development interventions. These reconstituted community mobilisations are articulating new framings of climate and development priorities, reestablishing old knowledge networks, and, as the next section will highlight, catalysing further strategies for engagement with municipal authorities.

The dialectic of urban adaptation innovations

Crucially, throughout Indore's climate adaptation planning process, the municipal authority has not directly funded any climate change projects in the city. The municipal water department has only indirectly supported projects such as the reverse osmosis facility by providing free connections to public services and subsidising water rates (Interview with town planner 2014). In spite of this, some awareness of climate impacts has begun to permeate into urban plans and policies. This section highlights these emerging municipal actions and unpacks the dialectical relationship between municipal decision-making and community-based mobilisations in implementing adaptation projects on the ground.

Many CBA projects in Indore have facilitated a renewed local focus on water conservation and protection as critical urban development priorities. As one AAS leader noted, experiences from Rahul Gandhinagar have catalysed changes within the municipal government itself:

The municipality is starting to talk about issues of water because we have got success in Rahul Gandhinagar. So now city people are interested in replicating this model in other areas. In fact, the leadership is very happy with the reverse osmosis plant, and in every speech they [talk about] this issue … so adaptation [is] being discussed in a public forum.

Galvanised by this community-level success, the municipality is now taking a more active role in pursuing projects that link urban water management and climate adaptation needs. For example, adequate storm water drainage has become a priority for new road development, while conserving green areas and promoting grey water reutilisation and treatment programmes will be featured in revisions of the *City Development Plan* after 2014 (Interview with town planner 2014). Other municipal adaptation projects supported by ACCCRN are listed in Table 14.2.

Table 14.2 Descriptions of different ACCCRN-supported adaptation projects in Indore

Project name	Budget	Actors	Description
Testing and Promoting Decentralised Systems for Differential Water Sources and Uses (Dec. 2010–June 2013)	US$239,850	TARU-Leading Edge, *Sewa Surbi*, local NGOs, local engineering and technical institutions, Indore Municipal Corporation	The project demonstrated alternative viable and sustainable models for cost-effective urban water management through community engagement. The project also included community surveys and developed tools for assessing water management options.
Strengthening Vector-Borne Disease Surveillance and Response Systems (Dec. 2011–Oct. 2014)	US$183,080	District Health Department, District Health Society, Indore Municipal Corporation, Urban Health Resource Centre, *Sahayata*	The project reduced incidences of vector- and water-borne disease outbreaks. The project facilitated daily collection of health data throughout the city and identified areas particularly prone to disease outbreaks. The project also supported awareness and capacity building programmes in communities.
Peri-Urban Lake Restoration to Create Emergency Water Management Options (Oct. 2012–Mar. 2016)	US$746,500	TARU-Leading Edge, real estate developers, various NGOs, Indore Municipal Corporation, Indore Urban Development Authority, Pollution Control Board, Lake Development Authority, MP State Urban Development Department	The project rehabilitated existing peri-urban lakes that were degraded due to urbanisation. The project also mapped existing urban and peri-urban lakes, built awareness amongst stakeholders, and devised integrated water management options.
Promoting Cool Roof and Passive Ventilation for Indoor Temperature Comfort (Aug. 2012–Jan. 2015)	US$556,120	TARU-Leading Edge, real estate developers, building material manufacturers, Indore Municipal Corporation, Indore Urban Development Authority, Association of Architectures and Builders	This project promoted indoor thermal management through identifying options for reducing heat inputs and passive ventilation techniques in buildings. Strategies included artificial shading methods, roof treatment and ventilation systems.

Source: Author's elaboration adapted from ACCCRN (2013).

Many of these municipality-led efforts continue to rely on community-based actors for legitimacy and implementation. Notably, the municipality and ACCCRN partners embarked on a project to conserve and rehabilitate four urban lakes that were degraded due to pollution and soil erosion (Chu 2015). The project started with biodiversity and household socio-economic surveys, which then resulted in comprehensive water quality protection plans and studies for the construction of community sewage treatment facilities. These decentralised efforts were supported by various ward committees as well as different *rehwasi sangh* (resident welfare associations). As one association member remarked:

> Only community members cannot work and only city government will not be helpful. We have to build the capacity of the city government and we have to orient the community through generating knowledge – then combine the two. The community is the first responder and the community will suffer, [but] the city government may not suffer. So there needs to be close coordination between city government and the community. There should not be a gap, one cannot work single-handedly.

The role of the *rehwasi sangh* (similar to the *basti vikas samiti*) is not only to provide legitimacy and experiential knowledge in the adaptation planning process, but to ensure interaction between community beneficiaries, the municipality and different local waste management agencies. This creates knowledge intermediaries between municipal and community actors that mimic historic pathways of community development interventions, but also reconstitutes them according to emerging climate change priorities. The municipality is seizing and reproducing locally powerful knowledge networks and implementing projects through alliances with pre-existing community groups.

Strong community advocacy networks have also catalysed changes in municipal policies. For example, to reduce stress on the public water infrastructure during extreme climate events, the government provides 6.25 percent property tax rebate for each private household that installs a water harvesting system (Interview with municipal officer 2013). The municipality also provides technical support for identifying and installing appropriate technologies. Furthermore, the municipality has introduced a budget line item entitled 'climate change safety expenses' that earmarks approximately US$9,000 per year for climate-related activities, such as replicating community-based pilot projects.

This section demonstrates that one must have a renewed understanding of urban climate adaptation based on a dialectical relationship between the municipality and the community. Municipal versus local knowledge is no longer the most meaningful division in theorising adaptation governance in cities. Rather, adaptation is a product of reconstituting and reframing local development networks in response to emerging climate priorities. This creates a robust knowledge-based infrastructure that reasserts the role of community actors in directing resources, implementing interventions and sustaining engagement processes.

Incremental adaptation and the prospects for urban transformation

This chapter began by identifying a gap in our understanding of how urban adaptation programmes shape (and are reshaped by) local development needs and knowledge of climate impacts. Much of the current literature on urban adaptation fails to adequately engage community-based institutions and their varying roles in framing local agendas, integrating development strategies and mobilising for influence within local government. The reality is that many local communities, including those in Indore, are already actively protecting assets, resources and livelihoods against climate impacts. These communities are doing so by building new (and reconstituting old) alliances with municipal actors, thus reasserting the role of local knowledge in urban adaptation planning processes.

Even though local NGOs such as AAS have partnered with both community-level actors – like the *basti vikas samiti* and *rehwasi sangh* – as well as ACCCRN partners within the municipality to promote awareness of climate impacts on the city's water resources, such decentralised and discrete efforts often only succeed because they are relatable, easy and cheap to implement. As one community organiser noted:

> We have identified some technologies and have conducted focus group discussions and shared [with them] which technologies would be for the community. Where the community cohesion is very high and the leadership is good, we have promoted interventions like the reverse osmosis facility. Where the capacity is limited, we have identified individual technologies, like storage tanks and water harvesting in individual houses.

So, in communities like Rahul Gandhinagar where there are strong and legitimate social institutions like the *basti vikas samiti*, extant decision-making capacities can be redirected to implement larger-scale adaptation strategies such as the reverse osmosis facility. These capacities are derived from utilising institutional structures that were created from working with external donors in the past. The AAS and *rehwasi sangh* were also pre-existing organisations that had the capacity to absorb emerging adaptation priorities perceived to be in line with their institutional objectives and interests. Thus the potential for the scaling up of these discrete adaptation interventions to redress citywide climate injustices remains unclear.

Finally, in theory, social mobilisations are characterised by clear linkages between actors through dense informal networks and by a distinct collective identity (Della Porta and Diani 1999). The goal, then, is to affect political change through mobilising human and material resources (Jamison 2010). However, in Indore, although local NGOs and community groups play a key role in generating awareness of climate impacts within city government, such discrete mobilisations are difficult to disseminate across different communities. As one community organiser remarked:

> One thing is the vision. The community-level vision is only for their community. If we are discussing with government officials, then their vision is for the whole city. So the vision is different. If the [municipality] agrees, the projects will be replicated in other communities also. Communities only care about their communities.

In sum, although various community activists all note the importance of community-based framings of adaptation needs and ownership over adaptation options, communities that lack the knowledge and experience of groups like the *basti vikas samiti*, *rehwasi sangh* or AAS are often unable to plan beyond the community scale. As a result, many adaptation projects rely on continuous capacity assistance from external actors such as the Rockefeller Foundation and DFID.

The two main barriers highlighted here – the lack of effective institutional structures to scale up discrete community-level projects and the unequal distribution of adaptive capacities between (and within) urban poor communities – are serious constraints that limit the ongoing sustainability and inclusivity of CBA interventions. There is also a danger that adaptation benefits may get co-opted by elite interests or that the poorest residents within slum communities will ultimately be left behind. Even though Indore has had some success in spurring projects that are in line with both developmental and adaptation needs of the urban poor, future research must also try to understand how these discrete gains set the stage for more structural transformations in urban climate governance (O'Brien 2011; Roggema et al. 2012; Bahadur and Tanner 2014; Pelling et al. 2014).

As climate impacts become more pronounced, municipal authorities in the Global South must focus on creating a knowledge-based infrastructure that places community representativeness, knowledge and legitimacy at the centre of adaptation planning processes. Even though external actors come and go, this knowledge-based infrastructure will ensure that community experiences and collective memories are carried forward to bridge future gaps in experimentation, local knowledge sharing and transformative climate action.

Notes

1 The Rockefeller Foundation's Asian Cities Climate Change Resilience Network (ACCCRN) program was a nine-year, US$59 million initiative to build climate resilience in Asian cities. Between 2008 and 2016, the ACCCRN programme partnered with ten cities across India, Indonesia, Thailand and Vietnam to develop city climate resilience strategies.

2 *Swarna Jayanti Shahari Rojgar Yojana* was launched in December 1997 and was implemented by various state governments in India. Under this scheme, between 1997 and 2006, the Indian government released 9.8 billion rupees to nearly 4,000 towns across India (Government of India 2013).

3 Launched in 2005, the Jawaharlal Nehru National Urban Renewal Mission (JNNURM) was designed to empower local governments, to facilitate urban economic development, and to improve the quality of life of urban residents. Initially piloted in 66 cities, JNNURM incentivised urban reforms through linking critical infrastructure and public

service development projects with conditional fiscal transfers from state and national governments (Government of India 2013). Phase I of JNNURM ended in 2014.
4 The Urban Water Supply and Environmental Project (Project Uday) was jointly funded by the Asian Development Bank, UN Habitat, the Madhya Pradesh Government, and the cities of Bhopal, Indore, Gwalior and Jabalpur. As of 2015, approximately US$113 million has been spent in Indore to improve urban infrastructure for water supply, solid waste management and drainage.

References

Asian Cities Climate Change Resilience Network (ACCCRN) 2013 *ACCCRN City Projects: Asian Cities Climate Change Resilience Network*. Bangkok Thailand: The Rockefeller Foundation Asian Cities Climate Change Resilience Network

Anguelovski I and Carmin J 2011 Something borrowed, everything new: innovation and institutionalization in urban climate governance *Current Opinion in Environmental Sustainability* 3 1–7

Anguelovski I Chu E and Carmin J 2014 Variations in approaches to urban climate adaptation: experiences and experimentation from the global south *Global Environmental Change* 27 156–167

Archer D Almansi F DiGregorio M Roberts D Sharma D and Syam D 2014 Moving towards inclusive urban adaptation: approaches to integrating community-based adaptation to climate change at city and national scale *Climate and Development* 6(4) 345–356

Ayers J and Forsyth T 2009 Community-based adaptation to climate change *Environment: Science and Policy for Sustainable Development* 51(4) 22–31

Aylett A 2010 Participatory planning, justice, and climate change in Durban, South Africa *Environment and Planning A* 42(1) 99–115

Bahadur A V and Tanner T M 2014 Transformational resilience thinking: putting people, power and politics at the heart of urban climate resilience *Environment and Urbanization* 26(1) 200–214

Barrett S 2013 Local level climate justice? Adaptation finance and vulnerability reduction *Global Environmental Change* 23(6) 1819–1829

Barrett S 2012 The necessity of a multiscalar analysis of climate justice *Progress in Human Geography* 37(2) 215–233

Bhat G K Raghupathi U Rajasekar U and Karanth A 2013 *Urbanisation, Poverty, Climate Change: A Synthesis Report – India*, Gurgaon, India: TARU Leading Edge and ACCCRN

Bulkeley H Carmin J Castán Broto V Edwards G A S and Fuller S 2013 Climate justice and global cities: mapping the emerging discourses *Global Environmental Change* 23(5) 914–925

Bulkeley H and Castán Broto V 2013 Government by experiment? Global cities and the governing of climate change *Transactions of the Institute of British Geographers* 38 361–375

Bulkeley H Edwards G A S and Fuller S 2014 Contesting climate justice in the city: examining politics and practice in urban climate change experiments *Global Environmental Change* 25 31–40

Bulkeley H and Tuts R 2013 Understanding urban vulnerability, adaptation and resilience in the context of climate change *Local Environment* 18(6) 646–662

Carmin J Anguelovski I and Roberts D 2012 Urban climate adaptation in the global south: planning in an emerging policy domain *Journal of Planning Education and Research* 32(1) 18–32

Carmin J Dodman D and Chu E 2013 *Urban Climate Adaptation and Leadership: From Conceptual to Practical Understanding* OECD Regional Development Working Paper 2013/48 Paris, France: Organisation for Economic Co-operation and Development

Chu E 2015 Urban Development and Climate Adaptation: Implications for Policymaking and Governance in Indian Cities in Garland A (ed) *Urban Opportunities: Perspectives on Climate Change, Resilience, Inclusion, and the Informal Economy* 6–29 Washington, DC: The Woodrow Wilson Center Press

Chu E Anguelovski I and Carmin J 2015 Inclusive approaches to urban climate adaptation planning and implementation in the global south *Climate Policy* 1–21

Ciplet D Roberts J T and Khan M 2013 The politics of international climate adaptation funding: justice and divisions in the greenhouse *Global Environmental Politics* 13(1) 49–68

Collins K and Ison R 2009 Jumping off Arnstein's ladder: social learning as a new policy paradigm for climate change adaptation *Environmental Policy and Governance* 19 358–373

Cooke B and Kothari U 2001 *Participation: The New Tyranny?* London: Zed Books

Della Porta D and Diani M 1999 *Social Movements: An Introduction* Oxford: Blackwell Publishing

Dipak S and Arti D 2011 Assessment and treatment of municipal wastewater of Indore city of India *Archives of Applied Science Research* 3(1) 450–461

Dodman D and Mitlin D 2011 Challenges for community-based adaptation: discovering the potential for transformation *Journal of International Development* 25(5) 640–659

Dodman D and Satterthwaite D 2009 Institutional capacity climate change adaptation and the urban poor *IDS Bulletin* 39(4) 67–74

Ebi K L 2009 Facilitating climate justice through community-based adaptation in the health sector *Environmental Justice* 2(4) 191–195

Ensor J and Berger R 2009 Community-Based Adaptation and Culture in Theory and Practice in Adger W N Lorenzoni I and O'Brien K (eds) *Adaptation to Climate Change: Thresholds, Values, Governance* 227–239 Cambridge, UK: Cambridge University Press

Ensor J and Harvey B 2015 Social learning and climate change adaptation: evidence for international development practice *Wiley Interdisciplinary Reviews: Climate Change* 6(5) 509–522

Few R Brown K and Tompkins E L 2007 Public participation and climate change adaptation: avoiding the illusion of inclusion *Climate Policy* 7 46–59

Forsyth T 2013 Community-based adaptation: a review of past and future challenges *Wiley Interdisciplinary Reviews: Climate Change* 4 439–446

Friend R and Moench M 2013 What is the purpose of urban climate resilience? Implications for addressing poverty and vulnerability *Urban Climate* 6 98–113

Government of India 2013 *Twelfth Five Year Plan 2012–2017* New Delhi India: Planning Commission Government of India

Gupta H K Gupta K Singh P and Sharma R C 2006 A sustainable development and environmental quality management strategy for Indore *Environmental Quality Management,* 15(4) 57–68

Hodson M and Marvin S 2010 *World Cities and Climate Change: Producing Urban Ecological Security* Maidenhead: Open University Press

Hughes S 2013 Justice in urban climate change adaptation: criteria and application to Delhi *Ecology and Society* 18(4) 48

Hughes S and Romero-Lankao P 2014 Science and institution building in urban climate-change policymaking *Environmental Politics* 23(6) 1023–1042

Huq S and Reid H 2004 Mainstreaming adaptation in development *IDS Bulletin* 35(3) 15–21

Indore City Resilience Strategy (ICRS) 2012 *Indore City Resilience Strategy for Changing Climate Scenarios* Available from: http://www.imagineindore.org/resource/30.pdf [Accessed: 28/10/15]

Intergovernmental Panel on Climate Change (IPCC) 2014 Climate Change 2014: Impacts, Adaptation, and Vulnerability Contribution of Working Group II to the Fifth Assessment Report of the Intergovernmental Panel on Climate Change in Field C B Barros V R Dokken D J Mach K J Mastrandrea M D Bilir T E Chatterjee M Ebi K L Estrada Y O Genova R C Girma B Kissel E S Levy A N MacCracken S Mastrandrea P R White L L (eds) *Climate Change 2014: Impacts, Adaptation, and Vulnerability. Part A: Global and Sectoral Aspects. Contribution of Working Group II to the Fifth Assessment Report of the Intergovernmental Panel on Climate Change* 535–612 Cambridge, UK: Cambridge University Press

Jamison A 2010 Climate change knowledge and social movement theory *Wiley Interdisciplinary Reviews: Climate Change* 1(6) 811–823

Karanth A and Archer D 2014 Institutionalising mechanisms for building urban climate resilience: experiences from India *Development in Practice* 24(4) 514–526

Magee T 2013 *A Field Guide to Community Based Adaptation* London and New York: Routledge

Nay J J Abkowitz M Chu E Gallagher D and Wright H 2014 A review of decision-support models for adaptation to climate change in the context of development *Climate and Development* 6(4) 357–367

O'Brien K L 2011 Global environmental change II: from adaptation to deliberate transformation *Progress in Human Geography* 36(5) 667–676

Paavola J and Adger W N 2006 Fair adaptation to climate change *Ecological Economics* 56(4) 594–609

Pelling M O'Brien K and Matyas D 2014 Adaptation and transformation *Climatic Change* 1–15

Pettit J 2004 Climate justice: a new social movement for atmospheric rights *IDS Bulletin* 35(3) 102–106

Puppim de Oliveira J A 2013 Learning how to align climate, environmental and development objectives in cities: lessons from the implementation of climate co-benefits initiatives in urban Asia *Journal of Cleaner Production* 58 7–14

Reid H and Huq S 2014 Mainstreaming community-based adaptation into national and local planning *Climate and Development* 6(4) 291–292

Roberts D and O'Donoghue S 2013 Urban environmental challenges and climate change action in Durban, South Africa *Environment and Urbanization* 25(2) 299–319

Roberts J T 2009 The international dimension of climate justice and the need for international adaptation funding *Environmental Justice* 2(4) 185–190

Rodima-Taylor D 2012 Social innovation and climate adaptation: local collective action in diversifying Tanzania *Applied Geography* 33 128–134

Roggema R Vermeend T and Dobbelsteen A 2012 Incremental change, transition or transformation? Optimising change pathways for climate adaptation in spatial planning *Sustainability* 4(12) 2525–2549

Sharma D and Tomar S 2010 Mainstreaming climate change adaptation in Indian cities *Environment and Urbanization* 22(2) 451–465

Solecki W D Leichenko R and O'Brien K 2011 Climate change adaptation strategies and disaster risk reduction in cities: connections, contentions, and synergies *Current Opinion in Environmental Sustainability* 3(3) 135–141

Uittenbroek C J Janssen-Jansen L B Spit T J M Salet W G M and Ruuhaar H A C 2014 Political commitment in organising municipal responses to climate adaptation: the dedicated approach versus the mainstreaming approach *Environmental Politics* 23(6) 1043–1063

UN Habitat 2006 *Water Demand Management Strategy and Implementation Plan for Indore* United Nations Human Settlements Programme (UN Habitat)

Verma G D 2000 Indore's habitat improvement project: success or failure? *Habitat International* 24(1) 91–117

Part V
Conclusion

15 Conclusion

Reconceptualising adaptation and comparing experiences

David Hulme, Manoj Roy, Michaela Hordijk and Sally Cawood

This final chapter draws out key findings and conclusions from the lived experience of urban poverty and climate change presented in this book. The cases from Bangladesh, Brazil, Colombia, India, Peru, South Africa and Tanzania demonstrate the various impacts, and incredible diversity of responses to climate change. Context emerges as central to understanding adaptation, making broad generalisation difficult.

The varied experiences reported here form part of a wider, ongoing debate about the uneven impacts of climate change and varying responses of specific locales and populations to impacts. This variation is increasingly recognised by local, national and global actors and institutions. Whilst the IPCC AR5 provides clear evidence that adaptation in urban areas is (and will be) central to reducing the damaging impacts of climate change on efforts to reduce poverty, the UN Sustainable Development Goals (SDGs) recognise the centrality of improving the prospects of the urban poor to achieve poverty reduction and social justice, integrating them into goals, such as Goal 11: 'Make cities and human settlements inclusive, safe, resilient and sustainable' (UN 2015). The SDGs are a significant advance on the MDGs, which had no specific goal on cities, applied a more '*ad hoc*' approach to formulating poverty reduction and environmental goals, and had relatively little to say about poor people in cities and towns. The SDGs furthermore have an explicit goal on inequality (SDG 10), something the MDGs were lacking.

Evidently, there is increasing recognition that urban areas and urban dwellers must be on the global agenda in a context where people living in informal urban settlements are the fastest growing group of poor in the world. Indeed, climate change could be used as a potential entry point for bringing the challenges facing poor and low-income people in urban areas to the attention of policy makers. The following section draws out cross-cutting themes from the chapters in each of the three book sections – Vulnerability, adaptation and the built environment; Understanding change and adaptation: from institutional interface to co-production; and From learning to knowledge, innovation to action. The chapter then broadens discussion over urban poverty and climate change, asking important questions about *who* is responsible and *who* has the power, knowledge and resources to make a difference.

Overview of chapter conclusions

It is now evident that climatechange-related hazards and weather variability exacerbates existing vulnerabilities for the urban poor. While this impact is uneven for many poor urban people, these changes have negative (sometimes severe) consequences for livelihoods, health and wellbeing. Sriram and Krishna's comparison of notified and un-notified slums in Bangalore, India (Chapter 3) demonstrates how these vulnerabilities are manifest in different settlement types, and vary between first- and fourth-generation migrants. Un-notified settlements and recent migrants have much less capacity to adapt to environmental problems than more established urban dwellers who have built up asset stocks and social and political relations. Furthermore, Mwanyoka et al. (Chapter 6) demonstrate the critical importance of engaging with health vulnerabilities associated with vector-borne diseases in Tanzania. Higher levels of health vulnerability are particularly significant for low-income households as many are 'one illness away' from health shocks that can cause extreme impoverishment (Krishna 2011). As indicated in Chapter 2, it is the accumulation of climatic and non-climatic shocks a household has to handle over time which is most detrimental.

The chapters presented here also demonstrate that households and communities are *already* actively adapting to climate change impacts, but that these impacts and adaptations are rarely distinguished from other compounding factors, such as low income, ill health, social and political exclusion and physical environment. Poor urban people respond to dynamic sets of multidimensional shocks and stresses, not the clearly discerned 'climate change' or 'economic environment' problems that external researchers often seek to identify. This was particularly evident in Sutherland et al.'s discussion of low-income dwellers redefining official boundaries around their daily needs and priorities for water and sanitation in Durban, South Africa (Chapter 4). Similarly, Parvin et al.'s chapter on adaptation in the built environment in Khulna, Bangladesh (Chapter 5) demonstrated how some households were actively adjusting their living space (e.g. ventilation, drainage) to address climatic shocks, but also reacting to (and taking advantage of) non-climatic changes in the local environment such as NGO projects and the construction of the city protection embankment.

Whilst there is abundant evidence that some poor urban people and communities are actively adapting, not all have the capacity or resources to cope, let alone adapt. This was particularly evident in Banks' contrasting of the differential responses of tenants and house owners (Chapter 7), and further explored in Hashemi et al.'s chapter on extremely poor households in Dhaka, Bangladesh (Chapter 12). Whilst tenants have little control over their housing and built environment, and often earn too little to cope with climate-related shocks, home owners and slum elites can use rent income and the services provided by NGOs to diversify their livelihoods and enhance the resilience of their households (through housing repairs, using higher-quality materials, increased mobility, etc.) This tenant/home owner contrast, and asymmetric tenant/landlord power relationships, adds to debate over romanticised notions of 'community' – cohesive, caring and egalitarian – that are often implicit in some interpretations of community-based adaptation (CBA).

Evidently, we must recognise heterogeneity *within* low-income households and communities, and that there are severe and varying constraints (e.g. financial, capacity for collective action, quality of governance) to household and/or community capacities to adapt. Fraser's discussion of home owners and displaced residents in landslide risk zones in Bogota, Colombia (Chapter 13) further demonstrates the varied capacity, ability and willingness of residents to adjust to (externally constructed) notions of landslide risk. Crucially, Fraser also highlights how the perception of risk and stressors is as (or more) important than *actual* risk. Indeed, risk and vulnerability are continuously negotiated and reconstituted by (and for) poor and low-income people in towns and cities.

As indicated by Hordijk et al. (Chapter 8), we must also acknowledge diversity *between* low-income communities, as evidenced in Peru and Brazil. For example, variation in leadership, strength of local institutions and geographical location affects the impacts of, and responses to, climate change impacts, such as increased rainfall and floods. Whilst such variation makes broad generalisation difficult and/or infeasible, this highlights the importance of context-specific responses that build upon (and link together) local, national and international knowledge and institutions. Stein and Moser's discussion of the Asset Planning for Climate Change Adaptation (APCA) methodology is one such 'tried and tested' example of a multi-level, multi-stakeholder initiative (Chapter 9). The authors argue that the APCA process in Cartagena, Colombia brought the local community, NGOs and municipal authorities into meaningful dialogue, enabling collaboration for the identification of priorities and feasible solutions. Critical questions remain, however, over whether local authorities can and/or will deliver on promises and commitments made through such processes. Whether APCA can be replicated in highly vulnerable contexts is also unclear. Opel's discussion of severe water shortages in two coastal towns in Bangladesh is a case in point (Chapter 10). The chapter raises critical questions over the inevitability of human displacement and relocation in areas of severe (saline) contamination of surface and groundwater, and where viable solutions are not affordable or accessible to low-income people.

This backdrop of uncertainty does not mean that innovative ways forward cannot be found. Nevertheless, Harriss-White and Rodrigo's work on innovation in India's informal economy (Chapter 11) demonstrates that there is a long way to go (and a lot to learn) about the implications and potential of this innovative sector for climate change mitigation and a 'low-carbon' agenda. Mitigation is not simply about official actors, high technology or innovative finance by formal institutions and scientists. Following the theme of innovation, Hashemi et al. (Chapter 12) outline an experimental approach to target those normally (knowingly or unknowingly) neglected by poverty reduction and climate change initiatives – the extreme urban poor. The authors outline how the DSK-Shiree project helped extreme poor households graduate from being 'risk prone' to 'risk averse' through a carefully designed and sequenced programme of asset transfer, training, savings and CBO engagement. Despite its many problems, initiatives like DSK-Shiree provide an opportunity (perhaps missed in this case) to align development (specifically urban poverty reduction goals) with climate change adaptation. This links to broader debates around the promotion of 'adaptive development' (Agrawal and Lemos 2015), which argues for the alignment of development and adaptation goals, moving away from the standalone approaches to climate change adaptation that aid donors prefer (as they want to be able to tell their domestic constituencies that they are funding discrete initiatives in response to clearly identified incidents of 'climate change').

Dynamic partnerships between low-income residents, NGOs, donors, governments and the private sector have an important role to play in 'adaptive development', as demonstrated in Chu's chapter on the role of multi-actor partnerships for climate change adaptation (Chapter 14). Chu demonstrates how the legacy and knowledge of local community organisations can be used (by and for communities) to reshape innovations around development and adaptation priorities. Whether this is 'innovation', or the reconstitution of climate change or adaptation funds as the 'new foreign aid', using the lessons of 'good' development (e.g. authentic participation, effective partnerships and local 'ownership' of programmes) requires sustained critical engagement.

The role of private actors and institutions is also worth noting in this context. Whether it is small-scale private home owners adapting their houses (and those of their tenants), or private firms and companies championing adaptation agendas, such as the Chamber of Commerce in Surat, India (see Karanth and Archer 2014), the future (and present) role of the private sector cannot be ignored. It is important to recognise that these partnerships are highly contextualised, formal and informal, and can even involve 'illegal' actors (e.g. slum elites and intermediaries/touts), as well as formal state and NGO institutions.

Nevertheless, as with the concept of 'communities' we must not romanticise the idea of 'partnerships' between the private sector and other actors. While some businessmen (occasionally women) and companies will participate in win–win opportunities, there are others – real estate companies, land speculators, City of London financiers and rich families – who are very powerful (in terms of finance, political connections and/or muscle) who will not allow the poor to obtain land, resources or knowledge and who do not wish to see residents of low-income settlements organise themselves.

In an increasingly unequal world, this group includes national and international plutocrats, sometimes called the '1 percent', who possess immense wealth and power (Credit Suisse 2014; Oxfam 2014). The voluntary or involuntary displacement of poor urban people is commonly the form of 'partnership' that these big players pursue. Often the identities and countries of residence of these elite are not transparent but their game plan is clear: 'we win, the poor lose'. In such contexts, coping will achieve nothing. Resistance is the priority but is often infeasible as the costs of resistance – harassment by thugs and the police, false legal cases, the threat of physical and sexual violence, actual violence – are much greater than the poor, and even public interest lawyers, are willing or able to risk. There are some examples of partially effective resistance – initiatives such as Slum/Shack Dweller

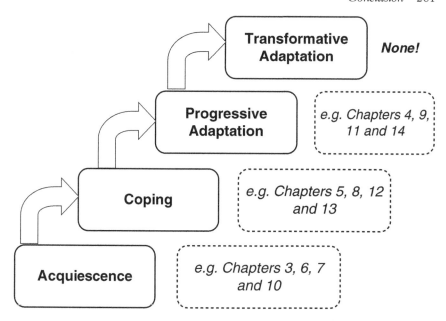

Figure 15.1 The ladder of adaptive capacity (and corresponding chapters)

Source: Authors' elaboration based on Agrawal (2010), Pelling (2011), Gurran et al. (2013) and Dodman et al. (2014).

International (SDI) and the Asian Coalition for Housing Rights (ACHR), where the urban poor, in collaboration with NGOs and academics, attempt to negotiate with powerful elites. However, in cities where urban land values are high and climbing (as in Dhaka), such resistance is unlikely to work as the commercial incentives for real estate companies and land developers – vast profits made rapidly and often extracted from a country without paying tax – sweep away all opportunities for collaboration with the urban poor. Simply keeping people uninformed about their foreseen relocation, as in the case of Tietê park in Guarulhos (Chapter 8), is another effective way of undermining collective resistance.

Dynamic adaptation: re-engaging with the ladder of adaptive capacity

The cases presented in this volume reveal the wide range of capacities of poor urban people to cope with climatechange-related stressors. Conceptually, these can be envisaged as a ladder of adaptive capacity, introduced in Chapter 2 (Figure 15.1).

The bottom step is *acquiescence*, when households and communities simply absorb the impacts of climate change and are not able to adapt in meaningful ways. They simply have to accept lower incomes or increased health problems or more stressful living conditions (excessive heat or waterlogging) and other adverse effects. For example, Banks (Chapter 7) highlights the limited options for coping that tenants have in Dhaka's slum settlements, whilst Mwanyoka et al. (Chapter 6) indicate the severe health costs of climate-related stressors for low-income people in Tanzania. This is perhaps best illustrated, however, in Opel's analysis (Chapter 10), when he envisages that poor people in southwest Bangladesh will have to involuntarily relocate as they are unable to adapt to the changes in their physical environment. Adaptation might be technically feasible, but the resources this would entail are not available to poor people.

On the step above acquiescence comes *coping*. This occurs when individual households and/or communities are able to make some adaptations that partially offset the impacts and increased vulnerabilities created by climate change. In the cases examined in this book, coping is the most common level of adaptation identified. Hashemi et al.'s discussion of how the extreme urban poor are affected by, and cope with, weather variability brought about by climate change (Chapter 12) is one such example. Other examples include Hordijk et al.'s discussion of floods in Peru and Brazil (Chapter 8) and Fraser's investigation of landslide risk in Colombia (Chapter 13). While it cannot always be assumed that coping strategies will be an effective means of reducing the negative impacts of climate change, such strategies may create the institutional and aspirational base for more dynamic engagement in the future – towards progressive adaptation.

This third step of the ladder – *progressive adaptation* – entails both a capacity to directly adapt to climate change (i.e. cope) alongside a capacity to develop new partnerships and/or create new institutional forms that enhance the prospects for communities to deal more effectively with future climate change impacts. Stein and Moser's discussion of the APCA initiative in Cartagena, Colombia (Chapter 9) provides an example of a formal strategy to shift communities from coping with, to progressive adaptation to climate change. In terms of CBA programmes, and climate change action plans, this shift from coping to progressive adaptation is perhaps the most common form of 'official' action. Chu's discussion of CBA initiatives building upon (and being reworked by) community knowledge in Indore, India (Chapter 14) is arguably an example of progressive adaptation. Whether such initiatives are 'transformative' remains to be seen.

Finally, drawing on AR5's (Revi et al. 2014) and Dodman et al.'s (2014) notion of radical or transformative adaptation, we conceptualise a 'top step' of *transformative adaptation*. This envisages the creation and/or evolution of new institutional frameworks that have the capacity to systematically analyse, plan and respond to climate change impacts. While such arrangements could not be guaranteed to ensure that adaptation is successful (i.e. ensuring that all households/communities experience no negative consequences), they would ensure that present and future climate change impacts are analytically tracked, that response options are identified and evaluated and that preferred options are implemented. Arguably, none of the cases in this volume achieve the transformative adaptation level. Only Chapters 4 (Sutherland et al.), 9 (Stein and Moser), 11 (Harriss-White and Rodrigo) and 14 (Chu) recognise it as a possibility. As noted in Chapter 2, transformative adaptation requires radical political choices for both distributive and procedural justice.

This *ladder of adaptive capacity* is a very simple analytical framework but it does facilitate the comparative analysis of the relative ambition and/or effectiveness of approaches to adaptation. While it might be inferred that all initiatives should seek to be transformational, this should not be assumed. We might need to opt for the short-term do-able actions that improve the current situation of the poor, without losing sight of the normative goal of climate justice. Strategies need to 'fit' their contexts and resource availability: seeking to strengthen household and community coping responses to climate change impacts may be the 'best fit' approach in many situations when institutions are weak and/or knowledge and resources are constrained.

Moving forward … what next?

Popular accounts of the impact of climate change in the early 21st century commonly adopted what Mike Hulme (2009) calls the 'myth of Apocalypse' scenario – global environmental collapse and the extinction of *Homo sapiens* (and most other forms of life) because of the failure of humanity to mitigate greenhouse gases. From this scenario, the best the urban poor can do is cope with climate change impacts until they are swept away – literally, or by famine and social breakdown. We are not so pessimistic! Yet, neither can we see Hulme's alternative, optimistic, extreme, 'the myth of Jubilee' coming to be – the scenario that the common threat that climate change makes for all of humanity leads to a rapid and unprecedented transformation of social norms and human behaviours that generates a fully functional set of global institutions able to deal with climate change (and all other threats and opportunities to/for *Homo sapiens*). Rather, we anticipate that an economically and socially belated response to climate change (individually, nationally and internationally) will eventually lead to more effective mitigation and enhanced adaptation.

Fortunately, the COP 21 climate summit in December 2015 appears to have broken through the climate change negotiations impasse. With US and Chinese leadership, the Paris Agreement won the support of the UN's 195 member states. This agreement aims to achieve a zero net anthropogenic greenhouse gas emission level during the second half of the 21st century, strive towards global warming not exceeding 1.5°C (which would mean zero net emissions before 2050) and have five-yearly stakeholder reviews of national contributions towards a low-carbon global economy. Crucially, the mechanisms are non-binding, with countries setting their own national targets for reductions, and stakeholder summits only 'naming and shaming' poorly performing countries, with no international compliance process. While world leaders proclaimed this as a great success, there were criticisms and concerns from civil society groups. For environmental radicals, Paris was a sell-out, charting a weak, reformist strategy that accepts species extinction and profound environmental degradation as inevitable. If achieved, the national contributions pledged at Paris would limit global warming to an estimated 2.7°C, well above the 2.0°C international guideline, so contributions must be increased in the future. This said, poor and low-income people living in urban areas (or their children) may benefit from this belated response, and will be important actors in creating that response.

How might poor urban people prosper as we move to a partially effective international response and, at the same time, how might they accelerate this belated response? Part of this has been charted in this volume – by acting independently and in partnership with others to achieve short-term, practical improvements in their lives through coping and progressive adaptation. This adaptation needs to be developmental (Agrawal and Lemos 2015) as there are other disruptive processes in operation – environmental, demographic, economic and social. Strong efforts will be needed to move from coping to progressive to transformational adaptation so that practical action supports strategic change. Strategic change is 'political', in that it seeks to redistribute resources and power, but does not automatically have to be confrontational. Transformational adaptation can adopt collaborative or confrontational tactics, depending on the goals and context. We live in a 'both … and' world as much as an 'either … or' world. Indeed, recent social and economic advances (gender, poverty reduction in Asia) would suggest that strategic advancement for the urban poor may need both collaboration and confrontation at one and the same time, with some pro-poor actors challenging established authorities (political parties, municipal councils, city and national elites) and others pursuing progressive forms of collaboration.

In this volume we hope we have been able to contribute to the understanding of practical action, coping and progressive adaptation: where practical achievements operate alongside efforts to start negotiating the reshaping of institutions and institutional partnerships so that they more effectively support the interests of poor and low-income urban people. While we have discussed transformative adaptation we recognise that none of our examples approached such a grand goal. Our colleagues David Dodman, Diane Archer and David Satterthwaite (2014) and Diana Mitlin and David Satterthwaite (2013 and 2014) have charted some of the territory of transformation. In addition, our future work with the EcoPoor project (see www.ecopoor.com) seeks to add to this. However, the outlines of what transformative adaptation will entail are emerging:

- Effective collective action by poor and low-income people and their neighbours to achieve short-term gains and raise capacity for future collective action.
- The co-production of knowledge and action with key partners – especially city and municipal authorities – so that knowledge and resources can be pooled and opportunities for cooperation strengthened.
- Cross-city/town and international communication and action (South/South, South/North and North/North), with a careful eye. Efforts by individuals, norm entrepreneurs, norm organisational platforms and leaders to challenge and change social norms (the living wage, property rights for women, reduced personal carbon footprints, inheritance tax, universal basic health

care) so that international social norms are steered towards the needs of all of us living on 'one planet' – poverty eradication, environmental sustainability, reduced inequality and social justice.

Around the world, poor urban people are struggling to adapt to complex sets of vulnerabilities that are most often produced by better-off people. We hope that the discussions in this book provide a little guidance as to how we might support their efforts to overcome these vulnerabilities, and the additional vulnerabilities created by anthropogenic climate change.

References

Agrawal A 2010 Local Institutions and Adaptation to Climate Change in Mearns R and Norton A (eds) *Social Dimensions of Climate Change: Equity and Vulnerability in a Warming World* 173–197 Washington DC: The World Bank

Agrawal A and Lemos M C 2015 Commentary: adaptive development *Nature Climate Change* 5 185–187

Credit Suisse 2014 *Global Wealth Report* Available from: https://publications.credit-suisse .com/tasks/render/file/?fileID=60931FDE-A2D2-F568-B041B58C5EA591A4 [Accessed: 26/10/15]

Dodman D Archer D and Satterthwaite D 2014 *Radical Adaptation: How Farsighted Cities Prepare for Climate Change* IIED Briefing Nov 2014 1–4

Gurran N Norman B and Hamin E 2013 Climate change adaptation in coastal Australia: an audit of planning practice *Ocean and Coastal Management* 86 100–109

Hulme M 2009 *Why We Disagree About Climate Change: Understanding Controversy, Inaction and Opportunity* Cambridge, UK: Cambridge University Press

Karanth A and Archer D 2014 Institutionalising mechanisms for building urban climate resilience: experiences from India *Development in Practice* 24(4) 514–526

Krishna A 2011 *One Illness Away: Why People Become Poor and How They Escape Poverty* Oxford: Oxford University Press

Mitlin D and Satterthwaite D 2013 *Urban Poverty in the Global South: Scale and Nature* London: Routledge

Mitlin D and Satterthwaite D 2014 *Reducing Urban Poverty in the Global South* London: Routledge

Oxfam 2014 *Even it Up: Time to End Extreme Inequality* Available from: http://policy-practice .oxfam.org.uk/publications/even-it-up-time-to-end-extreme-inequality-333012 [Accessed: 26/10/15]

Pelling M 2011 *Adaptation to Climate Change: From Resilience to Transformation* London: Routledge

Revi A Satterthwaite D Aragón-Durand F Corfee-Morlot J Kiunsi R B R Pelling M Roberts D C and Solecki W 2014 Urban Areas in Field C B Barros V R Dokken D J Mach K J Mastrandrea M D Bilir T E Chatterjee M Ebi K L Estrada Y O Genova R C Girma B Kissel E S Levy A N MacCracken S Mastrandrea P R White L L (eds) *Climate Change 2014: Impacts, Adaptation, and Vulnerability. Part A: Global and Sectoral Aspects. Contribution of Working Group II to the Fifth Assessment Report of the Intergovernmental Panel on Climate Change* 535–612 Cambridge UK: Cambridge University Press

United Nations (UN) 2015 *Sustainable Development Goals* Available from: https:// sustainabledevelopment.un.org/topics [Accessed: 16/10/15]

Index

Page numbers in **bold** refer to figures and tables.

For Product Safety Concerns and Information please contact our EU
representative GPSR@taylorandfrancis.com Taylor & Francis Verlag GmbH,
Kaufingerstraße 24, 80331 München, Germany

Printed and bound by CPI Group (UK) Ltd, Croydon, CR0 4YY
08/05/2025
01864319-0003